Japanese Culture and Behavior

Japanese Culture and Behavior

Selected Readings

REVISED EDITION

Edited by
Takie Sugiyama Lebra and William P. Lebra

 UNIVERSITY OF HAWAII PRESS / Honolulu

© 1974, 1986 University of Hawaii Press
All Rights Reserved
Printed in the United States of America

04 03 02   10 9 8 7

Library of Congress Cataloging-in-Publication Data
Japanese culture and behavior.
  Bibliography: p.
  Includes index.
  1. National characteristics, Japanese.
I. Lebra, Takie Sugiyama, 1930–   II. Lebra,
William P.
DS821.J343   1986   306'.089956   86–4367
ISBN 0–8248–1055–4

University of Hawai'i Press books are printed on acid-free
paper and meet the guidelines for permanence and durability
of the Council on Library Resources.

On New Year's Day of 1986,
William P. Lebra, co-editor
of this book, suddenly passed
away, not knowing that this
would be his last work. It is
hoped that this volume reflects
some of his accomplishment
as a medical/psychological
anthropologist and scholar.

Contents

Acknowledgments

THE editors wish to express our appreciation of the many who helped to make this volume possible. We are grateful, first, to the contributors, whose scholarly activities made the contents worthwhile. To the various publishers and professional associations who freely gave (or required silver for) permission to use their publications, we offer our thanks. Special recognition should be accorded to Frances Yuasa, who helped to compile and standardize the references. Both of us were able to use portions of sabbatical leave time, granted by the University of Hawaii, for this effort. And the Social Science Research Institute (UH) provided support in typing and photocopying. For these benefits and others, thank you!

Introduction

IN preparing this revised edition of *Japanese Culture and Behavior: Selected Readings,* we considered three problems or issues encountered since the publication of the first edition in 1974. One relates to responses to the original publication, received in a number of reviews published in scholarly journals and conveyed in personal correspondence. Most of these were kindly favorable and encouraging—encouraging enough to prompt us to do a second edition. We benefited from criticism as well as support. Following the comments of some reviewers, we decided to insert more editorial commentary so that the assortment of papers would exhibit greater coherence and integration. This new edition, therefore, begins with this enlarged introduction, where rationales are spelled out. Further, each of the four parts is prefaced by an editorial commentary on each of the chapters contained in that section.

In order to conserve space and to provide greater uniformity in the style of reference citation, all references have been placed at the end of the text in alphabetical order, and text citations have been standardized. A much-needed index has been added as well. We have taken the liberty of deleting most acknowledgments (unless the context prohibits such deletions) and, where contextually appropriate, some of the notes. However, the original texts (save for obvious typos and inconsistencies) have been preserved intact. For complete papers, the reader is urged to refer to the originals, which are cited at the outset of each chapter.

Second, among Japan specialists across disciplines we have witnessed in the last decade what might be called a protest movement against the allegedly established, popularized image of Japan that strongly empha- sizes group solidarity, as exemplified by the celebrated phrase "Japan, Inc." Established scholars have been charged with circulating their biased models for Japanese studies, which are variously designated "group model," "consensus model," "holistic model," or simply "ste- reotype." New models, by implication, should stress the individualistic, egoistic, conflict-ridden, and dissension-prone aspects of the Japanese.

This kind of debate could be seen as a dialectic step toward a new synthesis, or less narrowly construed, as a welcome development for greater enrichment of the field.

It is up to the reader to decide how this controversy is to be appraised and whether it can be understood, as tacitly implied by Moeran (chap. 5), as a tempest in a teapot. Undoubtedly many models, not just one or two, are desirable to understand a complex society and culture like Japan's, but whether one model is really incompatible with another is a question that requires careful and serious study.

Our position is that one might let something essentially Japanese slip away by counterposing the individual to the group, dissension to consensus, conflict to harmony, equality to hierarchy, egoism to altruism. It is more fruitful, we believe, to see the two opposites as both sides of a single coin, or to discern one as it is embedded in the other. If the face-to-face smile in neighborhood interaction is a mandatory ritual, the back-to-back grimace will be a likely accompaniment. If selfless dedication is always demanded, it will be balanced off by a strategic manipulation of the double standard of *omote* (front) and *ura* (back), or of *tatemae* (the publicly enunciated principle) and *honne* (the privately held feeling), whereby self-indulgence is made permissible. Underlying this generalization may be a functional model of the human actor.

Intimately linked with the above argument is the issue of deviance. Again, it seems to make more sense to see deviance as an integral part of the normative pattern, to account for anomaly in terms of normalcy. The neurosis called *taijin-kyōfu* (the phobia of interpersonal exposure) described by Kasahara (chap. 21), for instance, would be more understandable if connected with the rigid protocol adhered to by Japanese in normative social interaction than if taken as a distinctly pathological category contradictory of normal sociability. Consider also such problems as the school phobia and school violence that is plaguing today's Japan. It goes without saying that these problems are inseparable from, not opposed to, the nationwide obsession with educational achievement validated by passage of entrance examinations for selected high schools and universities. Such educational problems are further interlaced with a child's home life. We are told by clinical specialists that a "normal," "good," and "smart" child is suddenly transformed into a monster who cruelly abuses his or her parents to the total disbelief of the latter. The suddenness of this turnabout, paradoxically, seems to indicate a continuity, not a discontinuity, between the normal and aberrant, or at least to suggest how slight the demarcation line is between the two realms. It is from this pespective that we have included Kawai's chapter on "Violence in the Home" (chap. 17).

There remains another point to be made with regard to the second issue. Any selected characteristic of the Japanese is not inherent in being Japanese but emerges only in comparison with other cultural groups. The reason many observers, Japanese or foreign, characterize the Japanese as group oriented, for example, and keep doing so despite criticisms is because the Japanese are usually compared with Americans or Westerners in general.

Take for example the concept of *amae* (propensity to depend upon another's presumed indulgence), which is captured and superbly analyzed by Doi in chapter 8. Doi claims that it offers a key to Japanese personality and social organization, and this claim has been confirmed and reconfirmed by many observers, as shown by the wide circulation of the word. Doi's argument obviously rings a bell with a large number of Japanese, in view of the persistent popularity of *Amae no kōzō* (the original of *Anatomy of Dependence,* 1973) which has sold over a million copies. This famous work, too, involves a comparison of Japanese with independence-minded Westerners. But as the comparative reference shifts, quite another image of Japan is likely to arise. It is not surprising, therefore, that O-Young Lee, a Korean scholar, in his Japanese book (1982) refutes the proposition that *amae* is unique to Japanese, arguing that Koreans are endowed with an even more elaborate vocabulary of their version of *amae.* Lee goes on to strongly criticize many other concepts proposed by Japanese authors, and eagerly seized upon by Japanese readers, as clues to Japanese uniqueness in thinking and behaving. This oversight is blamed on Japanese intellectuals who looked up to the West exclusively, bypassing Korea, their nearest neighbor, as a comparative reference. Lee offers the concept of *chijimi* (shrinkage or miniaturization) as a truly "unique" Japanese proclivity.

There is no doubt of the need for more research involving non-Western cultures as reference points, and we wish to call attention to two chapters in this volume which provide comparisons with Koreans and/or Chinese (see chap. 4 by Lebra and chap. 13 by Brandt). Nevertheless, we believe that there remains a great need for books introducing the Japanese to an English-speaking audience, books written in English and comprehensible within the frame of English-speaking cultures. The present volume is intended primarily to be such a book. For explicitly cross-cultural comparisons of Americans and Japanese, in addition to those cited above, see chapter 16 by Lanham, and chapter 4 by Caudill and Weinstein.

The third issue is that of change within Japan. It is clear to all that, within the last decade alone, technologically propelled change has taken place at an accelerated pace and has affected the overall life-style of the Japanese. What is more, the Japanese are not merely poor victims of the electronic revolution, but are insatiable consumers of its latest products, hardware and software. By the time this book is published, the *wāpuro* (word processor), today's craze among Japanese, may have become obsolescent junk. The earlier-mentioned protest against the "group model" is in part a response to this speed of change, in that everything "established" is destined, so it seems, soon to be hauled away as outmoded, hopelessly unequipped to negotiate with the ongoing change.

It should be noted that change, like a cultural characteristic, is a relative matter, relative to constancy. Change is recognized as such with reference to what does not change, and vice versa. It is a common practice, therefore, in studying social change to presuppose an earlier, stable state of affairs called "traditional" as a point of departure. Through a comparison between a tradition and a departure therefrom, that is, a change, one will arrive at a better understanding of both states. Befu's chapter (11) on gift-giving is a case in point, showing a significant contrast between the traditional and a newly emerging mode of gift-giving. The reader will learn as much about the older form as the newer one, the two offering themselves as mutual references. The same holds true with three village studies, all published in 1978, by Dore, Norbeck, and Smith, respectively, which focus on the remarkable change that transpired in each village since their earlier studies. The point is that change cannot be handled within itself but must be referred to something constant, stable, or "traditional."

While Befu (in chap. 11) focuses on change itself, several other studies collected here deal with change more or less secondarily, and the rest say little about the matter. Every chapter, however, brings insight to one aspect or another of *contemporary* Japanese life. Pelzel (chap. 1) writes about the myths whose origins are rooted in the prehistoric oral tradition of what much later came to be known as Japan. But his main point is to unearth out of the legendary past the views of human nature and the world which he considers to have persisted into contemporary Japan. All the other papers present topics more directly related to the present-day Japanese, and some depict very recent, still recurring events or phenomena. But none is addressed to what is today's latest and tomorrow's antique, which is probably best handled by the media. If Pelzel's chapter illuminates present Japan from the forgotten past, the others throw light upon the past and future from more recent data (such as advertisements). In other words, "contemporary" is to be understood as of longer duration than here and now. We are interested in something historically continuous or repetitive within a given time span, something more constant than the slippery "latest." Even if the phenomenon under study is transitory, or even if the study is addressed to change per se, interpretations of these should be longer lived in shedding light on contemporary Japanese, as attested to by all the contributions in this volume.

If we seem to be belaboring the obvious, the reason is that there are too many people who, partly because of media dependency, confuse the most updated with the real. Japanese are no exception in having an inflated sense of change about their life-style and in taking the media presentation of "changing" Japanese for their "real" selves. The rural-urban continuum arouses a similar response, dismissing rural Japanese as insignificant (in numbers and influence). If Tokyo represents urbanity, then the rest of the country is rural in a relative sense; but we know there are "rural" enclaves within Tokyo as well. We do not subscribe to the notion that Tokyo is most representative of the Japanese, nor do we discern such a discontinuity between rural and urban.

To pursue the same point further, a typical response by a young Japanese to a question regarding "arranged marriage" brings a scoffing denial, "Nobody is as old-fashioned as to marry that way any more." We know this to be flatly untrue. On the contrary, arranged marriage thrives as ever through the commercialization and professionalization of the arranging agents as well as the computerization of matching. True, it is no longer a "traditional" form of arrangement and its function has changed somewhat, but this marriage industry would not have prospered so unless grafted on the traditional acceptability (and respectability) of the arranged, initially loveless marriage. In fact, the same woman who has given a response like the one above may be undergoing the *miai* (prearranged introduction of prospective spouses to each other). She is not consciously lying but only blind to herself, so entrenched is the notion that new equals good, and oblivious to what is left behind.

We are not advocating conservatism, but are saying that, no matter what ideological position is taken, one should be aware of the gaps which always exist between the newsworthy, latest mode and the prevailing, and therefore news-unworthy mode of life. Chapter 6 by De Vos helps us realize such gaps and understand the cultural-psychological mechanism for the persistence of a traditional mode such as arranged marriage. Likewise, Salamon (chap. 9) on the Japanese version of male tyranny will give a clue to why women's liberation is so tardy in Japan despite liberated women or career women occupying media space as a popular topic, and why a large portion of Japanese housewives are found through occasional large-sample surveys, to the surprise of many male and female readers, to be contented with their lot.

The foregoing discussion on change boils down to the common-sense viewpoint that while change is essential to life, there are limits in the magnitude, velocity, and directions of change. No life, after all, can tolerate total unpredictability. Colby (1966), following the linguistic discovery of the 50 percent redundancy in a message, suggests *"that life in general, like language, seeks an equilibrium of about 50 percent redundancy—an equilibrium between the new (unexpected) and the old (predicted)"* (p. 369, Colby's italics). As a dynamic analogy, Colby suggests the pendulum, swinging back and forth, passing a midpoint, and checking one swing by a counterswing so as not to go out of control in either direction. Well matched with this notion of pendulumlike motion is Rohlen's study (chap. 18) on the training of bank employees: the training aims to straighten out the new college graduates, presumably accustomed to self-indulgence and liberal ideology (a swing in one direction) as part of campus life, by instilling the "spirit" which is no less than an essence of the Japanese tradition (a counterswing).

The pendulum analogy also seems to fit the overall change that Japan is experiencing today. On the one hand, we have the impression that the traditional social order is threatening to break down, as summarized from reports on the rates and types of crime (e.g., crimes committed by law enforcement officers), the decline of schoolteachers' authority, family disintegration signaled by divorce rates, premarital pregnancy, and sexual laxity in general.[1] Looked at in a positive light, the Japanese appear to be enjoying an increasingly greater degree of freedom, individuality, privacy, variation, and equality, partly as the result of affluence, as well as of urbanization and a postwar value change. It might be said that Japan is fast moving toward a Western or American model, good or bad, steered or unsteered.

A steered or propelled movement would imply that the Japanese are still burdened with a sense of ethnic inferiority vis-à-vis the West, which urges them to catch up. If unsteered, the process might be understood as a confirmation of the convergence theory. According to this theory, which is a latter-day version of evolutionism, industrial technology, once it takes root, imposes its own mandate upon all other sectors of society to transform institutions and human behavior, regardless of cultural traditions, toward greater rationality, individuality, and impersonality. In this view, cultural differences would be reduced ultimately to technological lags. We cannot totally deny this aspect of change in Japan, as partially admitted by Dore (1973) in his "late development effect" thesis.

On the other hand, Japan's rise as a superpower through its phenomenal economic growth is generating a new level of self-confidence and pride among most Japanese. The growth in economic and technological strength is not alone responsible for this change. The academic performance of schoolchildren, measured by the results of internationally conducted tests, is also a contributing factor. The newly gained pride is not so much self-generated as it is a response to the praise and admiration of Japan's achievement by foreigners, notably Americans, who have so far believed themselves to be top of the world. Vogel's *Japan as Number One* (1979) stands as a symbolic watershed in the self-reappraisal of both Americans and Japanese. Earlier, Bayley's (1976) comparative study of police behavior in Japan and the United States contributed to the image of Japan as the world's safest country, the aforementioned rising crime rate notwithstanding. Doubtless these observers, eager to give lessons to Americans, exaggerate Japan's success and idealize Japan. These observations upset many Japanese, who believe that such idealizations will retard Japan's progress and intensify tendencies, particularly the undemocratic, authoritarian aspects of Japanese institutions, that should be eliminated. (For a more ambivalent, less idealized, view of the Japanese police, see Ames 1981.) But many more Japanese are receptive to whatever Westerners say about them. Having long specialized as a learner and emulator, Japan is now being promoted to the status of a teacher and model. Foreign leaders in many fields, business and education in particular, are visiting Japan to gain lessons from their host.

The implications of this change are far-reaching. The enhancement of Japan's status in the international prestige hierarchy is often credited to the Japanese tradition of culture and human relations going back to well before the war era. What interests the foreign learners is not Japanese products as such, but the so-called Japanese style of management, labor-management relations, and student motivation. Not unrelated to this trend is an enthusiasm among many Westerners for martial arts, Zen, tea ceremony, and other traditional arts of Japan. Reassured, Japanese leaders urge their people to reappreciate their national traditions, and patronizingly offer cultural tips to foreign novices. Some conservative politicians are trying to exploit this revivalistic current in order to restore Shinto, as symbolized by Yasukuni Shrine (for war dead) and Ise Shrine (for the Sun Goddess), as a national religion, and to "Japanize" the postwar constitution, a product of the Allied occupation. Japanese history textbooks are under revision, with a view to arousing in the young a sense of national pride. The thrust of this revision is the softening and deleting of the morally reprehensible marks of Japan's past. We get some of the same from scholarly quarters as well. There are scholars who espouse *wakon wasai* (Japanese spirit and Japanese ingenuity) to replace the old, familiar slogan, *wakon yōsai* (Japanese spirit and Western ingenuity), and who advocate the exportation of Japanese software (culture) as well as hardware (technology).

The pendulum seems to be in full swing, and we are not certain what new equilibrium Japan is moving toward. What is certain is that change is far from unidirectional, and that the process and directionality of change are interlocked with the vestiges of tradition, as well demonstrated by many chapters of this book.

Something else is certain. Exposed to the ever-amplifying international flow of goods, information, and, above all, people, Japan can no longer remain smug about its claimed homogeneity; it is joining most other large nations which are culturally heterogeneous and often torn by ethnic protests and antagonisms. An increasing number of foreigners come to Japan not as visitors, but as long-term residents, employees, refugees, or spouses of Japanese. Besides these foreign settlers and their "mixed" offspring,[2] Japan is facing the problem of how to handle the *kikokushijo* (young returnees from abroad), whose numbers are reaching a proportion that policymakers can no longer ignore. These children, usually born and raised abroad and only physically Japanese, are unable to adjust to the cultural environment of Japan, particularly to the strictures of the educational system. Their marginal status is indicated by such labels as *hen-japa* (odd Japanese) and *han-japa* (half-Japanese) (Kitsuse, Murase, and Yamamura n.d.). Japan is under mounting pressure to recognize and manage the problem of ethnic and cultural diversity, and its latest slogan is "Internationalization" of Japan. Nevertheless, this is where the traditional repertoire of Japanese culture is felt to be most inept in providing guidelines. Furthermore, the issue of ethnic heterogeneity, while it is new, revives the old issue of ethnic minorities. Apparently, many of the ethnic minorities—Ainu, Okinawans, Koreans, Chinese, and the "yet-to-be-liberated" people (the former outcastes)—would prefer to pass as Japanese. Others, especially Koreans, are displaying their minority identity, armed with pride and militant egalitarianism (Lee and De Vos 1981). We regret that limitations of space and appropriateness for this volume do not allow us to cover these issues of ethnic diversification and minorities. We do hope, however, that what is included in this volume will provide insights into the psychological plight of Japan's minorities, marginals, and outsiders.

As indicated by the title, this book is about interrelationships between *culture* and *behavior:* the cultural context of behavior on the one hand, and the behavioral manifestations of culture on the other. The part divisions reflect these modes of relationship between culture and the individual or behavior. Part 1 focuses on morality as a combination of culturally articulated and shared "value standards" both imposed upon the individual and held as individually internalized and expressed sentiments. Part 2 presents patterns of interaction, communication, and grouping as a social bridge between culture and the individual. Part 3 addresses some aspects of child rearing and one aspect of adult training.

Here culture-focused "socialization" is balanced off by individual-focused "development" or maturation. Part 4 turns to some manifestations of pathology which, while revealing a mismatch between cultural norms and individual behavior, are nevertheless explainable in terms of cultural expectations. A greater portion of this section, however, is devoted to a variety of culturally available therapies.

In selecting the contributions to this reader, we wished to present diverse perspectives and topics. Included are a mix of Japanese and Western scholars representing different disciplines—anthropology, psychology, psychiatry, sociology, and linguistics. At the same time we felt bound by the need to offer a coherent picture of Japanese culture and behavior so that one chapter would be reinforced, complemented, enriched, or balanced, but not totally cancelled out, by another chapter. We attempted to avoid presenting a jumble of mutually unrelated or grossly contradictory viewpoints which would frustrate and discourage the reader.

Ten out of the total twenty-three chapters were retained from the first edition, either because they have gained the reputation of being "classics" and thus would serve as an important point of departure, and/or because they remain quite relevant in explaining, if not describing, behavior of contemporary Japanese. The reader should recall our earlier comments about change.

We regret that many other papers which would deserve inclusion for their quality had to be omitted due to space constraints. Needless to say, responsibility for the arrangement of chapters and editorial comments rests with us alone.

TAKIE SUGIYAMA LEBRA
WILLIAM P. LEBRA

Notes

1. Sexual laxity may be exaggerated also in the minds of media-sensitive Japanese. According to a recent survey (Hayashi 1983), teenagers' sexual activities appear to be milder than might be expected. For example, as of 1981, kissing had been experienced by only 16 percent of boys and 13 percent of girls of fifteen years of age or younger; petting by 8 percent and 6 percent; and intercourse by 4 percent and 2 percent (Hayashi 1983:90–91). Coleman (1983), in his study of family planning in Japan, describes urban Japanese as sexually too inhibited for successful birth control by means other than abortion. Furthermore, whether the claimed sexual freedom is a sign of change or not depends upon what time span is taken for comparison. The sexual freedom among women in Suye Mura observed in the mid-1930s (Smith and Wiswell 1982) is a cautionary reminder in this respect.

2. See Strong 1978 for a psychosocial study of konketsuji (mixed-blood children).

PART ONE

Moral Values and Sentiments

Editorial Note to Part One

MORALITY refers to value standards by which a certain conduct is judged and sanctioned as right or wrong, good or bad, just or unjust, noble or ignoble, and so on. Focusing on Japanese concepts of morality, we regard culture foremost as a storehouse of such value standards. Individuals are disposed, though admittedly in varying degrees, to regulate or justify their conduct and to evaluate one another's conduct according to one or another standard drawn from that storehouse. Morality involves both constraints *upon* the individual and sentiments held and aroused *in* the individual.

Part 1 begins with John C. Pelzel's analysis of myths that appear in the *Kojiki* (Records of ancient matters) and *Nihongi* (Chronicles of Japan, also called *Nihon Shoki*), compiled by imperial order in A.D. 712 and 720, respectively. Pelzel's chapter may well be read as an introduction to the entire volume, in that it reveals intimate parallels between mythical motifs and "real" human life, whether the former are regarded as projections or metaphors of the latter (both projections and metaphors come under the umbrella of symbols in our view). Indeed, Pelzel does suggest such parallels between mythical dramas on the one hand, and human nature and human life on the other, as conceived by the early Japanese and still largely relevant to modern Japanese.

There is another reason that this article heads the first part of this volume. Value standards vary from specific to general, from situational to ultimate, from relative to mandatory. It is generally assumed that the general-ultimate-mandatory end of the scale is embedded in the realm beyond human jurisdiction, that is, the supernatural world. A supernatural being might be looked up to as an exemplary moral actor, or as a creator, proclaimer, and enforcer of a moral order. What is said and done by gods who appear in the mythical narratives, especially major gods in the Shinto pantheon, such as the Sun Goddess and her recalcitrant brother, Susanoo, may provide a clue to the nature of Japanese morality.

Before going into his analysis of the myths, Pelzel gives a summary of major cycles of myths, and here the reader might, if so inclined, find a number of oppositions, such as heaven versus earth, either of these versus the netherworld, sea versus land, pure versus impure, birthing versus killing, and the like, and even decipher the "grammar" of universal human thought. But Pelzel's interest lies elsewhere. He wants to delineate the "Japanese" thought process primarily in contrast to its Chinese or continental counterpart. This idiographic focus leads him to minimize rather than to capitalize upon such oppositions. What strikes him is, in fact, the relative lack of opposition between, in addition to those mentioned above, gods and humans, life and death, mortal and immortal, order and disorder, blessedness and misery, wild and tamed, nature and culture. Between these, there is no gulf, no confrontation, no dominance, no contradistinction; instead, one finds continuity, compromise, fusion, and duplication. So too is the relationship between good and evil. Hence we come to learn that the gods do not play the role of exemplary moral actors nor do they take full charge of maintaining a moral order. Moral standards are more or less relative and lack the kind of didactic assertions that feature in the rationally oriented Chinese myths and philosophy. What compels the Japanese individual as a moral actor, as extrapolated by Pelzel from the early myths, is his consideration of other persons, often worded as *giri* or *ninjō*. If there is anything close to an ultimate standard, it is, we are led to believe, the cleanness of the actor's heart.

The world of the *Kojiki* and *Nihongi* does not exhaust the Japanese sense of morality or worldview, however. Undeniably, Confucianism and Buddhism have had overwhelming impact upon Japanese culture and behavior, and the Japanese sense of morality cannot be captured without considering these. The point is that the long history of religious and philosophical transfusions from the Sinified continent and of the conglomeration of newer beliefs with the earlier "native" cult (which came to be known as Shinto) has not replaced the pre-Confucian, pre-Buddhist intuitions and sentiments symbolized by the myths. Not surprisingly then, we read about "the principle of harmony that admits no distinction between good and bad" (Smith 1983:47) as operating in today's Japan.

Pelzel's thesis finds its empirical elaboration in chapter 2, where Pamela J. Asquith, a British primatologist, reports on an event she witnessed involving a group of colleagues, Japanese primate researchers. Describing a memorial service for dead monkeys, this short essay reveals the status equivalence (or lack of opposition) between human and animal life which entitles the "souls" of monkeys to the same Buddhist rite as for the human dead. Something more may be read into this chapter, although it is not the author's point. While showing such humane compassion for the dead monkeys, the Japanese mourners apparently are not opposed to lethal experimentations on live monkeys. In other words, the Japanese, while holding a belief in the sacredness of all life, are not as extreme as antivivisectionists or the "right-to-life" groups of antiabortionists found in the West. Nor do they find suicide morally abhorrent. Their regard for life does not reach the dogmatic extreme of "absolute."

In chapter 3, Eiichirō Ishida, a Japanese cultural anthropologist, throws light upon Japanese moral values, conversely, by presenting his views of Germans, Christians, and Westerners in general, whose cultural ancestry he traces to the ancient warlike nomadic Indo-European peoples. From the Japanese standpoint, Westerners embody extreme, fierce, unrelenting emotions, as shown by the chapter title, and moral severity, intolerance, and tenacity in punishing wrongdoers. This implacability is symbolized, Ishida suggests, by the Nazi swastika and the Christian cross alike. The Japanese are characterized by an inclination toward compromise, pliability, and moral leniency. What underlies the Western extremism is the propensity to distinguish yes from no, friend from foe, likes from dislikes, to a logical extreme, while Japanese remain undisposed to dichotomize these so clearly. The reader need not be reminded that Ishida's viewpoint echoes Pelzel's thesis and Asquith's observation. Western culture, thus characterized, might be called a culture of oppositions.

Chapter 4 turns our attention to two East Asian cultures, Chinese and Korean, as comparative references for delineating the Japanese sense of morality. Takie Sugiyama Lebra analyzes the results of sentence-completion tests administered to samples of adult residents of Tokyo, Hong Kong, and Seoul, focusing on compensative justice (rewards for moral acts and punishments for immoral acts) and purposeful moral actions. While no cross-cultural difference is found in the respondents' expectations of rewards for "perseverance" and "kindness," and of retributions for "wrongdoing," the kinds of rewards and retributions are remarkably varied. Japanese surpass Chinese in stressing the human, subjective, inner consequences, while Chinese are more disposed to strive for success and goal attainment and to anticipate objective, external consequences. Koreans generally, if not always, stand in between. When the respondents articulate what sorts of resources are to be mobilized to attain a goal like "to build an ideal home life," Japanese and Koreans pay attention to cooperation and family relations, whereas Chinese emphasize diligence, rationality, and economy. These findings lead the author to conclude that there are two types of humanism, Japanese and Chinese. Among other findings is the difference in response styles: Japanese more frequently accept the vicarious role of the actor in the sentence, whereas more Chinese take a didactic, detached role in instructing the actor.

The quality of the individual's inner state has been noted by Pelzel and Lebra as a core of Japanese morality, and was speculated to be a basis for the individual's integrity against group conformity. In chapter 5, Brian Moeran leads us much further on this aspect of Japanese morality by capturing two terms, *seishin* (spirit) and *kokoro* (heart), as umbrellalike "keywords" embracing many Japanese concepts thereunder. Drawing illustrations from a broad array of popular idioms used in connection with nationwide high school baseball tournaments, art pottery, and advertisements, Moeran makes a semantic analysis to demonstrate how *seishin* and *kokoro* mingle together to make group ideology compatible with individual character and spontaneity, or to reinforce the Japanese tradition of morality while at the same time "smuggling" in Western ideas. All this is accomplished, claims the author, without capitulating to Western "individualism," which remains anathema in Japanese eyes. The controversy of the group model versus individualistic model (see Introduction) is thus reduced to "Japan's internal cultural debate."

Unlike the preceding chapters where moral values were identified and analyzed largely at an ideational level, chapter 6 delves deeply into the psychodynamic layer of morality, centering around guilt. The Japanese have been characterized, through Ruth Benedict's famous work (1946), as shame oriented, but De Vos reveals in them a strong undercurrent of guilt, together with shame, the former being stronger than the latter (see Lebra 1983 for a similar conclusion reversing Benedict's contention). Based on a sample of responses to a Japanese version of the Thematic Apperception Test (TAT) gathered in rural Japan, De Vos recognizes the guilt, instilled through childhood socialization, toward sacrificial parents. The guilt seeks its expiation, as projected in TAT narratives, through one's achievement or self-reform. In connection with marriage it is reflected in the projection of tragic consequences for a love marriage which has been carried out against the parents' wishes. Further, both male and female respondents tend to blame marital discord and the husband's profligacy on the wife's inadequacy as a wife and mother. Theoretically, this chapter brings into question the Freudian conceptions of guilt such as the presumed embeddedness of guilt in sexuality (see Pelzel's discussion of sexuality in chap. 1) and of the superego as distinct from the ego-ideal.

1

Human Nature in the Japanese Myths

John C. Pelzel

WHAT follows is an attempt to describe one traditional Japanese literary view of human nature, that pictured in the myth portions of the *Kojiki* and *Nihongi*. Though the quality seen in man is the main interest here, it has seemed desirable to describe also the myth's view of his context—the nature of the world and of mankind's role in it.

These sources constitute only one of the models that the basic literary tradition made available to later generations of Japanese. Buddhist and lay Chinese conceptions were in time absorbed, and in recent centuries ideas from the West, and we must assume that throughout history the native talent reworked the body of perceptions it had before it in varying ways. Nevertheless, the myths are the earliest repositories of this tradition, and in spite of many additions to Japanese eschatological literature and numerous fluctuations of fashion, the myths have not been rewritten, nor have they ceased to be well known and viewed with at least some measure of respect by even moderately well-educated Japanese. They are thus the most persistent, and at least one of the basic, sources of native literary views on these matters.

The behavioral relevance of such a model is an interesting problem. One may wish to argue that a society's basic literature offers cognitive limits and patterns according to which the native mind tends to build up its understanding of the world and of man. As values, the views of prestigious literature may be accepted by native individuals as proper judgments and can even affect the choices through which, in part, they form their own personalities. Nevertheless, and critical as the question of behavioral relevance undoubtedly is in many contexts, it is beyond the scope of the present paper, which will confine itself to the attempt to discern the mythic model itself.

What the *Kojiki* and the *Nihongi* have to say about the cosmos and

From *Personality in Japanese History*, A. M. Craig and D. H. Shively, eds. (Berkeley: University of California Press, 1970). © 1970 The Regents of the University of California, used by permission of the University of California Press.

man was not set out in any self-conscious or reasoned statement. These books are art forms, a mixture of narrative legend and poetry. But in this they are characteristic of the main form of the Japanese literary tradition, which in this respect contrasts so sharply with the Chinese corpus as to merit a reminder.

The bulk of the respected literature of China has been a formal ethics, identified with individual professional philosophers, and a history deliberately written to illustrate the conclusions of the philosophers. Chinese literature is thus rational and intellectualized, as well as didactic. Its thrust, moreover, is such as to counsel agnosticism about the nature of the cosmos, earthly pragmatism about the role of man therein, and disinterest in most aspects of human nature except the moral. Japanese literature, by way of contrast, has from its beginnings in the myths taken forms—such as poetry, fiction, and the drama—which are best suited to an approach by intuition and imagination rather than reason. This literature has been much given, moreover, to questioning and picturing the place of individual men in a cosmos that includes, but that goes far beyond, earthly society. Certainly, then, what the Chinese and the Japanese sources have to say about man differ not alone in the traits of personality they discern or emphasize, but even more basically in the approach to the human condition that they illustrate. Chinese literature had faith in conscious moral will and exhorted man to be what he should be in one overwhelmingly important segment of life. Japanese literature instead had faith in intuition and described men in terms of the whole existence they were seen to lead.

The context and the events of life are thus basic to the interpretation of the Japanese myths, and their narrative accordingly deserves to be recapitulated here. In details, the stories of the two books under consideration vary slightly, but both were well known and had roughly equal prestige.[1] The retelling that follows attempts to combine important elements from both tales, noting the textual divergence only when this seems to have a particular significance.

The myths fall into several cycles, most centering on certain major figures and events and roughly sequent to one another in terms of myth chronology. We may briefly divide this chronology into three myth eras, namely, Before the Creation of the Earth, the Creation of the Earth, and the Ordering of the Earth.

The Era before the Creation of the Earth

This first segment of the myths is extremely brief and, in contrast with what follows, aesthetically unrewarding. The story starts with heaven already in existence,[2] though we are told virtually nothing about it until the third and final era, and with the earth still a formless thing, floating about below heaven "medusalike," "like drifting oil." The first precursor of creation was the growth of a "thing like a reed shoot," which in its turn gave rise to three or four (varying with the source) deities described as "single," that is, each existing alone, at a different time, without discernible relation to the others, and, it may be added, without our learning anything about them other than their names.[3] These were followed by four or five generations, each of which comprised a pair of gods, one male and one female, described as "brother and sister." The last such pair, Izanagi (the brother) and Izanami, were the creator gods par excellence.

The Creation of the Earth

With this segment, the story comes to life. The creator siblings stood on the "floating bridge of heaven," stirred the formlessness below with the "heavenly jewel spear," and watched the brine dripping from its point curdle into an island, Onogoro. Descending to it, they erected there the "pillar of the center of the land" and proceeded to the work of creation.

In part, they created as their exuviae, articles of their clothing, and so forth turned into progeny. But in part they created through normal mammalian sexual reproduction, which is given by far the greater attention in this cycle. As it turns out, they must discover or invent sexual reproduction, and they perform a ritual to accompany it, a marriage rite, as well.

Izanagi, as though casting about for a method of creation, asked his sister how her body was formed. She replied that in one place it was "not complete." Noting that his own body at one point had "something left over," he then proposed, "How would it be if we were to fill in the place on your body that is not complete with the spot on mine where something is left over, and so give birth to the land?" She replied simply, "That would be good."

Izanagi likewise devised a ritual, which consisted in their circumambulating the pillar of the center of the land from opposite directions, he from the left and she from the right; on meeting on the other side, they would "perform the acts of the honeymoon chamber."[4] On the first attempt, however, the sister exclaimed first, on the far side of the pillar, "What a fine, lovely youth!"—a forwardness which her brother considered a breach of the proper male-female relationship. He therefore had them perform the circumambulation again and exclaim on one another's loveliness in the proper sequence. As a result of the breach of etiquette that had occurred, however, one of their children was born deformed.[5]

By sexual reproduction and something approaching parthenogenesis, therefore, the siblings created a large number of deities, many identifiable with the seas, islands, rivers, mountains, and vegetation of Japan and other (for example, the Sun Goddess) deities who came later to occupy key positions in heaven or in the process by which the created earth was put into order.

Only the *Kojiki* and certain variants cited by the compilers of the *Nihongi*, but not the text of the *Nihongi* itself, tell a version of the common Old World tale of Orpheus and Eurydice in Hades. According to the Japanese version, Izanami was badly burned by the birth of the Fire God and died, going to the "world of darkness." Mourning for her and wishing to persuade her to come back and continue the unfinished work of creation, Izanagi followed her, but when he met her he violated her order not to look at her and saw her in the corruption of her body. Frightened, he fled toward the upper world while she, in shame, sent avenging deities after him. He was able to trick them, however, and in the end took leave of his sister-wife at the Even Pass of Hades in enmity, she threatening to strangle earthly people, and he boasting that he could easily replace such losses, building "1,500 parturition huts a day." Back on earth, according to the *Kojiki*, he then saw other deities created from his exuviae, and according to both books he retired to a life of perpetual quiet on the islands of Japan.

The Ordering of the Earth

Much the longest and most circumstantial, this segment of the myths consists of several cycles depicting the events whereby the created earth was ordered into the particular life forms we know. Not only is it richer in detail than what goes before, there also is repeated variation between the two main texts, and numerous variants are cited by the compilers of the *Nihongi*.

The story begins with a cycle depicting the relations in heaven between the Sun Goddess, now ruling there on the authority of her parent(s), and her younger brother Susanoo (the meaning of whose name we do not know). Susanoo had from birth been a selfish, cruel, and unruly god, whose very presence "withered mountains and dried up rivers and seas" and encouraged the "sound of bad deities to be like flies in the fifth moon." His parent(s) therefore had ordered him to proceed to the nether world (or the sea) to be its ruler where he could not harm the things of earth, but instead, at the start of this cycle, he had risen up to heaven.

His rising made so fierce a commotion it alerted and alarmed his sister, who wondered if he came "with good intentions" or to rob her of her kingdom. Fearing the latter, she dressed and armed herself like a man, gave a battle cry, and went to question him on the "redness of his heart," i.e., his sincerity. He protested his innocence, saying he had only wished to bid his sister good-bye before leaving to take up his own realm far away. To test the purity of his intentions, however, brother and sister engaged in an ordeal which amounted to a symbolic act of incest. She chewed up his sword and spat out its pieces as children, while he did likewise with the jewels of her regalia. They then exchanged children, those treated as hers and as inheritors of her authority and ancestors of the imperial family being the sons her brother spat out from her regalia.

The result of the ordeal was accepted as vindication of his intentions, and he remained a visitor in heaven. However, he continued to perform acts which were aggressive and destructive—breaking down the dikes around his sister's rice fields, letting a piebald colt loose in her fields at harvest time, defecating on the floor of her palace, and so forth. The Sun Goddess did not protest these acts, however, in each case finding an excuse for them that was acceptable to her. For example, she decided that in tearing down the dikes among her fields he had been moved by a helpful intent, impractical as it was in actuality, merely to increase the area that could be planted to rice, and she imagined that what looked like excrement on her floor was really nothing but vomit that he had brought up during an otherwise forgivable bout of drunkenness.

Eventually, however, Susanoo broke a hole in her roof while she was weaving, and threw in the corpse of a piebald colt flayed backwards. She (or her maids) was so startled that she jumped up and wounded herself (or themselves) on the shuttle. Indignant at this personal outrage and harm, she withdrew into a cave, locked the door, and so reduced heaven to darkness. Thereupon, the *Kojiki* adds, the "voices of the myriad [evil?] deities were like the flies in the fifth moon as they swarmed, and myriad portents of woe all arose."

The heavenly deities met together in a riverbed and consulted on how to end this intolerable situation. They collected a number of objects and performed various rituals, but they also did things to pique the Sun Goddess's curiosity and vanity. Having birds fill the air with song, they also had a goddess perform a noisy dance so lewd ("pulling out the nipples of her breasts and pushing down her skirt-string to her private parts") that they all laughed. Hearing the sounds of apparent revelry outside and wondering how the deities could make merry with herself absent and the world dark, the Sun Goddess stuck her head out to see what was happening. A mirror was immediately pushed up in front of her face, and she was told that it was a "deity more illustrious than" herself. Quite upset, she came out farther until she could be grasped and was implored by the deities not to deprive them of herself again. The heavenly deities then took upon themselves the judgement of Susanoo. Fining him for the pollution he had caused, they banished him from heaven, in effect voting for the continued rule of the Sun Goddess.

In the next cycle, Susanoo descended to earth, at a spot known historically as Izumo, and after saving the daughter of a pair of "earthly deities" from a monstrous dragon, produced from her a progeny that was to rule earth for a period, the principal descendant being the so-called Master of the Land. Susanoo himself then proceeded to the nether world he had for so long avoided.

At this point, the sources vary considerably. It is clear from all that the earth was still untamed. As one variant says, "This central land of reed-plains had always been waste and wild. The very rocks, trees, and herbs were all given to violence." The text of the *Nihongi* notes that "earth had numerous deities which buzzed like flies. There were also trees and herbs, all of which could speak." This subcelestial world had to be "constructed . . . for the sake of the visible race of man as well as for beasts . . . in order to do away with the calamities [that occur to] birds, beasts, and creeping things," and all texts make it clear that the progeny of the Sun Goddess, who were eventually to rule Japan, did not want to take on so noisome a place until it had been made habitable.

However, the *Kojiki* and several of the variants cited by the compilers of the *Nihongi* have most of this taming task performed by the Master of the Land, earth-born scion of Susanoo, before the Sun Goddess's emissaries descended, and tell a number of tales in which he exerted his humanizing influence on earth. The *Nihongi* itself, in contrast, gives very little space to Susanoo's progeny and has the humanizing work performed by ministers of the Sun Goddess and the heavenly deities, thus implying the dereliction of Susanoo's line. It is in this that the text of the *Nihongi* perhaps most clearly edits the record in a way ennobling to the imperial family, which claimed descent from the Sun Goddess. The tales told of the Master of the Land by the *Kojiki* and the variants add much that is of cultural interest, however, and because they also were available to all readers of the myths they will be recapitulated here.

In one, the Master of the Land is pictured as at first the despised servant of his eighty lusty, aggressive, and selfish brothers, relegated by them to carrying their baggage while they go in pursuit of a desirable female. On the way, they met a hare which had lost its fur. The elder brothers, as a cruel joke, told it to bathe in sea water, but when it did and the water dried, its skin cracked and put it in great pain. The Master of the Land, feeling pity for it, told it to roll in pollen, which formed a soothing cloak, and the hare in gratitude promised him the hand of the princess. Angered because she therefore accepted him rather than themselves, the eighty brothers twice killed the Master of the Land, once by striking him with a searing hot stone and once by catching him in the fork of a split tree, but each time his own mother brought him back to life.

Going to the nether world, the Master of the Land married his half-sister, the daughter of his father, Susanoo. His cruel parent then submitted him to several tortures. Once confined to a pit of snakes and once in a house filled with centipedes and wasps, the son was in each case saved by a scarf, given him in secret by his wife, which served to ward off these loathsome creatures. Again, Susanoo shot an arrow into the moor and sent the Master of the Land to fetch it, but then set fire to the moor grass to kill him. The Master of the Land again was saved, this time by a mouse that showed him a hole in which to hide while the fire passed overhead and then showed him the location of the arrow, which he therefore was able to return to his father as ordered. In the end, Susanoo fell asleep while the Master of the Land was performing the filial task of picking lice out of his hair, which the son therefore tied to the rafters and, stealing his father's sword, bows and arrows, and lute, fled with his own wife. Starting up, Susanoo was delayed long enough by his hair's entanglement that the refugees were able to get past the Even Pass of Hades. Thereupon Susanoo, giving the accolade to success, called to the Master of the Land that he must become the ruler of the earth and put his eighty unruly elder brothers to death, which he did.

The *Kojiki* continues its special attention to the progeny of Susanoo, competitors-to-be of the imperial line, by picturing a series of love affairs the Master of the Land had with several women on earth after he had returned to it in the company of his wife. He took up again with the princess he had earlier won from his eighty elder brothers. Again, telling of his courtship of another girl, the myth is able to paint the type of scene that was to be popular in Heian literature at least three centuries later. The Master of the Land is shown standing all night outside her bedroom, rattling her locked door and imploring her to let him in, while she replies that she is, "like a drooping plant, my heart . . . a bird on a sandbank," and that she will not let him in until the next night, when she promises that his "arms white as rope of paper-mulberry bark shall softly pat [my] breast soft as the melting snow."

Predictably, the wife of the Master of the Land became jealous and must have threatened to leave him, for he sang that if she indeed left, her "weeping shall. . . . rise as the mist of the morning shower." She, trying then to appeal to his sympathy, offered him a drink and sang "[Thou], being a man, probably hast on the various island headlands that thou seest, and on every beach, . . . a wife like the young herbs. But as for me, alas! being a woman, I have no man except thee. . . ."

In spite of this appeal, the *Kojiki* ends this cycle of amorous tales by list-
ing the numerous progeny the Master of the Land subsequently had
with still other girls.

The same sources that tell the story of Susanoo's progeny on earth,
moreover, ascribe to the Master of the Land a series of the humanizing
tasks. It is said that "for the sake of the visible race of man as well as for
beasts, [he and his helper] determined the method of healing diseases,"
and also that they, "in order to do away with the calamities of birds,
beasts, and creeping things, established means for their prevention and
control." Again, it is noted that whereas formerly "the very rocks, trees,
and herbs were all given to violence," the Master of the Land has "now
reduced them to submission, and there is none that is not compliant.
. . . It is I, and I alone, who now govern this land."

In any event, there begins here the cycle of tales according to which,
with only slight variations, all sources agree that in spite of the Master
of the Land's ministrations the earth was still not a suitable place, and
tell of the steps by which the Sun Goddess's descendants take over its
control. Japan "is still painfully uproarious," "violent and savage
earthly deities are numerous," and rocks and vegetation still have the
power of speech. In sum, "that country . . . is a tumbledown land, hideous to look on," and the Sun Goddess's progeny refuse to descend to it
as they are ordered until things have been put right there.

In consequence, when the Sun Goddess decided that the son her
brother spat out from her regalia (or, in other versions, when another
god decided that her grandson through that son) shall rule the earth, a
congress of heavenly deities has first to be convened to decide which of
the gods should be sent to make the land fit for the divine children. The
emissaries so dispatched, it turned out, were not faithful, but instead
curried favor with the ruling Master of the Land, settled down with
earthly goddesses, and did not even report back to heaven. Ultimately,
however, a pair of emissaries was found who asked the Master of the
Land to stand down in favor of the heavenly line. Consulting his own
son, the incumbent ruler decided not to resist the intercession and
"became concealed" forever in the shrine of Izumo, still one of the principal spots of state Shinto worship. In all versions, Ninigi no mikoto,
grandson of the Sun Goddess, is the first of the heavenly line to descend
and rule the earth, after the emissaries who received the submission of
the Master of the Land pacified it and made it a fit place to live.

Among the heavenly grandchild's first acts on earth was his mating
with a beautiful girl. The *Kojiki* and some variants also say that he
refused to mate as well with this girl's ugly elder sister, and that because
of this act of uncharity the emperors of Japan were doomed to be mortal. In all versions, Ninigi no mikoto made his wife pregnant in only one

night and therefore expressed doubts that he could possibly be the father. Piqued, and submitting herself to an ordeal to prove his paternity, she set fire to her parturition hut and the children born therein were unharmed. At his death, the heavenly grandchild was the first of the long line of early emperors who were buried in the great *kurgans,* many of which are still known in western and central Japan.

In a final cycle, the two sons born to Ninigi no mikoto proved to have gifts for fishing and the sea, and hunting and the land. They decided to exchange tools and occupations for awhile, but soon became bored and the fisherman elder brother asked for his hooks back. The clumsy younger brother, however, had lost them, and though he made offers of restitution nothing would satisfy the overbearing elder brother except the return of the very hooks lost. The younger brother was in despair, but eventually made his way to the palace of the Sea God, at the bottom of the sea. Marrying the Sea God's daughter and recovering the lost hooks, he returned to land with his wife and a jewel that gave him control of the tide, which he used to make his elder brother liege to him. One of the sons (or, according to a variant, one of the grandsons) of the younger brother and the daughter of the Sea God came to be known as Jimmu Tennō, taken by traditional Japanese historiography to have been the founder of the imperial Japanese family.

At this point, what the Japanese considered to be the mythic portion of the tales ends. Though much of what follows in the *Kojiki* and *Nihongi* still smacks more of legend than of history, it is perhaps permissible to abandon the story here and turn to the attempt to analyze the myths.

Cosmology

On the whole, the cosmos pictured by the myth-makers is the earth the Japanese knew, and only the earth they knew. The features of the realm called "the land" are of course those of the Japanese islands, often given the place names they still had in historical times, and only one or two remarks indicate even an awareness of other regions of the globe, including those parts of the nearby continent known to Japanese long before the dates at which the present texts of the *Kojiki* and *Nihongi* were compiled.

The homogeneity and familiarity of this mythic cosmos go far beyond this, however. Realms other than earth are indeed pictured—heaven, nether world(s), and a land beneath the sea—but only in the tale describing Izanami's dark and physiologically corrupted hades is any of these shown as at all different from man's own world. Certainly the High Plain of Heaven is nothing but the mold from which the earth was cast—a land of familiar vegetation, rivers, and mountains; of villagers subsisting by irrigated rice agriculture and making their clothing in weaving halls; of government by a ruler who is little more than the executive of concensuses reached in town meetings; of a religion of familiar ritual and pollution taboos; and of gods who feel the same joys and pains, and exhibit the same aptitudes, as individual men on earth do.

If the forms of the cosmos are thus almost everywhere the same, so too are the processes at work in it, those that men find in their own experiences to be natural. Most features of the environment, and most gods, are born by normal mammalian reproduction, discovered as even human children left to themselves can discover it. Most behavior conforms either to cultural conventions quite like those of men or to individual motivations understandable to the human reader.

There are some events that do not have this familiarity—the aboriginal generation of something "like a reed shoot," the creation of certain beings by parthenogenesis, the resurrection of the Master of the Land, the "concealment" of some deities, the primeval mobility of plants and rocks, whatever force it may be that renders ordeals effective, and so forth. Yet many of these instances need not be considered unnatural. If immortality is natural for gods, then so is their "concealment," which it is clear is only the process by which they change from one form of life to another. Izanami's is the only such case in which the after life included physical change, but she continued to be active, even though in hades. In other examples, because the deity in question reappears later leading a normal life in heaven or the nether world, one must conclude that "concealment" amounted to no more than a physical transportation from one to another location. In still other instances, the "hidden" god in fact remains alive in this world, as the Master of the Land continues to farm his rice fields and to live with a retinue in his palace-shrine. He has merely, as the result of a spirit change, quite literally "hidden himself" from the eyes of others and taken on a role that no longer obtrudes itself on them. In the same vein, there is no suggestion, in the telling of the ordeal of Susanoo, that its efficacy needs to be guarded by supernatural, rather than human, means. It can be considered to be a form of the promise, a transaction between men, accepted or rejected in terms of the probity, the will, and the faith in one another of its human participants.

Other exceptions, unfamiliar to human experience as they may be, are presented as being irrelevant to men. The noisiness and aggression of plants and rocks was the state of affairs of antiquity, but had been corrected by the time the heavenly deities and their descendants came to occupy earth. Clearly also, the myth-makers treat the distinction between mammalian birth and parthenogenesis as immaterial. Even though the myths seem to have been compiled in part as a political apologia for the temporal supremacy of the imperial family, the two sources differ without comment on the form of birth, and the source of authority, of even the Sun Goddess. One has her created parthenogenetically and sent to rule heaven by her father alone; the other makes her the result of the mating of the creator siblings, and her rule take its legitimacy from the order of both these primal gods.

The earthly condition as men know it is thus presented by the myths as all but universal and, in any event, the only context men need seriously consider. Moreover, once the heavenly dynasty has taken possession of the world, there is little evidence that other regions of the cosmos can any longer even have much effect on men's realm. In the past, it is true, the gods came from heaven, and all Japanese are their genealogical descendants. The main political emphasis of the myths was to establish the biological tie between the ruler of heaven and the rulers of earth, but the descent of noble Japanese families from other deities was also, within that context, accepted. By the beginning of recorded history, at the latest, very large segments—if indeed not all—of the Japanese people may well have been considered genealogically related to the gods, presumably through some form of adoption to the aristocratic lines if not biologically.[6] Nevertheless, the myths tend to assure us that these physical links now have been broken, and give no evidence that the two realms are any longer in a position to affect each other very substantially.

Similarly, the main impression a reader receives of the nether world(s) is that it is significant only for those beings who must be excluded from the normal community—whether because of the kind of polluting physical accident that maimed Izanami, or for the qualities of personality that made Susanoo a source of constant trouble for those around him. There is here no suggestion that normal gods or men need expect this exile. Moreover, though hades can to a certain extent affect this world—as is clear from Izanami's threat to destroy earth's inhabitants—its impact also can be nullified from earth, for Izanagi maintains that he can easily repair her ravages. All things considered, the nether world(s) is merely a distant island, much like the major islands on which men and the gods live, where those who are beyond the social pale can live out their lives without harming their fellows.

In sum, the Japanese myths show few of the workings of a "metaphysical" imagination, and give a resounding priority and value to things of this world. Except for a very few, and surely Sinified exegeses, there is no suggestion of impersonal or unearthly processes, such as the Yin-Yang, karma, or even the absolute law of God, which have made much in the continental Asian cosmologies an engine amoral to and/or beyond the understanding of man.

Similarly, there is no hint that such cosmic forces as do exist can over-power life as man proposes to live it. The gods do not have arbitrary powers; an earth-nurturing Izanagi can counteract an earth-threaten-ing Izanami, and the heavenly deities were able to take control of earth only with the agreement of its previous masters. Even the imagery of the myths shows us little to fear or to marvel at. The only monsters appear in Izanami's hades—but not in that of Susanoo—and in the form of the eight-headed eight-tailed dragon, a brief nightmare, easily detroyed. The godly captiousness of so humanistic a mythology as that of Greece—Zeus of the thunderbolt or Hera of the jealous eye—have no counterparts in the Japanese stories, where gods and events pursue a gentle and sociable, an almost homely, course. Only the Sun Goddess's younger brother acts arbitrarily, and he is banished for behavior that conforms more to that of the American Peck's Bad Boy than to that of a devil.

The moral of the myths thus seems to be that life for men can be expected to follow courses that are almost wholly intelligible and action-able in earthly and human terms. More, one can expect them to run along a fairly even way, in sight of neither the abyss of frustration nor the mountain of miracle. One need not fear terror or hope for ecstasy of any ultimate proportions.

The Human World

It is tempting to say that the myths thus show the world to be "good," and indeed in one very important sense they do. Nevertheless, it is a kind of "good" for which the English adjective is not an apt translation.

Except for those who are physically maimed, there is no different world with which to contrast our own. For the generality of men and gods, even the "nonworld" of death is not clearly pictured, individuals either disappearing from the narrative without explanation, being exiled to other worlds much like ours, or "concealing" themselves in a new form of our life. We may wish to assume that the strict pollution taboos we know surrounded death in early Japan led the myth-makers to avoid mention of any different kind of life after death; their silence then would not indicate that they also refused to admit of mortality. Certainly much later Japanese literature seems bemused by a fear of death. Yet such an interpretation is also arbitrary, and it seems as eco-nomical to conclude that the myth-makers quite simply denied death as a final or different state, that they saw life, essentially as we know it on earth, universal in time as it is in space. The preoccupation of later Jap-anese literature with the waste of death can be seen as a natural reaction of a people with the myth-fed faith in the hopefulness and permanency of life, who subsequently have had to take cognizance of the imported South Asian heresy—that life is pain and its end to be sought.

If there are no states other than those of our world and our life, we must conclude that at this point in Japanese history the idea of fundamental value alternatives—of "good" and "evil" as an elemental dualism—did not exist. On this basis, it is meaningless to characterize the mythic view of the things of our experience as merely "good." Far more basically, they "are," and are compatible with one another.

So existential a view does not, of course, preclude evaluation. The myths do judge a great many things positively or negatively and together with the verbal judgment justify appropriately cathectic behavior—avoidance or expiation of the ritually unclean, joyous mating with the beautiful girl, and so forth. There is no sense, however, of that massive concentration of "evil" at one point and time, and of "good" at another, which is so characteristic of Chinese thought and of the theory of the dynastic cycle on the continent. Instead, what is evaluated in the myths are particular states, individual events, and beings, which one runs into only at random. We shall do well, therefore, to interpret things so evaluated simply as items in the "is-ness" of life which are appreciably above or below the mean and average, rather than as things foreign to life. Even the "evil" Izanami and Susanoo are merely banished to realms where they can live out more fully the particular characteristics that make them "evil" for most men. "Evil" thus is not destroyed. Indeed, to the extent that we are correct in our general understanding of this philosophy, the denial or destruction of evil, its removal from the cosmos of what "is," would be inconceivable. One can think only to isolate its harmful effects from the rest of life.

It is congruent with this kind of evaluation, clewed as it is only to the standards of life, that the judgments of particular things handed down in the myths recognize no priority among all the possible types of "good" and "bad." Rather than subordinating other cathexes to a metaphysical, or a moral, or any other single kind of good, the texts name what is valued in each case differently, isolating verbally now one, now another, kind of standard. Sometimes they call it by the catchall, as well as moral, terms "good" and "evil," but as often they call it "lucky" or "unlucky," "bright" or "dark," "clean" or "dirty," "beautiful" or "ugly," "good-hearted" or "evil-hearted," and so forth. It seems most useful to interpret such terminology as the expression of a catholic and on the whole unbiased appreciation of the many kinds of value a thing can have to the lives of men, and thus basically to an appreciation of things in terms of their facilitation or inhibition of human life.

It is not strange to find in this world, where life is the only criterion of value, that the state of being is equivalent to the possession of spirit, that impersonal or will-less forces do not exist. Gods and men of course are spirit, but one of the most nearly central, and unique, elements of the myth story records that at an early date plants and what we call "inorganic" matter also had identical attributes of life and spirit. For many plants and features of the topography we are given the genealogy, facts of birth, and names that personify them. For all, we are assured that they once possessed the powers of speech, movement, and violence.

Their use of these attributes was as troublesome to life for men as was Susanoo's behavior. The heroes of the Japanese myths therefore remedied this defect. Like many another cultural charter, therefore, the myths of Japan also celebrated the heroes of the significant process by which an aboriginal earth was made fit for men, and in the celebration validated a line of rulers and a system of rule.

Yet how enormously different are the Japanese and, for example, the Chinese myths in this regard! In the Chinese myths, physical nature is pictured as only a passive entity. It is troublesome for man because he still, at that early date, lacked the cultural artifacts to exploit its inertness for his own benefit. The continental heroes were therefore inventors of artifacts and custom—of ditches to drain the swamps, of plows to tear the grass-matted soil, of techniques for growing grain. The Chinese view thus assumed an absolute gulf of nature between man and even beasts, let alone the "lower" orders of life. Man adores man, and only man.

In the Japanese myths, in contrast, human culture much as it persisted well down into historical times is taken as already given, its origins of no interest, its celebration of no utility. The natural world has life and will that are all but identical with those of man, save that like Susanoo they often use these to antisocial ends. The task of the culture heroes was to make nature civil, removing from it the troublesome qualities of speech, mobility, and violence.

We must note that there is no suggestion that in doing so the heroes reduced physical nature to a lifeless and spiritless state, or made it into an order unworthy of man's attention. The myths are filled with an appreciation of the flora and topographic features of the islands of Japan, and the message of the hero tale is that this world is a harmonious union of the life of man with the life of nature. One sees here, in other words, the first literary expression of that acute and comradely sensitivity to physical nature that has been a hallmark of the customs of Japanese life down to our own day. One feels that as early as the time at which the myths were told, the Japanese genius already had avoided Rilke's "mistake of drawing too sharp distinctions" (Rilke 1939: "First Elegy," line 81). This view persists, so that it is not strange for even a contemporary Japanese novelist to say of his heroine, "Looking around

her garden, a little gone to seed [after a week's absence], . . . she felt
that each of its plants and trees, each in its own language, was speaking
to her" (Osaragi 1952:184–185).

Human Nature

There is as yet, in the myths, as little evidence of what Gilbert Murray
called a "failure of nerve" about man's capacity to achieve a satisfactory fate in this world as there was among the early Greeks. Nor need
there be. The universe conforms to worldly and human experience and
provides no more justification to the fatalist than it does to the Pol-
lyanna. Events oscillate fairly evenly about a mean that for man as a
whole is life-sustaining, and thus encourage neither pessimism nor opti-
mism. In time, Buddhist and continental imports, with their visions of
other worlds and idealized goals, would prepare the soil for those clichés
about the "transiency" of life, "regret" for the unrequited, and *akirame*
("giving up") the unattainable that were to be so characteristic of later
Japanese literature. But one senses that in the mythic view it is the fate
of mankind to succeed, with reasonable effort, in grappling with the
very material problems of daily life, as indeed it is his unconsciously
accepted goal.

Individual fates do differ, some men attaining more, others fewer, of
those earthly experiences and attributes that are "good" or "bad"
because they are above or below the mean. There is as yet, however, no
hint of Buddhist or Chinese explanations of these differences in terms of
karma or "hidden good and evil." There is no picture of differences in
individual fate so thoroughgoing as to impress one with the contrast
between misery and blessedness.

We thus sense no ontological gulfs dividing men or gods into fundamentally different types. This is, of course, congruent with the myth's
view of the descent of all men from the gods. The most basic elements of
man's nature is his spirit—that bit of the godhead dwelling in each Japanese, derived from one primal common source, and thus in the most
basic sense alike in all men. The myth-makers even extend their universalism in a way that is cross-culturally quite rare, for to them mankind
shares his descent from the gods, and his nature as spirit, with all other
things of this world. The way was thus open not only for that sense of
kinship with nature which has continued to characterize the Japanese,
but also for such modifications of imported concepts as the doctrine
which allowed Buddhahood even to what continentals considered "lower" orders.[7]

It is also true that later, as Japanese came to have contact with other
peoples, for whom a kindred descent from the gods could not be

claimed, they were forced into that pervasive ethnocentrism so characteristic of many isolated tribal peoples—an ethnocentrism that cannot accord even human status to others. In somewhat the same vein, the emphasis in the myths on man's nature as spirit would lead Japanese thinkers, from Shōtoku Taishi to men of our own day, into almost compulsive attempts to try to define what it is that best describes the "Japanese spirit." It even seems possible to argue that the stress on success in attaining worldly "goods" inevitably validated that hierarchialism which has been so characteristic of Japanese social relations; he who succeeds knows no reason for tempering his satisfaction or for querying its rightness, just as he who falls behind finds no legitimation for his resentment. The man who succeeds is patently, and in a most pervasive sense, "better" than the failure.

The assumptions of the myths about man's fate and nature thus would conduce to particularisms that other peoples and times would find corrosive or petty. But the compilers of the myths wrote as if they were unaware of these possibilities, and we as well must admit the real universalisms at home here.

It is against this background of a common nature and fate for all created things that the myths were able effectively to concentrate their attention on individuality. Each actor has particular characteristics—of beauty or strength, of skill, of sociability, and so forth. We remember clearly the sympathy of the Master of the Land for the naked hare and his elder brothers' cruel prankishness, the quickness of hand of the god who seized the Sun Goddess from her cave, the hunter and fisher sons of Ninigi no mikoto, the womanly pique of the Sun Goddess when she imagined that her neighbors could enjoy themselves even in her absence, Susanoo's irascibility. These texts do not, it is true, draw so full and unique a picture of each character as the best modern fiction does. But the Sun Goddess and her brother come close enough, and as Kroeber (1951) has pointed out, the later literature of Japan approached that of the West more closely than most in this respect. The actors in the myths are pictured much as we think of the members of our own family or closest friends—alike, but in ways so fundamental as seldom to arouse awareness, all our interest being concentrated on the quite individual quirks by which each person is stereotyped for identification by his intimates.

It was above all the emotions of the actors that excited the interest of the myth-makers, and it thus seems possible to say that at the individual level human nature was defined heavily in emotional terms. The principal emotions portrayed, moreover, fall into two opposing sets—love for the other person and love for oneself. Susanoo concentrates into his character most of the extreme examples of the latter, but love for others is described repeatedly, for numerous actors, and in a variety of forms. One can only conclude that in the mythic view love for others is the more common quality of mankind, as it is unhesitatingly, with no apparent *arrière-pensées* at all, judged "good."

A quite uncomplex sexual love reappears again and again, and in terms that forced the Victorian sensibilities of Chamberlain to render whole passages of the *Kojiki* into Latin. These are all cases, be it noted, of physical attraction at first sight, with immediate pleasurable copulation as their straightforward aim. To generalize the myth phraseology, when a boy and girl meet and are pleased with each other, almost his first remark is the simple "Let's go to bed. How about it?" and very few refusals are recorded.

In this picture of sexual love, mutuality is obviously the standard. There is no suggestion of brutal initiatives, of sadism or rape, of neurosis, and if a person refuses it is simply because he finds the other unattractive. The myths even make it clear that it is improper to deny a person who proposes love his or her pleasure merely because the attraction is not reciprocated, for the emperors of Japan are not immortal, it is said, because the Sun Goddess's grandson would not sleep with one goddess whom he found ugly. The aim of love is not merely to gain pleasure but, as important, to give it.

At no point do the myths picture sexual love as in conflict with social "goods," or as conditioned by the requirements of society. Kinsmen are not shown as having anything to do with one another's marriages, let alone love affairs, and there is no suggestion that the community need judge sexual relations. This emphasis on the absolute goodness and individual autonomy in judgment of the bond of pleasurable love is carried even to the point of an uncritical portrayal of what we, and at least historical generations of Japanese, were to consider brother-sister incest. The creator deities are of course full brother and sister. Though the relationship between the Sun Goddess and her brother may be considered to have been masked by the only symbolic form of their incest, the Master of the Land married his half-sister without attracting the myth-makers' condemnation. As late as the reign of the Emperor Ingyō, what the traditional Japanese view treats as history records the union of Crown Prince Karu with his full sister, and though they are punished by the exile of one (or both) of them, their relationship is described with some sympathy as a case of true love (Aston 1896:323–325).

It seems quite clear that this presentation of sexual love as something that does, and should, well naturally and undenied from the hearts of two people has remained the basic norm of the Japanese people to our time. In Heian literature, upper-class manners are shown as more complex, and in the upper class of the Tokugawa some currency was given to the imported Chinese convention that sexual love is legitimate only when harnessed, through the arranged marriage, to the machine of family politics. But by and large, the view of the myths that sexual love is an unconditional good, subject only to the mutual wills of those who share it, has continued to exert a strong appeal in the literature and the daily customs of the Japanese. *Yobai,* the visit of a youth to his girl's bedroom, is first acted out by the Master of the Land, and the curiously aroused mutuality (if not the constraint) of the modern geisha and her customer would not seem out of place if described in the myths. Even where the family-haunted conventions of China at last reduced the Japanese spirit, the values first celebrated in the myths have tempered them, for in Japan the principals play a far larger role in the marriage arrangement, just as their wishes help account for the great prevalence even into modern times of the *naien,* or common-law marriage.

Sexual love, however, is only one of a variety of gentle loves that characterize the relation of men or gods in the story. In a real sense, one can argue that it is love between individuals that begets all communal and societal morality. The Master of the Land, it will be recalled, helped the hare; he likewise determined the methods of healing diseases "for the sake of the visible race of man as well as for beasts." The bond between parents and children is never pictured as other than one of love, and the unilateral social obligation of filial piety that was so obtrusive in Chinese thought about this key bond never put down deep roots in Japan. Above all, the mechanism through which harmony is achieved and maintained within the social community can only be described as the working out of a steady mutuality among not merely the rights but, more important, the sensibilities of its members.

No doubt the formal social institutions of the village of the gods—the town meeting with its decisions reached by consensus, the obvious limitation on the ability of the Sun Goddess to make important decisions arbitrarily—were such as externally to constrain the individual to cooperation with his fellows, without any necessary commitment of his will to this end. No doubt also the form of the myths, as a creation of art rather than of reason, inhibited their statement of social duty in terms of abstract moral principles, and the absence of such statements is not evidence that these principles were not also operative. Nevertheless, even in later ages Japanese were not attracted to the Chinese habit of trying to produce moral behavior through conscious obedience to abstract principles. Moreover, in *giri*—a duty to a specific person—and in the compulsions ascribed to *ninjō,* as in the legal importance given confession, the Japanese have shown an interest in morality as a matter of the emotional commitment of the individual to others. It seems not inappropriate, therefore, to interpret the myths in the same terms, as a portrayal of morality achieved, or denied, in the personal relations of individuals.

Where behavior takes the form shown by Susanoo it is "evil." He makes loud noises that frighten others and acts impulsively, without the warning that would at least save their being startled. He tricks people, promising to be considerate but breaking his word, perhaps with intent to do so from the outset. He does not shrink from inflicting physical harm on others or from harming them through their possessions. Yet there is no suggestion that his behavior results from either long plotting or a perverted pleasure in harm for its own sake, as there is little evidence that he aims through his actions to gain any special material rights for himself. In other words, he is either a complete egoist or an emotional cripple. Needing only to express himself, he makes the freedom to do so his goal, so that in the end he admires his son for having exploited the same freedom to thwart him. He cannot, or will not, empathize with the pain his actions bring to others. He shows no capacity whatsoever to give, or to receive, consideration.

The quality of the Sun Goddess is not morally upright in any self-conscious sense. Rather, she shows understanding of how to mold herself with the people around her in a harmony that still does not deny the individuality of each. It seems no accident that she is typically termed "bright," a sign perhaps more of her humane than her astral attributes. She does not obtrude herself markedly on the lives of others, on the whole seeming to live and let live. When she acts as heaven's chatelaine, she asks more than she orders the behavior of others, letting herself be guided in major things by the consensus of the gods and gaining her ends by persuasion. She overlooks or forgives small errors and accepts their consequences, willing to give her brother and her recreant messengers to earth every benefit of the doubt. Yet she is not cowardly, and when she suspects her brother of evil she is willing to fight if need be. Nor does she lose the sense of the inner borders of her own individuality, for when her brother has clearly violated her trust she withdraws from society, sick at a world in which she can no longer maintain a minimal dignity. She is lured out of this withdrawal only by the firm evidence that her fellow gods are lonely without her, and are willing to act to change that world back to the one of reciprocal emotional trust that alone she can abide.

It thus does not seem amiss to say that morality lies in the total sympathy of one person for another, in the desire to give, not humanitarian "rights," but human fulfillment, even as he receives the same common and essential gift. In a real sense, morality derives from the forms of love.

Against this background, we should perhaps restate the myth's evaluation even of sexual love. It is not merely that they show no sense of "wrongness" attaching to this act and thus reduce it to the level of the behavior of the human animal. Instead, wherever man and woman want one another it is a "good" to take and give this pleasure, and perhaps even the most nearly idealistic of all rapports. One needs some such interpretation to explain the enduring romanticism of the Japanese literary treatment of this relation.

The emphasis given here to morality as emotional rapport between individuals comports poorly with the frequent contemporary view that Japan's is a "shame culture." If such a culture is one in which improper behavior is frequently prevented or punished by the negative reactions of other persons, the description of Japan in these terms is apt. As every Japanese child soon learns, if he errs in propriety or fails in an effort, he will be "laughed at," and ridicule, however gently applied by Western or Chinese standards, is unbearable. Likewise, if he sins deeply or repeatedly against others, he will be "abandoned," emotional as well as material support being withdrawn from him.

Nevertheless, it is nonsense to squeeze one's description of morality down to only negative sanctions against improper behavior. It is surely as much the habit of modern Japanese as it was that of their ancestors as portrayed in the myths to engage for the most part in proper acts, impelled thereto by positive sanctions—again, in the myths, to gain and earn consideration for themselves as sentient beings, as well as to give that consideration, and not merely by the fear of losing it.

The myths make it seem as clearly partial to claim that the main sanctions, whether negative or positive, are those imposed by other persons. Susanoo was not judged in terms of whether he did objective good or evil, and not even according to the opinion of the other gods on his actions. He was judged, rather, according to his own intentions—his will or "heart"—to do good or evil to others. The point of his ordeal is that it seemed to confirm his profession that his heart was "clean," and his sister was willing for a long time thereafter to forbear from judging what was in fact his disruptive behavior. She overlooked the harm he caused the fields as due to his ignorance of the field economy. She assumed that he was drunk when he vomited behind her chair; the seat of the moral will lies in that part of the mind that is given a vacation in drunkenness, and even today Japanese law and custom consider it not only forgivable but "good" that an individual give himself this holiday occasionally.

Susanoo ultimately was judged "evil" only when the Sun Goddess and her neighbors came to understand that he either wanted to visit evil upon them or was incapable in his own heart of distinguishing good from evil, crimes so polluting that he must pay an expiatory fine and be banished. The basic sanction to morality is thus the individual's own conscience, his compassion that not only, as Mencius put it, "cannot bear to see the sufferings of others," but wishes them joy.

Much of this view of the matter is still built deeply into the Japanese legal system. Its emphasis is not on whether an objective crime has or has not been committed, and not on restoring equity or punishing the offender, but on gaining from him that self-realization and repentance that is the true meaning of the confession so sought at every legal level (von Mehren 1963:426–427). The myths seem already to have contributed to this system the view that social evil is the failure, as good is the common success, of the individual will to be compassionate with others.

Notes

1. One man, Ō no Yasumaro, was the key amanuensis for both books, which were completed in A.D. 712 (the *Kojiki*) and in 720 (the *Nihongi*). Neither book is represented as other than a compilation from then-extant sources, not now identifiable but apparently consisting primarily of the archives of various noble families (including the imperial family) and oral traditions and documents, many of the latter having themselves been written down from oral tradition. Both compilations were made at imperial order, at a time when the throne was coming into a position to assert the cultural supremacy of the centralized state over the feudalism or tribalism of the noble families and at a time when Chinese influence over the lives and thought of the upper class was rapidly increasing.

The *Kojiki* is said to be the transcript of a record dictated to Yasumaro by one Hieda no Are, a person famous for the ability to memorize, though twenty-five years after he (or she) had been set to the task of committing at least some part of the extant sources to memory. The *Nihongi* is represented as having been compiled entirely from then-existent documents by Yasumaro and Prince Toneri. The forms of the books we have are consistent with the origins imputed to them. The *Kojiki* is a smoothly flowing narrative in colloquial Japanese, though transliterated by Chinese characters used phonetically, whereas the *Nihongi* is written in the Chinese language itself, which was used then for all official documents, and includes quotations as well as numerous variants from the differing sources said to have been used.

The question has been raised of whether the *Kojiki* we have is not a much later forgery. In evidence against this view, the book shows very few of those Chinese influences which were at the time of its reputed compilation only becoming known in Japan, but which were soon to become an inseparable part of the intellectual furniture of later generations of Japanese. Moreover, the *Kojiki* also is said to preserve many archaic Japanese linguistic usages which were not known to later generations. Thus, most authorities believe the *Kojiki* to be what it pretends to be. Probably equally authentic, the *Nihongi*, however, contains many more usages and ideas derived from the continent, and thus represents a further stage of that cultural fusion which was becoming fashionable during the generation and a half that the compilers say separated the original of these texts.

The English translations used and quoted here are, for the *Kojiki*, Basil Hall Chamberlain's "Kojiki, Records of Ancient Matters" (1882), and for the *Nihongi*,

W. G. Aston's *Nihongi, Chronicles of Japan from the Earliest Times to* A.D. *697* (1896). The Japanese text of the *Kojiki* used is that of Kurano Kenji, *Kojiki taisei* (1957).

2. The *Nihongi* states baldly that heaven emerged before earth as a "united body" out of an original chaos, "like an egg which was of obscurely defined limits and contained germs," but all commentators consider this a Sinified exegesis.

3. The *Kojiki* lists three "single gods" in existence in heaven prior to the appearance of the reed shoot, but none is given any prominence.

4. The text of the *Kojiki* is slightly less euphemistic than that of the *Nihongi*. The term here translated "*acts* of the honeymoon chamber" is glossed by Kurano (1957:53) as having meant "to exchange glances and consummate a marriage."

5. The *Kojiki* and a variant cited in the *Nihongi*, but not the text of the *Nihongi* itself, state that Izanagi and Izanami were commanded to their task of creating the earth by the "heavenly deities" and took counsel with them to discover, through their divination, the breach that had produced the deformed child. I have omitted these evidences of a complete and guiding heaven, however, for it is not shown as deeply involved in the creation of earth.

6. At least this is one interpretation that can be made of the evidence on the family system of the day. See Ariga Kizaemon, "Nihon kodai kazoku" (1948:103–150).

7. See Nakamura ([1960] 1964: chap. 34, esp. 356–360).

2

The Monkey Memorial Service of Japanese Primatologists

PAMELA J. ASQUITH

IN a small shady grove between two large enclosures containing chimpanzees and Japanese macaques stood a wooden table and chair facing a large rock on which is written in Japanese: "Monkey memorial stone (*saruzuka*) erected by the Primate Institute's volunteers in April, 1973." On the table which served as an altar were four neatly stacked offerings of bananas, apples, sweet potatoes and a box of sweet red bean-filled cake, a burning candle, and flowers. Beside the table were two or three graves of monkeys. A priest from a local Buddhist temple sat in the chair facing the table and memorial stone. It was 3 p.m. on 15 October, 1982 at Kyoto University's Primate Research Institute in Inuyama, Japan. The annual *sarukuyō*, or monkey memorial service, was about to begin.

In attendance were the head of the institute, administrative office staff, veterinarians and scientists and secretaries from the various departments. To begin the service, the head of the Institute's office staff said to the priest, "Shall we begin the ceremony of *sarukuyō*?" The director then made a short speech saying that because many monkeys had died from disease and experimental use, let us pray for them. A veterinarian next told how many monkeys had died that year: in experiments, 49; from disease, 50; from accidents, such as bites, 8; and from management mistakes, 7, giving a total of 114 animals. He said we must try to reduce the number of deaths from disease which about equalled those (unavoidable ones) from experiments.

The priest then read two sutra chants sitting in the chair facing the memorial stone, after which everyone went one by one to the altar to say a brief prayer. To my surprise and delight, the first to do this was a chimpanzee, which, accompanied by its keeper, laid a bouquet of flowers by the memorial stone.

From *Royal Anthropological Institute News* 54 (1983):3–4. Reprinted by permission of the Royal Anthropological Institute of Great Britain and Ireland.

Oshōkō refers to burning incense for the dead. Two dishes, one each of
unburned incense and of burning incense, are set side by side on the
table and before praying, one picks up a small amount of unburned
incense, brings it to the forehead and places it in the dish of burning
incense. This can be done once, twice or three times (three times is most
formal). Each person did *oshōkō* and said a prayer for the monkeys:
"Yasuraka ni nemutte kudasai" (Please sleep peacefully).

After everyone had paid their respects the food from the altar was fed
to the monkeys in the enclosures. Just beyond the *sarukuyō* area a long
table had been set up and in the equivalent of a wake that followed,
everyone helped themselves to *sake* (Japanese rice wine) and small
snacks and stood around or sat on the grass. A party-like atmosphere
prevailed and it went on for at least 1 1/2 hours or until the drink was finished. I was told that people were happy as they believe that the souls
(tamashii) of the monkeys have gone to a happy place.

So ended an annual ceremony that appears to reflect rather conspicuously an attitude to primates for which there is no real equivalent
among Western researchers. The independent development of primate
behaviour studies in Japan and the West has given rise to some comment on culturally based differences evident in and as an explanation
for the methodology and focus of the respective studies (Umesao 1960;
Frisch 1963; Watanabe 1974; Reynolds 1976; Asquith 1981). The
author is at present researching this in depth in Japan. Because of the
often made, but fairly ill-defined (because difficult to define) observation that the Japanese have a "special" or "closer" relationship to animals than do Westerners, I was interested to attend the memorial service for monkeys that have died in the course of researches made on
them.

Primatology is a relatively new science in Japan, as it is in the West.
Begun by Imanishi Kinji and the group that grew around him in 1948,
the first journal of Japanese primatology, *Primates,* (pronounced by the
Japanese as the Latin prēmǎ'těs as it refers to the taxonomic Order) was
published in 1957. Thus any special service connected with non-human
primates was likely also to be of recent origin. However, the feeling
there was a need for such a service may have been based on beliefs more
deeply rooted in Japanese culture. Such was my question as I enquired
further about the *sarukuyō*.

A similar ceremony is held by Osaka University's primatologists each
spring. Further, some large medical and physiology departments hold a
memorial service for other animals such as mice sacrificed in experiments. On asking various people what the service for monkeys means to
them or why they attend, I received the following answers. One said he
felt you should attend as it reminds you of the importance of animals

too. He does not really believe that animals' souls go to heaven or return in other bodies afterwards, but the service is important as a reminder not to needlessly kill animals. In answer to the question, "Do Japanese believe the souls of monkeys go somewhere, or exist at all?" one primatologist said he believed in the existence of souls of monkeys he had come to know, but not of monkeys he did not work with. Another in attendance said he felt he should go to the ceremony although he was a Shintoist, not a Buddhist, because everyone else goes and because all life is important. He also felt that making prayers for animals was a bit of a business proposition so far as the temple was concerned (there is a fee for the prayers). Another researcher dislikes experiments done on animals and goes to say "excuse me" to the monkeys. Another, not a scientist, was surprised to hear how many monkeys had died and felt one should pray for their souls. For some people this person felt the service was a way to say "excuse me" and also "thank you."

In these comments there is a basic affirmation of the importance of an animal's life, that it is not to be taken for granted. How extensive is this attitude and on what may it be based? The Buddhist priest who is hired to perform the *sarukuyō* at Osaka University is monk master at Toneyamagobō in Toyonaka-shi near Osaka. There are two temples on the grounds, one for animals (Shoanji) and one for people (Jōankuji). The animals' temple is undecorated while that for people is very ornate inside with gold paint and hand-painted screens, etc. The practice of performing a ceremony for animals was begun here only twenty-five years ago. I was told that scientists, veterinarians and other professionals who had to kill animals in their work first asked the monk master to perform a ceremony. Now, people bring their pets or favourite animals to be buried here, or rather some of their hair only is buried and the corpses are burned elsewhere in the interests of hygiene and space. Each grave is topped with a stick with the name of the animal (pet name), date of death and number. Since 1956 over 18,800 animals' souls have been prayed for there. Every year 700–800 animals are buried. The day I was there (May 22, 1982), the hair of number 18,845 was buried, a young Alsatian dog. There is in addition an annual ceremony held at the end of May to which 300–400 people come to pray for the souls of their animals.

A place filling this function is quite rare in Japan and even newsworthy. At the animal temple there were two thick scrapbooks of newspaper clippings and photographs of the history of these animal ceremonies, and the monk master pointed out the important people who had attended, such as the mayor of the city. It has its business side too and a price list of burial costs is displayed. Costs vary according to the size of the animal from 1,500 (£3.60) yen to 5,000 yen: 1,500 yen for a bird, small cat, etc., and up according to small, medium, large-size dogs or other animals such as a goat.

The animal ceremony has two names, *ireisai*, or prayer ritual for dead animals, and *kanshasai*, or thanking for animals. *Ireisai* breaks down into the following meaning; *i*—comfort, console; *rei*—soul; *sai*—festival. *Kanshasai* breaks down into: *kansha*—thanks; *sai*—festival. It is interesting that the idea of consoling ("excuse me") and thanking the (souls of) monkeys was very much present in the remarks of those attending the *sarukuyō* at the Primate Research Institute. The value of the animals' soul is evident too in Buddhist thought in that the Buddhist prayer book, *okyō*, uses the same prayers for both humans and animals.

What significance if any can be attached to the fact that such a ceremony occurs in modern research? Some care must be taken not to make too fine a point of a rather striking practice. Many primatologists in Japan have never attended a *sarukuyō*. Those who attended said that most Japanese now do not know the meaning of the chants or prayers said for the monkeys, nor the significance of the formality distinctions of doing *oshōkō* (burning incense for the dead) three times instead of two or one, nor the prayer said at the time of doing *oshōkō*, and so on. People are not *au fait* with the meaning of the details of the rituals, but this by no means implies that no importance is attached to *doing* the rituals. Nor do the recent origins of the ceremony (1956 for the general Toyona-ka-shi ceremony requested by scientists and 1973 for the Primate Research Institute's) lessen its cultural significance. On the contrary, it points to the strength and persistence of certain beliefs that may be said to need assuaging in the face of modern science. Something of a parallel to this has already occurred in a different context in Japan, as I shall explain.

The monkey memorial service is Buddhist. Buddhism entered Japan in the middle of the 6th century and was promoted on an extensive scale by Prince Shōtoku Taishi (574–621) at the end of the 6th century. Direct results of Buddhist teaching were a reluctance to kill animals and general use of a diet restricted to fish and vegetables. However, by the 1930's eating meat had become quite common, and butcher's guilds apparently had masses said regularly for the souls of slaughtered cattle (Eliot 1935:191). Here again the abuse of a belief needed to be compensated for.

Thus, paradoxically, the very novelty of the monkey memorial service reaffirms the existence among modern primatologists of anciently held feelings of awareness of and importance attached to the life of each animal. There is no direct equivalent to this in Western practices. Such clues lend some justification to enquiries into the effects of different cultural beliefs on the performance of science.

3

A Culture of Love and Hate

Eiichirō Ishida

One autumn after the war, I stopped my car in a small village near the Alps in southern Germany and dropped in at the cemetery behind the church. I had no particular aim in view, but soon I found myself drifting irresistibly among the graves, absorbed in reading the words of affection chiselled on each stone.

> *Dear wife, dear Ilse whom I can never forget,*
> *rest in peace!*

The grief common to all human beings who have lost what is dearest to them on earth strikes at the wayfarer's heart with a particular poignancy; the wild flowers offered up to the lately deceased are also affecting. Before I knew it, my own eyes were moist with tears.

But my memory also goes back to my life in Germany and Austria just before the war:

> *Juden sind verboten!*
> *Nur Arier!*

"Jews forbidden, Aryans only." The theaters, cinemas, restaurants, cafes, park benches, plastered with the lurid posters. The merciless seizure of property, the arrests and the detentions. I saw a man dragged about the town by the Nazi S.A. with a large placard about his neck saying, "I bought at a Jew's shop." He had gone shopping at a store with a poster proclaiming "Jüdisches Geschäft." Even at that time, things had already gone too far for me to understand, let alone sympathize. What, then, of the appalling massacre of six million people which was revealed to the world after the war, and fresh aspects of which are still being exposed today, at the Eichmann trial? It is intolerably de-

Reprinted from *Japan Quarterly* 8 (1961):394–402.

pressing to think that the same people who carved such poignant words of affection on those gravestones also perpetrated—or at least permitted —the massacre.

Do all human beings, then, have the possibility of these two extremes? One suspects that they do. Miss Inukai Michiko, who was present during part of the Eichmann trial, tells the following story:

"An American woman reporter sitting next to me prodded my elbow just as the trial was about to begin. 'Oh, he's only an ordinary man!' she said. Her face betrayed a certain disappointment."

"Things would be much simpler," Miss Inukai adds, "if he were a devil. . . . That is the terrifying thing; that he is, indeed, no devil, but an ordinary man. It is because he is the kind of ordinary man you might see anywhere that Eichmann is far more devilish than any devil."

The Japanese army itself committed atrocities "far more devilish than any devil" on the Chinese mainland and in the Philippines. The same factor that, under a particular set of conditions, can make the "ordinary man" commit unparalleled cruelty—the ordinary man who, leading the humdrum life of the ordinary citizen, would probably be an ideal husband and father—undoubtedly lurks within all human beings. Among members of the Nazi S.S. that I have met personally there were those whose character and abilities would have given them an honorable place among the elite of whatever society they found themselves in.

Yet despite this, many Japanese, when they see horrifying scenes of mass slaughter in films of the last war, feel with a shudder "a Japanese could never do such things." I do not believe one can dismiss this as merely Japanese hypocrisy or complacency. It is connected rather, I suspect, with a feeling many Japanese have about the particular quality of European reactions—with the opinion, often expressed privately, that Westerners are egotistic and unrelenting. If I may quote from an essay I wrote recently for a newspaper:

> The European is far more conscious of the distinction between friend and foe than the Japanese. This is true not only of everyday life. Religious and political conflict and struggles, for instance—as during the Reformation and the age of the Nazis—have time and again driven men into a world of terrible hatred. The Japanese are by contrast far more willing to compromise. The reverse side of the willingness to compromise, however, is half-heartedness. For example, love as portrayed in Western literature is deep, intense, and full-blooded in a way that leaves far behind the gentle pathos of its Japanese counterpart; it has its roots in the very nature of Western civilization, with its thoroughgoing loves and hates. My memories of life in Europe are an odd compound of inexhaustible goodwill and kindness on the one hand and an implacable severity in human relationships on the other. To study this question further one would have, I suspect, to go back to the very bedrock and mainsprings of the cultures of East and West.

I hope sometime to tackle this vast theme in a scholarly fashion, from the viewpoint of the cultural anthropologist or the cultural historian. So far, however, I am not qualified to do so. All I can attempt here is to outline the ideas that have long been germinating in my mind as hints or as possible pointers to a working hypothesis for the academic solution of the question, and to invite the criticisms of those who have themselves been brought up inside Western civilization. I would point out here that I have striven to keep what I write, whether dealing with Western or Japanese civilization, free from all personal, emotional, value judgments.

About the same time that I published the piece from which I quote above, the critic Takeyama Michio wrote something relevant to the question in "The City of the Barbed Wire," an article in the July, 1961, issue of the periodical *Bungei Shunjū* recording his impressions of Berlin today.

"Europe is part of Christendom, yet no trace of the Sermon on the Mount is to be found in these parts. The history of Europe affords few examples of forgiveness towards the enemy. Nor were the mighty humble before men. . . . The Christian peoples have persisted in blatant preying on the weak. In what sense, and to what extent, one wonders, are the people of Europe Christians?"

I have myself remarked before on the lack of tolerance to be found in practice in the history of Christianity, supposedly the religion of love, and of Christian civilization. This lack of tolerance, however, is not peculiar to Christianity. Hebraism, from which it sprang, as well as Islam—which draws on the springs of Hebraism and Christianity and worships a supreme god of the same generic type—both have elements in common with it; and despite the merciless struggle between the rival creeds, the characteristics with which each has stamped its own civilization all bear a family likeness.

God, teaches Christianity, is love. Yet in actual history the Christian God in whose name the witch hunts, the Inquisition, and the suppression of the Copernican theory took place was the same jealous God that sent thunder and hail to destroy the unbeliever and the heretic. During the conquest of the New World, Cortes converted the Aztec king Cuauhtemoc to Catholicism by force, and Pizarro did the same to Atahuallpa, emperor of the Incas—then both the converts were put to death. One cannot read any history of the Crusades or of the Orders of Knighthood without noticing the resemblances to the expeditions of Mahomet, made with sword and the Koran in his hand, to protect the cause of Allah against the infidel. Such things are far from the doctrine of, at least, the New Testament—from the spirit of Christ who said, "Love thine enemy."

Perhaps, then, one should seek the source of the fierce intolerance and implacable hatred of the foe that pervades European history not so much in Christianity as in some broader and deeper cultural stratum that created the whole spiritual framework of which Christianity is but one section—a cultural stratum which, one suspects, formed the nature of Christianity and its civilization with a force far mightier and more overwhelming than that of any reforms of a single prophet of Nazareth.

To turn back to the case of the Germans, one at once comes up against the Germanism which the Nazis extolled as the peculiar tradition of the German people prior to Christianity. Woden (Odin), the god of the storm who occupied chief place in the pantheon of the Germanic tribes at the time of Tacitus, together with Thor, the god of thunder, and Tyr, whom the Romans identified with Mars, were all gods of war. The very name Woden, the principal god who led the phantom *wütendes Heer* of dead warriors as they thundered through the stormy night skies, derives from a word signifying "rage" or "frenzy" and corresponding to the modern German word *wüten*. Nor is this quality confined to myths and legends and heroic epics: the strains of battle and victory, defeat and revenge echo throughout the whole history of the formation of the Germanic peoples. In time, the Christian cross—like the Nazi swastika later—was to become the symbol that spurred on the knights of the Middle Ages into the Holy Wars.

The tough, untamed quality of the ancient Germans is still today—as is their language—deeply rooted in the psychologies of the peoples of Western civilization. Even in England, one form of punishment until the comparatively recent past consisted of tying the criminal between two horses which then tore him apart, while as late as the reign of Elizabeth I it is said that a crowd castrated a man in the streets of London. Even the thoroughgoing way in which the British, till the beginning of this century, repressed any resistance from the peoples of the colonies of the British Empire betrays, one suspects, something of the same quality.

However, the Germanic peoples and their culture do not, any more than Christianity, supply the sole mainstream of modern Western civilization. The civilization of Greece, as it was transmitted through the legacies of the Roman Empire, forms one of the bases of Western culture alongside Hebraism. One cannot, in particular, understand modern thought and the modern outlook since the Renaissance without tracing its genealogy back to classical Greek civilization, a civilization which saw a unique flowering on the bed of the ancient civilization that stretched from the Orient to the Mediterranean.

One thing that can be said for certain, though, is that Greeks and Romans alike belonged in their language to the same Indo-European family as the Germans, the "barbarian tribes of the North," and that originally they spread across the southwestern portion of the Eurasian continent from a common source. There is no space here to discuss the academic question of where precisely this source lay, but the Indo-European peoples who in the first half of the second millenium before Christ began a mass move with their horses and chariots into Mesopotamia to the south, Iran and India to the east, and the Mediterranean and Danube areas to the west show marked common features in the breeds of horses, the form of their chariots and their gods of the chariot; and their culture exhibits many of the military qualities—the mobility and the organizing power—to be seen in the warlike nomadic peoples of historical times.

Now if one considers the derivation of our modern cultures very roughly in terms of spheres or strata of culture, the basic culture of the Indo-European peoples who have created modern European civilization cannot be called agrarian in the sense in which the word applies to the peoples of the Japanese archipelago or of Southeastern Asia. Their living habits put them closer to the nomadic peoples of Inner Asia than to the rice-cultivating peoples of the damp, rainy regions. They slaughtered large numbers of domestic animals, tanned their hides, spun their fur, made dairy products of every kind and even blood sausages, and cut and ate their meat with knives and forks, while their dress was derived from the horseman's trousers and narrow-sleeved jacket. Moreover, the Semitic peoples who gave birth to Judaism, Christianity, and Islam were still more dependent on animal breeding than the Indo-Europeans.

If one looks at ethnic culture in this way, as a number of layers piled on each other in chronological sequence, then Hebraism and the cultures of the Indo-Europeans, including the Greeks, Romans, and Germanic peoples, will be seen to have a common underlying basic stratum. I do not, of course, believe that the breeding of animals originally grew up on the grasslands in the interior of the Eurasian continent independently of and parallel with the agricultural culture of the southern fringes of the continent. The nomadic peoples and their characteristic culture as they appear in history were not born, I believe, until later than the agrarian culture of the Orient. Even so, it is undeniable, even assuming that the discovery of animal raising was made in sedentary agricultural settlements, that once the nomadic people who relied on large flocks of animals for the greater part of their livelihood began to range over the boundless plains in search of grass and water, a cultural sphere was formed that was essentially different from that of the older agricultural society.

Nor were the differences confined to those, such as food, clothing, and housing, which were dictated by differing environments and subsistences. The preeminence of the male in social and economic life led to a strong patriarchal authority, and the nomadic peoples, in contrast to the farming peoples who looked to the earth as the mother of generation and fertility, came to look on the heavens that reigned above their heads as in themselves constituting the supreme male god. Where the view of the world held by the farming peoples was non-rational or supra-rational, that of the nomadic peoples tended towards a coherent, monotheistic belief in a clear-cut providence ordering the whole world. The stubborn religious fight put up by the Jewish prophets who insisted that there was no god but Jehovah and orderd the destruction of the idols of Astarte, Baaloth, and other Mother Goddesses was surely a challenge aimed by the monotheists at polytheistic heresies.

The belief in a single providential Heaven of this kind can hardly have been unconnected with what they saw about them in their daily lives, as they wandered without let across the vast plains through the dry, clear air, constant witness to the orderly revolution of the crystalline arc of heaven. And I suspect that these cultural characteristics, which were common—so far as one can judge from historical sources—to all the nomadic peoples of the Eurasian continent, have given Western culture its present nature, even after a historical process which entailed multiple fission into Hebraism, Hellenism, Germanism, and the like.

This cultural-historical interpretation of Western civilization is reinforced still further by comparison with other, different cultural spheres. At a discussion on how the civilizations of Europe and Africa could understand each other, held at the Round-Table Conference on Civilization in Rome in February, 1960, the poet Leopold Sedar Senghor, later President of the Republic of Senegal, pointed up vividly the differences between the culture of the white man and the black man in terms of their different attitudes to the world and things. In Europe, he said, men were creatures of will, fighters, birds of prey, and as such they distinguished clearly between things. Black people, however, lived in a primitive night, dark as their skins. Black people did not *see* others, they felt them, for in the night all elements are alive.

This contrast with the civilization of Europe, made by a member of a culture born out of the dense depths of the vegetation of Negro Africa, awakes a considerable sympathetic response in us Japanese, who carry on an agrarian culture in common with Southeast Asia. The volume of the *Nihon Shoki** (*The Chronicles of Japan*) dealing with the Age of Gods says that, before the descent of the August Grandson Ninigi-no-

---

*Another name for the *Nihongi,* the eighth-century compilation discussed in chap. 1 of this volume.—EDS.

Mikoto, the "Middle Land Where Reeds Grow Luxuriantly"—i.e., the Japanese archipelago—was filled with "numerous deities which shone with a lustre like that of fireflies, and evil deities which buzzed like flies. There were also trees and herbs all of which could speak."[1]

This land of animistic *kami*, in which men and Nature were indistinguishable, is a far cry from that other realm where the bright light of day illumines so clearly the distinction between the self and others; it is a perfect specimen of a "night where all elements are alive."

The Buddhist culture from the continent which was to be superimposed on this cultural foundation was in itself the product of distinctly non-Aryan sources. In his *Travel Diary of a Philosopher* (1925), Count H. Keyserling declares that the phenomenology of Buddhism, which stresses the never-ending cycle of change to which all things are subject, could only have been understood against a background such as that of India, with its terrifyingly swift, never-ceasing proliferation of vegetable life. Buddhism, he says, is the gospel of the tropics, the doctrine of vegetable growth. Such cultural traditions, one feels sure, still live on in the feelings and actions of the Japanese today.

Here we must turn again to the love of compromise and the pliability —in a different light, the lack of consistency—of the Japanese which I referred to at the outset, and compare it with the tenacity and intolerance of the European. My knowledge of European society is, of course, imperfect, but it is safe to assert that there, even among close friends, likes and dislikes, "yes" and "no," are expressed with great clarity; one may hunt dictionaries of European languages in vain for the equivalent of, say, *haragei* ("belly-play").* As a result of this Western way of doing things, the other man may sometimes be temporarily put out—yet the question is thereby got over with, leaving no particular aftermath.

A Japanese, however, even when he means "no," will sometimes equivocate because the other's expression, his fancies, seems to require it. And that strange phenomenon, the "Japanese smile," though it may smooth over the surface at the time, is often the prelude to an unpleasant, ambiguous kind of relationship. Even where, for a European, soundly berating someone in a loud voice would be an end to the matter, for the Japanese it can often be the beginning of a new question. To the former, the way the Japanese feels is incomprehensible; to the latter, Europeans do not show enough respect for others' feelings in their speech.

Whatever happens in theory, one wonders how far ideas such as "hate the crime but not the man" or "virtue and vice go hand in hand"

---

*Tacit communication without resorting to words or outright expressions.—EDS.

play any part in actual society and politics in Europe. On this score, at any rate, Japanese society is astonishingly lenient. For instance, even though a man may have committed many times what amounts to fraud —a crime, according to accepted social ideas—yet if he has virtues and abilities in other spheres he may yet be esteemed socially as a leader in the political, financial, or even sometimes the academic world. A man fired for embezzling public funds may very shortly be taken on by the organization next door. I do not know to what extent similar phenomena occur in Occidental society, but the fate of individual leaders at times of serious political conflict—for example, in the totalitarian states —suggests that society as a whole is less easygoing, more rigorous and demanding.

Where the question of war crimes is concerned, for instance, the Germans' feelings are far less pliable than those of the Japanese. No sooner had the war ended than the Japanese could switch quite effortlessly from talk of "American and British devils" to talk of "repentance of the whole nation." The atrocities the Japanese committed on the neighboring continent, too, were quite forgotten in ten years or so. The occasional dragging to light of such matters in books or magazines is frowned on as somehow being an unnecessary reopening of one's fellows' wounds.

In Germany, however, the courthouse where the Nürnberg trials were held was defaced with constantly recurring swastikas. On the other hand, only recently—a full fifteen years after the war—some 200,000 feet of film about the Nazis have been collected in West Germany with the aim of compiling a new documentary tracing the history of Germany's own crimes. Again, on May 11, the West German television station broadcast an hour-long film, entitled "Trial of the Executioner," on the life of Eichmann. "All these things," the announcer pointed out repeatedly as scene of horror succeeded scene of horror, "were done in the name of the German people."

The swastikas and the self-accusation—these two contrasting phenomena reveal very clearly the nature of Western civilization: the proud stubbornness, and the insistence on pursuing every question through to its logical conclusion. The two things almost certainly spring from the same cultural roots.

There have been quite a few well-known writers in modern Japan, Tanizaki Junichirō and Nagai Kafū among them, who fell under the spell of European civilization in their youth, only to return to things Japanese in the latter half of their lives. They respect and envy Western culture for its indomitable will to live and its fierce affirmation of human existence, yet in the end the pace proves too much for them, or they react against the unrelentingness, the excessive emphases of Western culture, and come to seek spiritual relief in an "Oriental" tranquillity. In the European's frantic pursuit of life, on the other hand, one senses an almost terrifying thoroughness.

A man in whose life I feel a strong interest, and who seems to me to stand for the typical European, is Heinrich Schliemann, the first to excavate Troy and Mycenae. Born the son of a poor pastor in a small village in northern Germany, he was excited as a child by the legends of knights, giants, and ghosts that clung to the old tombs in the village and the ruins of its medieval castle, and he conceived an extraordinary fascination for the unknown and the mysterious. Hearing the Homeric tales of the Trojan wars from his father, he decided at the age of eight that the mighty walls of Troy must still survive somewhere, and resolved that he would one day discover them for himself. Through a life full of difficulties in which he worked as shop assistant, steward on a ship, and messenger for a trading company among other things, he continued his studies in the hope of realizing his childhood dream. Finally, after building up a fortune as a merchant, he was at last able, in his late forties, to take spade in hand and set about making his life's dream come true.

The account of his thwarted love for the girl Minna—described quite briefly in the first chapter of his autobiography—strikes the reader with a purity of heart and a nobility that the *hakanai koi* ("fleeting love") of the Japanese language cannot express. The warm sympathy that germinated between the two as children led to a vow, made with a childish simplicity, to love and be faithful to each other forever; thereafter, the hope that Minna would accompany him in his excavations of Troy was a constant spur to his enthusiasm. When, after many years of separation, he achieved economic independence and proposed to Minna, he learned that she had married another man only a few days previously. In Schliemann's plain, unadorned account of this episode, commonplace in itself, I seem to sense something fundmental to the nature of all Europeans. In the fact that it was this same German people that produced Hitler and Eichmann I found the first incentive to write this article.

I am well aware that the above brief notes may be criticized as betraying a one-sided view. I have merely compared the culture of the West with that of the Japanese and deliberately avoided such words as "Oriental culture," since this involves too many different streams. I have not mentioned how a long history of conflict and struggle within a comparatively limited area distinguishes the civilization of Europe from that of America and has helped give it its characteristically uncompromising quality. Nor must it be forgotten that what I have lumped together as "Western civilization" itself includes strong currents of pre-Indo-European cultures from the Orient and the Mediterranean. I have not touched on the differences among individuals common to both East and West, and I foreswore from the outset any attempt to discuss the "human nature" common to all mankind in any part of the world. It goes without saying, moreover, that national character, patterns of culture, and the like are not eternally fixed and immutable. Even so, even after all these points have been taken into consideration, it seems to me, at least, that the individual characteristics of the cultures of both Europe and Japan harbor certain basic elements that will not easily prove susceptible to change.

Note

1. Aston's translation.

4

Compensative Justice and Moral Investment among Japanese, Chinese, and Koreans

TAKIE SUGIYAMA LEBRA

Background and Objective

THIS is an inquiry into the moral values based on a cross-cultural comparison involving three East Asian cultures. Two motives underlying this study are derived from my primary interest in delineating Japanese culture. In the first place, my previous research on generation gaps in moral values among Japanese has left me with the impression, among other things, that "difference between youth and adults is not so much in the former's alienation from moral values in general as in their resistance to the traditional morality of Japan" (Lebra 1974). It was not certain, however, whether the deviation from traditional moral codes on the part of the younger generation really implied an eventual value change in Japan and was, therefore, really indicative of a generation gap; or if it was only a matter of life cycle so that today's youth, on reaching adulthood, would turn out to replicate the moral posture of their parents. This uncertainty has brought me back to the starting point with the question, What is Japanese traditional morality? It has been my argument that Japanese culture is "sociocultic" and that Japanese morality is regulated by the highly sensitive social radar built into each individual actor. Now the question arises, Is this argument empirically sound? If the adult sample revealed higher social sensitivity in their moral orientations, one must first decide whether this meant the adults were more Japanese, more tradition-bound than the youth, or whether social sensitivity is part of adult culture in general. To repeat the question: What is Japanese traditional morality as distinct from adult morality? This question prompted an expansion of my research perspective into non-Japanese populations.

Adapted from *Journal of Nervous and Mental Disease* 157:287–291. Copyright © 1973, Williams & Wilkins. Reproduced by permission.

The second motive stems from the scarcity of cross-cultural informa-tion as well as the dominance of the Western-centric frame of reference in the available cross-cultural literature. Those major books on Japan which have become anthropological classics, including the works by Benedict (1946), Dore (1958), and Vogel (1965), are either single-cul-ture ethnographies or based upon an explicit or implicit comparison between Japanese and Western cultures. The single-culture approach may be a "necessary evil" concomitant to the anthropological emphasis upon the wholeness and complexity of a culture which might be sacri-ficed under the constraint of cross-cultural methodology. Indeed, many of the psychological attitude studies comparing Japanese and American students along one or another American-invented scale of measurement simply offend the anthropological version of empiricism. The primacy of Western culture as a comparative reference is also understandable since most of such major works were done by Westerners with the West-ern audience in mind. However, Japanese authors whose works have been widely circulated among Japanese readers also tend to depict the Japanese in terms of their deviations from a Western model or ideal (for instance, Maruyama 1956); and Nakane's work (1967), though not devoid of non-Western references, is basically no exception. It is my belief that, while we owe much knowledge of Japanese culture to these past contributions made mainly in light of East-West contrast, that knowledge needs further elaboration and validation by cross-cultural comparison involving non-Western, especially other Asian, cultures.

This paper is part of findings on three cultures—Japanese, Chinese, and Korean. My objective is to shed light upon Japanese morality by locating it in relation to its Chinese and Korean counterparts and thereby to go a step beyond the familiar dichotomy between "Orien-tals" and "Occidentals."

Samples and Method

For sample selection, attention was paid to a proper balance among three requirements: a) representativeness of a population under study which would be maximized by randomization; b) cross-cultural com-parability based upon cross-sample uniformity in socioeconomic and other basic attributes which, carried to the extreme, would defy the intracultural representativeness of each sample; and c) actual accessibil-ity to the sample which might conflict with the other two requirements. Relatively loose criteria were used and the personal judgment and dis-cretion of the "native" consultants—psychiatrists and psychologists— were heavily relied upon. Two generations of residents of Tokyo, Seoul, and Hong Kong were drawn from secondary high school students (seniors or juniors) and their parents or grandparents. Schools were supposed to be selected from among those which ranked average in terms of both academic reputation and socioeconomic status, although this ideal had in fact to be compromised with accessibility to the sample such as the personal interest and co-operation of school principals. The likely sample bias was somewhat checked by the inclusion of public and private schools. The expected sample size was 400 for each culture, equally divided by generation and by sex.

The sample subjects, thus selected, were given a sentence-completion test which partially overlapped with the test used for the aforementioned preliminary research. The test consisted of 20 sentence fragments formulated in order to elicit morally relevant responses in completing the sentences. The content was made tangible and routine rather than abstract and lofty so as to arouse a spontaneous response. The test results were translated into English by native bilinguals at the University of Hawaii who were cautioned to retain, as much as possible, the native meaning of each sentence. The coding scheme was designed and redesigned, its validity being tested by a group of coders (University of Hawaii students) who had met regularly to discuss the matter. In final coding, two judges participated for each sample, and all the disagreements and uncertainties were overcome through group discussion or judgments by native informants and myself. I am not as yet in a position to report more than my initial impressions of the coded data.

This paper deals only with adult samples, disregarding the generation variable. Perhaps the most serious problem of sampling lies in the choice of Hong Kong for China, which however was insurmountable as of 1971 to 1972 because of inaccessibility to other mainland cities. Moreover, some cross-cultural discrepancies among samples were noted in age and education. The Hong Kong Chinese were the oldest with the mean age of 48.6, the Japanese in the middle with 46, and the Koreans the youngest with 44. Probably reflective in part of this age discrepancy was the gradation of levels of education in a reverse order: the Chinese were the lowest with about half of the sample having completed elementary school or less education; whereas the Japanese were intermediary and the Koreans the highest (the overwhelming majority of the latter two groups were educated at high school or college levels, but more Koreans than Japanese had a college education). These variables, important as they are, will not be controlled in this paper. With these sample discrepancies as well as bias, this paper should be taken as little more than an inconclusive report subject to modification.

Attention will be paid, however, to one crucial variable—sex. First of all, across the sample, male respondents were consistently older and better educated than female respondents. Secondly, one should recall the patrilineal ideology and ritual male superiority that predominate in the traditions of all three of these cultures. For these reasons we should expect to find significant differences between men and women in their moral orientations. Space being limited, only 4 instead of 20 sentences will be included in the following analysis.

The frame of reference for the following discussion is derived from the premise that the individual does or does not bind his action by a moral code in accordance with the degree of confidence he holds in the efficacy of moral order in society. The efficacy of moral order depends in a large measure on compensative justice which insures a reward for morally endorsed action and a punishment for violation of a moral code. In short, confidence in compensative justice may be said to underlie moral commitment. The analysis will focus primarily on compensative justice which will be supplemented by a brief discussion on moral commitment under the assumption that these two validate each other.

1. Compensation for perseverance. For convenience, the sentence fragment given as a stimulus will be called *S*, and the fragment added by the respondent called *R*. Let the four *S*s selected for this paper be numbered *S*1, *S*2, *S*3, and *S*4, and corresponding *R*s as *R*1, *R*2, *R*3, and *R*4. Cross-cultural similarities and differences in compensative justice were sought, first, in responses to those *S*s which form conditional clauses beginning with *if*. We should first consider *S*1 "If you persevere through all the hardships that you encounter." The assumption implied here is that perseverance is a morally desirable action or attitude and therefore should be rewarded in one form or another under the rule of compensative justice. Table 1 is a summary of responses classified under seven categories including the last residual one. Each category is illustrated by quoted examples of *R*1. M, F, and T stand for male, female, and total respectively. Figures represent percentages except in the bottom row where total numbers of responses, each of which constitutes 100 per cent, are indicated.

The first four categories refer to one or another form of expected compensation for perseverance. Since most respondents of every cultural group fall under these four, it is safe to say that there is no cultural difference in anticipation of some positive compensation for perseverance. Responses showing mistrust or doubts about compensation or denigrating perseverance, as in category 6, are negligibly few throughout.

A closer examination of Table 1 reveals cross-cultural differences in the specific forms of compensation. The first category, which includes responses anticipating goal attainment, successful outcome, problem

Table 1. Compensation for Perseverance; S1: "If you persevere through all the hardships that you encounter"

R1	Sex	Japanese	Chinese	Koreans
1. Goal attainment, success, problem solution "I believe you will succeed later." "You can bring about the result you want." "Nothing will be impossible to accomplish." "I think anything can be solved."	M	21.9	59.2	21.4
	F	24.1	53.4	16.1
	T	23.0	56.2	18.6
2. Other rewarding end products "There will be a day when you can live well." "The fruit will surely ripen." "Sweet after bitter." "A fortune will come." "You might be rewarded." "A road will open up." "You will be blessed."	M	49.0	24.4	60.2
	F	40.7	34.0	61.3
	T	44.6	29.4	60.5
3. Maturational, experiential benefit "You will become a man of perseverance." "You will mature." "That will be good for you." "You will become self-confident." "You will realize the truth of life." "It will not only help improve your personality, but also be of help to your future in one way or another."	M	12.5	4.1	2.9
	F	15.7	4.9	2.7
	T	14.2	4.5	2.8
4. Inner contentment, emotional pleasure "Your joy will be great." "You will feel refreshed." "You will smile a smile of satisfaction." "Perhaps you may get fun out of it." "You will feel happy."	M	14.6	5.1	14.6
	F	15.7	2.9	8.0
	T	15.2	4.0	11.2
5. Positive implications of perseverance without explicit reference to compensation "You can continue to persevere." "It is the most proper thing to do." "Work!." "In case the result is not good it is important not to be disappointed." "You must have a firm belief."	M	0	6.1	1.0
	F	1.9	1.9	6.3
	T	1.0	4.0	3.7
6. Mistrust or doubts about compensation, negative evaluation of perseverance, other negative responses "They say you will be rewarded, but that's not necessarily the case." "I do not think any particular result will come." "The world will treat you as a fool." "I wonder if there will be any gain." "I do not want to persevere."	M	2.1	1.0	0
	F	0.9	1.0	2.7
	T	1.5	1.0	1.4
7. Other	M	0	0	0
	F	0.9	1.9	3.6
	T	0.5	1.0	1.9
Total number of responses (N)	M	96	98	103
	F	108	103	112
	T	204	201	215

solution, or achievement in general, is represented by more than half of the Chinese respondents. Japanese and Korean responses in this category constitute only about 20 per cent each. Koreans are a little lower than Japanese in this goal-attainment orientation, and that difference stems from female responses only. Korean women are least anticipatory of goal attainment or success and less so than Korean men, whereas Japanese women slightly surpass their male compatriots in this orientation.

The cross-cultural differences revealed here, particularly the Chinese dominance in success orientation over the other two groups, will make sense when this category is compared with the next category. Category 2 includes all responses referring to beneficial, rewarding outcomes as end products which cannot be included in category 1. This category turned out to be more meaningful than "residual." After coding was completed, I came to realize that this category refers primarily to the respondents' confidence in an immutable moral order such that one only has to wait, after persevering through hardships, for a reward to come automatically. "Some day there will be something good" or "You will have an easy life later" is a typical expression of such confidence. More specifically, it might be postulated that this confidence is rooted in the perceived irresistibility of natural order of cause and effect, as illustrated by metaphorical references to the natural growth of a plant: "Some day it will sprout"; "It will flower and bear fruit"; "The fruit will surely ripen."

The difference between this orientation and anticipation of goal attainment is now quite clear. Goal attainment involves the subjective committment as well as rational assessment and decisions on the part of the actor, whereas confidence in the natural order of compensation frees the actor from such subjective or rational involvement which might interfere with natural order.

Figures in Table 1 present these two categories as mirror images of each other. In category 2, Koreans by far surpass the other groups, followed by Japanese, and goal-oriented Chinese are lowest. If we can assume that these two categories—goal attainment and confidence in natural order—are mutually exclusive, bipolar orientations, we can say that the Chinese and Koreans are at opposite poles, the Japanese finding themselves somewhere in between. The validity of this tentative generalization must be tested by a further examination of the data.

The following two categories involve compensation other than in the form of final product. Category 3 refers to contributions of perseverance to the moral, emotional maturation or character development of the individual as a person. A beneficial end product may eventually come by, but for the moment the respondent is more concerned with building up the basic human resources which would be of use in the future. Although this category is decidedly lower in frequency than the previous ones across the samples, we find an interesting cross-cultural variation. Here the Japanese and Koreans are mutually opposed with the Chinese standing in the middle. The distinct dominance of the Japanese here seems to imply that their goal orientation is based on a long range career in view, and that they place more importance than do the other groups on the "human" consequence, instead of an external outcome, of perseverance.

Before making the last statement conclusive, we should proceed to category 4 referring to inner or emotional satisfaction or happiness. Here again the Japanese rank highest. This finding underscores what was said in the previous paragraph with reference to the "human" preoccupation, and further confirms the stereotypic image of a Japanese with an introspective propensity, with gravity toward the inner state of feeling. The success-oriented Chinese are understandably lowest in this category; and Koreans stand in between but much closer to the Japanese, with no difference between Japanese and Korean men on this score. The relative strength of the Koreans in this category appears inconsistent with their weakness in maturational, "human" concerns, and therefore calls for an interpretation. According to Crane, Koreans seem to share with Japanese the importance of maintaining the *kibun* (feeling) in an optimal state and the awareness of its vulnerability, and this is particularly true with the *kibun* of a person of higher status (Crane 1967:8). It is logical, then, that Korean males, occupying a higher status than females, reveal as much introspective orientation as the Japanese sample. This characteristic shared by the Japanese and Koreans may be partly related to their socialization techniques, which are distinct from the Chinese counterpart. Both Japanese and Korean mothers seem to cultivate the inner sanction in the child by appealing to his shame or guilt, whereas Chinese mothers tend to use a more direct threat or punishment. A Japanese mother is likely to discipline her child by saying, "If you do so, people will laugh at you," or "I, your mother, will be laughed at." But a Chinese mother would scold her child by saying, "Be quiet," or "You will be beat up." A Korean mother appears more like a Japanese mother in this respect, although both Chinese and Korean mothers seem to resort to physical punishment much more frequently than Japanese mothers do. Japanese mothers seem much more solicitous than Chinese and somewhat more than Korean mothers of the child's empathetic compliance by saying, for instance, "Please understand how I, Mother, feel."[1]

Category 4 is similar to category 3 in that both refer to the "human" consequence of perseverance, but they are not identical in the qualities of humanity. Category 3 delineates the moral or emotional strength, maturity, durability, or discipline of an individual, whereas category 4 involves a more "fleeting," transitory, or esthetic aspect of human quality, namely, his inner feeling or sentiment. Sensitivity to the latter is shared by Japanese and Koreans and least by Chinese, while the concern for the former is most characteristic of Japanese and least so of Koreans.

    2. Compensation for kindness. Cross-cultural similarities and differences thus far inferred from "compensation for perseverance" need more substantiation from another perspective. This section will delineate compensative justice anchored in social action involving reciprocal exchange of favors. The relationship between justice and reciprocity or exchange has been of sociological interest (Adams 1965; Blau 1964; Gouldner 1960; Homans 1958; Yuchtman 1972). We shall consider *S*2, "If you are kind to others" in a search for cross-cultural variations primarily in terms of the stress upon reciprocity as part of moral order.

    As in Table 1, one can see that the three cultures share expectations of some positive outcome from kindness. Negative responses of category 6, including those distrustful of a rewarding outcome as well as those disapproving kindness, are negligible in number.

    Category 1 "Direct, reciprocal, equivalent repayment" refers to the compensation contingent upon the sense of debt on the part of the receiver of kindness as bound by the rule of reciprocal exchange of equivalent values. Kindness is expected to be repaid by the same kindness or other "social" forms of benefit such as love or respect. The social relationship involved in this exchange appears more or less symmetrical, dyadic, and well spelled out in that one can tell who is the repayer and who the receiver of the repayment.

    The majority of the Chinese fall under this category, whereas only 14 per cent of Japanese indicate an expectation of reciprocal return. This finding is not surprising in view of the Chinese rationality in pursuit of a goal, in contrast to the Japanese "naturalistic," "human," and "introspective" preoccupations. It may be argued that the Chinese rationality, when applied to interpersonal relationships, results in the expectation of keeping balance between debts and credits. It is true that the norm of reciprocity is shared by the Japanese as well under the culture-loaded concept of *on* (moral/social debt). However, *on* for Japanese implies moral asymmetry, where it is imperative for the debtor to repay but the creditor's claim for pay-off should be suppressed. An explicit anticipation of reciprocal pay-off for kindness on the part of the creditor would therefore be rather distasteful to the Japanese, whereas the Chinese appear much less suppressed and more openly rational in an economic sense.

Table 2. Compensation for Kindness; S2: "If you are kind to others"

R2	Sex	Japanese	Chinese	Koreans
1. Direct, reciprocal, equivalent repayment "They too will be kind to you." "You will be thanked." "The kindness will come back to you." "They will respect you." "You will be well treated." "Give and take." "If you are kind to others, you will get that much in return."	M	11.5	57.6	41.3
	F	15.6	49.0	36.9
	T	13.7	53.2	39.1
2. Other beneficial outcome for the kind actor "Certainly you will get something good." "You might gain something." "It will pass around until it is returned to your children." "You will be blessed." "You can make many friends."	M	37.5	18.2	6.7
	F	28.5	27.6	9.0
	T	32.7	22.9	7.9
3. Inner satisfaction "Your heart will be brightened." "You will feel good." "It will stay with you as a heart-brightening memory." "You, yourself, feel satisfied and always happy." "It is a kind of service that can make both sides happy."	M	40.6	3.0	23.1
	F	50.5	4.9	25.2
	T	45.9	4.0	24.2
4. Benefit for others or society as a whole, or stress on altruism "They will be pleased." "Everybody will be in harmony with everybody else, and they will love and respect each other." "Society will become more healthy and make more progress." "The world will be a better place to live in."	M	6.2	3.0	22.2
	F	3.6	1.0	23.4
	T	4.9	2.0	23.3
5. Approval or instruction, without reference to compensation "That is a natural thing to do." "Be so with a smile." "Try hard to be so." "This is the way of being friendly with neighbors." "It is what everybody should do."	M	4.2	13.1	3.9
	F	0	13.7	4.5
	T	2.1	13.5	4.2
6. Negative response "To expect a reward would be a conceit." "You should not impose kindness." "It can cause other people to misunderstand you." "Some people might not accept your kindness; therefore it can be a waste of effort."	M	0	3.0	1.9
	F	0.9	3.9	0
	T	0.5	3.5	0.9
7. Other	M	0	2.0	1.0
	F	0.9	0	0.9
	T	0.5	1.0	0.9
Total number of responses (N)	M	99	96	104
	F	102	109	111
	T	201	205	215

Category 2, where the Japanese are strongest and Koreans weakest, refers to the expected return of benefit other than in an explicitly reciprocal direct, equivalent form. As illustrated by "You might gain something" neither the source nor the form of the compensation is clear; or a third party is involved either as the sender or receiver of the benefit in expanding or interfering with the reciprocal dyad. The fact that Japanese are highest in this orientation suggests that they expect a beneficial compensation for kindness as much as the Chinese do, and yet, because of the moral suppression of a creditor's claim, are compelled to express such expectation in vague, diffuse, indirect, nonequivalent terms. If Koreans were not so low here, I would be tempted to add that this category corresponds with confidence in the natural order of compensation (Table 1).

Category 3 calls special attention as an overpowering reinforcement of category 4 of Table 1. Japanese distinguish themselves in seeking compensation for kindness in the inner state of mind or feeling, and cross-cultural difference here is almost fantastic. When a moral action is oriented toward other people, Japanese are even more introspective than when engaging in a more individual-centered action like perseverance. This seems to confirm my previous characterization of adult Japanese as equipped with a sensitive social radar (Lebra 1974a). The Japanese actor may be so sensitive to the inner feeling of another person, the receiver of kindness, that he, the giver of kindness, may be able to share, inwardly, the pleasure felt by the receiver. This sort of "social echo" may be contributing to the primacy of inner satisfaction among Japanese respondents.

By contrast, Chinese score as low as one tenth of the Japanese counterpart. This cross-cultural gap makes one suspect that the Chinese sensitivity is quite different from that of the Japanese. According to Rin, a Chinese individual is more sensitized to what other people have verbally expressed in criticizing him than to their inner, unexpressed feelings. Compared with this, Rin argues, the Japanese sensitivity to the feelings of others is certainly unique (Rin 1972:995). In the same vein, Tseng and Hsu state that "most Chinese traditional novels concentrate on what the characters do in their roles as persons rather than what the characters think and feel as individuals" (Tseng and Hsu 1969–1970:6).

The open, unsuppressed expectation of reciprocal repayment and the expectation of inner compensation seem to form the mutually opposite extremes; and the Japanese and Chinese hold the extreme positions and Koreans are in the middle in both categories. What was said above regarding sex difference in Korean introspectiveness does not hold true with Table 2: women are slightly more introspective; and for that matter the female dominance here runs across cultures, unlike introspection with regard to perseverance. My speculation is that introspection, stimulated by kindness, reflects a socially empathetic and accomodating sensitivity—the sensitivity with which females are endowed in a greater degree.

Koreans stand out in category 4, which stresses a beneficial outcome of kindness for its receivers, society or the world as a whole, rather than for its giver. Implied here are altruism, suppressed self-interest, and lofty morality. The Korean strength in this orientation may be due to the more compulsive internalization of Confucian doctrine than among either Chinese or Japanese, or, more probably, nationalistic aspirations for unification.[2]

Category 5 includes those responses which, instead of expressing an anticipated compensation for kindness, give approval, instructions, or other comments on kindness. Here the respondent appears aloof from the interaction between the giver and receiver of kindness by assuming the role of an instructor. It is interesting that so few Koreans and Japanese responded in this way while there is substantial representation by the Chinese. It would seem that the Chinese tend to look at a given situation as an uninvolved witness, whereas both the Japanese and Koreans are more inclined to become involved and to place themselves in the position of either the kind actor or his alter. (To a lesser degree, the same can be said of the instructional responses that appeared in category 5 of Table 1.) The point I wish to argue is that what might be called "role vicariism" is operating more among Japanese and Koreans. In part, it may be this personal involvement that makes the Japanese morally resistant to reciprocal expectation, and that induces Koreans to be altruistic. The Chinese are not compelled to suppress self-interest because they are not taking the vicarious role of the kind actor. This finding, viewed in this light, is consistent with the other aspects of cross-cultural differences and similarities discussed so far.

3. *Retribution for wrongdoing.* While *S*1 and *S*2 are if-clauses invoking anticipations of *rewards* for a morally desirable action or attitude, *S*3 refers to past commitments of wrongdoing, and implies consequential *punishments*. This section is meant briefly to reinforce some of the previous statements from the point of view of negative compensation. *S*3, "After having committed all sorts of wrongdoing" aroused responses indicating some form of retribution across the samples. Cross-cultural differences are nonetheless interesting. More Japanese, as shown in Table 3, than Chinese or Koreans responded in the manner of category 1, where retribution takes a subjective form, that is, the wrongdoer feels guilty, uneasy, remorseful, or eventually reforms himself. Conversely, in category 2, which indicates objective occurrences of misfortune or nega-

Table 3. Retribution for Wrongdoing; S3: "After having done all sorts of wrongdoing"

R3	Sex	Japanese	Chinese	Koreans
1. Subjective retribution: guilt, repentance, reformation "You feel uneasy at heart." "He will feel regretful and guilty." "One can never die peacefully." "He settled down to work seriously." "I am living an honest life now." "Some people turn out to become more human."	M	23.2	10.1	13.7
	F	23.1	8.9	14.8
	T	23.2	9.5	14.3
2. Objective retribution: punishment, bad outcome "He was ruined." "He was rejected by the world." "After death, he was not even admitted to hell." "You will become the scum of society." "Finished." "You will be criticized and blamed." "I will be unable to reincarnate." "I will meet many miseries." "The next generation will suffer."	M	64.2	83.8	79.4
	F	66.7	87.1	78.7
	T	65.5	85.5	79.0
3. Lack or opposite of retribution "It has the same result as those who do many good deeds." "(I recall) it was fun." "He will keep on doing (it)." "I will just go ahead in my way of life." "There is no result." "Sometimes the person will become rich." "He lived a long life." "He became a company president."	M	6.3	4.0	3.9
	F	4.6	3.0	0
	T	5.4	3.5	1.9
4. Other	M	6.3	2.0	2.9
	F	5.6	1.0	6.5
	T	5.9	1.5	4.8
Total number of responses (N)	M	95	99	102
	F	108	101	108
	T	203	200	210

tive outcomes as retributions and where the majority of every group falls, Chinese stand out, Japanese being the lowest. This finding seems to confirm part of the previous tables, showing a greater proclivity among Japanese for inward orientation, whether involving inner gratification or repentance.

It must be admitted that the above generalization does not square with another point I have made. I speculated in discussing Table 1 that Japanese, like Koreans, tend to feel confident of the efficacy of compensative justice as a matter of natural course. If so, their responses in category 2 in Table 3 should be of higher frequency to the extent that objective retribution is considered a natural course of events. It might be wondered, in the same vein, why Japanese rank highest in category 3, which denies retribution for immoral conduct. Far from demonstrating a sense of efficacy of natural order in compensative justice, the response here suggests a sense of moral absurdity. The only explanation I can offer for these inconsistencies is that Japanese may be confident of moral efficacy if it entails a positive outcome, but not if it brings about a negative one; if a reward, but not a punishment, is expected.

4. Investment for an ideal home life. Let us turn to *S*4, "In order to build an ideal home life," meant to elicit responses indicating moral investment or commitment with the stated goal in mind. The finding here should either validate or invalidate the foregoing analysis of compensative justice in a logically reversed order: *S*1 and *S*2 specified moral investment, and *S*3 referred to immoral acts committed, the compensation for which was elicited, while *S*4 has the goal specified in advance and elicits responses identifying investments for that goal.

Table 4 consists of two classes of *R*4s: the first five categories, including the residual one, all involve characteristics of human action or actors, and the sixth and seventh categories refer to more or less environmental or external conditions or settings. Responses to *S*4 turned out to be loaded with richer information than those to *S*1, *S*2, and *S*3. This made it necessary for us to allow one response to be included in either one or two, but no more, categories simultaneously. For instance, "The whole family should co-operate with each other" and "Harmony between husband and wife" are coded under categories 1 and 6; "I am willing to work hard and undertake responsibility for my family" and "Both husband and wife should make efforts" are included in both 3 and 6; "A well organized economic plan is required" comes under 4 and 7, and so forth. The total numbers of responses are inevitably much larger than those in the previous tables, although each total thus enlarged is nonetheless made to stand for 100 per cent.

Since space does not permit covering this table in detail, the following analysis will throw into relief only a few salient aspects in conjunction

Table 4. Investment or Condition for Home Life; S4: "In order to build an ideal home life"

R4	Sex	Japanese	Chinese	Koreans
1. Co-operation, solidarity, mutual understanding "We should forgive and tolerate one another." "Mutual concession and orderliness." "You must trust and love each other." "The whole family should co-operate with each other." "Children should be polite to the elders and the elders should be kind to the youngsters."	M	48.5	9.2	40.9
	F	46.4	14.5	38.6
	T	47.4	11.8	39.7
2. Individual's moral attitude or personality "We should be patient." "One must become a respectable person." "Honesty and cheerfulness are necessary." "I, myself, should be more perfect." "One's personality must be good." "He must have confidence and (economic) ability to support his family."	M	13.2	10.5	7.3
	F	6.5	17.8	13.0
	T	9.7	14.1	10.3
3. Diligence, energy expenditure, effort "I am willing to work hard and undertake responsibility for my family." "They should endeavor in everything and live peacefully." "Both husband and wife should make efforts (for that purpose)." "You cannot avoid working hard." "One should try hard."	M	5.9	28.1	7.3
	F	12.4	26.3	9.8
	T	9.3	27.2	8.6
4. Rationality, plan, intelligence, judgment "A well organized economic plan is required." "I must have a well prepared family plan beforehand." "You must cultivate your intelligence." "You must study, keeping abreast of the times."	M	2.2	21.6	6.1
	F	2.6	18.4	3.8
	T	2.4	20.0	4.9
5. Other or ambiguous qualities of action or actor	M	2.9	0.7	2.4
	F	2.0	2.0	1.6
	T	2.4	1.3	2.0
6. Family condition "Harmony between husband and wife." "The first thing to do is to find a good mate." "Children should respect parents." "Let us the whole family try hard." "Father should show love (to his family) as the family head."	M	20.7	13.1	32.9
	F	21.5	7.9	26.1
	T	21.1	10.5	29.3
7. Economic condition "Earn as much money as possible and have birth control." "There must be a steady economy." "The first thing is money." "You must inherit property from your parents and be helped by good friends." "The first important thing is to make a strong economic foundation and then the family will have to be friendly with each other."	M	0.7	13.7	2.4
	F	1.3	5.9	5.4
	T	1.0	9.8	4.0
8. Other (health, education, occupation, etc.)	M	5.8	3.3	0.6
	F	7.3	7.3	1.6
	T	6.5	5.2	1.2
Total number of responses (N)	M	136	153	164
	F	153	152	184
	T	289	305	348

with the preceding points of discussion. Category 1, delineating human interaction with the emphasis upon co-operation, harmony, and solidarity as a necessary investment for an ideal home life, is clearly over-represented by Japanese, and to a slightly smaller degree, by Koreans, and under-represented by Chinese. The positions of Chinese and Japanese or Koreans are exactly reversed in categories 3 and 4. The Chinese are more oriented toward hard work as well as rational planning than toward harmonious interaction, while the opposite is true of Japanese and Koreans. The Japanese in particular stand out in neglecting the importance of rationality. It seems that both Japanese and Koreans, concerned with and sensitive to one another's feelings, find smooth, harmonious, co-operative human interaction most indispensable for achieving a goal. The Chinese, on the other hand, are more focused on individual action, outwardly oriented energy expenditure, and rational co-ordination of means and ends.

This difference further corresponds with another distributional difference in categories 6 and 7. Koreans and Japanese refer to family conditions far more often than do the Chinese, while the latter precedes the others in pointing out economic conditions as basic. This is no surprise in view of the Chinese stress on rationality and the rational, external manipulability of money, and of the Japanese and Korean focus upon interpersonal co-operation and empathy, which is most likely to be associated with family membership.

This brief summary of Table 4, I believe, validates rather than refutes what was delineated in the previous sections. Implications are that the type of confidence in compensative justice and the type of moral investment are in mutual support.

Conclusion

Despite the incomplete, tentative nature of this paper, there has emerged a rather clear picture of three East Asian cultures with respect to a portion of moral values. While some differences betwen male and female responses were noted in each culture, within-culture variations by sex have turned out to be small enough to be overridden by between-culture variations which stand out in an incomparable degree. In conclusion I would like to reiterate some salient points of cross-cultural contrast and to venture further speculations. Japanese will be centrally focused upon, Koreans and Chinese relegated to a comparative status.

First, although the Japanese in general tend to believe themselves to be unequalled in their preoccupation with success and goal attainment and many foreign observers seem to concur, our data suggest that they are surpassed by the Chinese in this orientation as far as their responses to "perseverance" are concerned. Instead, Japanese are more confident than Chinese, though less so than Koreans, of the natural order of compensative justice whereby one's perseverance is destined to bring about a reward as naturally as a plant bears fruit. From this contrast it can be inferred that success-oriented Chinese attach more importance to the subjective planning, decision making, and commitment on the part of the actor whereas Japanese would rather leave nature as it is instead of interfering with its order by human designs. Indeed, this inference obtained confirmation from another set of data indicating the Chinese tendency to single out the actor's rationality and judgments as a necessary resource for a goal attainment like "home life building." Japanese responses, in contrast, conspicuously overlook this factor. There seems to be what might be called "cultural allergy" to design and artifice among Japanese, and for that matter, among Koreans as well.

One may speculate as to whether this reflects the stronger Buddhist influence over the Japanese along with the idea of Karma or destiny; or whether Maruyama (1972) is right in characterizing the Japanese sense of history in terms of *naru* (become, grow, or emerge), as distinguished from *tsukuru* (make, construct, or design), which is rooted in the "ancient layer" of Japanese culture. The same orientation may be locked either with pessimistic fatalism and resignation or an optimistic faith in a bright future.

Second, Japanese are concerned with the "human" implication of moral action, as seen in their preoccupation with building up a morally or emotionally strong, mature personality. Japanese goal orientation, then, appears to be directed toward a human "means" as well as toward an end result, while Chinese are much more exclusively biased for the latter and Koreans pay least attention to cultivation of the human means. In this sense, we must qualify the first point made above regarding success orientation *vs.* confidence in natural order: Japanese may be as success oriented as Chinese, but constrained by the priority of the inner quality of man over an external successful outcome and by a long ranged view of a human career.

Related to this is the Japanese introspective propensity—our third point of discussion. Japanese tend to seek compensation for moral or immoral action in the inner state of feeling. Introspective sensitivity is heightened when action is socially addressed and social feedback is expected, as if one assumed one's inner feeling to echo that of another and *vice versa*. The Japanese proclivity for introspection, or "convolution," thus seems intertwined with social empathy and masochistic self-denial. The asymmetric weight of *on* morality reinforces this convolution, suppressing an egoistic, extravert, rational expectation of balanced reciprocal exchange which is taken for granted by Chinese.

On the scale of introspective convolution, Chinese are at the bottom, Koreans following closely behind Japanese.

The last two points differ from each other in that one emphasizes the strong, mature, durable aspect of personality while the other refers to the fleeting, ephemeral, sensitive, or esthetic aspect of man's inner quality. Relatively speaking, Japanese are sensitized to both values, Koreans to the latter only, and Chinese to neither.

Fourth, the Japanese introspectiveness based upon social sensitization results in attaching foremost importance to social cohesion as a necessary condition for goal attainment. It may be that social co-operation and harmony are not only necessary but most readily available as resources: Japanese are willing to make an investment in cohesion as well as inclined to regard it as indispensable. Diligence, hard work, and striving are not as important, while the reverse is true with Chinese. Here again we are reminded that the Japanese self-image as the most hard-working people does not hold strong. Japanese and Koreans who are mindful of social cohesion naturally pay much more attention to family relationships, whereas the rationally minded, work-oriented Chinese are as much concerned with economy as with family.

Fifth, there is evidence from the responses given to our sentence-completion test that Japanese tend to put themselves in the role of the actor in the sentence. Such "role vicariism" underlies Korean responses as well, while Chinese remain relatively more aloof or external to the given situation and take the role of an instructor or judge. This last finding seems either to confirm or explain the above points.

These characteristics of Japanese moral attitude, particularly the last four, put together, may be said to form a Japanese version of humanism. It was BenDasan (1970) who characterized Japanese in terms of their humanism under such labels as *ningenkyō* (humanistic religion) and *ningenteki-benshōhō* (human dialectic) in contradistinction with Jewish transcendental dogmatism. One might wonder if "humanism" is not a misnomer or whether this characterization of Japanese does not pose a logical contradiction with the first point above. We have seen the Japanese allergy to human intervention with the natural order, in contrast to the Chinese propensity to impose a human will and design upon nature. The term humanism then sounds more applicable to Chinese. Indeed, Chin (1971), another popular bicultural writer, attached this label to the Chinese in the sense that they trust man, and man alone, unlike Japanese.

If "humanism" can be used for both Chinese and Japanese, one should suspect different meanings implied therein. Chinese humanism, it appears, derives from an insistence upon the supremacy of *Homo sapiens* over the universe, over both the supernatural and natural spheres. Japanese humanism on the other hand is imbedded in confidence in human beings as part of the natural order, or in human "nature" as such (Pelzel 1970). Nature for the Chinese is more subjected to man's will, energy, and design, whereas the imposition of an arbitrary will upon nature goes against Japanese humanism. Chinese humanism is armed with civilization, man-made principles and standards, and even "formalism" (Chin 1971). For the Japanese, humanity should lie intact over, outside, or behind these artifices; as put by Ben-Dasan, the Japanese believe in *rigai no ri* (reason beyond reason), *hōgai no hō* (law beyond law), and *gengai no gen* (word beyond word). What constitutes Chinese humanism is what is rejected by Japanese humanism.

The Japanese concern for the human consequence of moral action, then, refers to the inner quality of personality such as discipline or feeling whereas Chinese appear more outwardly oriented toward external environment. Two types of subjectivity are involved. The Japanese subjectivity is distinctly inward-looking and focused on feelings, whereas the Chinese subjectivity is more outward and rational. Koreans stand in the middle on this score.

The empathetic-convolute theme of Japanese culture is likely to contribute to discrediting verbal, explicit communication and to glorifying an intuitive, subtle exchange of messages. While the Chinese anthropocentrism is inseparable, as stressed by Chin, from the imperative of verbal communication and strenuous persuasion between man and man, Japanese find the ability to communicate without verbalization adorable and truly "human." It then follows that the Japanese concern for social cohesion and harmony is based on the availability of untold, spontaneous, mutual co-operation among people involved. Chinese, on the other hand, may regard social cohesion as something to be created under strong leadership with an organizational design.

Although I am in no position to speculate upon Korean humanism, I suspect it to be closer to Japanese humanism.

Finally, I am tempted to suggest a possible relationship between our findings and depression. Depression is relatively prevalent among Japanese psychiatric patients as reported by Caudill and Schooler (1969). Not only "patients" but normal, healthy adult Japanese tend to exhibit a recurrence of mild depression as a matter of their culturally sanctioned life style. Among Chinese, however, depression is a rarity: they have no word for a depressive mood, and "feel embarrassed to express feelings of loneliness and sadness." Instead, they tend to somatize (Tseng and Hsu 1969–1970:10–11). This difference may have something to do with the two types of humanism. We would be on a firmer ground in this argument if information on Korean depression were available.

Notes

1. For those comparative observations on socialization, among others the author relied upon Wolf (1972), Rin (1972), and personal communication with Y. S. Kim Harvey, James Watson, and William P. Lebra.

2. It might be relevant to point out in this connection that one study has discovered Korean college students to be more severe in moral judgment than American students (Rettig and Pasamanick 1959). Another study (Gondo 1970) compared Korean with Japanese students on the view of life; among the findings was the difference in the types of individuals selected as most respected by the respondents. While many Japanese respondents picked more or less ordinary citizens, including their own parents, because of their ability to lead a steady life, Korean students selected great national heroes who had contributed to national independence, peace and prosperity, and the struggle against Japan.

5

Individual, Group and *Seishin:*
Japan's Internal Cultural Debate

Brian Moeran

Introduction

In his book, *The cultural definition of political response*, David Parkin* sees culture as a system of communications and responses. Custom, he says, consists of conventionalised activity, concept and lexicon, and he suggests that none of these need necessarily reflect the others consistently. Each is thus to some degree autonomous and it is *words* which Parkin argues are the most likely part of custom to persist, even though the context of what they describe may change. These words he refers to as "key verbal concepts" which "shape people's perceptions of changes in the group's environment of opportunity, which may in turn redefine the lexicons and taxonomies" (Parkin 1978:26). This leads one to suggest that, in contradistinction to the Whorfian idea that a people's world view is shaped by the grammar of the language it speaks, a people's perceptions are affected rather by *lexical* categories.

Parkin further distinguishes between what he has called "set words" (or "invariable words" [1976]) and "variable phrases," to show how new conventions can become labelled and old ones relabelled or forgotten about entirely. In order to accommodate change, keywords (as I shall proceed to call the "set" or "invariable" words) have to be conceptually ambivalent. Parkin's primary interest was in the study of poly-

---

*This article applies Parkin's notion of "internal cultural debate" to an analysis of Japanese social organisation. By considering the keywords found in such diverse cultural spheres as high school baseball, advertising, and pottery aesthetics, it is shown that neither the "group" model nor "social exchange" model can satisfactorily deal with the relation between group and individual in Japanese society. A hypothesis is made concerning the relation between keywords of evaluation and types of social organisation, and it is suggested that anthropological theory is itself limited, and to some extent determined, by the internal cultural debates of the societies studied by anthropologists.

From *Man* (N.S.) 19, no. 2 (June 1984): 252–266. Reprinted by permission of the Royal Anthropological Institute of Great Britain and Ireland.

gyny, bridewealth transactions and segmentary lineage organisation among the Luo in Kenya. He showed how, in public speech, keywords were used by those in power in an endeavour to maintain the *status quo,* while in private speech certain interest groups would make use of variable phrases in order to reinterpret the meaning of keywords. Precisely because keywords were conceptually condensed and lexically and syntactically predictable, it became possible to smuggle in new meanings.

I wish in this article to adopt a similar approach to the study of Japanese social organisation. My concern is primarily with a parochial problem, that of the relation between individual and group in Japanese society, but for those whose interests lie outside this somewhat narrow strip of oriental anthropology, I have endeavoured to set my data within the more general theory of Parkin's "internal cultural debate." During recent research into the production, marketing and aesthetic appraisal of art pottery in Japan, I discovered that a considerable part of the aesthetic vocabulary used by potters, critics and general public was to be found in other spheres of Japanese culture—sports, advertising, tourism and so on.[1] It became clear to me that there are a number of keywords which occur right across the board in Japanese society and that these can largely be grouped for convenience under the heading of *"seishin,"* or *"spirit,"* a concept which although officially looked down upon after the Pacific War because of its former association with nationalism and militarism, now appears to be regaining some of its former status among the Japanese. In this article, I want to examine the notions that are seen to make up the concept of *seishin,* and to this end I have brought in observations on high school baseball, art pottery and advertising language. My aim is to point out the way in which Japanese society is trying to grapple with the problem of individualism which is commonly feared to accompany Westernisation, modernisation, urbanisation and industrialisation. I shall argue that the ambivalence of certain keywords within the concept of *seishin* allows individualism to challenge the notion of "selflessness" inherent in the *seishin* model. Yet this same ambivalence prevents Japanese society from jumping—lemming-like—into the abyss of Western individualism, and allows it to retain strong community values.

Models of Japanese Social Organisation

Over the years, there has been some discussion among those anthropologists studying Japan concerning the role of the individual in relation to that of the group in Japanese social organisation. Recently, anthropologists such as Embree (1939), Benedict (1946) and Nakane (1970a) have been attacked for expounding a "group" model which fails to take account, it is said, of a number of facts in Japanese society which contradict the model.

Let us start by examining what is meant by the term "group model." In fact, its content is easily grasped, if only because for some time now it has been used by the Japanese themselves to project an image of their country here in the West. We have learned to accept this model and even in some cases—in particular where economics and art are concerned—to imitate its tenets. Briefly put, the group model of Japanese society assumes that people prefer to act within the framework of a group and that such a group will be hierarchically organised and run by a paternalistic leader. The psychological process underlying this structure is called *"amae,"* or "passive love." Doi (1981:38) argues that the parent/child relationship naturally creates *amae* and that this feeling comes under the rubric of *"ninjō,"* or "spontaneously arising feeling." When this parent/child relation of indulgence and dependence is introduced into other relationships, we have what is known as *giri,* or "socially contracted dependence." It is the combination of *giri* and *ninjō* which permeates all social relationships, in particular those between leader and subordinate in a group.

According to this model, members of a group are expected to conform and co-operate with one another, to avoid open conflict and competition. The emphasis, therefore, is on harmony, and behaviour tends to be ritualised and formal in order to reduce or eliminate conflict or embarrassment. Ideally, in this kind of group, people are supposed to subordinate individual interests to group goals and to remain loyal to group causes. In return for their loyalty and devotion, the leader of the group treats his followers with benevolence and magnanimity (Befu 1980:170–171).

The trouble with the group model as outlined here is that it fails to encompass certain paradoxes. For example, despite the emphasis on hierarchical forms of organisation in Japanese society, egalitarian forms do exist (witness, for example, the *kō-gumi** type of rural community found in the southwest of Japan). Moreover, paternalistic leaders do not necessarily look after the welfare of their subordinates. This can be seen in the organisation of smaller businesses in particular, where employees for their part are not so loyal to their employers. In other words, the group model fails to account for behaviour that goes against group norms. Finally, the ideology of harmony does not explain the conflict and competition rife—believe it or not—in Japanese society.[2]

Kō-gumi is one of various terms designating an association of households organized primarily for mutual aid.—EDS.

Befu rightly argues that the group model does not account for these differences between ideology and behaviour, and that it fails to explain how groups as such are related to one another *ex*ternally, since it concentrates on their *in*ternal structure. He suggests, therefore, that we accept the "group" model as "behavioral ideology" and then considers the notion of social exchange, together with the concept of *"seishin,"* as an alternative means of explaining the paradoxes outlined above. This social exchange model is far more practical and less overtly ideological than the group model. It assumes that the individual has certain resources such as wealth, knowledge, skills or influential friends, which he can exchange with others for resources that he does not possess. Here the individual will tend to "maximize his opportunities by strategically allocating his resources, distributing them to individuals who need them most and are most likely to bring him bountiful returns" (Befu 1980: 179). This does not mean that group ideology and social exchange are mutually exclusive. A company can advocate "benevolence," but be benevolent only in so far as it is profitable for the company to be so; workers can advocate loyalty to the company, but leave the company if greater loyalties take precedence. Thus the group model is motivated by altruism, the social exchange model by self-interest (1980:180).

Befu's suggestion that we consider social exchange when analysing Japanese society is sensible. It allows us to take account of the role of personal networks *(tsukiai)*, which have been almost totally ignored by anthropologists espousing the "group" model.[3] Yet one frequently finds that people make use of *tsukiai* to break down the altruistic morality of their own group and to threaten the solidarity of an outside group.[4] The group model of Japanese society is unable to explain this.

Finally, Befu suggests that *seishin* is an analytical concept which can be used objectively to explain Japanese social organisation. He takes the concept to refer to individuals *qua* individuals without reference to their social obligations. But, in fact, *seishin* is part of that which he observes, and so the concept cannot be applied in this way. He thus unreflexively uses a Japanese cultural principle to explain Japanese society, and so himself becomes victim of the Japanese group ideological model of which *seishin* is itself a part. Befu ends up talking about the way people say things ought to be done, and not about the way things actually are done.

So what is *seishin?* In that it is a key verbal concept and hence ambivalent, it is virtually impossible to say precisely what constitutes Japanese "spirit." Essentially, *seishin* refers to one's inner being which often derives spiritual fortitude from self-discipline. Both Confucian and Buddhist ideals are found in *seishin*, which relies on physical training as a means towards attaining spiritual well-being and harmony within the self. *Bushidō,* the way of the samurai, and other martial arts such as *kendō, jūdō* and *karate,* together with a number of more "refined pursuits" such as the tea ceremony, flower arrangement, *sumi* ink painting and calligraphy, all contain strong elements of *seishin* in their instruction and practice. It is only by cultivating *seishin* that one can begin to grasp the "real essence" of these activities.

High School Baseball Tournament

Probably the best way to start my examination of *seishin* is to look at the Japanese high school baseball tournament which is played annually at the beginning of August at Kōshien Stadium, Osaka. From early in July, high schools all over the country compete in knock-out competitions played at the prefectural level. These are written up in some detail in the newspapers, in particular by the *Asahi* which acts as official sponsor of the annual tournament. The winners of each prefectural tournament are then eligible to play at Kōshien, the shrine-like Mecca to the game of baseball in Japan. Each team makes the pilgrimage to Osaka and the cameras of the press are ready to record for posterity the looks and actions of these teenage players as they find themselves stepping onto the turf of the vast arena. It is here that the nation's summer ritual takes place.[5] For ten days, approximately fifty teams battle in gladiatorial combat to receive the accolade of being Japan's "No. 1" high school team. During these ten days, more than 400,000 people come to watch the games being played at Kōshien. In addition a very large percentage of the population watches the games that are played in temperatures frequently exceeding 35° Centigrade. As the competition proceeds towards its climax, tension mounts all over the country. Teams are discussed, pitchers and batters assessed, and favourites for the coveted title picked out. There is always the excitement of an upset victory, of some distant country team scrambling through to the quarter finals to challenge the giants—the schools like P. L. Gakuin, Waseda Jitsugyō, or Chūkyō in Aichi Prefecture—which tend to get through to the last stages of the competition year after year. For the winners of each round there is always the next match to be played; for the losers there are only tears, tears which mingle with the sweat and dust on the players' cheeks at the end of the day. And at the end of the tournament comes *o-bon,* the mid-summer All Souls weekend when the ancestors are believed to return home from the land of darkness. And after All Souls the summer is generally deemed to have "finished," in that the hot and sticky weather can only get cooler. The high school baseball tournament thus heralds All Souls *o-bon* and *o-bon* heralds the end of the summer.

Every team brings with it its cheer-leaders and supporters. These are marshalled in the enormous Alps Stand, filling the 1st or 3rd base side of the home plate, depending on which of the two dug-outs their team is occupying. Supporters bring with them their own brass bands (which one after the other proceed to play exactly the same music, every game all day, every day all the tournament). They have uniform-clad boys with arm bands and head bands inscribed with the almost magical words *"hisshō"* ("certain victory"). In their white-gloved hands they hold open fans which they swish dramatically through the lifeless, heavy air in order to get their supporters shouting for their team. Down the aisles between seats, girls in bright yellow or pink frilly short dresses wave pom-poms in unison, and the supporters themselves may well be wearing headbands inscribed *"hisshō"* and shouting the repetitive chant of *"Wasshoi! Wasshoi!"* as they rhythmically beat out their band's tune with wooden spoons for serving rice. The whole scene is reminiscent of American college football with its climax at the Rose Bowl, and the tournament has been compared in significance with the Stanley Cup play-offs in ice hockey and the World Cup finals in soccer (Whiting 1977:2). *N.H.K.*, the Japanese National Broadcasting Company, televises every game in the tournament, from nine in the morning to six in the evening, and as the days go by, it sometimes seems as though there is hardly a radio or television set in the country which is not tuned in to the live coverage. Japanese themselves admit that *kōkō yakyū*, as high school baseball is called, is one of Japan's last remaining festivals. In that television has made this "festival" available to the whole nation, one could argue, I think, that high school baseball is one of the very first truly *national* festivals, participated in by a vast majority of the Japanese people, from taxi drivers in Tokyo to fishermen in Hokkaido and potters in Kyushu.

Now, if the annual high school baseball tournament is, as I have here suggested, a modern Japanese ritual, we need to consider the way in which radio and television commentators present the rites. For it is they who act as "high priests" for the nation, they who decide what to emphasize or ignore as they intone the "prayers" surrounding each game. The language that they use is the language through which the nation unites. They may decide to characterise two opposing teams as "guile" versus "strength" *(waza tai chikara),* and use this as a theme around which to build their commentaries. Alternatively, they may decide to call one team by a nickname such as the *"sawayaka* eleven" and so stress the "fresh" attitude to the game taken by an out-of-town team which can only muster eleven players in all. Each team, then, tends to be given some kind of characteristic, some point by which it may be recognised in future matches if it survives the present contest. The easiest way for commentators to do this is to concentrate on the pitcher, or "ace" as he tends to be termed. It is the pitcher's performance which is generally discussed 90 per cent of the time any team is in the field, and the whole of each game revolves around the pitcher's ability to master opposing batters. The cameramen follow the announcers' cue and zoom in on the pitcher's face. We see every twitch of his mouth, every bead of perspiration that breaks out on his neck and brow. We are forced into sharing his agony when things go wrong, into shedding tears of joy with him when he finally wins a game. The pitcher is the "hero" when his team wins; he is the sacrificial victim if his team loses. He is interviewed at the end of every game by a bevy of reporters who ask his reactions to certain stages in the progress of the contest.[6] His answers are short, his demeanour humble for a "hero," for he has to conform to social expectations. Just as Nelson expected every man to do his duty at Trafalgar, so do the Japanese as a whole expect every pitcher and every high school baseball player to do his duty during the tournament. Above everything else, regardless of whether one wins or loses, the rite must be performed in the correct manner.

Ultimately, what is deemed to be responsible for a "correct manner" is *seishin,* or "spirit." It is a player's "spiritual" attitude and strength which makes or breaks him when it "comes to the crunch" *(ōzume o mukaeru).* It is here that the commentators really come into their own, for they can draw upon a large vocabulary of keywords to describe the spiritual battle which every pitcher is expected to fight and win if the team as a whole is to survive until the next round. They will use a word such as *"shōbu,"* that inimitable oxymoron of "win" and "lose" meaning "competition" or "contest." The pitcher throws a *"shōbu"* ball which, if all goes well, will find an "austere" *(kibishii)* corner of the strike zone. But if a runner reaches 1st or 2nd base, the mood switches to one of anxiety. The pitcher is facing a "pinch," a tight spot that can develop into a Sisyphean-like "mountain" *(ōki na yama)* if things get worse. Then he is expected to "endure" *(gaman)* the situation, to "compete to the bitter end" *(ganbaru)* and be "staunch" *(shikkari shite moraitai).* And if the pitcher somehow succeeds in overcoming the odds against him, in getting a double play for example, he is then praised for "sticking to it" *(nebari)* and for showing his "fortitude" *(shimbōzuyoi).* As things get better, the commentators will extol the pitcher's "conscientious" *(teinei)* hurling, the way he "sticks his chest out" *(mune o haru),* and throws with "resolve" *(omoikitte).* He "gives everything" *(isshōkenmei ni)* to the game and wins thereby the final accolade.

This is the way in which almost every game is portrayed in high school baseball. (It is also, of course, the way in which many English public schools like to teach their aspiring gentlemen pupils the art of such team sports as rugger, hockey and rowing.) The teams which reach the final of the tournament are those which have shown real spirit, which have shown "no wish to escape" *(nigeru kimochi nai)* mental hardship. Finally, it is all over. In the Lévi-Straussian way (1966:32), from two teams that started as equals, one has emerged the winner. And yet the "disjunction" of the game is at the very same time "conjoined" by the ritual of the tournament as a whole and by *seishin* in particular. The pitcher of the winning team is embraced; the players run to the home plate to line up and doff their caps to the opposing team and umpires. The winners then line up for the last time to hear their school song played over the tannoy system and to watch their school flag being run up the masthead above the scoreboard. Cameras zoom in once more on the tear-stained faces of the victors, and on the crouched bodies of the losers who kneel dejected in the dust and scoop up handfuls of sacred Kōshien stadium earth to put in their kitbags and take as souvenirs back home. The commentators praise the losers, and then the song of victory is played.[7] We come to the Closing Ceremony, with its speeches pointing out that the winners "have given their all to the last moment" *(saigo made zenryoku o tsukushite)* and "adorned history" *(rekishi o kazaru)* with the "marvellous quality" *(rippa na naiyō)* of their game. Now there is only "next year" to look forward to, with this year's competition "full of memories" and "impressions" that will remain imprinted on our minds. Gold medals with crimson ribbons are placed around the necks of the winners; silver medals with purple ribbons around those of the runners-up. Then both teams march to the scoreboard to participate in the final flag lowering ceremony. The "tournament song" is played, and then the national anthem as the *hinomaru* Japanese national flag is lowered. The ritual is finally over. Goodbye heroes! You have played your part and given back the Japanese people their "spirit" for another year.

Seishin and the Group Model

In his *City Life in Japan,* Dore (1958:67) comments that: "the old Japanese belief that *seishin*—spirit, will-power—could conquer matter, that the human body would endure loss of sleep, starvation and physical pain to an almost unlimited degree provided the will was strong enough, has demanded some modification ever since the central wartime inference from this premise—that Japanese spirit would be superior to American guns and bombs—has been falsified." While he suggested that the ideology of *seishin* was not nearly as important as it used to be, Frager and Rohlen, writing almost twenty years later, have argued to the contrary, and show how *seishin* acts as a kind of interpretative lens through which the Japanese like to view their own culture and society. After showing how broadly the concept is used throughout Japanese society—by companies, government agencies, schools of art and religious bodies—Frager and Rohlen stress its ideological importance to the notion that Japanese society is "unique" and "group oriented." One passage is, I think, worth quoting to see the resemblance between the concept of *seishin* and the group model criticised by Befu.

> The seishin outlook does not see the world as inherently divided into class or other interest groups; it chooses to view individuals less in terms of age, wealth, and the like, and more in terms of "spiritual" strength or weakness; it urges a sense of gratitude to others and to society rather than criticism or cynical detachment; it de-emphasizes the possibilities for doctrinal discussion or dispute in favour of psychological change and awakened personal experience; it considers order, individual sacrifice, dedication, hierarchy, thorough organization, a disregard for material disadvantages, and group activity to be expressions of proper attitudes and spirit; and it views traditional teachings and practices as consistent with modern science and industrial society, in effect saying that there is much more that is of timeless value in the tradition. (Frager and Rohlen 1976:270)

Here we find a number of concepts that I have already mentioned in my description of the high school baseball tournament: "strength," "fortitude" and "perseverance" (*nebari, shimbō, gaman, nintai, kurō, ganbaru*, etc.); "single-mindedness" (*omoikitte, seijitsu, makoto*) and "group spirit" (*dantai ishiki, minna to issho*). At the same time, the concept of *seishin* also includes ideas of "self discipline" (*enryo*), "loyalty" and "devotion" (*giri, on, chū, kō*), which have been used by scholars such as Benedict (1946) and Doi (1981) to explain the workings of Japanese society. Indeed, I remember very well one evening towards the end of my four-year stay in Kyushu when I was called away to attend a meeting of parents at the local primary school. There was a "discussion" during which the problems of modern youth were talked about (in the kind of rambling, monologue-type speeches that the Japanese adopt to discuss things): why were the young taking to violence? Why didn't they do as they were told any more? Why was the family not as strong a social unit as it used to be? The answers that were provided by the school headmaster were all to do with *seishin*, and included mention of Mencius, Confucius, as well as of "discipline" (*kiritsu*), "order" (*chitsujo*), "meekness" (*sunao*), "responsibility" (*sekinin*), "goodwill" (*kōi*), and so on and so forth. The situation illustrated precisely the paradox pointed out by Frager and Rohlen: that the concept of *seishin* is likely to thrive in a Japanese society undergoing change. As Austin (1976:8) puts it in his introduction to their article: "the more rapid the change, the more traumatic its effects and the more in demand the qualities of endurance, strength and perseverance that provide a stable set of values to grasp as an empirical aid in coping with a society that fosters insecurity." *Seishin* is being called upon to combat what are seen to be the evils of Western capitalism and individualism. Somehow people—especially young people—have to be guided into identifying with a "Japaneseness" which will conquer these evils.[8]

Aesthetics and Advertising

If this supposition is correct, we should expect to find the concept of *seishin* being used not only in baseball (or other sports), but right across society. I have already shown how in fact anthropologists dealing with Japan have tended to rely on aspects of *seishin* in their interpretations of the structure of Japanese society. Now I consider keywords used in the criticism of art pottery and in newspaper, magazine and television advertising to see whether we cannot in fact isolate certain other concepts which are part and parcel of the Japanese "spirit." It is here that I will turn my attention to Japan's "internal cultural debate."

Japanese art pottery is a fairly recent phenomenon which first came to public attention during the Taishō period (1912–1926). Although pottery came to be included in the Imperial Art Exhibition *(teiten)* in 1927, it was not until the 1950's, with the establishment by the government of a system of Important Intangible Cultural Properties, that potters were able to get their work accepted as "art" by Japanese society in general (Moeran 1982–1983).

With the birth of pottery as an art form, critics have come to play an important role in publicising the way in which pottery ought to be made and appreciated. In describing modern art pottery, critics tend to use words such as "staunch" *(shikkari shita)* or "stable" *(antei shita)* to describe form. These are words frequently used of baseball pitchers, volleyball teams, professional golfers and so on. The potter is admired for his "brave" *(yūki)* and "conscientious" *(teinei)* work in just the same way as sportsmen are admired. If a potter is to be criticised, then he will be criticised in much the same manner as is the high school baseball pitcher. Words like "soft" *(amai)*, "weak" *(yowai)* and "dull" *(nibui)* will be used by both critic and commentator alike, who are convinced that both artist and sportsman must "suffer" *(kurō/kurushimu)* to achieve success. The life of the artist is as "austere" *(kibishii)* as that of the sportsman, and such austerity should be readily perceptible in his work.

All these words would appear to fit the *seishin* model outlined earlier. Yet another factor which is seen to make a pitcher's hurling or potter's throwing at the wheel good is the concept of "life." A ball "without life" *(ikite'nai)* will be hit into the stands; a pot "without life" will never become accepted as "art." So commentators and critics alike look for the ball or pot that is alive *(tama/katachi ga ikiteiru)*. Although it is clearly difficult, if not impossible, to decide by objective criteria what constitutes "life" in either of these contexts, it would appear that such a characteristic can come only from a sportsman's or potter's "heart" *(kokoro)*.

The concept of "heart," like all important keywords, is not just polysemic. Speakers also vary widely in their views on the appropriateness of its use in a given context. Some might prefer to translate the term by the word "mind" rather than "heart," but for reasons which will, I think, become clear I shall retain the word "heart." At times, *kokoro* is used as part of the "disciplined" spirit discussed at such length here. In the closing speech of the high school baseball tournament, for example, one of the officials praised the players' "assiduous hearts" *(kokoro no tannen)*. At other times, however, *kokoro* would appear to be opposed to *seishin*. In the appreciation of pottery, for example, I have heard the concept of "heart" being used in direct antithesis to "skill" *(gijutsu bakkashi, kokoro nashi,* "all skill and no heart"), and since a potter's mastery of technical skill is generally thought to depend on his *seishin*, "heart" and "spirit" here find themselves in opposition. Yet, at the same time, "skill" is a word used with some pride by manufacturers of consumer goods (cf. "the skill of Citizen" *[gijutsu no Citizen]*; "the advanced skills of Nissan, loved by all the world" *[sekai ni aisareru, senshin gijutsu no Nissan]*). This suggest that, in other circumstances, *kokoro* could stand for "Japaneseness" vis-à-vis Western technology. Thus it seems to me that *kokoro* in Japanese currently occupies a somewhat ambivalent position in the country's internal cultural debate, and that it is being used to play a double role, half in, half out of, *seishin*. This can be seen in the way critics expect potters to "put their heart" into their work *(kokoro no komotta shigoto)*, while at the same time demanding that their heart be filled with "pleasure" *(kokoro no tanoshisa)* and "play" *(kokoro no asobi)*. But notions of "pleasure" and "play" are normally alien to the concept of spirit *(seishin)*.

The point to note here is that art pottery is not simply a product made by man; it is a consumer item, transformed by the qualities perceived to exist in it by people who appreciate pottery. As in much English or European art criticism, the qualities of the artist are seen by the Japanese to pervade the pottery that he or she produces. In this way the art object serves to link consumer to producer, and it is the heart, or *kokoro*, which does this. Whatever else it may be unable to do, a pot must "strike the heart" *(kokoro ni uttaeru)* of the person who sees it.

It is not surprising to find, therefore, that the much discussed aesthetic concepts of *sabi*, translated by Kenkyusha's dictionary as "elegant simplicity," and *wabi*, or "quiet taste," are seen by one critic to mean "the involvement of one person with another" *(hito to hito to no kakariai)*.

This attitude is frequently found in advertising, where "contact between hearts" *(kokoro no fureai)* is a popular catchphrase in Japanese
copy writing. Indeed, the word *kokoro* was the most commonly used
word in advertising in Japan during the 1970's.[9] Other words common
to both aesthetic criticism and to advertising are "generous" *(ōraka)*,
"tranquil" *(odayaka)*, "fresh" *(azayaka)*, "invigorating" *(sawayaka)*,
"abundant" *(yutaka)*, "intimate" *(shitashii)*, and so on. All these words
connote properties attributable to the "heart" and are spontaneous
aspects of an individual's purposeful action, rather than of what I
regard as the socially imposed discipline of *seishin*. Words used as
expressions of the "heart" are not nearly as socially constraining as
those like *gaman, shimbō, nebari* and so on which form the Japanese
"spirit." They include, moreover, a number of English loanwords such
as "sharp," "clear," "vitality," "rhythm," "dynamic," "originality,"
"simple"—all of these frequently taking the place of Japanese words of
fairly equivalent meaning.[10] When Japanese talk about the "heart,"
they talk also of "human life" *(jinsei)*. Pottery should be imbued with
"the charm of human life" *(jinsei no uruoi)*; Heineken beer with "the
taste of human life" *(jinsei, ajiwatte ikitai)*. And closely connected with
"human life" is the newly fashionable word "individual" or "idiosyncratic" *(kosei)*. Art pottery has to be "individually creative" *(koseiteki na
sakuhin)* to be beautiful; Gauloises cigarettes are advertised as "individual to the very end" *(doko made mo koseiteki)*; a Daihatsu car as "individual is beautiful" *(koseiteki'tte utsukushii)*; and Fuji xerox copiers as "fresh
. . . precise . . . and individual" *(azayaka de are . . . seikaku de are . . .
koseiteki de are . . .)*. *Kosei* is rapidly joining *kokoro* as the "in word" of the
1980's.

This brings me to the related problems of group and individual,
Japan and the West. In a survey which I conducted recently, visitors to
art museums in Japan were asked to distinguish between the concepts of
"traditional beauty" *(dentōbi)* and "modern beauty" *(gendaibi)* in Japanese art pottery. One word that was typically used to describe "modern" beauty was "individuality" *(kosei)*; another that I found to be typical of "traditional" beauty was "no mind" or "no heart" *(mushin)*.
These two words were almost invariably used mutually exclusively. In
other words, people felt that it was only by being without mind, by
being "detached" if you like, that "traditional" beauty could be born
(in the days before Westernisation), but that nowadays a potter had to
put some of his "individuality" into his work in order to create "modern" beauty (and the passive/active distinction of "being born" and
"creating" was also made). Here we have an opposition not simply
between "individuality" and "no mind," but also between "heart"
(kokoro) and "no mind" *(mushin,* which is written with the character for

"heart" with a negative prefix). *Mushin* is very much part of the *seishin* ideal in which the self is subordinated in the interests of harmony; *kokoro* is also part of the *seishin* ideal, and yet *kokoro* cannot logically exist side by side with *mushin,* for it expresses the presence of heart or mind.

Clearly, *kokoro* is a pivotal keyword in Japan's internal cultural debate because it allows non-Japanese ideas to be included in people's perceptions of society. I have already mentioned how English loanwords (which include concepts such as "originality" generally alien to Japanese aesthetics) are brought in under the umbrella of *kokoro.* Here we see *kokoro* moving right out of the *seishin* model to incorporate essentially Western concepts. Similarly, we find advertising messages such as "Bring about the revolution of the heart!" *(kokoro no kakumei o okosu),* and "You have heart, you have abundance" *(kokoro ga aru, yutakasa ga aru),* where "abundance" ultimately refers to the affluence that accompanies capitalism.

And yet *kokoro* does not necessarily have to support Western ideals that go against the concept of *seishin.* A large number of advertisements tend to emphasise the personal relations that Japanese value so greatly. "Dial a phone number and dial a heart" *(denwa o kakeru . . . kokoro o kakeru),* "Your heart is delivered, your heart smells so fragrant" *(kokoro ga todokimasu, kokoro ga kaorimasu),* and other such catchphrases stress the importance of relationships between people in Japanese society. Thus, however individualistic you are invited to be, you are often invited to be individualistic for *somebody.* Hence a catchphrase such as "Your heart, your beauty" *(anata no kokoro, anata no utsukushisa)* is an invitation for you to become beautiful both for yourself and on behalf of others. In the background, the concept of *seishin* looms again, for—as in art—you are being advised that ultimately beauty derives from an inner spiritual discipline.

Here then, I see a second role for *kokoro.* As I said earlier, *seishin* tends to dictate the way in which people *ought* to behave in Japanese society; it prescribes formal relations of *giri,* duty, and *on,* indebtedness. *Kokoro,* even within the *seishin* model, allows for variations and stresses the alternative to *giri,* the concept of *ninjō,* or "spontaneity." We have seen that *giri* is socially contracted interdependence and *ninjō* a spontaneous feeling. Emphasis on the former, I suggest, gives rise to the group model explanation of Japanese society; emphasis on the latter to that of social exchange. However, as Befu admits, neither can exist without the other. The ever-present danger is that *ninjō* can become ego-centred action. Thus, by using the word *kokoro,* the Japanese aim at solving, first, the inherent problem of the relationship between *giri* and *ninjō;* and secondly, the external problem of group vis-à-vis individual, of Japan against the West.

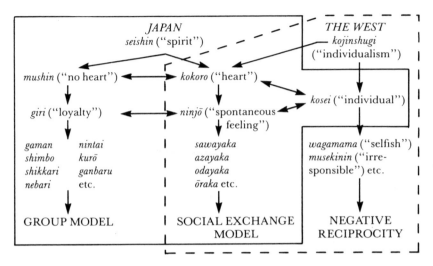

Fig. 1. Interpretations of Japanese social organisation through keywords

And yet, because of the flexibility of *kokoro,* which has now come to be used as a keyword in Western-style capitalist consumerism, *kokoro* is also found in a dialogue with *kosei,* or the individual. This dialogue would seem directly to contradict the "selfless detachment" of *mushin* and to tread a semantic tightrope strung between the two points of spontaneity and social exchange, on the one side, and outright individualism and "negative reciprocity," on the other (see fig. 1).

But I say "would seem to contradict" with reason. Ultimately, I am not convinced that *kosei* actually is equivalent to what we know as "individualism" in the West. The Japanese are extremely suspicious of such "individualism," and the interesting point is that the word for "individualism" *(kojinshugi),* is in fact viewed entirely *negatively.*[11] In other words, the Japanese see only the worst aspects of Western-style individualism in *kojinshugi* ("negative reciprocity" in the diagram). The good side of our "individualism" is not to be found in the concept of *kojinshugi,* but in that of *kosei.* This means that the Japanese are in effect denying that there is any good at all in Western individualism and that *kosei* is in fact entirely original and hence "uniquely Japanese." In this way, the advantages of Western individualism are being neatly adopted and adapted into *seishin,* or "Japanese spirit." To adopt the parlance of Le Carré's spy circus, *kokoro* is thus a double agent, while *kosei* is the "mole" in the internal cultural debate, in which the West was defeated long ago without ever realising it.

So we are back to square one. That *kokoro* is the most popular word in

Japanese advertising copy represents at one level the triumph of irrational "feeling" over rational "mind"; it suggests that all debate on the
issues of capitalism, of which advertising is the mouthpiece, is stifled
(cf. Williamson 1978:13). At another level, *kokoro*'s use poses a more
fundamental question concerning the relation between the Japanese
and Western concept of "mind." Western culture and Western technology are seen by the Japanese as products of Cartesian rationalism. They
have revered Western culture and technology over the past century,
only to discover that both leave much to be desired. There is something
"missing"; the Western mind is too limited in its horizons and the Japanese mind feels that it has grasped all that can be offered by the West
and has room to spare. This is where *kokoro* comes in. It is essentially a
Japanese concept which, it is claimed, understands beyond mere "intel-
lectualism." It suggests that such issues as individualism—generally
regarded as the inevitable companion of capitalism—are irrelevant to
Japan. *Kokoro* is thus used as though it were the melting point of all Japanese in one harmonious unity of *seishin*. It also intimates that an understanding of *kokoro* might also lead towards a united mankind.

Conclusion

I wish to make two points by way of conclusion: one concerns the concept of keywords; the other the relation between anthropology and a
society's internal cultural debate.

Parkin has suggested that the use of key verbal concepts is closely
connected with formalised speech, and this has been the gist of the argument put forward by Bloch (1975). The work of both these writers has
centred on the political usage of keywords and on how they may stifle
the exchange and expression of new ideas and so maintain the *status quo,*
with Parkin stressing how their ambivalence over time allows contradictory ideas to be expressed. Obviously, the use of keywords is not limited
to politics, but is to be found in other spheres of culture—as this discussion of sports, aesthetics and advertising has shown. What intrigues me
is the fact that in Japan the same set of words crops up time and time
again—almost like a ritual refrain—throughout society; it is not limited
to any one sphere of culture. There is, then, a "hard core" of keywords,
numbering perhaps not more than a hundred, which seems to deal adequately with all aspects of Japanese culture.

In England, on the other hand, this does not appear to be the case.
Keywords making up a vocabulary of evaluation certainly exist. But
neither are the keywords of politics necessarily those of advertising, nor
are the keywords of advertising usually those of aesthetics. The domains
in which keywords are found are more or less separate. There is a "hard
core" of keywords in English society (democratic, right, individual,

freedom, justice, classic, tradition, and so on), but in that their domain overlap is not so great as that of Japanese keywords, the hard core is smaller. At the same time, I would suggest that there is probably a greater number of less polysemic keywords used in English society, precisely because the domains of advertising, politics, sports, religion, aesthetics and so on do *not* overlap. This leads me to the following suggestion concerning the connexion between keywords of evaluation and social organisation which, although tautologous, may have heuristic value: the greater the hard core of keywords, the more pervasive their existence in cultural domains and hence the more condensed their meaning.[12] This situation is characteristic of a close-knit social organisation such as is found in Japan. On the other hand, the smaller the hard core of keywords, the less their domain pervasiveness and semantic condensation. This situation is characteristic of a fairly loose-structured type of society, of which England and the United States are examples.[13]

And so to my second conclusion. It can be seen, I think, that the argument about the role of the individual vis-à-vis the group among anthropologists dealing with Japan merely reflects the argument taking place in Japan's internal cultural debate. Not only this, but anthropologists dealing with Japan have long been accustomed to forming their own "unique," closed-in social cliques. Hence we become not anthropologists, but Japanologists whose interests rarely coincide with what is deemed to be mainstream theory in anthropology. While there may be several explanations for this,[14] and while we should not ignore the fact that Sinologists and Indianists may well feel out on a limb and yet still manage to contribute to anthropological theory, I suspect that every society to some extent dictates anthropology's approaches to it; it only allows us to study what it, the society, wants us to study, and so moulds us in its image. Hence I would suggest that anthropology itself ends up part and parcel of the internal cultural debate, both of the society being studied and of the society from which the anthropologist herself or himself comes. This is why perhaps anthropological theory will never be able to consist of a set of absolute, objective, scientific facts. Because it is closely bound by a continuing dialogue within and between cultures, theory can only consist of socially relative, subjective, and—in that such theory can be said to be pleasing to one's sense of elaborated form—aesthetic intuitions. In short, anthropology is the "mole" in the social science circus and we, its artists, smile at people's delusion.

Notes

This article is based on nine years of residence in Japan between 1967 and 1982.

1. I have briefly discussed some aspects of the language of tourism in Moeran 1983.

2. More recent discussions of the way in which group harmony has been upset in rural communities are to be found in studies of Kurusu (Smith 1978) and Sarayama (Moeran 1984).

3. Nakane, while not denying the importance of networks (Nakane 1978), does not appear to regard them as performing a structural role in the organisation of Japanese society.

4. I remember an afternoon in the pottery community of Sarayama when two men came into a potter's workshop and tried to persuade him—very politely, of course—to make and fire clay badgers. The potter reluctantly explained that Sarayama was renowned for its traditional folk craft ware (known as Onta pottery) and that badgers were not considered by potters, critics or general public to be included in this category of pottery. After considerable difficulty, he managed to get rid of the two men. It transpired that one of the men was a dealer; the other, with whom the potter had had some dealings in the past, was a member of the Committee for the Protection of Prefectural Cultural Properties, of which Onta pottery was officially designated one. Yet here was this committee member (associate professor at one of the prefecture's minor universities) trying to persuade a Sarayama potter to make something that went against the whole notion of "cultural property" and "tradition" which he was—in his official capacity—supposed to protect! It was *tsukiai* which had put the dealer in touch with the academic and which had led the academic to approach the potter.

5. Some may object to my use of the words "ritual" and "rite" to describe a baseball competition. Although I have toyed with alternatives such as "festival," "performance" and "cliche," I feel that, in the end, the notion of "ritual" is most appropriate to the event described here. The sense in which I use the word is, however, more akin to Barthes's *mythologique.*

6. Friends have pointed out that after baseball games in the United States, announcers and camera teams go into the team locker rooms and ask each of the players how the game looked from short stop, left field, and so on. It is interesting that a nation which prides itself on "individualism" should here focus on the "group" and team sports, while one that identifies with a "group" ideology should indulge in so many "individualistic" sports (*sumō, kendō, jūdō, karate,* and so on).

7. The ubiquitous victory-cum-congratulatory song played on such occasions in Japan is in fact the same tune as the Death March from Handel's oratorio *The Fall.* Charles Lamb later wrote a libretto for the tune, which includes the lines:

Toll for the brave, the brave who are no more—
All sunk beneath the waves far from their native shore.

This supports the adage that the Japanese do not copy; they adapt!

8. Hence, perhaps, the current fashion for *nihonjinron,* or "Japanese-ology."

9. *Kokoro* is cited 94 times in the *Kōkoku Bunan Jiten* advertising copy dictionary, published in 1980 by Sendan Kaigi, Tokyo.

10. I hope to discuss the problem of semantic displacement in Japanese by English loanwords in another article.

11. In fact, *kojinshugi* is probably rather close to the term *rikoshugi,* which means "egoism."

12. It is perhaps worth noting that cultural domains may be marked by social phenomena other than language. It is therefore possible for a number of domains to share the same evaluative keywords and yet remain distinct in the minds of actors through differences of, for example, dress, style and purpose.

13. I am aware that an analysis of differences in the degree to which words are polysemic or semantically condensed could instead make use of such distinctions as

denotation and connotation, reference and sense, etc., but I do not think that, for the purposes of this article, they are necessary.

14. In the light of Whorf's principle of "linguistic relativity," it is intriguing to note here that frequently it is the difficulties involved in acquiring and translating the Japanese language which are cited as reasons for Japan's anthropologists' isolation from the central theories of their subject. The view that the Japanese language is unique thus gives rise to the parallel view that the culture of Japan is also unique.

6

The Relation of Guilt toward Parents to Achievement and Arranged Marriage among the Japanese

GEORGE DE VOS

THIS paper, based on research materials gathered in Japan, suggests certain interpretations concerning the structuring of guilt in Japanese society.[1] Especially pertinent are Thematic Apperception Test (TAT) materials in which the subjects invent stories about a series of ambiguous pictures, which were taken from Niiike, an agricultural village of central Honshu. It is possible to obtain from the stories involving themes of achievement and marriage relationships indirect verification of hypotheses concerning the nature of internalization of the Japanese social sanctions that have been influenced by the traditional neo-Confucian ethics sustained by the dominant samurai class in the past.

A central problem to be considered is whether the Japanese emphasis on achievement drive and on properly arranged marriage may possibly have its motivational source in the inculcation of shame or guilt in childhood. It is my contention that this emphasis is not to be understood solely as a derivative of what is termed a "shame" orientation, but rather as stemming from a deep undercurrent of guilt developed in the basic interpersonal relationships with the mother within the Japanese family.

The characteristic beliefs, values, and obligatory practices that provide emotional security and are usually associated in the West with religious systems and other generalized ideologies—and only indirectly related to family life (Kardiner 1939:89–91)—are related much more directly to the family system of the tradition-oriented Japanese. The structuring of guilt in the Japanese is hidden from Western observation, since there is a lack of empathic understanding of what it means to be part of such a family system. Western observers tend to look for guilt, as it is symbolically expressed, in reference to a possible transgression of limits imposed by a generalized ideology or religious system circum-

From *Psychiatry* 23 (1960): 287–301. Copyright © 1960 by The William Alanson White Psychiatric Foundation, Inc. Reprinted by special permission.

scribing sexual and aggressive impulses. There is little sensitivity to the possibility that guilt is related to a failure to meet expectations in a moral system built around family duties and obligations.

Piers and Singer (1953; see also French n.d.), in distinguishing between shame and guilt cultures, emphasize that guilt inhibits and condemns transgression, whereas shame demands achievement of a positive goal. This contrast is related to Freud's two earlier distinctions in the functioning of the conscience. He used *shame* to delineate a reaction to the ego ideal involving a goal of positive achievement; on the other hand, he related *guilt* to superego formation and not to ego ideal. A great deal of Japanese cultural material, when appraised with these motivational distinctions in mind, would at first glance seem to indicate that Japanese society is an excellent example of a society well over on the shame side of the continuum.

Historically, as a result of several hundred years of tightly knit feudal organization, the Japanese have been pictured as having developed extreme susceptibility to group pressures toward conformity. This strong group conformity, in turn, is often viewed as being associated with a lack of personal qualities that would foster individualistic endeavor.[2] In spite of, or according to some observers because of, these conformity patterns, which are found imbedded in governmental organization as well as in personal habits, the Japanese—alone among all the Asian peoples coming in contact with Western civilization in the nineteenth century—were quickly able to translate an essentially feudal social structure into a modern industrial society and to achieve eminence as a world power in fewer than fifty years. This remarkable achievement can be viewed as a group manifestation of what is presumed to be a striving and achievement drive on the individual level.

Achievement drive in Americans has been discussed by Riesman (1950), among others, as shifting in recent years from Puritan, inner-directed motivation to other-directed concern with conformity and outer-group situations. Perceived in this framework, the Japanese traditionally have had an other-directed culture. Sensitivity to "face" and attention to protocol suggest that the susceptibility to social pressure, traced psychoanalytically, may possibly derive from underlying infantile fears of abandonment. Personality patterns integrated around such motivation, if culturally prevalent, could possibly lead to a society dominated by a fear of failure and a need for recognition and success.

Intimately related to a shift from Puritan patterns in America were certain changes in the patterns of child-rearing. Similarly, it has been observed in Japan that prevailing child-rearing practices emphasize social evaluation as a sanction, rather than stressing more internalized, self-contained ethical codes instilled and enforced early by parental punishment. In spite of some earlier contentions to the contrary based on a few retrospective interviews,[3] the child-rearing patterns most evident in Japan, in deed, if not in word, manifest early permissiveness in regard to weaning and bowel training and a relative lack of physical punishment.[4] There is, moreover, considerable emphasis on ridicule and lack of acceptance of imperfect or slipshod performance in any regard. There is most probably a strong relationship between early permissiveness and susceptibility to external social sanctions. In line with the distinctions made between shame and guilt, the Japanese could easily be classified as shame oriented, and their concern over success and failure could be explicable in these terms. Somehow this formula, however, does not hold up well when reapplied to an understanding of individual Japanese, either in Japan or in the United States.[5] Emphasis on shame sanctions in a society does not preclude severe guilt. While strong feelings of anxiety related to conformity are very much in evidence, both in traditional as well as present-day Japanese society, severe guilt becomes more apparent when the underlying motivation contributing to manifest behavior is more intensively analyzed. Shame is a more conscious phenomenon among the Japanese, hence more readily perceived as influencing behavior. But guilt in many instances seems to be a stronger basic determinant.

Although the ego ideal is involved in Japanese strivings toward success, day-by-day hard work and purposeful activities leading to long-range goals are directly related to guilt feelings toward parents. Transgression in the form of "laziness" or other nonproductive behavior is felt to "injure" the parents, and thus leads to feelings of guilt. There are psychological analogs between this Japanese sense of responsibility to parents for social conformity and achievement, and the traditional association sometimes found in the Protestant West between work activity and a personal relationship with a deity.[6]

Any attempt to answer questions concerning guilt in the Japanese raises many theoretical problems concerning the nature of internalization processes involved in human motivation. It is beyond the scope of this paper to discuss theoretically the complex interrelationships between feelings of shame and guilt in personality development. But the author believes that some anthropological writings, oversimplifying psychoanalytic theory, have placed too great an emphasis on a direct one-to-one relationship between observable child-rearing disciplines culturally prevalent and resultant inner psychological states. These inner states are a function not only of observable disciplinary behavior but also of more subtle, less reportable, atmospheric conditions in the home, as well as of other factors as yet only surmised.

Moreover, in accordance with psychoanalytic theory concerning the mechanisms of internalizing parental identification in resolving the Oedipal developmental stage, one would presume on an a priori basis that internalized guilt tends to occur almost universally, although its form and emphasis might differ considerably from one society to another. This paper, while guided by theory, is based primarily on empirical evidence and a posteriori reasoning in attempting to point out a specifically Japanese pattern of guilt. Developmental vicissitudes involved in the resolution of Oedipal relationships are not considered. Concisely stated, the position taken in this paper is as follows:

Guilt in many of the Japanese is not only operative in respect to what are termed superego functions, but is also concerned with what has been internalized by the individual as an ego ideal. Generally speaking, the processes involved in resolving early identifications as well as assuming later adult social roles are never possible without some internalized guilt. The more difficult it is for a child to live up to the behavior ideally expected of him, the more likely he is to develop ambivalence toward the source of the ideal. This ideal need not directly emphasize prohibited behavior, as is the case when punishment is the mode of training.

When shame and guilt have undergone a process of internalization in a person during the course of his development, both become operative regardless of the relative absence of either external threats of punishment or overt concern with the opinions of others concerning his behavior. Behavior is automatically self-evaluated without the presence of others. A simple dichotomy relating internalized shame only to ego ideal and internalized guilt to an automatically operative superego is one to be seriously questioned.

Whereas the formation of an internalized ego ideal in its earlier form is more or less related to the social expectations and values of parents, the motivations which move a developing young adult toward a realization of these expectations can involve considerable guilt. Japanese perceptions of social expectations concerning achievement behavior and marriage choice, as shown in the experimental materials described in this paper, give ample evidence of the presence of guilt; shame as a motive is much less in evidence.

Nullification of parental expectations is one way to "hurt" a parent. As defined in this paper, guilt in the Japanese is essentially related either to an impulse to hurt, which may be implied in a contemplated act, or to the realization of having injured a love object toward whom one feels some degree of unconscious hostility.

Guilt feelings related to various internalization processes differ, varying with what is prohibited or expected; nevertheless, some disavowal of an unconscious impulse to hurt seems to be generic to guilt. In some instances there is also emphasis on a fear of retribution stemming from this desire to injure. Such seems to be the case in many of the Japanese. If a parent has instilled in a child an understanding of his capacity to hurt by failing to carry out an obligation expected of him as a member of a family, any such failure can make him feel extremely guilty.

In the following materials taken from the rural hamlet of Niiike,[7] an attempt will be made to demonstrate how guilt is often related to possible rebellion against parental expectations. Two possible ways for the male to rebel are: (1) Dissipating one's energies in some sort of profligate behavior rather than working hard, or neglecting the diligence and hard work necessary for obtaining some achievement goal. (2) Rejecting arranged marriage by losing oneself in a marriage of passion, a so-called "love marriage."

In women, guilt seems related to becoming selfish or unsubmissive in the pursuit of duties involved in their adult role possibilities as wife and mother. This could mean, as in the case of men, refusal to accept the parents' marriage arrangement, or, after marriage, failure to devote oneself with wholehearted intensity, without reservation, to the husband and his purposes and to the rearing of the children. Failure to show a completely masochistic, self-sacrificing devotion to her new family is a negative reflection on the woman's parents. Deficiencies in her children or even in her husband are sometimes perceived as her fault, and she must intrapunitively rectify her own failings if such behavior occurs. TAT stories taken from the Niiike sample bring out in both direct and indirect fashion evidence to support these contentions.

The Relation of Guilt to Achievement

The Japanese mother has perfected the technique of inducing guilt in her children by quiet suffering. A type of American mother often encountered in clinical practice repeatedly tells her children how she suffers from their bad behavior but in her own behavior reveals her selfish motives; in contrast, the Japanese mother does not to the same extent verbalize her suffering for her children but lives it out before their eyes. She takes on the burden of responsibility for her children's behavior— and her husband's—and will often manifest self-reproach if they conduct themselves badly. Such an example cannot fail to impress. The child becomes aware that his mother's self-sacrifice demands some recompense. The system of *On* obligation felt toward the parents, aptly described by Ruth Benedict (1946), receives a strong affective push from the Japanese mother's devotion to her children's successful social development, which includes the standards of success set for the community. As discussed in a previous paper (Caudill and De Vos 1958), the educational and occupational achievements of Japanese-Americans also show this pattern, modified in accordance with American influences.

The negative side of accomplishment is the hurt inflicted on the parent if the child fails or if he becomes self-willed in marriage or loses himself in indulgence. Profligacy and neglect of a vocational role in Japan —and often in the West as well—is an attack on the parents, frequently unconsciously structured.

The recurrence of certain themes in the TAT data, such as the occurrence of parental death as a result of disobedience, suggests the prevalence of expiation as a motive for achievement (Wagatsuma 1957). Themes of illness and death seem to be used not only to show the degree of parental, especially maternal, self-sacrifice, but also seem to be used as self-punishment in stories of strivings toward an ideal or goal with a single-minded devotion so strong that its effects may bring about the ruin of one's health.

These attitudes toward occupational striving can also be seen in the numerous examples in recent Japanese history of men's self-sacrifice for national causes. The sometimes inexplicable—to Western eyes at least —logic of the self-immolation practised in wartime by the Japanese soldier can better be explained when seen as an act of sacrifice not resulting only from pressures of group morale and propaganda stressing the honor of such a death. The emotions that make such behavior seem logical are first experienced when the child observes the mother's attitude toward her own body as she often exhausts it in the service of the family.

To begin the examination of TAT data, the relation of guilt to parental suffering is apparent in certain TAT stories in which the death of the parent follows the bad conduct of a child, and the two events seem to bear an implicit relationship, as expressed in the following summaries (*W* indicates a woman, *M* a man):[8]

> *W, age 16, Card J13:* A mother is sick; her son steals because of poverty; mother dies.
>
> *M, age 41, Card J6GF:* A daughter marries for love against father's will; she takes care of her father, but father dies.
>
> *W, age 22, Card J6GF:* A daughter marries against her father's opposition, but her husband dies and she becomes unhappy.
>
> *M, age 23, Card J18:* A mother strangles to death the woman who tempted her innocent son; the mother becomes insane and dies. The son begs forgiveness.

In such stories one may assume that a respondent first puts into words an unconscious wish of some kind but then punishes himself by bringing the death of a beloved person quickly into the scene.

One could also interpret such behavior in terms of cultural traditions. Punishing or retaliating against someone by killing or injuring oneself has often actually been done in Japan in both political and social arenas. Such self-injury or death became an accepted pattern of behavior under the rigid feudal regime, where open protest was an impossibility for the suppressed and ruled. Numerous works on Japanese history contain accounts of the severe limitations on socially acceptable behavior and spontaneous self-expression.

Understanding the "emotional logic" of this behavior, however, requires psychological explanations as well as such valid sociological explanations. This "moral masochistic" tendency, to use Freud's terminology, is inculcated through the attitudes of parents, especially of the mother. Suffering whatever the child does, being hurt constantly, subtly assuming an attitude of "look what you have done to me," the Japanese mother often gains by such devices a strong control over her child, and by increasing overt suffering, can punish him for lack of obedience or seriousness of purpose. Three of the above stories suggest that a mother or father is "punishing" a child by dying. Parents' dying is not only the punishment of the child, but also more often is the final control over that child, breaking his resistance to obeying the parental plans.

This use of death as a final admonishment lends credence to a story concerning the Japanese Manchurian forces at the close of World War II. The young officers in Manchuria had determined to fight on indefinitely, even though the home islands had surrendered. A staff general was sent by plane as an envoy of the Emperor to order the troops to surrender. He could get nowhere with the officers, who were determined to fight on. He returned to his plane, which took off and circled the field, sending a radio message that this was the final directive to surrender. The plane then suddenly dived straight for the landing field, crashing and killing all on board. The troops then promptly surrendered.

It is not unknown for a mother to threaten her own death as a means of admonishing a child. In a therapy case with a delinquent boy,[9] the mother had threatened her son, with very serious intent, telling him that he must stop his stealing or she would take him with her to the ocean and commit double suicide. The mother reasoned that she was responsible and that such a suicide would pay for her failure as a mother, as well as relieve the world of a potentially worthless citizen. The threat worked. For the man, this kind of threat of possible suffering becomes related to the necessity to work hard in the adult occupational role; for the woman, it becomes related to working hard at being a submissive and enduring wife.

In other of the TAT stories the death of a parent is followed by reform, hard work, and success. Examples of these stories are:

W, age 16, Card J7M: A son, scolded by his father, walks out; the father dies; son works hard and becomes successful.

M, age 39, Card J5: A mother worries about her delinquent son, becomes sick and dies; the son reforms himself and becomes successful.

M, age 54, Card J13: A mother dies; the son changes his attitude and works hard.

W, age 17, Card J7M: A father dies; son walks out as his mother repeatedly tells him to be like the father; when he meets her again, she dies; he becomes hard-working.

W, age 38, Card J9: Elder brother is going to Tokyo, leaving his sick mother; his sister is opposed to his idea; his mother dies; he will become successful.

M, age 15, Card J6M: A son becomes more thoughtful of his mother after his father's death; he will be successful.

Emphasis on hard work and success after the death of parents clearly suggests some expiatory meaning related to the "moral masochistic" attitude of the mother in raising her child. The mother's moral responsibility is also suggested by other stories, such as a mother being scolded by a father when the child does something wrong, or a mother—not the father—being hurt when the child does not behave well. The feeling experienced by the child when he realizes, consciously or unconsciously, that he has hurt his mother is guilt—because guilt is generated when one hurts the object of one's love. The natural ambivalence arising from living under close parental control supplies sufficient unconscious intent to hurt to make the guilt mechanism operative.

The expiatory emphasis on hard work and achievement is also evident as a sequel in TAT stories directly expressing hurt of one's mother or father:

M, age 17, Card J11: A child dropped his father's precious vase. The father gets angry and scolds the mother for her having allowed the child to hold it. The child will become a fine man.

M, age 53, Card J18: A child quarreled outside; his mother is sorry that his father is dead. The child makes a great effort and gets good school records.

M, age 24, Card J11: A mother is worrying about her child who has gone out to play baseball and has not yet come back. When he comes home he overhears his mother complaining about his playing baseball all the time without doing his schoolwork. He then makes up his mind not to play baseball any more and to concentrate on his studies.

Although the realization of having hurt one's parents by bad conduct is not stated in the following story, it is another example of the use of working or studying hard—obviously as the means to achievement—to expiate possible guilt:

W, age 17, Card J3F: A girl worries about the loss of her virginity, consults
with someone and feels at ease. She studies hard in the future.

In the same context, if one fails to achieve, he has no way to atone.
He is lost. The only thing left is to hurt himself, to extinguish himself—
the one whose existence has been hurting his parents and who now can
do nothing for them. Suicide as an answer is shown in the following
stories:

M, age 57, Card 3BM [original Murray card]: A girl fails in examination;
kills herself.
W, age 32, Card J3F: Cannot write a research paper; commits suicide.

On the level of cultural conditioning, the traditional teaching of *On*
obligations enhances the feeling of guilt in the child, who is repeatedly
taught by parents, teachers, books, and so forth, that his parents have
experienced hardship and trouble and have made many sacrifices in
order to bring him up. For example, financial strain and, significantly,
ill health because of overwork may haunt the parents because of this
child. Of course the child did not ask for all this sacrifice, nor does he
consciously feel that he has intentionally hurt the parents, but there
seems no way out; all this suffering takes place somewhere beyond his
control, and he cannot avoid the burden it imposes. Certainly the child
cannot say to himself, "I did not ask my parents to get hurt. Hurt or
not, that is not my business," because he knows his parents love him
and are also the objects of his love. What can be done about it then?
The only way open to the child is to attain the goal of highest value,
which is required of him; by working hard, being virtuous, becoming
successful, attaining a good reputation and the praise of society, he
brings honor to himself, to his parents, and to his *Ie* (household lineage), of which he and his parents are, after all, parts. If he becomes
virtuous in this way, the parents can also receive credit. Self-satisfaction
and praise from society go to them for having fulfilled their duty to *Ie*
and society by raising their children well. The pattern repeats itself; he
sacrifices himself masochistically for his own children, and on.

My assumption is, therefore, that among many Japanese people such
a feeling of guilt very often underlies the strong achievement drive and
aspiration toward success. If this hypothesis is accepted, then it can easily be understood that the death of a parent—that is, the culmination of
the parent's being hurt following some bad conduct of a child—evokes
in the child a feeling of guilt which is strong enough to bring him back
from delinquent behavior and to drive him toward hard work and success. This is what is happening in the TAT stories of parental death and
the child's reform.

Guilt in Japanese Marriage Relationships

The feeling of *On* obligations generated in the family situation during childhood is also found to be a central focus in Japanese arranged marriages. This feeling of obligation is very pronounced in women. In a sense, a woman expresses her need for accomplishment and achievement by aiming toward the fulfillment of her roles as wife and mother within the new family she enters in marriage. The man does not face giving up his family ties in the same way. Interview data suggest that for a Japanese woman, failure to be a dutiful bride reflects on her parents' upbringing of her, and therefore any discord with her new family, even with an unreasonable mother-in-law, injures the reputation of her parents.

Marriages which go counter to family considerations and are based on individual passion or love are particularly prone to disrupt the family structure; they are likely to be of rebellious origin, and any subsequent stresses of adjustment to partner and respective families tend to remind the participants of the rebellious tone of the marriage and, therefore, to elicit guilt feelings.

The TAT stories give evidence of guilt in regard to both types of "unacceptable" marriage behavior—they show the wife's readiness for self-blame in marriage difficulties with her husband, and they express self-blame or blame of others, on the part of both men and women, for engaging in possible love marriages.

The Wife's Self-Blame in Difficulties with Her Husband

Of the stories involving discord between a man and his wife, several indicate a woman's feeling herself to be wrong in a situation which in America would be interpreted as resulting from the poor behavior of the husband. There are no cases of the reverse attitude—of a man's being blamed in an even slightly equivocal situation.

Four of five such stories are given by women. The man's story involves a need for reform by both partners, who are united in a love marriage and therefore apparently conform to the guilt pattern of such marriages, which I shall discuss shortly. In summary, the four women's stories are:

W, age 26, Card J3F: A wife quarreled with her husband when he returned from drinking. She leaves her house to cry, feels guilty for the quarrel.

W, age 54, Card J4: A husband and wife quarrel because the former criticized her cooking. The wife apologizes to him.

W, age 37, Card J4: A husband and wife quarrel, and after it the wife apologizes to her angry husband.

W, age 22, Card J5: A husband comes home very late at night; the wife thinks it is for lack of her affection and tries hard; he finally reforms.

Such attitudes also seem to be reflected in other test data, such as the "Problem Situations" material[10] collected in Niiike village. It is especially interesting to note that a husband's profligacy can be attributed by women to the wife's failure. It seems that the husband's willfulness—as is also true of a male child—is in some instances accepted as natural; somehow it is not his business to control himself if he feels annoyed with his wife. The wife nonetheless has to take responsibility for her husband's conduct. In one therapy case of a psychotic reaction in a young wife,[11] the mother-in-law blamed the bride directly for her husband's extramarital activities, stating, "If you were a good and satisfying wife, he would have no need to go elsewhere."

In connection with this point it may be worth mentioning that on the deepest level probably many Japanese wives do not "give" themselves completely to their husbands because the marriage has been forced on them as an arrangement between the parents in each family. Wives often may not be able to adjust their innermost feelings in the marital relationship so as to be able to love their husbands genuinely. They may sense their own emotional resistance and believe that it is an evil willfulness that keeps them from complete devotion as dictated by ethical ideals of womanhood. Sensing in the deepest level of their minds their lack of real affection, they become very sensitive to even the slightest indication of unfaithful behavior by the husbands. They feel that the men are reacting to the wives' own secret unfaithfulness in withholding. They cannot, therefore, blame their husbands but throw the blame back upon themselves. They may become very anxious or quickly reflect upon and attempt to remedy their own inadequacies—as when their husbands happen to be late in getting home. Another hypothetical interpretation is that, lacking freedom of expression of their own impulses, Japanese women overidentify with male misbehavior; hence, they assume guilt as if the misbehavior were their own.

This propensity for self-blame in women is not necessarily limited to the wife's role. In the following story a younger sister somehow feels to blame when an older brother misbehaves.

W, age 17, Card J9: An elder brother did something wrong and is examined by the policeman; he will be taken to the police station, but will return home and reform. The younger sister also thinks that she was wrong herself.

One might say, in generalization, that the ethical ideal of self-sacrifice and devotion to the family line—be it to father or elder brother before marriage, or to husband and children after marriage—carries with it internalized propensities to take blame upon oneself and to express a moral sensitivity in these family relationships which no religious or other cultural sanctions compel the men to share.

Love Marriages and Other Heterosexual Relationships

Of the Niiike village TAT stories involving marriage circumstances,[12] 13 directly mention an arranged marriage and 24 mention a love marriage. While 9 of the 13 arranged marriage stories show no tension or conflict between the people involved, only 2 of the 24 stories mentioning love marriage are tension-free. The rest all contain tension of some kind between parents and child or between the marriage partners. In other words, many of the men and women in Niiike who bring up the subject of love marriage still cannot see it as a positive accomplishment but, rather, see it as a source of disruption. As mentioned, love marriage carried out in open rebellion against the parents is punished in certain stories by the death of a beloved person.

M, age 41, Card J6F: They are father and daughter. The mother has died. The daughter is sitting on a chair in her room. The father is looking in, and she is turning around to face him. He is very thoughtful of his daughter, and as she is just about of age [for marriage], he wants to suggest that she marry a certain man he selected. But she has a lover and does not want to marry the man her father suggests. The father is trying to read her face, though he does know about the existence of the lover. He brought up the subject a few times before, but the daughter showed no interest in it. Today also—a smile is absent in her face. The father talks about the subject again, but he fails to persuade her. So finally he gives in and agrees with her marrying her lover. Being grateful to the father for the consent, the daughter acts very kindly to him after her marriage. The husband and wife get along very affectionately also. But her father dies suddenly of apoplexy. The father was not her real father. He did not have children, so he adopted her, and accepted her husband as his son-in-law. But he died. He died just at the time when a baby was born to the couple.

W, age 22, Card J6: The parents of this girl were brought up in families strongly marked with feudal atmosphere—the kind of family scarcely found in the present time. So they are very feudal and strict. The daughter cannot stand her parents. She had to meet her lover in secret. She was seeing her lover today as usual, without her parents knowing it. But by accident her father came to find it out. She was caught by her father on the spot. When she returned home her father rebuked her severely for it. But she could not give up her lover. In spite of her parents' strong objection, she married him. [*Examiner:* Future?] The couple wanted to establish a happy home when they married. But probably she will lose her husband. He will die—and she will have a miserable life.

There are a number of stories about unhappy events in the lives of a couple married for love. Many of these are found in response to Card 13 of the TAT, which shows a supine woman, breasts exposed, lying on a bed. A man in the foreground is facing away from the woman with one arm thrown over his eyes. A low table with a lamp is also in the room. Since responses to this card bring out in clear focus some basic differences between guilt over sexuality in Americans and in the Japanese, it will be well to consider them in some detail. Card J13 in the Japanese series is a modification of the original Murray TAT Card 13, with furniture and facial features altered.

Comparing Japanese and American responses to Card 13, it is obvious that while Americans rarely express remorse in connection with a marriage, the Japanese of Niiike express remorse in a heterosexual situation *only* in the context of marriage. In Americans, Card 13 is apt to evoke stories of guilt related to intercourse between partners not married to each other, with the figure of the woman sometimes identified as a prostitute, or sometimes as a young girl. When the figures are identified by Americans as married, the themes are usually around the subject of illness. In contrast, in the sample of 42 stories given in response to this card in Niiike village, not one story depicts a theme of guilt over sexuality between unmarried partners. Remorse is depicted only when it is related to regret for having entered into a love marriage.

Most of the Japanese stories given about this card fall into one of three categories: sex and/or violence (10 stories); marital discord (10 stories); and sickness or death (20 stories). Some striking differences in themes are related to the age and sex of the subjects.

Card 13: Sex and/or violence. Six stories involve themes of extramarital sexual liaison. In three, the woman is killed by the man. Five of the six stories are given by men, who were with one exception under 35 years of age, and one is given by a woman under 25. The young woman's story depicts a man killing a woman because she was too jealous of him. One young man sees a man killing an entertainer who rejects him. Another sees a man killing a woman who was pursuing him "too actively." Another young man gives the theme of a student and a prostitute. In this story the man is disturbed by the prostitute's nakedness, not by his feelings of guilt over his activity.

The man over 35 sees the picture as depicting disillusion in a man who unexpectedly calls on a woman with whom he is in love, only to find her asleep in a "vulgar" fashion. As is true in the stories of other men over 35, which pertain to marital discord, the man is highly censorious of the woman's position on the bed. The Japanese woman is traditionally supposed to be proper in posture even when asleep. To assume a relaxed appearance reflects a wanton or sluttish nature.

Japanese men are apt to split their relationships with women into two groups: those with the wife and those with entertainers. Other evidence, not discussed here, supports the conclusion that for many men genuine affection is directed only toward maternal figures. Conversely, little deep affection seems freely available toward women perceived in a sexual role. Moreover, the Japanese male must defend himself against any passivity in his sexual relationship, lest he fall into a dependent relationship and become tied. By maintaining a rude aloofness and by asserting male prerogatives, he contains himself from involvement.

Men can resort to a violent defense if threatened too severely. Younger women especially tend to see men as potentially violent. Three women under 35 see a man as killing a woman, in two cases his wife. In addition to the jealousy mentioned before, the motives are the wife's complaint about low salary (a man must be seen as particularly sensitive about his economic prowess if such a complaint results in murder), and regret for entering a love marriage. The latter story, which follows, is particularly pertinent to understanding how guilt is related not to sexuality per se but to becoming "involved."

> *W, age 22:* He got married for love with a woman in spite of opposition by his parents. While they were first married they lived happily. But recently he reflects on his marriage and the manner in which he pushed his way through his parents' opposition—and the present wife—he wishes his present wife would not exist—he attempts to push away the feeling of blame within his breast. One night on the way home he buys some insect poison and gives it to his wife to drink and she dies. What he has done weighs on his mind. He gives himself up to the police. He trustfully tells his story to them. He reflects on how wicked he has been in the past. He completes his prison term and faces the future with serious intent.

This story indirectly brings out a feeling of guilt for attempting to carry out a love marriage. Since such a marriage is psychologically forbidden fruit, the tasting of it brings upon the transgressor punishment, much like what happens for sexual transgressions out of wedlock in the fantasies of some more puritanical Westerners.

Card 13: Marital discord. The nature of the stories concerning marital discord is unique to the Japanese. Seven of the 21 Niiike men giving stories about Card 13 mention marital discord. Five of these men and all three women giving such stories are between 35 and 50 years of age. The men tend to see the marriage as ending badly, whereas the women are more optimistic about seeing the discord resolved. Both sexes usually place the blame for the discord on the women.

As in one of the stories mentioned previously, the men take a cue for their stories from the position of the woman in the bed. Rather than seeing the woman as ill, as do many of the women responding to this card, the men use the woman's posture as a basis for criticizing her. One of the chief complaints found in these stories is that such a woman obviously does not take "proper care" of her man. The following stories bring out the nature of some of the feelings leading to the castigation of the wife for "looseness" and lack of wifely concern for her husband. The man, too, is castigated in some of the stories, but not with the strength of feeling that is turned toward the woman.

M, age 39: This is also very difficult for me. What shall I say—I can't tell my impressions—what shall I say—it seems to me that they do not lead a happy life. The man often comes back home late at night, I suppose. But his wife does not wait for her husband. She has decided to act of her own accord, I suppose—he is back home late again, and his wife is already asleep. He thinks that it might be well to speak to her. I suppose there is always a gloomy feeling in this family. Well, if they lead a peaceful life, such a scene as this would never occur. It is customary that a wife takes care of her husband as she should when he comes home—and afterward she goes to bed. But, judging from this picture, I suppose this wife wouldn't care a bit about her husband. Such a family as this will be ruined, I think. They should change their attitude toward each other and should make happy home. [*Examiner:* What about the future?] They will be divorced. It will be their end. [*Examiner:* Do you have anything to add?] Well, I expect a woman to be as a woman should be. A man also should think more of his family.

M, age 41: This is also—this man is a drunkard, and his wife also a sluttish woman. And the man was drunk, and when he came back his wife was already asleep—and, well—finally, they will be ruined. They have no child. They will become separated from each other. This wife will become something like *nakai,* or a procuress. The husband will be held in prison—and the husband will kill himself on the railroad tracks. And—the wife will work as a *nakai,* and after contracting an infectious disease will die. An infectious disease which attacks her is dysentery. They worked together in a company and were married for love. That is their past. [*Examiner:* What does it mean that they will be ruined?] He became desperate. He became separated from his wife, so that he became desperate. If a man committed a bad thing, nobody cares for him. He could not hope for any help, so that he killed himself.

M, age 35: Well, this man and woman married for love. The woman was a café waitress and married the man for love. But they have not lived happily, so the man repents the marriage very much. Well, this man used to be a very good man, but he was seduced by the waitress and lost his self-control, and at last he had a sexual relationship with her. Afterwards, he becomes afraid that he has to think over their marriage. If their married life has any future at all, I hope they will maintain some better stability. But if this woman doesn't want to do so, he needs to think over their marriage, I suppose.

The latter story especially brings out strong feelings of guilt related to an attempt to carry out a love marriage. The story directly depicts the guilt as being related to losing self-control and becoming involved with an unsuitable woman, not with the sexual activity per se.

Implied, too, is the criticism that any woman who would make a love marriage is not really capable of being a very worthy wife. Therefore, in addition to depicting guilt for going counter to the parents in a love marriage, Card 13 indicates the potential avenue for projecting guilt on to the woman who is active enough to enter a love marriage. Such a woman's conduct obviously does not include the proper submissiveness to parental wishes and attention to the needs of her spouse.

This castigation of the woman is therefore directly related to an expectation that the wife, rather than being a sexual object, should be a figure fulfilling dependency needs. The man sees his wife in a maternal role and is probably quick to complain if his wife renders him less care and attention than were rendered him by his mother. Since the wife-mother image tends to be fused in men, there is little concept of companionship per se, or sharing of experience on a mutual basis. Also, the wife's acting too free sexually excites aspects of sexuality toward the mother that were repressed in childhood. The wife-mother image cannot be conceived of in gross sexual terms. It is speculated by some that the mistress is a necessity to some men, because their sexual potency toward their wives is muted by the fused wife-mother image. Certain free sexual attitudes on the part of the wife would tend to change the mother image of her to a prostitute image and cause castigation of her as morally bad.

One may say that this fusion of images has a great deal to do with the conflict often arising between the young bride and her mother-in-law. The mother-in-law's jealousy is partially due to her fear of being directly replaced in her son's affection by the bride, since they are essentially geared to similar roles rather than forming different types of object relationship with the man. The wife becomes more intimate with the husband after she becomes a mother, and essentially treats him as the favorite child.

These sorts of attitudes were present in Hirano's case, mentioned previously, wherein a woman's psychotic episode was precipitated by her mother-in-law's attacks, including the interpretation that the dalliance of her son with other women was further proof of the wife's incompetence. It was interesting to note that during the wife's stay in the hospital the husband was able to express considerable feeling of concern for her. There was no doubt that he loved her. In effect, however, this feeling was more for her as a maternal surrogate than as a sexual partner. His mother knew she had more to fear from the wife in this respect than from liaisons with other women, with whom the husband never became too involved. He, on the other hand, had no manifest guilt for his sexual activities—in effect, they were approved of by his mother in her battle with the wife.

Card 13: Sickness or death of wife or mother. In six instances (five women, three of them teen-agers), Card 13 is interpreted as a mother-son situation with the mother either sick or dead. The son is pictured specifically as working hard or studying; in one story the son steals because they are so poor. The younger girls especially seem to need to defend themselves from the sexual implications of the card by inventing a completely de-sexualized relationship. Unable to make the card into a marital situation, much less a more directly sexual one, some fall back on the favored theme of a sick mother and a distraught, but diligent, son. Emphasis on studying hard suggests the defensive use of work and study to shut out intrapersonal problems. Diligent work to care for the mother is again unconsciously used to avoid any feelings related to possible guilt. The way out is the one most easily suggested by the culture. Seeing Card 13 as a mother-son situation is rare in American records, even in aberrant cases.

Seeing Card 13 as illness or death of a wife is the most characteristic response of women; fourteen women, most of them over 35 years of age, gave such stories. Six men, including four of the five in the sample over 50, selected this theme. The middle-aged women were strongly involved in their stories about the death of a wife. Such stories were the longest of any given to the card. In sharp contrast to the derogatory stories directed toward the women by the men, the women use respectful concepts, such as *Otoko-naki* ("manly tears"), in referring to the men. On certain occasions it is expected that "manly tears" are shed. Although a man is usually expected not to cry freely when sober, the death of a wife is an occasion on which he is expected to cry. Much emphasis is placed on the imagined love felt toward the wife by a husband, on his loneliness, and on his feeling of loss because of the absence of wifely care. Concern with potential loneliness and possible loss of such care is certainly reflected in the fact that the older men in most instances select similar themes. The women in all but one case see the wife as dead or dying; the man is frequently seen as remarrying. Conversely, the men are more optimistic about recovery of a wife from illness and more pessimistic about remarriage if she does not recover.

One woman constructs a story of the noble self-sacrifice of a sick wife who commits suicide so as not to be a burden to her husband. This type of story, which recalls many sentimental novels written in Japan, is considered very moving by the Japanese, since it is supposed to reflect the degree of devotion of a wife for her husband and his goals and purposes. Tears are brought to the eyes of the older members of a *Kabuki* audience when such a story unfolds. To the Westerner, the stories seem to be excessively masochistic and overdrawn. The Japanese ethical ideal of the self-sacrificing role of woman is here emphatically displayed.

Conclusion

The foregoing materials from a farming village, which other evidence suggests is deeply imbued with traditional attitudes, are consistent with the interpretation that the potentiality for strong guilt feelings is prevalent in the Japanese. Such feelings become evident when there is failure in the performance of expected role behavior. Guilt, as such, is not as directly related in the Japanese to sexual expression as it is in the persons growing up within cultures influenced by Christian attitudes toward sexuality. As first pointed out by Benedict (1946), there is little pronounced guilt or otherwise negatively toned attitude directed toward physical expression of sexuality per se. Rather, there is concern with the possible loss of control suffered by becoming involved in a love relationship that interferes with the prescribed life goals of the individual.

From a sociological standpoint, Japanese culture can be considered as manifesting a particularistic or situational ethic as opposed to the more universalistic ethic built around moral absolutes found in Western Christian thought.[13] This evaluation can be well documented but does not mean that the Japanese evidence a relative absence of guilt in relation to moral transgressions. Whereas the applicability of the more universalistic Western ethic in many aspects may tend to transcend the family, the Japanese traditional ethic is actually an expression of rules of conduct for members of a family, and filial piety has in itself certain moral absolutes that are not completely situationally determined, even though they tend to be conceptualized in particularistic terms. This difference between family-oriented morality and a more universalistic moral system is, nevertheless, a source of difficulty in thinking about guilt in the Japanese.

Another reason for the failure to perceive guilt in the Japanese stems from the West's customary relation of guilt to sexuality. Missionaries in particular, in assessing the Japanese from the standpoint of Protestant moral standards, were often quoted as perplexed not only by what they considered a lack of moral feeling in regard to nonfamilial relationships but also—and this was even worse in their eyes—by a seeming absence of any strong sense of "sin" in their sexual relationships. It seems evident that the underlying emotional content of certain aspects of Christianity, in so far as it is based on specific types of repression and displacement of sexual and aggressive impulses, has never appealed to the Japanese in spite of their intellectual regard for the ethics of Christianity. Modern educated Japanese often recognize Christianity as advocating an advanced ethical system more in concert with modern universalized democratic ideas of man's brotherhood. As such, Christianity is favored by them over their more hierarchically oriented, traditional system with its rigidly defined, particularistic emphasis on prescribed social roles. To the educated Japanese, however, the concept of sin is of little interest in their attitudes toward Christianity. The lack of interest in sin is most probably related to the absence of childhood disciplines that would make the concept important to them.

Traditional Western disciplinary methods, guided by concern with the inherent evil in man, have been based on the idea that the child must be trained as early as possible to conquer evil tendencies within himself. Later, he learns to resist outside pressures and maintain himself as an individual subject to his own conscience and to the universalist laws of God. The traditional Western Protestant is more accustomed in certain circumstances to repress inappropriate feelings. "Right" thoughts are valued highly, and one generally tries to repress unworthy motives toward one's fellow men. Justice must be impartial, and one must not be swayed by the feelings of the moment or be too flexible in regard to equity.

In Japanese Buddhist thought one finds a dual concept of man as good and evil, but in Shinto thought, and in Japanese thinking about children generally,[14] the more prevailing notion is that man's impulses are innately good. The purpose of child training is merely the channeling of these impulses into appropriate role behavior.

The definitions of proper role behavior become increasingly exacting as the child grows and comes into increasing contact with others as a representative of his family. As such, he learns more and more to be diplomatic and to contain and suppress impulses and feelings that would be disruptive in social relations and put him at a disadvantage. He is not bringing a system of moral absolutes into his relations with others any more than the usual diplomat does in skillfully negotiating for the advantage of his country. The Japanese learns to be sensitive to "face" and protocol and to be equally sensitive to the feelings of others. He learns to keep his personal feelings to himself as a family representative. It would be just as fallacious to assume, therefore, that the Japanese is without much sense of guilt as it would be in the case of the private life of a career diplomat.

The fact that so much of conscious life is concerned with a system of social sanctions helps to disguise the underlying guilt system operative in the Japanese. This system, which severely represses unconscionable attitudes toward the parents and superiors, is well disguised not only from the Western observer but also from the Japanese themselves. The Westerner, under the tutelage of Christianity, has learned to "universalize" his aggressive and other impulses and to feel guilt in regard to them in more general terms. The modern Japanese is moving toward such an attitude but is affected by the traditional moral structure based on the family system, or if expanded, on the nation conceived of in familial terms.

Lastly, some difficulty in perceiving Japanese guilt theoretically, if not clinically, is due to the fact that psychoanalysis—the psychological system most often consulted for help in understanding the mechanisms involved in guilt—tends to be strongly influenced by Western ethical values. Psychoanalytic writers, in describing psychosexual development, tend to emphasize the superego on the one hand and concepts of personal individuation and autonomy on the other. A major goal of maturation is freedom in the ego from irrational social controls as well as excessive internalized superego demands. In understanding the Japanese, this emphasis is somewhat out of focus. Maturational ideals valued by the traditional Japanese society put far more emphasis on concepts of "belonging" and adult role identity.

In studying the Japanese, it is helpful, therefore, to try to understand the nature of internalization of an ego ideal defined in terms of social role behavior. Concern with social role has in the past been more congenial to the sociologist or sociologically oriented anthropologist,[15] who in examining human behavior is less specifically concerned with individuation and more concerned with the patterning of behavior within a network of social relations.

However, the sociological approach in itself is not sufficient to help understand the presence or absence of a strong achievement motive in the Japanese. It is necessary to use a psychoanalytic framework to examine the psychological processes whereby social roles are internalized and influence the formation of an internalized ego ideal. The ideas of Erikson (1956), in his exploration of the role of "self-identity" in the latter stages of the psychosexual maturation process, form a bridge between the psychoanalytic systems of thought and the sociological analyses which cogently describe the place of role as a vital determining factor of social behavior. The avenue of approach taken by Erikson is a very promising one in understanding the Japanese social tradition and its effect on individual development.

Notes

1. This paper will not discuss subcultural variations. Niiike village is representative of a farming community that has well internalized the traditional, dominant values held by the samurai during the Tokugawa period (about 1600–1868). Other local rural traditions emphasize other values. For example, material from a fishing community wherein the status position of women is higher than in the farming

community considered shows far different results in the projective tests. Women are perceived in TAT stories as more assertive, even aggressive, toward their husbands. Guilt is not expressed in stories of self-sacrificing mothers. Love marriages are accepted and not seen in the context of remorse, and so on. A comparison of the attitudes of the farming village with those of the fishing village is presented in detail in the following article: George De Vos and Hiroshi Wagatsuma, "Variations in Traditional Value Attitudes Related Toward Status and Role Behavior of Women in Two Japanese Villages," submitted for publication, *American Anthropologist.*

2. See, for example, Lafcadio Hearn's statement that Japanese authoritarianism is that of "the many over the one—not the one over the many" (1905:435ff.).

3. For example, Gorer (1943).

4. See, for example, the empirical reports by Lanham (1956) and Norbeck and Norbeck (1956). Norbeck and De Vos (1972) present a more comprehensive bibliography, including the works of native Japanese, on child-rearing practices in various areas in Japan.

5. The five clinical studies of Japanese-Americans in *Clinical Studies in Culture Conflict* (Seward 1958) consistently give evidence of depressive reactions and an inability to express hostile or resentful feelings toward the parents. Feelings of guilt are strongly related to an inability to express aggression outwardly, leading to intrapunitive reactions. Feelings of worthlessness also result from the repression of aggressive feelings. The Nisei woman described by Farberow and Schneidman in chap. 15, demonstrates the transference to the American cultural situation of certain basic intrapunitive attitudes common in Japan related to woman's ideal role behavior. The Kibei case described by Opler in chap. 13 well demonstrates a young man's perception of the manifest "suffering" of Japanese women. The case described by Babcock and Caudill in chap. 17 as well as other unpublished psychoanalytic material of Babcock's, amply demonstrates the presence of deep underlying guilt toward parents. Such guilt is still operative in Nisei in influencing occupational selection and marriage choice. Seward, in a general summary of the Japanese cases (p. 449), carefully points out the pervasive depression found as a cohesive theme in each of the cases. She avoids conceptualizing the problems in terms of guilt, perhaps out of deference to the stereotype that Japanese feel "ashamed" rather than "guilty." She states, "Running through all five Japanese-American cases is a pervasive depression, in three reaching the point of suicidal threat or actual attempt." Yet she ends with the statement, "Looking back over the cases of Japanese origin, we may note a certain cohesiveness binding them together. Distance from parent figures is conspicuous in all as well as inability openly to express resentment against them. In line with the externalization of authority and the shame-avoidance demands of Japanese tradition, hostility is consistently turned in on the self in the *face-saving devices* of depression and somatic illness." (Italics mine.)

6. Robert Bellah, in *Tokugawa Religion* (1957), perceives, and illustrates in detail, a definite relationship between prevalent pre-Meiji Tokugawa period ethical ideals and the rapid industrialization of Japan that occurred subsequent to the restoration of the Emperor. A cogent application of a sociological approach similar to that of Max Weber allows him to point out the obvious parallels in Tokugawa Japan to the precapitalist ethical orientation of Protestant Europe.

7. See the comprehensive, five-year study of this village by means of various social science disciplines by members of the Center for Japanese Studies of the University of Michigan (Beardsley, Hall, and Ward 1959).

8. The TAT cards used in the Japanese research were in most instances modifications of the Murray cards, with changed features, clothing, and background to con-

form to Japanese experience. The situations in the original Murray set were maintained. New cards were added to the modified set to elicit reactions to peculiarly Japanese situations as well. The numbers given for the stories used illustratively in this paper refer to modified cards resembling the Murray set with the exception of J9 and J11, which represent original Japanese family scenes.

9. Reported in unpublished material of a Japanese psychiatrist, Taeko Sumi.

10. This test included items specifically eliciting a response to a hypothetical disharmony between wife and mother-in-law. In such cases the results indicate that the wife often sees herself as to blame for failing in her duty as a wife. She "should" conduct herself so as to be above reproach.

11. Described by the Japanese psychiatrist Kei Hirano.

12. A total of 80 persons gave 807 stories: 33 persons gave one or more stories involving marriage circumstances.

13. See Parsons (1951:175) for a description of the particularistic achievement pattern. This category suits traditional Japanese culture very well.

14. It is significant that the Japanese usually use Shinto ceremonials in regard to marriage and fertility, and to celebrate various periods in childhood, whereas Buddhist ceremonials are used mainly in paying respect to the parents—that is, in funerals and in memorial services at specified times after death. It must be noted that the material in this paper does not include any reference to fear of punishment in an afterlife; although present in traditional Buddhism in the past, such feelings are not much in evidence in modern Japan. Relatively few modern Japanese believe in or are concerned with life beyond death (see De Vos and Wagatsuma 1959: esp. 13ff). It is my contention that fear of punishment either by the parents, society, or God is not truly internalized guilt. Insofar as the punishment is perceived as external in source, the feeling is often fear or anxiety, as distinct from guilt.

15. This approach is also evident in the theorist in religion. Also, the recent interest in existentialist psychiatry is one attempt to bring in relevant concepts of "belonging" to the study of the human experience.

Interaction, Communication, and Grouping

Editorial Note to Part Two

PART 2 presents patterns of interaction, communication, and grouping observed in various social situations. While moral values and sentiments, dealt with in part 1, may be held by the individual internally without necessarily being manifested in observable behavior, interaction, communication, and grouping involve what is acted out for social purposes. In that sense, this part captures more faithfully what the Japanese actually do, not just what they think they ought to do.

In chapter 7, Harumi Befu engages us with his sensitive description of the dinner-entertainment style. He analyzes the subtle communication between host and guest where what is said is not what is meant—a remarkable illustration of the patterned arbitrariness of culture. We are further conducted into the tatami-floored interior of the *ryōtei* (the so-called teahouse) where business negotiations may be taking place, and the sake party where participants follow the subtle etiquette for pouring and accepting sake and exchanging and circulating sake cups. All of these seem very esoteric to outsiders, and yet ring a bell with most Japanese; foreign visitors who have been invited to a Japanese party will recall their puzzlement and *faux pas*. Befu presents the Japanese protocol of hospitality as a culturally staged drama in which actors perform their parts flawlessly according to an unwritten but well-understood script. The successful production of such an entertainment drama presupposes a social sensitivity on the part of actors to one another, which in turn is likely to be fostered through intimate interaction and interdependence.

Takeo Doi, writing on *amae* in chapter 8, throws psychological light upon interpersonal relationships. Through his clinical experience, the author came to realize the overwhelming drive of *amae* (the propensity "to depend and presume upon another's benevolence") present in neurotic patients, often in the form of its frustration. *Amae* is linked with many other words so that it emerges as a keyword. Doi does not say *amae* is unique to Japanese; on the contrary, he sees a Western parallel in what Balint calls "primary love" or "passive object-love." What does

make a difference, Doi says, is that it is accessible to Japanese, thanks to
the word *amae* or its verb form *amaeru,* whereas for the Westerner, lacking such an expression, "primary love" becomes "accessible only after
a painstaking analysis." To put it another way, we might say that the
relationship between symbol (word *amae*) and its referent (*amae* inclination) is more direct for Japanese. Further, as Doi observes, *amae* is
socially sanctioned and therefore, if frustrated, continues to be sought
even by adult Japanese, whereas the Western primary love is deeply
repressed. In passing, it might be noted that Doi recognizes that Ainu
and Koreans have words similar to *amae,* which Lee (1982) fails to acknowledge.

Even though his basic data comes from therapist-patient interaction,
Doi does not hesitate to generalize *amae* and related phenomena to the
normative Japanese culture and personality, and goes on to propose a
counterbalancing relationship between *amae* and *on* (social indebtedness) so that an excess of one stifles the other. While prewar Japan had
on in excess, concealing *amae,* postwar Japan is experiencing moral
chaos, says Doi, under the predominance of *amae.*

Following Doi is chapter 9 by Sonya Salamon on husband-wife interaction, where *amae* reappears in a twisted form. Salamon attempts an
emic explanation for what strikes Western women as an offensive "male
chauvinism" on the part of Japanese men. The sample of Tokyo
women, highly educated and married to middle-level executives, were
found to be at that stressful stage of their marital careers where realign-
ments were forcing husband and wife apart and away from their earlier
conjugal intimacy, one toward an overtime involvement with work-
career and the other as a home-bound mother of small children. To cope
with this situation, as interpreted by the author, the husband displays
"problematical" behavior which upsets the wife and which boils down
to male tyranny, the Japanese equivalent of machismo. The wife, having no option, comes to accept this by redefining the relationship, and
by reinterpreting his tyrannical behavior as an expression of *amae* which
amounts to "love." Hence the interesting title of this chapter.

The next chapter by Takao Suzuki, a linguist, gives a sensitive analysis of Japanese speech with a particular focus on the speaker's usage of
terms for self-reference and for addressing others. He spells out how a
Japanese speaker resorts to a variety of such terms depending upon the
kind of person he happens to be addressing, in contrast to an English
speaker, for instance, who consistently adheres to "I" and "you"
regardless of addressee. The chapter thus throws light, from a linguistics perspective, upon the Japanese conception of the self-other relationship. Suzuki attributes this speech pattern to the cultural psychology of
self-definition through an empathetic assimilation of the object person.

While the exchange of speech is a major form of communication, a portion of which we have seen in the chapter by Suzuki, the exchange of goods or money as gifts is another significant communicative act. In discussing gift-exchange behavior, Harumi Befu begins with the folklorist interpretations of gift, and comes up with several significant manifestations of change from the rural/traditional to the urban/modern forms of gift-giving. In conjunction with the traditional forms, the Japanese sense of obligation called *giri,* tied to the principle of reciprocity, is examined; the new forms suggest a direction of change in Japanese lifestyle toward individuation. As an editorial note it might be added that, the changes notwithstanding, the Japanese continue to engage in gift-exchange intensively and that gifts exchanged today seem to be more extravagant than ever. No longer contented with giving money or a commodity, fashionable Japanese give coupons for concerts, theaters, traveling abroad, and so on.

Chie Nakane (chap. 12), unlike the previous authors who have focused on specific aspects of interaction and communication, proposes a broad generalization of Japanese human relations and groupings. Offering a bipolar typology of "attribute" and "frame" as criteria for group formation and group identity, she characterizes the Japanese case as frame oriented in contrast to the attribute-oriented Westerners and Hindus. Frame is rooted, Nakane argues, in the traditional structure of the *ie,* the household, which she defines as a corporate residential group apart from kinship. The *ie* as an archtype is replicated, the author claims, by all Japanese organizations, and notably by modern enterprises and companies.

The group orientation of the Japanese, as stressed by Nakane, is reinforced and vividly illustrated by Vincent Brandt. In this short essay Brandt shares with us his participatory observations of three groups of skiers—Japanese, Korean, and American—at a Korean mountain resort. On and off the slopes, the Japanese skiers noticeably stood out in group discipline, loyalty, and exclusiveness.

These findings seem to confirm the persistence of collectivistic orientations among the Japanese. In fact, it is not just a matter of persistence, but from the point of view of some opinion leaders, something to be recaptured and reenergized to meet contemporary needs, such as the quality control of manufactured products. Totoki Akira, president of the Japan Management Association, expressed it thus: "Not so long ago, however, such group-centered behavior, so typically Japanese, was beginning to be thought old fashioned and a thing that should be corrected and modernized. But today the pendulum is swinging back and we are thinking that the traditional practice has its better side—benefits that should be put to effective use" (Totoki n.d.).

7

An Ethnography of Dinner Entertainment in Japan

HARUMI BEFU

ENTERTAINMENT in Japan is a highly ritualized activity, full of set procedures and etiquette. Limiting the analysis to entertainment in *ryootei,* or the Japanese-style restaurant, essentials of these procedures and etiquette are outlined. Aside from the sheer behavioral side of the entertainment ritual, symbolic meaning given to such behavior is complex and often too subtle to be perceived by untrained eyes. The paper discusses how symbolism is used in entertainment interaction.

Superficial understanding of a culture is often said to be worse than no understanding at all. The reason is, of course, that a little bit of knowledge is a dangerous thing: it gives one a false conviction that he knows it all. Foreigners who have been living in Japan for a while and begin to manage their daily routines often lodge the allegation that Japanese say or do things that they do not mean, implying the insincerity of Japanese. True, a Japanese would offer a gift of a bottle of Johnnie Walker Black Label scotch, saying, "Please accept this worthless gift. . . ." Or, when you are invited to a Japanese home, the hostess is likely to say in an embarrassed voice, "Our house is in a cluttered mess, but please come in," but you will find the house immaculately clean. It is only the foreign novitiates to Japanese culture who are surprised by the contradiction. A Japanese guest would expect the house to be clean. If the house is in fact the cluttered mess the hostess says it is, the guest is entitled to surmise that he is not as honored a guest as he thought he was.

I recall the time I was invited to a Sunday lunch by a Japanese friend when I was collecting data on gift-giving in Kyoto. I was temporarily alone in Kyoto, my family having gone to visit a relative in western

From *Arctic Anthropology* 11-Suppl., 196–203. © 1974 The Regents of the University of Wisconsin System, reprinted by permission of the University of Wisconsin Press.

Japan. The friend, in the course of conversation about various and sundry things, found out I was alone and asked if I would come next Sunday. First, I had to judge whether my friend indeed meant to invite me or whether the invitation was a meaningless *pro forma*, uttered simply to fill time and to convey friendship and no more, much as Americans say, "Hi, how are you. . . . oh, I'm just fine," not as a way of conveying a message about one's state of affairs but merely to indicate one's readiness to enter into further interaction. Invitations are often extended in Japan without meaning to invite anyone when (and because) the context of the invitation makes it obvious that an invitation is not really intended and the invited person is expected to politely decline. Had I sensed that the invitation was of this variety, of course I should not have accepted it. Interpretation of the invitation was tricky in this instance, not only because of the dual possibilities of the invitation, but further complicated by local custom. On one hand, Kyoto people are known for extending "false invitations" more sincerely than other Japanese and are fond of ridiculing others in private for misinterpreting them and, on the other hand, this hostess was unusually insistent on inviting me, even for a native-born Kyoto woman. Did she mean it or didn't she? Since etiquette requires me to decline any invitation initially anyway, I took advantage of the time required in the repeated give-and-take of declining and inviting several times to weigh all evidence to see if she really meant it. I finally decided that she really meant to invite me and I accepted the invitation. To this day, however, I do not know, and I probably never will, if my interpretation was in fact correct.

Be that as it may, when I accepted the invitation, the hostess asked me what I would like to have for lunch. I was, of course, quite well aware of the Japanese etiquette of not making demands on others. So I told her that anything would do. But she insisted that I specify what I wanted. I kept insisting I had no preference, knowing full well I would soon have to tell her what I wanted. However, I knew that protocol required that I wait until the hostess had made several urgings, after which to state one's wishes would not seem too forward. Following what I judged to be an appropriate number of urgings, I said to the hostess that *ochazuke* would be just fine. *Ochazuke,* a bowl of rice with hot tea poured over it and served with one or two pickled dishes to increase the appetite, is one of the simplest meals in the whole Japanese culinary repertory. The hostess said fine, that she would serve me *ochazuke* as I requested. The following Sunday she did indeed serve me *ochazuke*. It turned out, however, to be the last, small appendage to a sumptuous luncheon served with elegant heirloom utensils starting with a bowl of fine soup and vinegared vegetables. *Sake* was served with fish of the season and a half dozen varieties of *tsukundani* (vegetable and sea food preserves—which are specialties of Kyoto) were brought out as hors d'oeuvres. At last, almost as an anticlimax, *tsukemono* (pickled food) and *kamaboko* (fish preserve). Was I surprised? Yes and no. Indeed, I asked for the simplest dish imaginable and got a feast instead. I should be surprised. On the other hand, knowing my relationship to the hosts, something more than a bowl of rice with tea poured over it was definitely in order, although the meal might have been a trifle more elaborate than I had expected. I would have been indeed surprised had the hostess simply served a bowl of rice with tea over it. It would not have been far from the mark in interpreting the event to mean either that the friend's luncheon invitation was actually *pro forma* and I shouldn't have accepted it, or that the invitation was meant but I wasn't highly thought of. Knowing my relationship with the hosts, I felt they meant to invite me and I was reasonably sure they respected me. Knowing this then, the feast I was offered was no surprise. But the rub is in the fact, or in the cultural rule, that the guest in this situation ought to act as if he was surprised. Like a good Japanese, I expressed much surprise with such a treat, while saying to myself, "this is about what I expected."

Now, did my hosts tell me a lie? Were they insincere? Or did they try to mislead me when they had agreed to treat me to *ochazuke?* If you assume that people always have to say what they mean literally, then the answer is yes. But an intriguing part of the cultural assumption operating in this context is that both hosts and guests are supposed to say what they do not mean, that they are supposed to know that they are supposed to say what they do not mean, and moreover that they each know what the others really meant to say but did not say without being told. Hosts and guests are thus in collusion, acting out their parts in the everyday drama of Japanese social life.

Japanese do not have monopoly over such contrived behavior. Variance between intention and declaration is something we see everyday among Americans, who take pride in their being straightforward, in saying what they mean, and chastise people who are roundabout and cannot come right out and say what they have on their minds. As Sunday dinner guests leave, an American host is likely to say, with a big happy smile, "Good-bye, now. Come back any time." But he would be most surprised if any of them returned the next morning unannounced. He can tell such a blatant lie because he knows his guests know that he does not mean it. To take another example, "if there is anything you need, just let me know" may be a way for your newly acquired friend to say, "I like you, let's be friends." But the court would not honor your claim for a breach of contract if he refused to give his $50,000 home for the asking. Here again is a collusion. Both parties know what is claimed is not to be interpreted on its face value. That is in fact why a lie can be told with such sincerity.

A representative of a business firm in Japan, when negotiating a contract with another firm, is often invited by his counterparts in the other firm to play mah-jongg. The counterparts, who are normally very good players, then begin to lose one game after another, while placing heavy bets. The representative, knowing all the different ways in which Japanese firms try to entice contractors, would suspect, and correctly so, that he is being allowed to win, that this is a form of semi-sophisticated bribery, the money having been probably supplied through the company's expense account. Upon detecting this, the representative must not only continue to play games of mah-jongg, but also play the game of pretending to play a serious game of mah-jongg. There should not be even a hint that they are intentionally losing the game and that the money the representative won is meant to be a bribe. But after the game is over, without anyone telling him, he would try his best to get a contract with that company.

In sum, then, face-to-face interaction is like a drama, in which each actor knows what the others are supposed to say. Part of what this means is that multiple meanings of expressions are correctly sorted out by participants and behavior appropriate for each meaning is acted out in appropriate contexts.

Dinner entertainment in Japan illustrates workings of numerous cultural assumptions such as the above, many of which remain implicit and unstated. Spelling out these assumptions will hopefully help understand the general nature and quality of Japanese human relations in a way in which they are not ordinarily discussed.

Japanese prefer to entertain their business associates at a restaurant rather than at home, whereas Americans very often do entertain such guests at home. Japanese say that their homes are too small, that their kitchen is inadequate for preparing foods for guests, or that the wife lacks appropriate culinary skills. Such factors are not to be denied, of course, but business executives with large homes and adequate kitchen facilities still entertain their guests by and large in restaurants, which suggests that there may well be other factors.

There is indeed a very important social reason for not entertaining business associates at home. Home for Japanese is very private. Besides their own families, it is generally open only to relatives, long-time friends, children's friends and, occasionally, a man's subordinates at work. These are mostly people with whom one shares a great deal of affect and intimacy. They are, in other words, people with whom one need not be businesslike. Even subordinates at work, when visiting, tend to discuss personal matters or family problems about which they seek psychological support as much as, or more than, practical solutions.

Penetrability of American homes is seen by the eagerness with which

the hostess will show her guests around the house, all the way to bedrooms and even bathrooms, as if they deserve the special admiration of
the not-so-interested guests. This is a symbolic gesture which parallels
the expression, "my home is yours; please feel at home." Of course such
an expression is another of those agreed-upon lies, but it nonetheless
does indicate the relative openness of American homes. Not so in
Japan. There is no Japanese expression comparable to "my home is
yours." Guests are expected to act like guests. They are never shown
around the house. They are taken to a room specifically designed for
outsiders known as *kyakuma* (guest room) or *oosetsuma* (reception room),
where guests stay put.

Japanese have invented the neologism "my-home-*shugi*" or "my
homism" to express the idea that the home is a fortress of privacy closed
to people with whom affect is not shared to a great extent. Neighbors,
shopkeepers who come around to take orders and others who are
excluded from the circle of intimacy must stand at the entrance *(genkan)*
or the service entrance *(katteguchi)* and carry on their business, even
though the business may take half an hour or a whole hour. The mistress of the house, being a paragon of propriety, will bring out a cushion
(zabuton) for such people to offer a comfortable seat, but implicitly to
convey the message that the visitor belongs at the entrance and no further inside the house. This parallels an American housewife who stands
at the front door, fully open but otherwise blocked by her bodily presence, to indicate to a Fuller brushman that she intends to cut him short
and not to let him into the house where he can spread out his merchandise. I have seen a handful of neighborhood housewives with shopping
baskets in their arms huddled together at street corners in Kyoto, where
I lived in 1969–1970, talking for hours on end. Since they all do not
want their neighbors to enter their homes just to sip tea and gossip, a
street becomes a convenient open parlor for housewives to come and go
and join and leave as time allows.

If neighbors are generally excluded from visiting, so are business
associates whose visits home, in a sense, are tantamount to invasion of
privacy. Excluded from the home, the only alternative is to entertain at
a restaurant. While there are both Western-style restaurants serving
Western dishes and Japanese-style restaurants serving Japanese dishes,
practically all dinner entertainment of business associates, if done in
style and if they can be called entertainment at all rather than just dinner, is done in a Japanese-style restaurant generally called *ryootei* or
ryooriya rather than a Western-style restaurant. For the sake of brevity,
we will refer to *ryootei* for Japanese-style restaurants. "Restaurant"
would mean Western-style restaurants.

There are several reasons why *ryootei* are preferred to restaurants for entertainment. First of all, sitting in chairs is not the most relaxing posture for Japanese. At work, in school, and at other places like trains and buses, Japanese do, or course, sit Western style. But when they want total relaxation, they like to move their center of gravity close to the floor. No restaurant in Japan offers this comfort. Secondly, in restaurants, except for a large group, one has no privacy since the dining room has to be shared with numerous strangers, whereas in a *ryootei* each group of diners has a private room.

Thirdly, the role of service employees is different in the two situations. In a restaurant, waiters or waitresses are what Erving Goffman has called "non-persons." They interact with guests only to take orders and serve food; for the purposes of the dinner guests, they do not exist. Dinner guests ignore their comings and goings and recognize their presence only in connection with serving food. In a *ryootei*, the people serving dinner guests, who are always women, are not even called by the same name as their counterparts in restaurants. In a restaurant, they are called *kyuuji* or *jokyuu*, unless English terms such as "boy," "waiter," or "waitress" are directly used. In a *ryootei*, they are *nakai, neesan, okami-san, geisha, geiko,* etc. Far from being a non-person, a *ryootei* service worker is an integral part of the dinner entertainment. She is expected to participate in conversation, although unless she is a *geisha*, her role is by and large passive, speaking up when spoken to and not taking initiative in directing the trend of conversation. The extent to which she participates, however, is a function of the degree to which dinner guests are affected by alcohol, the size of the group, and other factors. When dinner guests are drunk and jovial, she too must join in to help maintain the joviality by being, for example, a little more risqué in her remarks, a little louder in speaking, etc. Her initial, reserved giggles should give way to uninhibited laughter. These changes must be executed even if she is not affected by alcohol herself. She is likely to receive offers of *sake* from time to time which she is expected to accept, but only in moderation so that she would not become truly intoxicated and fail to perform her duty in play-acting her intoxicated role.

In a *ryootei,* service workers serving in one private room are serving only one group of guests. At least during the time she is in the room, her services are monopolized. Even if they have other rooms to serve, they do not give a hint of it, so as to maintain an appearance, at least, of monopolized service which is not possible in a restaurant.

In *ryootei* entertainment, ordering of food is done by the host alone. Often this is done beforehand by telephone. And after the dinner is over, the host excuses himself from the dining room momentarily and pays the bill in the guests' total absence; the bill may alternatively be sent to the host's home or to his company if the entertainment is on the company expense account, as it often is. Thus guests do not see the menu with prices of each item printed or the total cost of the dinner on the check. All this helps to remove pecuniary aspects of dinner entertainment and helps to create a homelike atmosphere. This is a fourth reason why *ryootei* are preferred to restaurants for entertaining guests.

Fifthly, *ryootei* entertainment lends itself to creating a social environment conducive to group cohesion, at least for Japanese, because everyone—hosts and guests—have the same set of dishes. In a restaurant, each individual carefully studies the menu and orders his own unique combination of hors d'oeuvres, soup, salad (and salad dressing), main dish (not forgetting how the meat is to be cooked), side orders, and dessert as a symbolic way of asserting each individual's unique existence. In contrast, in the *ryootei,* by everyone having the same dishes, emphasis is placed on common sharing of experience. *Ryootei* entertainment thus strives toward negation of individuality and denial of uniqueness of each participant. Instead, it strives to create an atmosphere conducive to communion through commonality by emphasizing the sameness of everyone, by everyone having an identical set of dishes in front of him as it is in home dinner entertainment.

I have not exhausted all the factors of preference for *ryootei* over restaurant for entertainment. In fact, I have reserved probably the single most important reason, namely, that *sake* is served in *ryootei* while it is not served with Western dishes and therefore not in restaurants. The whole ritual surrounding *sake* drinking is unique, and is not replicated in drinking Western alcoholic beverages. For one thing, Western beverages, except for wine and beer, are generally not drunk with meals; they are more apt to be before-dinner aperitif or after-dinner "dessert." Drinking of grape wine has not caught on on any wide scale in Japan yet, and its significance in Japanese dinner entertainment is still negligible. Beer alone has come to acquire some of the features of the *sake*-drinking ritual and is often used as a substitute.

Japanese folklorists tell us that *sake* was originally a sacred beverage produced as an offering to the gods. Mortals drank *sake* in a ceremony called *naorae,* which was held in front of the gods' altar, and drank it in communion with the gods. Mortals would assemble in front of the altar and share the spiritual essence of immortals by sharing the *sake* and other foods once offered to the gods and now given back as the gods' gifts. *Naorae,* while an occasion for communion with the gods, was at the same time an occasion for conviviality and re-affirmation of communal mutuality. Now, drinking *sake* is a completely secularized affair; its sacredness is gone. But still, its "communal" functions are deeply imbedded in ordinary dinner entertainment because the etiquette and numerous rules of *sake* drinking insures conviviality and communion.

One of the elementary rules of the *sake* party is that one does not pour for himself. Pouring is done for and by each other. It is a symbolic gesture of indicating that each is at the other's service. Since *sake* cups, except those used for solitary drinking called *guinomi,* are so small and allow only a few sips out of each cupful, this gesture requires constant surveillance of cups in front of others around you and an offer to pour as soon as a cup is empty or near-empty. At the same time, one should engage in absorbing conversation, an art which requires considerable training. An experienced host would, in fact, not wait until a cup is near-empty; he would hold a bottle of *sake* in front of a guest, slightly tilted (nonverbally communicating his readiness to pour), and urge him to empty or "dry" his cup so he can pour more.

When *sake* is being poured, the "owner" of the cup is expected to hold the cup in his hand rather than leaving it on the table. Leaving it on the table while *sake* is being poured makes it possible for one to ignore the service another is rendering. One would thus be inadvertently impolite not to show proper appreciation for the service. Holding the cup in hand, on the other hand, requires one to attend to the pouring and obligates the expression of appreciation.

Pouring *sake* without spilling requires coordination between the pourer and the one holding a cup to be poured. A *sake* cup is small and at the same time, the bottle has a relatively large opening. Since the bottle is opaque, it is hard to know how much liquid is still in the bottle and how much the bottle should be tilted. There are three general ways of guessing how much liquor is left in the bottle, none of which is foolproof. One is to judge from the total weight. Since the weight of the bottle itself varies a great deal, past experience is not of great help. A second method is to remember how much one had to tilt the bottle the last time he poured. Since the same bottle is usually passed around from one end of the table to another, one does not always know how much to tilt the bottle he happens to be holding at a particular moment. The third means is to shake the bottle near one's ear if it seems light, and judge from the splattering sound of the liquid inside how much liquor remains.

After a considerable amount of alcohol is consumed, the man holding his cup and the man holding the bottle may not have perfect control of their arm and hand muscles, let alone of their swaying torsos. Yet both parties are sober enough to know spilling is bad manners. There is momentary concentration by the two individuals on the act of pouring and coordinating of hands to avoid spilling.

If a guest has had enough *sake* and wants to accept—only out of politeness—just a little more but not a full cup, then before the cup is full, he must move the cup higher and higher to prevent pouring of more *sake* while mumbling something to the effect that it is enough. A good Japanese host is not one who necessarily respects the other's wishes. He is more concerned with forcing his hospitality upon the guest. He is thus prepared for the contingency of the guest attempting to refuse by raising the cup. The moment he senses this defense strategy of the guest, he counteracts by holding the bottle higher and higher, raising the bottle at precisely the same speed as the guest raises the cup, so that he can keep pouring *sake*. To do this, and do it without spilling a drop, especially after both parties are intoxicated, is no easy feat. I might add parenthetically that Japanese do not spend a great deal of time practicing pouring *sake*.

Numerous activities requiring various eye-hand coordination engaged in from childhood—goldfish scooping, using chopsticks, making paper-folding figures, playing with beanbags, etc.—all prepare Japanese for their adult life, an adult life which includes pouring of *sake* as an essential skill.

After the pouring is over, there have to be some gestural or verbal cues on the part of the receiver to indicate his thanks. He may bow ever so slightly or mumble something like, "aaaa . . ." or *"doomo . . ."* or combine the two.

Etiquette requires that the host first pour *sake* for the guest, the host symbolically being the servant of the guest, and that the guest then reciprocate. It also requires that if a person of lower status wishes to exchange drinking with a person of higher status, the former first pours for the latter, and then the latter reciprocates. Also, if their seats are far apart, as they may be in a large party, the junior person is required to come to the senior person and ask him for the privilege of pouring *sake* for him.

This, incidentally, is a convenient ploy for a very junior person to approach a very high status person as a means of establishing an acquaintance, otherwise known as "buttering up." Offering to pour *sake* is a way of showing one's respect and paying homage to a high status person. It is thus socially correct, and offers a legitimate way for a lowly person to sit next to or in front of a high status person, a position he cannot otherwise occupy without seeming to be excessively forward. Thus he plays the game at two different levels at the same time. At one, he is showing respect to his superior and being formally correct; at another, he is furthering his personal gain by impressing the superior with his presence.

A practice unique to *sake* drinking is the offering of one's own cup to another person after drinking the contents. While pouring starts from a lower status person to a higher status person, or from the host to the guest, in offering a cup, the higher status person has the privilege of offering it first to a lower status person, or the guest to the host. This is followed by the same cup or the cup of the other person being offered to the superior or to the guest. Each such exchange is a symbolic handshake or embrace and is a re-affirmation of the social pact uniting those exchanging the cup.

When a cup is offered to someone, he is not required to return it immediately. Since normally a person drains a cup in several sips, putting it on the table at intervals of a few minutes, often someone else comes along to offer another cup before he finishes the first. When one finishes the first cup offered, he might offer it to the second person if he happens to be engaged in conversation with him. The upshot of this is that the route a cup travels forms a complex pattern indicating social statuses, cliques, ulterior motives, etc. Also, after a while cups are unevenly distributed, some people having several in front of them—typically high status persons to whom others have paid homage—leaving none in front of some of the lower ranking individuals. Since it is improper to leave people without cups to drink from, the *ryootei* management, concerned about customers' consumption (for which they can present a fat bill) as much as social propriety, will bring extra cups and leave them in the center of the table for this type of contingency. Thus, those without a cup may help themselves from the center of the table. High status persons should not hoard cups, however. They should try to drink up and redistribute them as fast as they can. Herein lies the reason why Japanese business executives are mostly heavy drinkers and why ability to absorb great quantities of alcohol is almost a *sine qua non* for upward mobility in Japan.

What makes excessive drinking inevitable in this sort of dinner entertainment is that there are no socially acceptable ways of refusing an offer of *sake* and at the same time making the occasion a success. Turning one's cup upside down and placing it on the table thus is a socially recognized way of saying, "No thanks, I cannot drink any more." But this is admittedly a socially poor thing to do, and if one must do this, he profusely apologizes for his ineptitude. If only one out of ten or twelve people is a teetotaller and if he is not a principal guest, then the atmosphere would not be affected appreciably since he may be ignored entirely and the entertainment can proceed without his social presence. But if there are more than one such persons in a small group and if they cannot be ignored because of their number or because of their position in the group, then the party cannot help being a failure.

On the other hand, succumbing to the insistence of the host and forcing oneself to drink when one does not wish to may not be pleasant at all. At least, however, it has the virtue of complying with the group norm and manifesting the willingness to sacrifice personal welfare for the good of the group. In the end, the participant may be dead drunk. He may say or do things he would not remember or prefer not to remember. But others observing him tend to be quite lenient in their judgment of his behavior. They are likely to show sympathy and some may wish he had a little more self-control. But one would not morally chastise him since such misbehavior is not a moral misdeed, it is simply social misconduct. By the same token, even if drunkenness and possibly getting sick and throwing up at the end may be due to unswerving insistence of the hosts, who often equate the amount of hospitality forced upon guests with the degree of success of the entertainment, it is quite improper for a guest to be angry with the hosts. The opinion of the community is on the side of the host, on the side of those who help lubricate social relations.

While a good deal of alcohol may be consumed in the course of a dinner, how drunk participants get is not absolutely a function of alcoholic intake. Socially defined rules of drunken behavior, varying from situation to situation, dictate how drunk one should appear. The help which alcohol provides in acting drunk is not to be minimized, of course. But we all know that the same amount of alcohol consumed in a party of congenial friends produces radically different results from that taken at home all alone. In a party, it takes very little alcohol to induce loud talking, shouting, loud laughter, singing and clapping of hands in unison with a wild, off-tune chorus of school songs. When the fun of the party is all over and it is time to go home, everyone except the few who lost control and are sound asleep by this time, regains his sobriety almost instantly and acts almost like a different person, like a group of actors leaving the stage after the curtain comes down. It is thus not strange that one almost never hears in Japan of a drunk, walking the narrow downtown streets without sidewalks and teeming with cars day and night, being run over by a car or hit by a bus. Of course, he is almost invariably helped home by his more sober companions.

One important rule to be followed in dinner entertainment of a small party of five or six persons is to center the conversation of the entire group on one topic. Breaking up into groups of twos and threes rather than keeping the whole group united in a dinner situation is a sign of conspiracy, a gesture indicating lack of interest in the major theme of the play being enacted, and therefore an outright expression of a lack of respect and discourtesy to the honored guests of the party.

Those of higher status in the party should be allowed to dominate the conversation most of the time. Others are the supporting cast in this production. They should pitch in from time to time to punctuate the conversation and make it more interesting, throwing in little jokes and light remarks now and then, but they should make sure to leave any punch lines to the honored members of the party so that the dominant role of the principal actors of this drama is unmistakable to anyone. Supporting cast roles in this play are, of course, to enhance the dominant roles played by principal actors. The latter should be allowed to speak longer, introduce new topics more often, and make somewhat belittling remarks about comments of the supporting cast. They are privileged to cut into sentences of others, but the others must politely listen until they finish their remarks. The supporting cast might play its role by asking questions an honored member can answer with authority, so that in answering them he can reassert his dominant role, for example, by giving a glowing report of his recent trip to a place no one else in the company has been to, or by divulging some secret information he happens to be privy to. Supporting casts are supposed to express exaggerated interest, surprise, and other appropriate effects.

The drama cannot be enacted only with the effort of the supporting cast, obviously. Principal actors must know their roles well and read their script without making errors. When hosts expect the guests to dominate the scene, they must dominate. In order to dominate, they must know how to dominate. They must know interesting topics of conversation and know how to make conversation interesting. At the same time, even if the guest's talk is not too interesting, a good host would put on the appearance of being interested and attentive. In short, both sides—hosts and guests—must cooperate, saying what is appropriate at the right moment, giving cues to one another so that each knows when to offer a cup, pour *sake,* laugh, shake hands, etc. Seeing the appropriate and expected responses, others take this as a cue to proceed to the next scene of the play.

Flawless enactment of the entire drama and a smooth flow of each episode thus requires hosts and guests all be familiar with the rules. This insures that the scenario is read flawlessly by all actors. This is more difficult than enacting a real play since, unlike real plays, the script is not written beforehand, but is being written from moment to moment as scenes unfold. Without rehearsal, each participant must play his part. As for the script, each participant must improvise his lines without delay as the drama develops.

Rehearsal of the play and the practice of improvising the script are actually found in each participant's daily living from time of birth. Learning to speak Japanese and learning all the hidden meanings and reversals of meaning, the meanings of hand and body gestures and the social system of hierarchy are all preparations for enacting the next drama of life.

When an American is invited to a dinner party in a *ryootei,* he naturally goes in without rehearsal and without the practice of improvising lines in the way appropriate to a Japanese social scene. He lacks the social accouterment necessary to act with grace and without flaw. The result is somewhat like an American wrestler having to play a match of *sumoo* with a *sumoo* athlete using *sumoo* rules. The result is a most awkward match. Since Japanese are too polite to tell their guests they are clumsy people, guests leave the scene believing they played their part according to the script. But actually, as in a real play, when one actor cannot play his part well other actors must strain themselves to make up for the deficiency, making their cues excessively obvious and covering up the mistakes made by the clumsy actor. Having an honored guest who does not know his part well in a dinner party requires that others help him to play his role so that they themselves can continue to play the hosts' role. If a clumsy actor is one who plays a minor role in the play, he can be almost ignored without causing much damage to the play. When the principal actor, which an American guest usually is, does not know the part and know the script, the amount of effort required by the supporting cast is heartrending. It is almost like Fred Astaire trying to dance gracefully with a 200 pound woman who never danced before. After entertaining Americans, one often hears Japanese say they are all worn out. This is precisely because they try so hard to help Americans play the principal role without *faux pas* or try so hard not to make *faux pas* look like *faux pas* and even try to make them look as though they are charming improvisations of the correct script. In short, they try so hard to make American guests believe they play their role like Fredric March that in reality the Japanese are the Fredric Marches heroically helping clumsy and inexperienced American actors.

8

Amae: A Key Concept for Understanding Japanese Personality Structure

L. TAKEO DOI

I am particularly interested in the problem of personality and culture in modern Japan for two reasons. First, even though I was born and raised in Japan and had my basic medical training there, I have had further training in psychiatry and psychoanalysis in the United States, thus exposing myself for some time to a different culture from that of Japan. Second, I have had many opportunities of treating both Japanese and non-Japanese (mostly American) patients with psychotherapy. These experiences have led me to inquire into differences between Japanese and non-Japanese patients and also into the question of what is basic in Japanese character structure. In this paper I shall describe what I have found to be most characteristic in Japanese patients and then discuss its meaning in the context of Japanese culture.

The essence of what I am going to talk about is contained in one common Japanese word, *amae*. Let me therefore, first of all, explain the meaning of this word. *Amae* is the noun form of *amaeru*, an intransitive verb that means "to depend and presume upon another's benevolence" (Doi 1956). This word has the same root as *amai*, an adjective that means "sweet." Thus *amaeru* has a distinct feeling of sweetness and is generally used to describe a child's attitude or behavior toward his parents, particularly his mother. But it can also be used to describe the relationship between two adults, such as the relationship between a husband and a wife or a master and a subordinate. I believe that there is no single word in English equivalent to *amaeru*, though this does not mean that the psychology of *amae* is totally alien to the people of English-speaking countries. I shall come back to this problem after describing some of the clinical material through which I came to recognize the importance of what this word *amae* signifies.

It was in my attempt to understand what goes on between the therapist and patient that I first came across the all-powerful drive of the
patient's *amae*. There is a diagnostic term in Japanese psychiatry,
shinkeishitsu, which includes neurasthenia, anxiety neurosis, and obsessive neurosis. Morita, who first used *shinkeishitsu* as a diagnostic term,
thought that these three types of neuroses had a basic symptom in common, *toraware*, which means "to be bound or caught," as by some
intense preoccupation. He considered *toraware* to be closely related to
hypochondriacal fear and thought that this fear sets in motion a reciprocal intensification of attention and sensation. In psychoanalytic work
with neurotic patients of the *shinkeishitsu* type, I have also found *toraware*
to be a basic symptom, but I have evolved a different formulation of its
significance (see Doi 1958). I have observed that during the course of
psychotherapy the patient's *toraware* can easily turn into hypersensitivity
in his relationship with the therapist. This hypersensitivity is best
described by the Japanese word *kodawari*. *Kodawari* is the noun form of
kodawaru, an intransitive verb meaning "to be sensitive to minor
things," "to be inwardly disturbed over one's personal relationships."
In the state of *kodawari* one feels that he is not accepted by others, which
suggests that *kodawari* results from the unsatisfied desire to *amaeru*.
Thus, *toraware* can be traced back through *kodawari* to *amae*. In my
observations, the patient's *toraware* usually receded when he became
aware of his *amae* toward the therapist, which he had been warding off
consciously and unconsciously up to then.

At first I felt that if the patient became fully aware of his *amae*, he
would thereupon be able to get rid of his neurosis. But I was wrong in
this assumption and came to observe another set of clinical phenomena
following the patient's recognition of his *amae* (see Doi 1960). Many
patients confessed that they were then awakened to the fact that they
had not "possessed their self," had not previously appreciated the
importance of their existence, and had been really nothing apart from
their all-important desire to *amaeru*. I took this as a step toward the
emergence of a new consciousness of self, inasmuch as the patient could
then at least realize his previous state of "no self."

There is another observation that I should like to mention here. It is
about the nature of guilt feelings of Japanese patients (see Doi 1961).
The word *sumanai* is generally used to express guilt feelings, and this
word is the negative form of *sumu*, which means "to end." *Sumanai* literally means that one has not done as he was supposed to do, thereby
causing the other person trouble or harm. Thus, it expresses more a
sense of unfulfilled obligation than a confession of guilt, though it is
generally taken as an indication that one feels guilty. When neurotic
patients say *sumanai*, I have observed that there lies, behind their use of

the word, much hidden aggression engendered by frustration of their wish to *amaeru*. So it seems that in saying *sumanai* they are in fact expressing their hidden concern lest they fall from the grace of *amae* because of their aggression. I think that this analysis of *sumanai* would also apply in essence to the use of this word by the ordinary Japanese in everyday life, but in the case of the neurotic patient *sumanai* is said with greater ambivalence. In other words, more than showing his feeling of being obligated, he tends to create a sense of obligation in the person to whom he makes his apology, thus "forcing" that person eventually to cater to his wish.

I have explained three clinical observations, all of which point to the importance of *amae* as a basic desire. As I said before, the state of *amae* originally refers to what a small child feels toward his mother. It is therefore not surprising that the desire to *amaeru* still influences one's adult years and that it becomes manifest in the therapeutic situation. Here we have a perfect example of transference in the psychoanalytic sense. But then is it not strange that *amaeru* is a unique Japanese word? Indeed, the Japanese find it hard to believe that there is no word for *amaeru* in European languages; a colleague once told me that he could not believe that the equivalent for such a seemingly universal phenomenon as *amae* did not exist in English or German, since, as he put it, "Even puppies do it, you know." Let me therefore illustrate the "Japaneseness" of the concept of *amaeru* by one striking incident. The mother of a Eurasian patient, a British woman who had been a long-term resident of Japan, was discussing her daughter with me. She spoke to me in English, but she suddenly switched to Japanese, in order to tell me that her daughter did not *amaeru* much as a child. I asked her why she had suddenly switched to Japanese. She replied, after a pause, that there was no way to say *amaeru* in English.

I have mentioned two Japanese words that are closely related to the psychology of *amae: kodawaru*, which means "to be inwardly disturbed over one's personal relationships," and *sumanai*, which means "to feel guilty or obligated." Now I should like to mention a few more words that are also related to the psychology of *amae*. First, *amai*, which originally means "sweet," can be used figuratively to describe a person who is overly soft and benevolent toward others or, conversely, one who always expects to *amaeru* in his relationships with others. Second, *amanzuru*, which is derived from *amaeru*, describes the state of mind in which one acquiesces to whatever circumstances one happens to be in. Third, *tori-iru*, which means "to take in," describes the behavior of a person who skillfully maneuvers another into permitting him to *amaeru*. Fourth, *suneru* describes the behavior of a child or an adult who pouts and sulks because he feels he is not allowed to *amaeru* as much as he wants to, thus harboring in himself mental pain of a masochistic nature. Fifth, *higamu* describes the behavior of a child or an adult who feels himself unfairly treated compared to others who are more favored, often suggesting the presence of a paranoid feeling. Sixth, *tereru* describes the behavior of a child or an adult who is ashamed of showing his intimate wish to *amaeru*. Seventh, *hinekureru* describes the behavior of a child or an adult who takes devious ways in his efforts to deny the wish to *amaeru*.

One could readily say that the behaviors or emotions described by all these Japanese words are not unknown to Westerners and that they appear quite frequently in the therapeutic situation with Western patients. But there remains the question I raised before: Why is there no word in English or in other European languages that is equivalent to *amaeru*, the most central element in all these emotions? To this, one might answer that the absence of a word like *amaeru* is no inconvenience, since it can easily be represented by a combination of words such as the "wish to be loved" or "dependency needs." That may be so, but does not this linguistic difference point to something deeper? Perhaps it reflects a basic psychological difference between Japan and the Western World. Before discussing this problem further, however, I would like to mention a theory of Michael Balint, a British psychoanalyst, which has much bearing on what I am talking about now.

In his psychoanalytic practice Balint observed that "in the final phase of the treatment patients begin to give expression to long-forgotten, infantile, instinctual wishes, and to demand their gratification from their environment" (Balint 1952a). He called this infantile desire "passive object love," since its primal aim is to be loved; he also called it "primary love," since it is the foundation upon which later forms of love are built. I imagine that he must have wondered why such an important desire is not represented by one common word, for he points out the fact that "all European languages are so poor that they cannot distinguish between the two kinds of object-love, active and passive" (Balint 1952b).

By now it must be clear that the "primary love" or "passive object-love" described by Balint is none other than the desire to *amaeru*. But then we have to draw the curious conclusion that the emotion of primary love is readily accessible to Japanese patients by way of the word *amaeru*, while to Western patients, according to Balint, it can become accessible only after a painstaking analysis. In my observations I have also noticed that the recognition of *amae* by Japanese patients does not signify the final phase of treatment, as it did in Balint's patients. I think that we have to try to solve this apparent contradiction very carefully, because therein lies, in my opinion, an important key to understanding the psychological differences between Japan and Western countries.

The reasoning behind Balint's observation that primary love appears in its pure form only in the final phase of treatment is as follows: The primary love of an infant is bound to be frustrated, leading to the formation of narcissism; as though he said to himself, "If the world does not love me enough, I have to love and gratify myself." Since such narcissism is part of the earliest and most primitive layer of the mind, it can be modified only in the last stage of treatment, at which time the long-repressed urge to be loved can re-emerge in its pure state. Then what shall we say about the Japanese, to whom this primary desire to be loved is always accessible? Does it mean that the Japanese have less narcissism? I think not. Rather I would say that the Japanese somehow continue to cherish the wish to be loved even after the formation of narcissism. It is as though the Japanese did not want to see the reality of their basic frustration. In other words, the Japanese, as does everybody else, do experience frustration of their primary love, as is well attested to by the existence of the rich vocabulary we have already encountered relating to the frustration of *amae*. But it seems that the Japanese never give up their basic desire to *amaeru*, thus mitigating the extent of violent emotions caused by its frustration.

In this connection I want to mention an interesting feature of the word *amaeru*. We do not say that an infant does *amaeru* until he is about one year old, thereby indicating that he is then conscious of his wish to *amaeru*, which in turn suggests the presence of a budding realization that his wish cannot always be gratified. Thus, from its inception, the wish to *amaeru* is accompanied by a secret fear that it may be frustrated.

If what I have been saying is true, then it must indicate that there is a social sanction in Japanese society for expressing the wish to *amaeru*. And it must be this social sanction that has encouraged in the Japanese language the development of the large vocabulary relating to *amaeru*. In other words, in Japanese society parental dependency is fostered, and this behavior pattern is even institutionalized into its social structure, whereas perhaps the opposite tendency prevails in Western societies. This seems to be confirmed by recent anthropological studies of Japanese society, notably that of Ruth Benedict, who said: "The arc of life in Japan is plotted in opposite fashion to that in the United States. It is a great U-curve with maximum freedom and indulgence allowed to babies and to the old. Restrictions are slowly increased after babyhood till having one's own way reaches a low just before and after marriage" (Benedict [1946] 1961). It is true that the restrictions Benedict spoke of do exist for adults in Japanese society, but it should be understood that these restrictions are never meant to be drastic so far as the basic desire to *amaeru* is concerned. Rather, these restrictions are but channels through which that desire is to be duly gratified. That is why we can speak of parental dependency as being institutionalized in Japanese society. For instance, in marriage a husband does *amaeru* toward his wife, and vice versa. It is strongly present in all formal relationships, including those between teacher and student and between doctor and patient. Thus William Caudill (1961), in his observations on Japanese psychiatric hospitals, spoke of the mutual dependency he encountered in all relationships.

In this connection I cannot resist mentioning an episode that happened when I gave a talk on some characteristic Japanese words to a professional group in the United States. *Amaeru* was one of those words. After my talk, one distinguished scholar asked me whether or not the feeling of *amaeru* is something like what Catholics feel toward their Holy Mother. Apparently he could not recognize the existence of such a feeling in the ordinary mother-child relationship. And if his response is representative of Americans, it would mean that in American society the feeling of *amaeru* can be indulged in perhaps only in the religious life, but here also very sparingly.

I would now like to mention a study by a Japanese scholar, Hajime Nakamura, professor of Indian philosophy at the University of Tokyo and an authority on comparative philosophy. In his major work, *Ways of Thinking of Eastern Peoples* (1960), he presents a penetrating analysis of thought patterns of Indians, Chinese, Japanese, and Tibetans on the basis of linguistic studies and observations on variations in Buddhist doctrine and practice in these four countries. What he says about the Japanese pattern of thought is parallel to what I have been saying here, though he reaches his conclusions from an entirely different source. He says that the Japanese way of thinking is greatly influenced by an emphasis on immediate personal relations and also that the Japanese have always been eager to adopt foreign cultural influences, but always within the framework of this emphasis on personal relations. To state this in psychoanalytic terms: the Japanese are always prepared to identify themselves with, or introject, and outside force, to the exclusion of other ways of coping with it. This character trait of the Japanese was touched upon by Benedict, too, when she said that "the Japanese have an ethic of alternatives" and "Japan's motivations are situational," referring particularly to the sudden complete turnabout of Japan following the defeat of the last war.

This leads, however, to the very interesting and important question of whether or not Japanese character structure has changed at all since the war. I think that Benedict was quite right in assuming that Japan as a whole willingly submitted to unconditional surrender because it was the emperor's order, that Japan wanted only to please the emperor, even in her defeat. But it cannot be denied that things have been changing since then. For instance, the emperor had to declare that he no longer wished to be considered sacred. Also the Japanese have been disillusioned to find that the paramount virtue of *chū*, that is, loyalty to the emperor, was taken advantage of by the ultranationalists, who completely failed them. With the decline of *chū* there was also a decline of *kō*, that is, of filial piety. In other words, the tradition of repaying one's *on*, that is, one's spiritual debts to an emperor and to one's parents, was greatly undermined. Thus there developed the moral chaos of present-day Japan.

I think, however, that the nature of this chaos has a distinctly Japanese character and can best be understood by taking into account the psychology of *amae*. It seems that heretofore the stress upon the duty of repaying one's *on* to the emperor and to one's parents served the purpose of regulating the all too powerful desire of *amae*. Since the Japanese were deprived of this regulating force after the war, it was inevitable that their desire to *amaeru* was let loose, with its narcissistic element becoming more manifest. That perhaps explains why we now find in Japan so many examples of lack of social restraint. I wonder whether this recent tendency has also helped to increase the number of neurotics. I think it has, though we have no reliable statistics to confirm it. But I am quite certain that an analysis of the psychology of *amae* such as I am attempting here would not have been possible in prewar days, because *amae* was concealed behind the duty of repaying one's *on*. It certainly was not visible to the outside observer, even to one as acute as Ruth Benedict. I would like to give you one clinical example to illustrate this point.

One of my recent patients, who was a student of law, revealed to me one day his secret thoughts, saying, "I wish I had some person who would take the responsibility of assisting me." The remarkable thing about this confession was that the Japanese word that he used for "assist" was a special legal term *hohitsu*, which was formerly used only for the act of assisting the emperor with his task of governing the nation. In saying this, as the patient himself explained, he wanted, like the emperor, to appear to be responsible for his acts but to depend completely on his assistant, who would really carry the burden. He said this, not jokingly but, rather, with complete seriousness. It is obvious that his confession revealed his secret desire to *amaeru*, about which he spoke more clearly on another occasion. But what I would like to point out here is that in prewar days the patient could hardly have made such a confession, using a special term reserved only for the emperor. Of course, this is a special case, and the fact that the patient was a law student accounted for his use of such a technical term. Yet I think that this case illustrates the point that I want to make, that is, the more emphasis placed upon repaying one's *on,* the less clearly seen is one's desire to *amaeru.*

In this connection, let me say a few words about the nature of so-called emperor worship, which served as the Japanese state religion in prewar days. It is true that the emperor was held sacred, but the element of taboo was greater than that of divinity. It is really tempting to apply what Freud said about taboo to the Japanese emperor worship. As a matter of fact, he did mention the Japanese emperor in his book on *Totem and Taboo,* but not from the viewpoint of what is being discussed here. I will not go into this subject any further now, except to add one more comment concerning the effect of elimination of the emperor taboo and its related system, apart from the already discussed release of the desire to *amaeru.* Some Japanese critics voiced the opinion that the tight thought control deriving from the emperor and the family system in prewar days stifled development of healthy selfhood, that one could assert himself in those days only by way of *suneru* and *higamu,* which are interestingly enough the very same Japanese words that I have described before as indicating frustration of *amae* (Maruyama 1960; Isono 1960). I agree that this opinion is generally true, but I do not believe that elimination of the emperor and family system alone can lead to development of healthy selfhood or personality. This is shown by many patients, who confess that they are awakened to the fact that they have "not had self" apart from the all powerful desire to *amaeru.* Then what or who can help them to obtain their "self"? This touches upon a very important problem of identity, which I will not attempt to discuss in detail. I can say only that the Japanese as a whole are still searching for something, something with which they can safely identify themselves, so that they can become whole, independent beings.

In closing I should like to make two additional remarks. First, it may seem that I am possibly idealizing the West in a way, since I have looked at the problem of personality and culture in modern Japan from the Western point of view. I do not deny that I have. In fact I could not help doing so, because Japanese culture did not produce any yardstick to judge itself critically. I really think that it is a fine thing for the West to have developed such a yardstick for critical analysis. And it seems inevitable that it involves a kind of idealization when the non-Westerners attempt to apply such a yardstick to themselves. I know, however, that in the psychoanalytic circles of Western countries, idealization has a special meaning and is not something commendable. So they would certainly not call their use of the analytical method idealization. But I wonder whether they are entirely right in assuming that their use of the analytical method stands on its own without involving any idealization on their part.

Second, though I have stated that there is no exact equivalent to the word *amaeru* in all European languages, I do not say that *amaeru* is unique to the Japanese language. I have some information that the language of Korea and that of Ainu have a word of the same meaning. There seems to be some question about whether or not the Chinese language has such a word. I am now most curious to know whether or not the Polynesian languages have a similar word. I have a feeling that they may have. If they do, how would their psychology compare with that of the Japanese? It is my earnest hope that these questions will be answered by anthropological and psychological studies in the not-too-distant future.

9

"Male Chauvinism" as a Manifestation of Love in Marriage

SONYA SALAMON

THE images of Japanese womanhood held by many in the West can be classed into two categories. One is the JAL stewardess, trained in a thousand year tradition to serve beautifully and gracefully; the other, as the feminists see her, is the shy female enslaved by men and by the society of which she is a part (Millet 1973). When I went to Japan, these stereotypes were part of my anthropological baggage. Upon seeing certain male patterns of behavior toward women I interpreted these as outright "male chauvinist pig" (MCP) acts, and I was continually outraged for the women with whom I identified. As I delved further and began to ask myself what was happening, I saw that the pattern was indeed MCP on the etic, or culturally universal, level. But what seemed to be hideous sexism was more complex when one began to interpret it on the emic, or culturally unique, level. I found that certain forms of Japanese MCP behavior have crystallized out of conjugal relationships through many generations. These patterned ways of acting have acquired names and marks of recognition. Because they are commonly recognized they also are expectable. Japanese wives may not especially welcome them, but they are "normal"—and thus perhaps not personally threatening.

I want to examine the dynamics of Japanese marriage in its early stages, and the reasons why partners need to realign their relations. But first I need to explain whom I am talking about and then to sketch a paradigm of the early stages of marriage, in order to show the developmental context for the behavior I will discuss.

My data were collected from two groups of women in Tokyo during 1971, and from a preliminary study in 1965–66. The women were all middle class, in their early thirties, married for more than five years, graduates of universities or junior colleges, and had two or three children. Their husbands were middle level executives in government or

Reprinted from *Adult Episodes in Japan*, David W. Plath, ed. (Leiden: E. J. Brill, 1975).

business bureaucracies. My husband also was a source of data since he participated as a member of a work-based group at a university and was able to give me insights into male behavior. I made use of interviews, observations, and telephone logs; but above all I benefitted from group discussions which began as English conversation classes and ended as mutual exchanges and even consciousness-raising sessions. The women I will describe are not in farming or small business families where husbands and wives share an everyday work world and where men therefore may not be able to act arbitrarily toward the women who work beside them.

Stages of Marital Relations

Figure 1 shows four ideal-typical stages for the early course of a marriage. The ages are approximations, with men generally two to three years older than the women they marry. The Asahi yearbook of statistics for 1973 reports that in 1960 the age at first marriage was 27.2 for males and 24.4 for females; 1970 showed 26.9 for males and 24.2 for females. The lower part of Figure 1 is a demonstration that the stages reflect broad trends in Japanese attitudes across the young adult life course. The graph is based upon replies to the question, "What do you consider to be most important in life?"

During Stage I many college graduates in urban Japan continue to live within their natal families. Because they remain economically dependent, though often earning a salary, we must view young adults as participating in a parent-child relationship until they enter marriage with its relational equality. Young men are faced with the major adjustment of moving from student freedom to a lifetime commitment to one organization. However, young women, who usually make no such commitment, enjoy a latency period of independence, self-indulgence, and considerable testing of different interests. Throughout this pre-marital phase, parents continue to indulge their children in a degree of dependence uncommon in the West (Lifton 1965; Caudill 1970).

When readiness for marriage is reached, Stage II finds men and women on the lookout for a suitable mate. Many young women acknowledge that they chose to work in order to find a husband on their own. The preference is for a love marriage. Even if men and woman avail themselves of the fail-safe mechanism of an arranged marriage, their ideal is to marry for love. Akiko, who had had an arranged marriage, hastened to tell me, "But it was love." Blood (1967) and Waller (1938) both emphasize that the form of courtship and engagement affect the expectations of the partners entering a marriage and the subsequent development of their relationship. Young people launching a marriage

Stage	I	II	III	IV
Age	21–24	25–27	27–33	33–48
Turning point	Pre-romance Post-college	Courtship Marriage Pre-children	Parenthood Preschool-age children	Parenthood School-age children
Place	Natal family	Own home	Own home	Own home
Focal career male	Life commitment work	Work Husband	Work Husband/father	Work Husband/father
Focal career female	Non-career work Unmarried daughter	Work Wife	Housewife Mother	Housewife/mother (Part-time work)

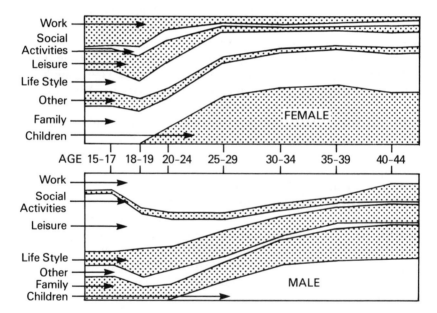

Fig. 1. Marital stages and purposes in life. Graphs indicate the percentage of persons specifying that item in answer to the question, "What is the most important thing in life to you?" This material has been adapted and redrawn from p. 43 of Munesuke Mita, *Gendai no ikigai: kawaru Nihonjin no jinseikan*. Tokyo: Nikkei Shinsho 128 (1970).

via an arranged courtship are seen by Blood to have lesser expectations about equality and companionship than those marrying via a love match. However, most men and women who marry in Japan do so holding idealized notions of love, companionship, and mutuality as do their counterparts in the West.

After marriage the couple shares a short interlude, before starting a family. In the culturally dictated life course in Japan, when one marries it follows that one has children, and the sooner the better. The husband continues at his job; so does the wife unless marriage involved a geographic move for her. Though she is working she is able to cater to her husband, and he in turn woos his wife—they have "dates" and he makes an effort to be chivalrous (Blood 1967). This stage is difficult mainly for the bride who has moved away from friends, relatives, and possibly work; and who is therefore isolated until she has a baby, and thus gains entrance into the sorority of neighborhood mothers.

Stage III—the focus of this paper—is critical in determining which direction the marital relationship will take. The couple no longer has the time or inclination to cater and woo one another; the husband increasingly is drawn away from his family by the demands of work, and the wife must care for the children and the house. All of this occupies, but may frustrate, her. As they draw apart, the couple must in some way realign their relationship from the ideal they held at the outset, and reconcile it with the reality of present demands.

With Stage IV the children enter school, the marriage typically having reached a kind of détente; a steady state in which the husband focuses on his work, and the wife is at home. With the children away, the options widen for women. Some wives consider working, but most husbands say, as Hiroko reported, "You may work if you wish, but make no changes in our home life at all." These conditions effectively rule out any working career for most women unless they have been able somehow to keep up contacts or part-time work through the previous stages. In general, women continue the emphasis on their children, and plunge into PTA and school-related activities. The famous *kyōiku-mama*, or "education mother," is a woman who, as a result of coping during the previous stage with a denigrating or unsympathetic husband, plus a lack of confidence in her own abilities, is unable to make use in any other way of the widening options open to her.

The Realignment

The early years of Stage III find both partners entering "crunch" periods in other careers, which draw off time and emotion from one's career as husband or wife. Becoming a mother forces working wives

into unemployment. Even those who previously were specialist housewives now must divide their attention between baby and husband. Japanese middle-class motherhood is characterized as "being nailed in the
house," cut-off from social contacts, and occupied with the drudgery of
household routine. Husbands complain of a wife's constant nagging for
money—an all too common behavioral trait.

With time, the demands of work begin to increase and, as the husband begins to rise on the promotional ladder, his attention to wife and
family is seen to decrease accordingly (Nakane 1970:122). The meaning
attached to a man's occupational niche carries, in addition to the life-
time commitment, a loyalty to the organization first and family second,
just as in the past it was first to his lord before his family. Accompanying
the allegiance to his employer is another commitment to a small work-
based social group within which the self develops and whose interaction
spills over into the after work hours (Nakane 1970:120–130).

An ambitious man faces a critical advancement period at this stage.
While we have no similar data for white-collar workers, Cole (1971)
found for blue-collar workers that the crucial period begins around age
thirty—or about the seventh or eighth year of employment. Increasing
age brings stronger competition, which culminates with worker interest
in promotion to foreman at around age thirty-five. For white-collar
workers we might assume that the peak comes a few years later. Cole
found for blue-collar workers, and I found for my sample of white-collar
workers, that the work-career crunch period overlaps the period of
starting a family and having pre-school age children, Stage III in the
paradigm. In order to advance at work the husband must shift his focus
from home to work, for advancement carries with it the burden of full
commitment.

Middle-class Japanese men can find a great deal of symbolic support
for a withdrawal from their families. The mass media depict nagging
wives, and husbands who react by disconnecting themselves from their
families in favor of work and its associated group. The man's work-
based group places great demands on him to produce, and it also makes
great social demands and enforces a stereotype of maleness. One is not
a man unless he is free—not encumbered by attentiveness to a wife. My
husband found in the work group in which he participated that any
attempt to telephone his wife before embarking on an evening of drinking was treated derisively. He was told that American men are not masters of their homes and wives as Japanese men are. Calls to a wife are
made later, in front of the group, at the bar, when the act is a *fait accom-
pli,* and where group support encourages assertive behavior.

From the male point of view the wives are to blame for forcing them
to withdraw from the home. A male informant recounted how an old

college intimate, Shin, described his career of separation. After having met and fallen in love at a university, Shin and his wife had, in a few years of marriage, become distant. They had frequent arguments over money. A baby helped ease the strain for a time, but Shin's wife continued to nag about money though he was endeavoring to save for their future. Finally deciding, "What the hell," Shin started playing golf, bought a car, and did what *he* wanted to do. In his view, he could never do enough, so he decided, "Why bother?" My informant added that his own elder brother had followed a similar career.

> At the beginning he was a typical sort of guy. He devoted all of his time to family and wife. He came home right after work at five, and didn't go out with his group because his wife was at home. This lasted five years—he made it last . . . Now he has changed.

An important factor which influences whether the husband or the wife will take the initiative to realign the relationship is the asymmetry of alternatives open to each. The husband may decide to opt out of the marriage in favor of work, or alternatively to devote himself to his home and family—termed "my-home-ism" and looked on somewhat derisively (Morris 1972). Most men choose to dedicate energy and self-development to the arena of work. But whichever choice a man makes, his wife must react to it and cope with it, for she has no real alternatives once she has a baby. As most women see it, Japanese men are too poor to pay alimony, and no one wants a wife with children; further, employers are not favorably disposed toward married women, let alone mothers. Thus the couple are differentially willing or able to engage in acts which change the structure of the marital relationship (Denzin n.d.). While the family is young, a woman has only the alternatives of total devotion to children, and/or a parallel withdrawal from her spouse.

Realignment Dynamics

As the husband begins to feel the buildup of tension created by the demands of work and his peers, he reacts at home in ways that facilitate his withdrawal, or as Goffman (1952) terms it, he does "de-courting." Goffman describes the dynamics of how a "mark" may be "cooled out"; the involuntary loser in a situation being finessed into accepting disappointment, change of self-concept, finally compromising and carrying on. The one who does the "cooling" protects himself from guilt by rationalizing that the mark is at fault, or perhaps is not worthy of the attention. The following discussion tries to show how a wife—the mark—is made to accept realignment and is cooled out—accepts, without rancor, a relationship where both she and her husband view him as a "lodger" in their home.

One method for achieving distance without also creating undue rancor is to make oneself a problematic performer so that fellow interactants are relieved when one is absent (Denzin n.d.). With time, and the demands of work, Japanese middle-class husbands have few periods when they actually meet with the family for focused interactions. These cluster around the routine features of the domestic order: meals, dressing, returning home, and bed. Akiko describes a situation in which her husband's questionable arrival makes mealtime problematic:

> I don't know whether he will be back early for dinner or not. I want him to tell me, it is my greatest wish. He says it is impossible to let me know. I don't understand why it is impossible. I have to cook and it is difficult. We have dinner two to three times a week together. I don't necessarily want more, but I *want to know* when they will be.

While at home, many husbands make themselves problematic by calling into question their wife's competence, by being critical of how she manages the house, or by denigrating her or her stand-in-objects (Goffman 1952). Yōko says, "Usually he is angry. I move too slowly, and he likes a woman who moves quickly." Yukiko's husband always claims to be able to cook or clean better than she. He jokes to his sons, "Look at your mother as an example, never marry anyone like her."

Many wives attempt to maintain their pre-marital friendships by talking on the telephone. A wife's long sessions on the telephone are a focal point for criticism and denigration. Husbands all say their wives use it "as a toy." One husband went so far as to claim his wife was possessed by a telephone demon. Akiko says, "My husband says the phone is not for enjoying; it is only for business. But I enjoy it." Few husbands recognize the telephone to be, as Hiroko said, "A young mother's only relaxation."

Disruption of daily routines also is manifested in staged outbursts. Akiko relates:

> Every morning he doesn't put on his jacket. Every morning—on purpose. He asks me to bring it to him at the door before he leaves for work. I ask him why he does it? He says "It is not my work, it is your work."

In another instance Yuriko told of a common occurrence in her home:

> We have breakfast at 8:30, and Ichirō is sleeping. Then I get dressed to go somewhere. And just when I am leaving, he demands, "I want a cup of coffee."

These two instances of a husband's problematic behavior can be viewed as institutionalized within Japanese society to the extent that they have linguistic labels which are commonly recognized. When Akiko told the story about her husband and his jacket, several women commented independently that he was doing *amaeru*. And Yuriko related her episode as a clear example of a particular type of behavior: "I would tell him, you are being very *teishu kampaku* this morning," she said. I feel that the two terms are related, and a semantic discussion is necessary before we look at their meaning within an interactional framework.

Amae and Teishu Kampaku

Takeo Doi views *amae* as a structural feature in Japanese society which colors most interpersonal relationships. *Amaeru*, a concept for which we have no word in the West, is an active verb which designates the seeking or causing of oneself to be loved, nurtured, and indulged by others. It is an active attempt to make oneself into a passive love object. Doi sees *amae* in its idealized form as the relationship between mother and infant. But (as seen in Stage I) it often is encouraged and indulged between adults such as superior/inferior, and our major concern, between men and women.

Teishu kampaku can be roughly translated as "petty tyrant." Like *amae*, it has no simple equivalent in English. It is a behavioral concept which must be viewed within an interactional context. The term categorizes male behavior which demands services, attention, and indulgence by women in an authoritarian manner, with the expectation of being obeyed. Being teishu kampaku (from here referred to by the abbreviation TK) can range from making mild demands to bring tea, to behavior which is currently designated as "male chauvinism" by feminists. TK behavior is one overt manifestation of the superior/inferior male to female relationship in Japanese society, for it is never seen in its obverse. But it has analogues for other Japanese behavioral subunits which involve junior-senior relationships. Though the behavior is personally objectionable to most women, because it is labelled, normal, and even typical, it is somewhat de-emotionalized. Yuriko says, "When I say Ichirō is teishu kampaku, other women can laugh with understanding."

Because TK behavior is viewed as normal there are institutionalized ways of dealing with it. Vogel terms the way women cope with TK, as "the art of husband management" (1963:200–203). He likens a wife's treatment of her husband to that of her eldest son. Waller describes how the insightful member of a marriage is kept subordinated by the very fact of being insightful, thereby assuming the burden of adjustment. He sees the control of the relationship, at a cost of mutuality, going to that partner who ruthlessly and without sensitivity does as he wishes (Waller 1938:355–357). By means of his TK behavior the husband makes himself a problematic performer within the order of the home. He must be watched, and therefore cannot be relied upon (Goffman 1970:377).

TK behavior also has meaning outside of the domestic order. When a man calls his wife from a bar and asserts his independence, he is being TK to her, but is seen as virile by his fellows. TK thus can be viewed as an aspect of what it means to be a man in Japan—a Japanese form of *machismo*. Yōko related a story that points up the importance of this image:

> A friend of mine was recently married. Her husband made her promise one thing before they got married. "Please allow me to to be teishu kampaku outside the house. You can do anything at home—even if I don't want you to, you can do it. But don't do it outside our home."

In another instance Yuriko says:

> When we visit my inlaws Ichirō pretends he is really teishu kampaku. For Ichirō's parents he is the first son, so he must be teishu kampaku, that is the right way. It is serious business.

The fact that acting out of TK behavior relates to qualities of maleness is recognized by both men and women. When in the course of a group discussion Yuriko complained extensively about her husband being TK, the other women told me she was really boasting (*norokeru*, "to boast about one's sweetheart") about what a man he was. David Plath reports that one woman's neighbor inquired if her husband was adopted, since he was so kind to her in public.

In addition to its other manifestations, TK behavior may also be viewed as a peculiarly male manifestation of amae. Thus when Kenzō demands Akiko to help him with his jacket he is being TK in his expectation that she will do it, but in addition he is showing amaeru, as our discussion group pointed out when Akiko told the story.

When a wife speaks of her husband as her eldest son, because she has to deal artfully with TK behavior, she is commenting on having shifted to a mother/child relationship with him. The wife may not like this realignment of status, but when potentially deviant or disruptive behavior can be de-emotionalized by viewing it as normal and thus routine, it is perhaps more acceptable and easier to cope with (Denzin n.d.). By means of TK behvaior a man is able to achieve a transition from lover to quasi-son while at the same time maintaining and reinforcing male authority. This maneuver places a woman in the position of resenting male chauvinism, but understanding TK behavior as an expression of dependency and, by implication, love. Doi explains that thoughtless demands made via amae behavior are evidence that there is the most love and interdependence within the family since amae flows freely and without concern for others (1973:41).

Men are able to resolve the conflicting pulls of work and home on themselves by being problematic performers, upsetting household routine through criticism, denigration, and TK behavior to the extent that their wives would just as soon not have them at home. The following quotes express the resignation that comes with acceptance of routinized problematic behavior:

> I am a "good wife." . . . I used to complain when I was young [the speaker is 34] about my husband's activities, but now I never complain.

> I think it is easier to live in Tokyo than in the United States if your husband is teishu kampaku. In America he comes home at 5:30, but in Japan he doesn't come until after 7.

Tokyo's thousands of restaurants with their all-male clientele are a testament to the uniformity of structure which evolves in middle-class marriages. After the early years of marriage most men eat only breakfast and Sunday meals in their homes, the rest of the time they eat at work or with work companions in public bars and restaurants.

Détente is not simply a unilateral phenomenon. Husbands make the domestic routine difficult without replacing it with anything but their absence or continual problematic behavior. The wives cope with the withdrawal but also display more subtly a parallel withdrawal. As Yōko and Yukiko express it,

> I don't do more than the minimum tasks expected of a wife. I don't complain about my husband's behavior outside of our home. Therefore, I think he is grateful to me.

> I am a bad wife. . . . My husband usually goes while I'm still in bed in the morning. I prepare his tea for him, but I don't pour it. I usually go to bed by 12, so sometimes I don't see my husband for two days. Kazuko and my husband meet each other at the bus stop. . . . I think I might not be able to recognize my husband unless she tells me what he is wearing.

The implication of many of these examples is that the men have been more successful in placing a wedge between themselves and the wives than they ultimately desire. Wives can and do engage in similar acts. Many refuse to entertain for their husbands.

> When my husband works at home I don't do anything for him. He wants me to bring tea or something, but I don't let that bother me because I don't want to.

Akiko talks on the telephone, though it annoys her husband:

> I enjoy the telephone with one ear, and with the other listen to my husband's complaints. My husband tells the children "Make Momma stop," but I don't listen to them either.

Just as their husbands receive support from their work group, so women draw upon friends, female siblings, and neighbors. Many a woman turns to her mother as a source of concern, support, and companionship. I see this as a parallel to the husband's repositioning of himself into a parent/child relationship vis-a-vis his wife. Through an intimate mother/married-daughter tie, women too are able to maintain or return to an amae relationship. Doi (1973) sees this as a basic need in Japan. Even their children observe this return to a Stage I relationship, as in Sumi's case where they say, "Why are you like a child when you talk with grandma?"

Remedial Acts

The détente which evolves is built upon mutual needs that husband and wife alone can fulfill for one another. Their mutual separation is modified and softened by remedial acts, both joint and solitary, which help to create some unity as well as to reinforce the underlying sentiment which persists. Every train station is surrounded by cake and fruit shops at which husbands can be seen, late at night, buying gifts to carry home as tokens of thought or appeasement. Sunday has become father's day, a time for outings as a family or for children to be alone with their fathers. Caudill (1970) sees these activities as evidence for an intensification of marital relationships, but I see them as an effort to maintain ties despite the separation of spouses.

Most women call their husband, "my closest friend," one with whom they can discuss major family problems, purchases, or plans. Underlying their distance is a bond of affection, perhaps based on amae. For the husband, the family and his wife represent the arena in which amae can flow freely. She allows him a freedom he cannot find in group interactions; and though disengaged he must make some effort to maintain her goodwill in order to sustain his dependency (Doi 1973). Some of her resentment might come from wishing that their relationship, at times, was more than the amae structured, quasi-parental nature.

The paradox of the entire situation is that once the husband achieves the repositioning which allows him freedom, once he opts out, he cannot come back. A common saying of women who have been through the realignment is, "How fortunate it is to have a husband who is healthy—and at work." Once his TK behavior is accepted as normal, he must go on producing it to maintain the status quo, and he can do little or knows little else to do, through time. Middle-class Japanese today have few alternative models in their behavioral repertoire for mutuality between spouses.

TK as Love

Until a man marries, the dependency relationships he has all involve amae flowing from senior to junior. After marriage, he is placed in the awkward position of finding himself dependent on one who is junior to him by virtue of being female, a wife, and younger. Nothing culturally gives him an option of looking weak in relation to her. If we are to believe Doi that amae and its needs are a lifelong bent, the husband is not only torn between family and work, but put into a status equality position with one who is his chief source of amae.

Thus during the courtship and wooing of Stage II we don't know the extent to which a man is building a foundation of good will in order that he may openly express dependency in later years. TK is an expression of dependency. If we are to grant respect for the Japanese dependency pattern described by Doi as love, then, TK behavior also is an expression of love.

In the United States where the feminist movement has raised female consciousness nationally, TK behavior—deliberate assertion of authority by virtue of being male—would lead to an emotionally charged interaction. The receiver, particularly if she is middle or upper class, would feel that such behavior is personally insulting to her as a woman. However, this raises an issue well worth further comparative study. The characteristics which I find associated with white-collar marriages in Japan seem to be associated more often with *blue*-collar marriages in the West (Bott 1957; Gans 1962; Young and Wilmott 1957).

In Japan, however, the fact that TK behavior is not only expectable but typical, has caused it to be seen as a nonemotional and understandable aspect of maleness. Therefore women in Japan come to feel personally not threatened, are not emotionally aroused, by "male chauvinist" behavior on the part of their husbands. In order to maintain harmony within their homes Japanese women cope with TK behavior and indulge their husbands in amae. While not falling into a definition of love as epitomized in a Shakespearean sonnet, TK behavior as expression of dependency must be viewed as a manifestation of love. Love then is at the root of maintaining the status quo in male/female interpersonal relations in Japan. When people ask me, "How do Japanese married women stand it?" I must answer, "Out of love."

10

Language and Behavior in Japan: The Conceptualization of Personal Relations

Takao Suzuki

Words for Self; Words for Others

Whenever a Japanese holds a conversation there is always one critical question which he must confront. That task is to make quite clear just who is talking to whom. If one asks a native speaker of English or French what word a speaker uses to indicate himself, he will uniformly get the answer, "I," or, "je." Most European languages are identical in this respect, so that the formulae "first person = speaker"; "second person = addressee," still have validity today. And Japanese scholars, based on this approach, have come to believe that there are multiple Japanese personal pronouns: First person = *watakushi, boku, ore . . . ;* second person = *anata, kimi, omae . . .*

But the Japanese situation, in fact, is completely different from that in the European languages.

Upon examination it becomes clear that although the Japanese use so-called personal pronouns, we also use many other words in conversation to identify speaker and addressee. For example, in many families today fathers identify themselves in conversation with their children as *otōsan* (father-polite) or *papa.* But if that same man who calls himself "papa" to his children is, let us say, a schoolteacher, then he will probably call himself *sensei* (teacher) when he is talking to his pupils in school. And should he find a lost child crying by the roadside, he will like as not call himself *ojisan* (uncle; general term for male adults when addressed by children), and say something like, "Stop crying, now. Ojisan will see that you get home all right."

The same may be said for modes of identifying the addressee in a conversation. In the last example of the man who found the lost child,

Reprinted from *Japan Quarterly* 23, no. 3 (1976): 255–266.

he might well have said, "Oniichan (big brother, endearing), stop cry-ing," and the child could just as well have answered, "Does Ojichan (mister) know where I live?" When looked at this way, words for identi-fication of speaker and addressee in Japanese conversations are more complex than generally thought. Personal pronouns are, if anything, in the minority.

I have decided to call the phenomenon of speakers using different words to indicate themselves "speakers' linguistic self-definition." Lin-guistic self-definition constitutes a determination of the speaker's loca-tion of himself along the axis of language. Further, I call the speaker's behavior in choosing a word to identify the addressee, "linguistic other-definition." This too sets a linguistic coordinate, and, in tandem with linguistic self-definition, serves to confirm linguistically the human rela-tionship involved.

In the past the existence of numerous personal pronouns in Japanese has been dealt with as a part of respect language, and there was at one time a movement to seek to explain them as of vestiges of a feudal status system. However, I have tried to see this question from the rather differ-ent standpoint of socio-linguistics, not merely as a question of personal pronouns, as already noted, but rather to deal with it comprehensively, in relationship to such hitherto ignored vocabulary categories as kinship terms, status and occupational terms. Moreover, I have tried not to remain simply within the framework of the Japanese language in study-ing this question. But I have tried to make comparisons and contrasts with similar phenomena in the European languages, Turkish, Arabic, and the languages of the Eurasian subcontinent. I have thus been able to point out several interesting problems, such as the characteristics of the mode of conceptualizing human relationships, a uniquely Japanese mode, I think, in which the psychological tendency is to assimilate the self into the other (addressee), resulting in identification of views of both self and addressee. This analysis makes it clearer than ever before how thoroughly inseparable are these psychological factors from the struc-ture of language itself.

Rules for Self-Specifiers and Other-Specifiers

I have conducted a study of how an individual Japanese conducts lin-guistic self-definition and linguistic other-definition in conversations with the various people surrounding him (subject male). In the discus-sion which follows I shall call words by which the speaker indicates him-self "self-specifiers" and those by which he indicates his partner in con-versation as "other-specifiers." (For the current purposes we shall omit third parties from the discussion.)

Figure 1 is modeled on a hypothetical 40-year-old male elementary

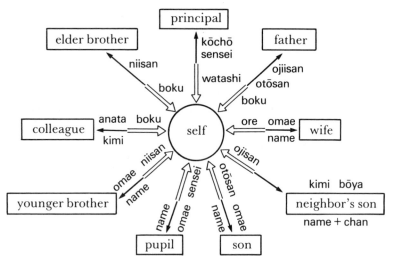

Figure 1

school teacher. It is not a complete set of specifiers, but represents responses to the question, "What do you usually say in this situation?" In those cases where multiple responses were offered for the same situation (i.e., the same category of speech partner) I have selected only the first, instant response. In this example we find seven self-specifiers: "watakushi" (I, formal), "boku" (I, informal), "ore" (I, intimate & vulgar), "ojisan" (uncle), "otōsan" (father), "sensei" (teacher), and "niisan" (elder brother). Besides the second person pronouns "anata" (you, formal), "kimi" (you, informal), "omae" (you, intimate & vulgar), we find as other-specifiers the person's name, "ojiisan" (grandfather/old man), "otōsan," and "niisan," among others.

As a result of a survey of models representing persons of various ages, statuses, and occupations, I have been able to compose a fairly comprehensive set of rules for the use of self-specifiers and other-specifiers. Most basic are the contrasting concepts of superior and inferior (subordinate) status. When we consider the various phenomena of respect language in Japanese this is quite natural. There is indeed a marked vertical polarization apparent in the use of interpersonal relations terminology. In order to simplify the explanation I have graphically represented a set of intrafamilial vertical relationships in figure 2. Persons of generations older than oneself are superiors, while persons of the same generation are divided into superior and inferior status *vis-à-vis* oneself according to whether they are older or younger. It is possible to differen-

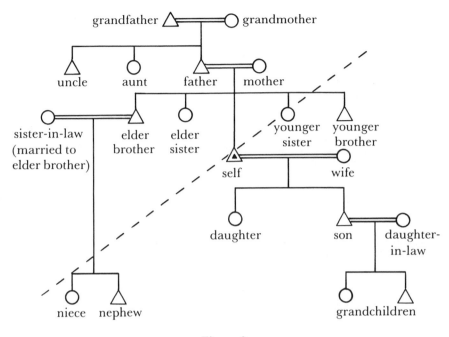

Figure 2

tiate Japanese interpersonal relations broadly into intrafamilial and extrafamilial categories, but in general the principles of the intrafamilial system are merely expanded to form those of the extrafamilial system, so we will for the moment limit the discussion to intrafamilial situations.

Intrafamilial (Intrarelational) Self-Specifiers and Other-Specifiers

A. The speaker (self) cannot address other relatives above his locus in the family by means of personal pronouns. He is not permitted, for example, to address his father as "anata" or "kimi," and the same strictures apply when he addresses, say, his elder brother.

B. The speaker addresses people above his station in the family, as a rule, by use of terms denoting their relationship to him. But he does not address people below himself by the terms for those relationships. He would not, for example, call his younger brother vocatively with a phrase like, "Hey! Otōto (younger brother)!" nor would he ask pronominally his daughter, "Where is Musume (daughter) going?"

C. The speaker may not address people located above himself by their names alone (unless suffixed by an appropriate kin term), but may so address those located below him.

D. Speakers, especially female speakers, may, in addressing people above themselves, use their own names as self-specifiers, but may not do so in conversation with people located below them. Thus, Yoshiko (daughter) may say to her mother, "Momma, Yoshiko hates that," but her mother may not use her own name in a similar situation in conversation with her daughter.

E. In conversation with relations below himself the speaker may use as a self-specifier the term indicating his own relationship to the addressee, but a junior speaker may not do this in speaking to a senior one. In a conversation between brothers, for example, then, the elder brother may specify himself by saying "niisan," but the younger brother may not use "otōtochan" to indicate himself.

In these five principles, the boundaries of superior and inferior are congruent, and comprise all the rules for self- and object-specification among the members of a family or relational group. Of course, these are principles, and some families may not comply with all of these, for whatever reason. For example, in recent years we have observed the phenomenon, in urban families, of sisters of approximately the same age addressing each other by name alone.

Empathetic Identification

There is a further interesting phenomenon in the system of intrafamilial appellation in the Japanese family, a phenomenon which we may call the fictive use of relational terminology. There are many families in Japan today in which, for example, a wife will address her husband as "papa," or "otōsan." The reason I call these a fictive use of relational terminology is that they do not accurately reflect the relationship between speaker and addressee.

There is a consistent underlying structure in this phenomenon, in which the speaker views the addressee, not from his own position, but by empathetic identification of himself with a third party.

We shall try to explain this using the example of a wife who addresses her husband as "papa." From the wife's position, of course, he can only be her husband, but she is empathetically identifying with the position of her children. From the children's point of view her husband is their father. From the position of the wife, identifying with the children, she can call also her husband "papa." And when an older woman calls her own daughter "mama," she is doing nothing less than identifying with her own grandchildren.

Intrafamilial appellations in the Japanese family are generally structured around the self-identification of the younger members of the family. Thus, when a mother addresses her older children with words embodying the concepts of elder siblings, "oniichan," "oneechan," it is rendered possible only by her empathy with the youngest of her children. Intrafamilial appellations are, after all, reciprocal. One man's father is another man's son, and another's younger brother.

But in the Japanese family the standards for relational terminology tend to harmonize with the position of the children, and in fact with the very youngest of those, so that relational terminology tends to become absolute, and even to take on certain aspects of proper nouns. A grandfather, for example, will be called "ojiisan" not only by his grandchildren, but by his children and his wife as well, and will probably identify himself as "ojiisan," too. The word "boku" (I, informal), also tends to have absolute value. Families with very young sons tend to call them "boku," and although other adults around that child might as well call him "omae" or "bōya" when viewing him from their own point of view, they empathize with the child's position, so that they, too, become "boku," and it is with this term that they call him.

Extrafamilial Self-Specifiers and Other-Specifiers

The principles for the use of intrafamilial (relational) self-specifiers and other-specifiers tend simply to be expanded for application to use in extrafamilial situations in the society at large. Some examples: 1. As a rule we do not address our teachers or other superiors with personal pronouns like "anata"; 2. It is common to address superiors with a title or status name like "sensei," "shachō" (company president), or "kachō" (section-chief = supervisor). But teachers can not address their pupils, "Hey, pupil!"; 3. The dividing line between superior and inferior is fairly strictly observed in regard to the use of names (surnames). In addressing a teacher or superior at work it is rare simply to use the surname, it being the rule to affix some status or positional term, as in "Tanaka-sensei"; 4. It is acceptable for an inferior to use his surname alone, as in "Chief, leave this job to Yamamoto (me)," but the reverse is not possible; 5. In regard to specifying oneself by title, again, a teacher may speak of himself as "Sensei" in addressing his pupil, but a pupil may not identify himself as "seito" (pupil).

Many other specific examples could be offered, but as a general statement it is fair to say that the principles which govern intrafamilial usage are also applicable in extrafamilial situations. The same is true for fictive usage. An adult may address a child on the street as "oniichan," because he has posited a younger child and identified with that imaginary child; he calls the child before him "elder brother" from the fictive child's viewpoint. No other hypothesis can explain how he could address a child far younger than himself with a term denoting the concept of "elder brother."

Similarly, when a doctor or teacher calls a child's mother "okaasan," he clearly does not mean his own mother. Rather, he defines the addressee thus precisely because he empathizes with the child.

A Structural Analysis of Self-Specifiers and Other-Specifiers
Self-Definition from the Viewpoint of the Addressee or Third Parties

We have noted above that speakers of English, French, German and other European languages almost invariably identify themselves in conversation by using first person pronouns. But all the first person pronouns in these languages can be traced back to the same source. The German "ich," English "I," French "je," Russian " Я," and Latin "ego" may all be regarded as differently shaped branches sprouting from the same tree. They are no more than the various transformations of one and the same word (in the pre-historic mother tongue). That is, the first person pronouns in all these European languages have preserved their original character for several thousands of years. In similar manner, the first person pronouns of the Semitic languages (Arabic, Hebrew) and of the Turkic languages (Turkish, Tatar), or for that matter, in Chinese as well, remain qualitatively essentially unchanged since antiquity. The function of first person pronouns in these languages is simply to indicate verbally that the self is the speaker. The act of a speaker pronouncing, for example, the Latin word "ego," is the verbal indication that, "The person speaking now is none other than me."

It is a characteristic of this type of linguistic behavior that the speaker's linguistic self-identification is conducted autonomously and independently, without reference to the addressee or to surrounding circumstances. Moreover, we can even say that prior to recognition of the addressee, there is self-recognition. This is because it is only on the postulation of a linguistically confirmed "ego" that one obtains a linguistic expression for the "tu" of the addressee. The order of consciousness, then, is ego → tu (in English, I → you).

In Japanese, however, there is no other way to account for the structure of personal pronouns except by precisely the reverse analysis. Let us consider for example the case of a person who calls himself "papa" within the family. In order for him to define himself linguistically as "papa" he must arrive at the linguistic consciousness, first, of having a child, and second, that his addressee is that child. Only upon empathetically assimilating his own position into that of the child he is addressing can he begin the definition of himself as "papa." From anyone else's position he is neither "papa," nor anything else, so he can't be identifying himself from the position of any other specific addressee. This is what I mean when I say that in Japanese, unlike the European languages, definition of the addressee precedes self-definition. (cf. Baby talk in English)

The situation of a schoolteacher calling himself "sensei" when he speaks to his students is structurally identical. Or, in terms of fictive usage, when someone addressing a child he or she does not know refers to himself or herself as "ojisan," or "oneesan," he or she is first considering his or her position as viewed from the standpoint of the child. This is the basis for my assertion that, in comparison with the absolute self-definition of the European languages, where the speaker is defined first as an active language user, irrespective of the identity or even the presence of an addressee, linguistic identification in Japanese is, on the whole, object-dependent.

This structure fits even when a Japanese uses a so-called personal pronoun as a self-specifier. In general an adult male Japanese makes the operational choice between the (first-person pronouns) "watakushi" and "boku," "boku" and "ore," to accord with the situation and the addressee. This appears to be a set of choices reflecting power differences and gradations of social distance. Even so, since he chooses only after determining whom he is addressing, it is still true that his linguistic self-definition is object-dependent. Seen in this light we may even say that the Japanese self is in an undefined, open-ended state until the appearance and determination of a specific addressee. This may well be the explanation for the unease and discomfort Japanese experience when dealing with people we cannot define.

In any language, of course, the adjustment of speech to accord with the addressee or the situation is a matter of degree, and all languages have variations in terms of address to fit the social position of the addressee. But I do not think there are very many languages in the world where, as in Japanese, one actually alters the linguistic definition of the self to accord with changed conditions. There seems to be a slightly similar phenomenon in Vietnamese, Thai, and a few other Southeast Asian languages, but no detailed research has been done on them.

Indication and Confirmation of Tangible Roles

I shall here take the term "role" to mean the concept of a specific behavioral pattern generally accepted as normal within the social context, of a person with a specific combination of status and characteristics. For example, soldiers, teachers, or policemen all engage in occupation-specific behavior, and other people expect this behavior of them. We see quite different behavior patterns in children and in old people, and so their roles are different. Thus, there are many, many roles in a given society.

There are roles which have a relatively long duration, such as the congenital distinction of gender, status in societies which preserve distinctions of class, as well as all sorts of occupationally or familially determined roles, as in the situation between parent and child. On the other hand, there are many and variegated relatively short-lived roles, such as in the interaction of a shop-clerk and customer, or of the fellow-passengers on a train, or of the speaker and addressee in a conversation. When we bring this concept of role into the analysis of linguistic self-definition and other-definition the differences between Japanese and other languages, especially the European languages, become even more clear.

As we saw above in the cases of Latin and English, speakers first express themselves by using first person pronouns, and then call the addressee by use of second person pronouns. But as the conversation progresses and the person who had been the addressee begins to speak, he now uses the first person for himself, while the original speaker becomes the second person. This transfer between first and second person pronouns is a clear demonstration that the use of the first person pronoun at root states that "The person who is speaking now is myself," that is, it is the linguistic expression of the speaker's role, while the second person pronoun says to the addressee, "You are the listener at this point in the conversation." Looked at it in this way personal pronouns appear quite naturally as characteristic expressions of the roles in a conversation.

Personal pronouns in Latin and English, then, have no relation to the tangible characteristics of the speaker or the listener (status, age, sex, etc.), having instead the sole function of expressing the quite abstract roles of active or passive members in a scene of linguistic behavior. Just as the actors in a theater change masks or make-up to fit the role they happen to be playing at the moment, as the role changes, so does the linguistic mask. In fact, the reason why this class of words is called *personal* pronouns in European languages is that they are pronouns which possess the characteristics of a *persona*, or a player's mask. The interpersonal relationships visible in the interchangeable Latin "ego" → "tu" transformation, or the English "I" → "you" transformation is correspondingly symmetrical. It is true that French, German and many other European languages in recent centuries have developed a double second person pronoun system, thus deviating somewhat from the model laid out above, but the essential structure of personal pronouns is as I have described it.

Let us now see how a Japanese conversation looks when analyzed from the point of view of role, taking a conversation between a father and son for a model. A father will generally call himself "papa" or "otō-san" when addressing his son. He usually calls his son either "omae" (you), or calls him by name. The son will also call the father "papa" or "otōsan," but he will not use pronouns or his father's name. He will commonly refer to himself as "boku" (I) or, on occasion, use his own name. As even this single set of examples makes plain the structure of

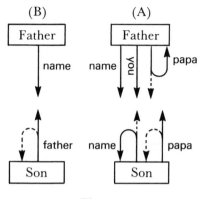

Figure 3

self-specifiers and other-specifiers in Japanese conversations is in principle asymmetrical.

The father's act of calling himself "papa" can be taken as linguistic confirmation of his role as father as seen from the viewpoint of the person addressed. Furthermore, although this is indirect and implicit, he is thereby assigning to his addressee the subordinate role of his own child. This is because the concept of "father" is only established in contradistinction to the concept of "child" (son, daughter), and so it is only in addressing his own children that a father may express himself linguistically as "father."

Similarly, when the son calls his father "papa" there is a two-layered process of role confirmation involved. First, he is directly and explicitly assigning and confirming the parent role of his addressee. But at the same time he is implicitly expressing his acknowledgment of his willingness to assume the role of the addressee's son. Furthermore, the father's use of the son's name to address the son in conversation expresses his assumption of the superior role *vis-à-vis* his addressee (son), and the fact that only the father can use personal pronouns in conversations between them strengthens confirmation of his superior status role. These relationships have been represented graphically in figure 3.

As the diagram shows, in a conversation between a father and son, confirmation by the father of his superior role is continuously expressed directly and explicitly by three different linguistic means, and indirectly and implicitly by a fourth. The child confirms his inferior position by two direct-explicit means and two indirect-implicit means, also for a total of four. Thus in any conversation between these two there are in operation eight different procedures for mutal role confirmation and role assignment. Of course, this does not represent the full range of potential self-specifiers and other-specifiers for these two people. For simplicity of explanation I have here chosen to take up only those terms which bear directly on the question of role confirmation (figure 3-A).

A conversation between speakers of English will serve as a good contrast. In most cases, unlike Japanese, conversations are conducted with the "I" → "you" exchange described above. Thus the only times when confirmation of the roles of father and child come into play are when the father calls his child by name, or when the son calls his father "father," "daddy," etc. This is represented graphically in figure 3-B.

The role-confirming function inherent in a son calling his father "father" is precisely the same as that in Japanese, and has both the explicit and implicit meanings described above. However, unlike Japanese, in certain situations a father may call his son "son," as when the father feels a strong sense of identity with his son, or feels especially affectionate toward him. But this is a much more limited usage than is the son's use of "father" to address his father. And the point that normal usage permits only the father to use his addressee's name, and not the son, is exactly like Japanese usage, and serves as an explicit, direct confirmation of the father's superior role.

This analysis yields the information that as between a father and son in an English speaking society there are three linguistic forms of mutual role confirmation: two from the child's side, one direct and one indirect; and one direct method from the father's side. If we add in the extremely limited usage of a father addressing his son as "son," then two more methods may be included. When we compare this with the eight methods available for mutual linguistic role confirmation in the case of a Japanese conversation we get an idea just how much importance Japanese place on role.

Of course, there are also nonlinguistic means of role assignment and confirmation, so we are not free simply to take these linguistic differences and conclude that they represent the difference in attitudes toward role in the two societies as a whole. But to the extent that linguistic behavior is more articulate than other forms of behavior, it has a much more strongly explicit character, so that the determination of whether people regularly engage in linguistic confirmation or not when they enter into a relationship with another person is a powerful potential index of such differences.

The Relationship between the Structure of Language and Behavior Patterns

Fixed and Unified Roles

It is possible to analyze the determinants of role and status into two broad categories. The first, including age, sex and, in class societies, social status, are congenital, that is, they are given, and beyond the range of the individual's option to determine. The second set is those acquired characteristics gained by virtue of the individual's own strengths, and thus dependent on his or her will. Expanding this analysis, we can say that those personal relationships determined by blood are congenital, while those created by promise, contract, etc., are acquired. The relative importance placed on the former or latter set of characteristics varies with society and culture. Japan, which still gives favor to lifetime employment, promotion based on seniority, and male dominance/female submission, is a society which places greater value on congenital characteristics, standing in contrast to a society like the United States, in which distinctions of individual ability, occupation and even wealth are considered to be acquired characteristics.

However, leaving aside for the moment such objective distinctions as age and sex, many of the distinctions made between ascribed and acquired characteristics in a given society are in fact the result of interpretations made by that society. Thus the determination of just how a particular individual's character and circumstances will be analysed must be tested empirically. In the previous section I analysed Japanese linguistic behavior from the standpoint of role. Now I would like to analyse linguistically the question, "Do Japanese place greater stress on role as related to ascribed characteristics, or as related to acquired characteristics?" by reference to a few linguistic facts.

We have already noted the fact that most modern Japanese couples address each other with such terms as "papa" and "mama," or as "otō-san," "okāsan." But there are many couples who say that when they were first married they called each other by name, and the situation of the husband calling his wife by name, while she addressed him as "anata" (you) was most common. But no sooner do they have a child than they switch over to calling each other "papa," "mama," or "tōsan," "kāsan." That is, they start to use terms implying the concept of parentage. How should we analyse this phenomenon?

We may view the members of a marriage as having entered into a kind of contract. Since both the husband role and the wife role are roles taken by choice, we may look on them as having a consciously "played" aspect. So we may say that there is a certain instability in a marriage which has only a husband and wife who have not yet had a child. But when a child is born, then the wife becomes the child's mother, and the husband the child's father. These roles as father and mother are not elected, played roles, but given roles. For once one has become a person's father, he can no longer dissolve this relationship simply by his own will. The relationship between parent and child, at least in Japan, is regarded as of a higher order of stability than that between husband and wife. Therefore, by restructuring their relationship through the assigned relationship of father and mother of the child they have in common, a husband and wife try to enter into a more enduring and stable condition. May we not then interpret their behavior as reflecting their transformation into types subsumed by the appellations "father" and "mother"? If this analysis is correct, then Japanese parents behave more as father and mother of their children than they do as husband and wife, which is true, I think, when compared to the situation in the United States for example.

Americans are said to place more emphasis on autonomously chosen roles than on roles assigned without action of their own will, and in comparison to Japanese couples their appearance in the husband and wife roles is far more dominant. Their marriage starts with the exchange of rings symbolizing their mutual bond, and they expend great effort in the preservation of their husband-wife relationship. The constant exchange of terms of endearment, the exchanges of gifts on birthdays and wedding anniversaries, these are all nothing other than a ritual strengthening and reconfirmation of the contractual condition of marriage. So a decrease in the use of explicit terms of endearment comes to mean a breakdown of the marital condition itself. Japanese couples use practially no overt terms of endearment, and there are no such saccharine terms (to use anthropological jargon) like "honey," or "darling," which have attained a formalized place in the society. This is because for the Japanese the marital condition is not a dynamic, directly contractual personal relationship, preserved with constant reconfirmation of mutual affection. Rather, is it not a "given" relationship, through the medium of the unchanging static parent-child relationship, which is neither deniable nor dissoluble?

There is yet another characteristic Japanese behavior pattern which deserves attention in the context of a discussion of roles. As explained in the previous section, in our psychological make-up we tend to determine the self only on the basis of the determination of a specific, tangible addressee. It is for this reason that we dislike having to deal at one and the same time with two or more persons of differing character whose presence demands mutually contradictory, or even precisely opposite behavior.

At the height of the student demonstrations on campus there was a reflective mood among the faculty, with frequent discussion of the reform and improvement of the educational aspect, if not the research aspect, of the university. At that time I proposed as one partial solution that faculty members audit each other's courses. From the standpoint of both pedagogy and of knowledge, it seemed to me that there was much to be gained from professors, who are used to being king of the hill, to listen to the lectures of their colleagues, and that teachers, with their peers out in the audience would put forth their best efforts. I presented both of these desirable results as my overt reasons for the proposal.

The rebuttal to this proposal was very interesting. We teachers lecture in the classroom in order to educate students. But if our peers or superiors appear in the classroom the temptation will be to show off, and the lecture will turn into a technical research presentation of no immediate educational interest to the students. Since I have frequently seen professors at American and Canadian universities regard it as an honor to be asked by their colleagues for permission to sit in on their lectures, I could only believe that I had here hit upon another cultural difference.

North Americans treat colleagues, even senior colleagues, as students if they come to audit their classes. They address questions to them, and if the class happens to be a recital class, the auditing faculty member is assigned to recite. They do not bring their outside social position or personal relations into the classroom, and enter smoothly into the contractual relationship of teacher and pupil. The auditing professor, now treated like a student, questions and argues without restraint.

Things do not work this way in Japan. In a word, it simply becomes more difficult to conduct a class. This isn't simply a problem with colleagues. Things would be just as difficult if one's wife, children, or other family members were to appear. I know teachers who have had colleagues take over a class for them because their own child was in the classroom as a student. In the United States it's not just one's children; it is not even unusual for a wife to take a course her husband is teaching.

At such a time the Japanese is not simply embarrassed. He can't go on because the mutual role expectations of senior and junior colleague, peers, parent-child or husband-wife are fixed, and it is difficult to change roles to fit time and circumstances. If A and B are husband and wife then it is difficult to transform the relationship of the AB pair into that as between, say, teacher and pupil.

A teacher becomes anxious when a senior teacher is mixed in among his students. His role-definition and self-definition *vis-à-vis* his superior and his role-definition and self-definition *vis-à-vis* his students are on a collision course. Even linguistically, he is confronted with the problem of whether to call himself "boku" or "watakushi." If his wife is in the class then his problem is that much more difficult. For the private character of the Japanese marriage relationship is very strong, while in public they behave, as much as possible, as if there were no relationship between them. So it is that many Japanese men strongly dislike having their wives show up at their place of work, or phone them there. Their relationship to their wives is of a different order, a different nature, and is mutually irreconcilable with the relationships of the workplace.

In effect, relations between two specific Japanese are binomial and fixed. By comparison, interpersonal relations among Americans have a strongly polynomial aspect. It is precisely for this reason that a husband and wife may at times be student and teacher, friends, or even competitors. It is common for an American graduate student, after he received his doctorate, to call his former professors by their first names. This is because in America the concept of "colleague" is an equalitarian status concept superseding distinctions of senior and junior, age, scholarly attainment. By comparison, even today I cannot address the old professor who taught me at the university I graduated from more than twenty years ago as anything other than "sensei."

Thus, the fact that the roles for a given pair of Japanese tend to become fixed, and tend not to accept changes imposed by changes in place or the flow of time, cannot be unrelated to the fact that linguistic mutual definitions in Japanese possess too concrete a structure. Many are the old tales of the loyal retainer, assigned to teach the martial arts to his lord's son, who has incurred disfavor for failing to pull his punches. It is precisely because Japanese find it so difficult when a person of lower status is placed in a position of leadership that these stories have their appeal.

Special Japanese expressions like ". . . no kuse ni" ("And you call yourself a . . . !"), or ". . . rashiku" ("Like the . . . [he/she is].") are intimately linked to the psychological structure of fixed roles, a point which we will not take up here in detail in the interest of brevity.

The Meaning of Other-Dependent-Type Self-Definition

I have already noted that the other-dependent format in which the self is defined in relation to the addressee, only after having assimilated oneself into the addressee's position, is a characteristic of linguistic self-definition among the Japanese. The fundamental distinguishing characteristic as between Japanese and others, that Japanese tend easily to assimilate the observing self into the observed object, while in other cultures the distinction between self and other is *a priori*, has been noted before. But I do not believe that the inseparability of this psychological structure and linguistic structure has been pointed out heretofore.

There are many vocabulary items in Japanese which are built on this foundation of assimilation.

Terms which describe a person's character, such as "Sasshi ga yoi/warui" ("He's perceptive/unfeeling."), or "Ki ga kiku/kikanai" ("He's considerate/inconsiderate."), are extremely difficult to translate into European languages. But it is perfectly natural if one remembers that in other cultures besides Japan's it is the norm not to make suppositions about another's feelings until he has expressed his views or desires in language. Such terms as "unwelcome favor" ("arigata-meiwaku"); or "failing to recognize a favor unsought for" ("hito no ki mo shiranaide"), indicate that it is normal to attempt to pre-assess the addressee's feelings or wishes.

So it is only natural to call Japanese culture a "culture of anticipatory-perception," or a "culture of consideration." Because it is important to sympathize with one's addressee the function of language as a means to reconcile conflicting interests, or as a medium for the exchange of intentions between one individual and another, is held to a minimum. In the worst instance this type of communication can degenerate from trying to know what one's addressee is thinking, or guessing his feelings, to simply minding everyone else's business. But on the other side of the coin it also contains the potentiality for such expressions of the philosophy of the tea ceremony as, "Be circumspect with fellow guests." Taken beyond this, the psychological structure of object-assimilation has value in the very fact that it transcends the distinction between self and other. Thus it is that this structure links up with that rare phenomenon in the world, the spirit of what Doi Takeo (1971) has chosen to call "dependence." The high degree of cultural, racial and religious homogeneity which makes this sort of interpersonal interaction possible has been argued many times before and needs no repetition here.

In closing, I would simply like to add that, so long as the interaction is between Japanese people, in Japan, then whether one calls it "dependence," or "object-assimilation," it is precisely because this phenomenon is operative that problems do not arise. But only let a Japanese come into contact with someone else, someone who is not a Japanese, and this Japanese characteristic ceases to be functional. We, used to assimilation and dependency, expect to project ourselves onto the other, and expect him to empathize with us. We have great difficulty with the idea that so long as our addressee is not Japanese we can't expect to have our position understood without strong self-assertion. But establishing our own viewpoint or position before our addressee has understood it is not our forte. That is why Japan is always getting a late start in its foreign negotiations, whether diplomatic, political or economic. It is because we cannot place ourselves until we have gotten a reading of the overall situation.

So when Japanese, who aren't good at foreign languages, don't show their true ability in international conferences and scholarly meetings, it is less because of their language skills than because of the weak development of the will to express themselves linguistically to sufficient degree. It lies furthermore in the underdeveloped ability to stand apart from the position taken by another and at least assert oneself to the extent of saying, "This is where I stand at this moment."

11

Gift-Giving in a Modernizing Japan

HARUMI BEFU

Introduction

THE prevalence of gift-giving in Japan is well known. Even the casual visitor sojourning in Japan for a few weeks will find himself presented with a gift from his Japanese friends or business associates. The full-page ads of midyear-gift *(chūgen)* sales by major department stores, the rows of gift shops in any resort town, the displays of gift-wrapped presents in stores at railroad stations, these are among the innumerable indications of the extent to which the Japanese are involved in gift exchange. Although no one knows for sure how much the Japanese spend on gifts every year, since no adequate statistics are available, the figure is undoubtedly high.[1]

Indeed, gift-giving is a minor institution in Japan, with complex rules defining who should give to whom, on what occasions he should give, what sort of gift is appropriate on a given occasion, and how the gifts should be presented. To take an example, a properly wrapped gift for a happy occasion should bear an intricately folded decoration known as *noshi* (nowadays, however, it is enough to have its picture printed on the wrapping); but a gift on an inauspicious occasion would not have the decoration on the wrapping. This practice goes back to the days when *noshi* was a strip of abalone, which, when attached to a gift, indicated that the occasion did not call for abstention from meat owing to death or other misfortune in the family. It is for this reason that a dried fishtail or fin is used in some rural areas as a substitute. For the same reason, a gift of fish does not require a *noshi,* since the nature of the gift itself indicates that abstention is not necessary and that the occasion is a felicitous one (Japan, Nat'l Comm. for UNESCO 1958:950; Sakurada 1957; Segawa 1964:245; Yanagita 1940:249–274). Most Japanese, particularly young urbanites, are no longer aware of this origin of *noshi,*

Reprinted from *Monumenta Nipponica* 23 (1968): 445–456.

which indicates the extent to which gift-giving customs have changed. In this paper I wish to explore the origin of gift-giving in Japan and consider recent changes in it. I hope that this little exercise will help clarify the process and the present status of Japan's modernization.

Methodological Remarks

Reconstructing the past is not easy—even for a culture like Japan's which has a long written history—when the task is to outline the origin and development of a commonplace custom like gift-giving, which few literati and historians have thought worthy of documentation or study. Rather than to the historians and historical documents, then, we must turn to the folklorists and folk customs. As in so many instances, it has been the Yanagita school of folklore study that has contributed most in unraveling the past of the custom of gift-giving. To accomplish this, Yanagita and his students have had to analyze varied but similar and related gift-giving practices in many different regions of rural Japan, often in isolated communities and on offshore islands, to compare these variant practices, to dip into the etymologies of terms related to gifts and gift-giving, and to juxtapose past customs remembered by old-timers with present practices.

One major methodological problem that confronts us in using folklorists' data and interpretations concerns the temporal referent and sequence, a blind spot in folklore study which the anthropologist Eiichirō Ishida (1963) has noted in his sympathetic assessment of Yanagita's scholarly contributions. Folklorists, working almost exclusively with oral tradition and unrecorded folk practices, have generally been reluctant to specify the definite point in time for any event. They discuss events of the past in terms simply of the "past," without indicating the absolute time referent. Consequently, it is extremely difficult to work out a sequence of stages or of events leading up to the present.

What follows is a composite picture of how, in general, gift-giving practices have originated and developed in Japan over an undefined period of time, based in good part on the findings of folklorists and also on a comparison of rural and urban practices. Urban data were mostly obtained through the writer's own investigation.[2]

The Supernatural Past

The custom of offering foods to gods and other supernatural beings— still a common practice in Japan—may seem unrelated to our concern, but in fact is an appropriate starting point.[3] Examples are numberless. In many households today, rice is offered to family ancestors at the household altar every morning. Village Shinto shrines and roadside *jizō* shrines are offered glutinous rice cake and other foods from time to time. The New Year is the time to offer rice cake to the New Year's god. And so on. Folklorists have shown that such food offerings are historically related to *naorai*, the custom according to which gods and mortals shared foods together (Minzokugaku Kenkyūjo 1951:418–419). *Naorai* is now commonly understood to refer to the feast held after a religious ritual proper, but this is evidently a later modification. In the original form of *naorai*, offerings to gods were gifts to gods, and these gifts were returned by gods as their gifts for mortals to share with them, so that the mortals might partake of the divine power of the gods to whom gifts were originally offered (Sugira 1935:128–132; Yanagita 1940:191–197; Wakamori 1947:199–200). The symbolic significance of communal eating has been well argued by De Vos in his recent study of outcasteism (De Vos and Wagatsuma 1966:370–372). He argues that the abhorrence of commensalism with members of an outcaste group is an essential psychodynamic ingredient of outcasteism. For us, this abhorrence is simply the other side of the "deeply social act [of eating together] symbolizing a form of communion, whether it exists as part of a ritual or as part of the daily habits of life" (De Vos and Wagatsuma 1966:370–371).

The ritual importance of sake is also apparent, as the practice of offering it to gods is still very much alive. Originally, the sake was first offered to gods, and then shared by mortals in *naorai* (Shiibashi 1942). This custom is still alive in Shirakawa, Gifu Prefecture, where once a year *doburoku* (a type of raw sake) is prepared in a large tub, offered to the tutelary god of the village, and consumed communally by all villagers and also by visitors who wish to receive supernatural power from the local god.

The pervasive custom in Japan of giving the first crop of the field to neighbors and relatives is also derived from the past practice of offering the first fruits to gods, and thereafter sharing them among the community (Mogami 1935; Wakamori 1944:447–448). The word *otoshidama*, which nowdays refers to the New Year's present to children (usually money), also originally denoted offerings to the god of the New Year, which were later eaten by men as the god's gift (Kurata 1943:497–502).

It is because communion with supernatural beings was achieved primarily through commensality that offerings to gods were, and still are, largely foodstuff, and also that even now food is considered the traditional type of gift in Japan and that in fact it is the most popular type of gift (Sakurada 1954).

In the past, commensality was not only a device for transferring supernatural power to man, but also a means by which members of the community could partake in one another's power and be brought into a mystical union. After all, the gulf between mortals and gods was not felt to be great; what gods were capable of, men were capable of, too, to a lesser extent. Otherwise, how could men hold communion with gods in *naorai?* Indeed, because of the belief that men are simply less powerful gods, but still susceptible to magical contagion through commensality, it happened that when *naorai* came to be separated in time and place from the ritual proper, the feasting retained its supernatural efficacy. The belief in magical contagion accounts for the banquet held for a person of an unlucky or "calamitous" year *(yakudoshi)*, in which the combined power of all the guests was believed to dispel the danger of misfortune (Norbeck 1955:105–120). In addition to the magical function, such communal feasting of course served to reinforce the social solidarity of the group (Embree 1939:104; Wakamori 1944:447–448).

If magical power could be shared by mortals through a communal meal, as Yanagita has argued, it could also be shared by the giving and the receiving of a gift of food. For example, folk medicine practiced in many rural areas of Japan until recent years prescribes that a person suffering from an eye disease should go to houses in the neighborhood and beg for food (Yanagita 1935:101–129). By consuming food from families in which no one was suffering from the disease, one could absorb magical power from these families to help cure the disease. In fact, giving a food gift to a sick person—something frowned upon in the U.S. for medical reasons—was generally thought to be a way of giving the power of health inherent in the giver, so that the sick might recover from illness through the power of the healthy. Another custom related to gift-giving to a sick person is also based on the magical power of a food gift. Ordinarily, when a gift is given in Japan, the receiver returns a token gift, such as a box of matches or a bundle of paper, at the time the gift is made.[4] When the gift is to a sick person, however, the custom is not observed owing to the belief that such a return gift has the power of making the healthy person sick. The same belief in ritual pollution through commensality with a ritually impure person explains the customs of avoiding gifts from a person of an unlucky or calamitous year (Segawa 1964:228). The customs of giving food gifts to a newborn baby and of having a seven-year-old child solicit food from seven neighbors, which have been seen in many rural areas of Japan until recently, are also believed to be means of building up strength by "borrowing" power from others (Ōomachi 1935).

The Traditional Social Framework[5]

The folklorists' work on the supernatural origin of gift-giving has tended to give the impression that the origin of gift-giving in Japan was entirely magical and religious. To claim that gift-giving in Japan used to be entirely supernatural in its significance is to claim an unproven and probably false proposition. We have discussed the supernatural aspects of some gift-giving customs only because most of us know Japanese gift-giving in its secular forms. It is important to note that in rural Japan these gift-giving practices, whether supernatural or secular, were, and still are, imbedded in the traditional social structure, in which we find the household as a basic social unit, the values of *giri* and *on*, and the principle of social reciprocity. Let us examine the ways in which gift-giving is related to these elements of the traditional Japanese social organization. (I do not suggest that this social framework operates only in rural Japan. It is very much alive in urban Japan, too; but there one finds new social elements manifested in gift-giving practices, as we shall see later.)

The importance of the household as a basic social institution in Japan has been reiterated by generations of anthropologists, both Japanese and Western, and scarcely needs emphasis here. Suffice it to add that even when a gift is seemingly intended for one individual—e.g., a sick member of a household—and is sent from a certain individual—e.g., the sick person's uncle—the gift is still regarded as a gift from the uncle's household as a corporate unit to the sick person's household as another unit. Magically, as we saw above, such a gift may be intended for a given individual; but in terms of the working of the society, it is a gift to a group, of which the individual is merely a member. The significance of this fact will be seen when we consider how the principle of reciprocity operates.

In rural Japan, probably the most important motivating force behind gift-giving is the concept of *giri*. *Giri* is a moral imperative to perform one's duties toward other members of one's group. Gift-giving falls squarely in the sphere of *giri;* one is morally obligated to give a gift when custom demands it. *Giri* is bound up with the institution of gift-giving in another way, namely, reciprocation. To the extent that one man's relation to another in Japanese rural society is defined in reciprocal terms, in which the give-and-take of social relations should be fairly rigidly balanced, the concept of *giri* evokes in the tradition-minded rural Japanese the obligation to reciprocate. Since gift-giving is an act of *giri,* and since *giri* requires reciprocation, a gift naturally calls for a return gift. The moral obligation to give, to receive, and to return gifts is as much a part of traditional Japan as it is of the archaic societies with which Marcel Mauss (1954) concerned himself in his famous essay on the gift.

So important is the concept of *giri* in gift-giving that many rural Japanese interpret *giri* to mean strict observance of the etiquette of gift-giving (Furukawa 1952:291; Mori 1937:162; Wakamori 1947:198; Wakamori 1951; Wakamori 1953; Minzokugaku kenkyūjo 1951:164). Dore's account of Shitayamachō in Tokyo shows how important the concept is in the operation of gift exchange even in cities (Dore 1958:260–262).

We have seen that the institution of gift-giving requires that giving be balanced by returning. The operation of this principle of reciprocity in its most elementary form is readily seen in the customary donation of "incense money" *(kōden)* at funerals. The family of the deceased keeps a careful record of each donation, and when death occurs in a family which has given incense money, an identical amount of money is returned.[6] Similarly, when the roof of a farmhouse is to be rethatched, neighbors and relatives donate labor and materials, such as bundles of grass and rope. When the time to rethatch the house of one of the helpers comes around, exactly the same amount of labor and material is returned.

Reciprocation, however, need not be in kind. A gift may be given for a favor done, or vice versa. When the relationship between households is a vertical, hierarchical one, this type of "heterogeneous" exchange is likely to take place. A man brings gifts to his *oyakata* in the New Year, or to his landlord at *o-bon* in thanks for the *on*—the past favor granted and assistance received. Or again, a recovered patient may bring a gift—in proportion to the seriousness of his illness—to this doctor to thank him for the medical attention given. On such a gift-giving occasion, the social superior does not reciprocate with a gift of the same type or value. For the gift is already a return for the past favor, and to return in kind and in value would reduce the status of the superior to that of the giver.

In short, in rural Japan, whether and how well a person observes the rules and etiquette governing the who, the what, the when, and the how of gift-giving are important ways of judging his social character. One who observes them meticulously is a responsible, trustworthy individual; he is *giri-gatai*. If, on the other hand, a person sent a gift disproportionately cheaper than the social equation of gift-giving calls for, people would gossip about the cheapness not only of the gift but also of the giver's character.

Modern Changes and Innovations

In modern urban Japan, the religious origin and significance of gift-giving discussed above has been forgotten by most people. By contrast, the social context in which gift-giving is practiced in rural areas is still of critical importance for the city dwellers. They are quite conscious of the concept of the household as a unit in gift-giving, and the continuation of their household-based customary gift exchange is very much motivated by the concept of *giri*.

This is not to say that city people uniformly approve of the traditional etiquette of gift-giving. The more educated urbanites feel very much constrained by the social obligation of *giri,* which they contemptuously label "feudalistic." It is because *giri*-based gift-giving is looked on as a nuisance and with disfavor that the Japanese often scarcely consider the appropriateness of the content of a gift. Instead, gift-giving is treated as an empty formality. One simply buys a piece of merchandise of proper monetary value. Or, as it so often happens in returning from an extended trip, one simply buys so many dozens of the same kind of gift to be distributed among those to whom one by *giri* owes a gift, irrespective of the individual tastes of the receivers. It is in this context that we can understand the practice of *taraimawashi,* in which a gift that a person receives, for which he (and anyone else, for that matter) would have no conceivable use, is simply passed on to another to meet the obligation of giving and returning. One reason why *giri*-based behavior, including gift-giving, persists in cities, in spite of the negative attitudes toward it, is that such behavior is social insurance, as Dore puts it (Dore 1958: 258–262). In case of an emergency, a person just might have to depend on neighbors and friends. If he had been recalcitrant and ignored *giri*-based etiquette, he might not be able to expect a helping hand at critical moments.

The strain of tradition thus presses heavily upon urbanites. And city life, which does not depend very much any more on the kind of solidarity maintained by the traditional human relations and values of rural society, has to some extent permitted the discontinuation of the gift-giving that symbolized such solidarity. For example, in rural areas, at *o-bon* a social inferior traditionally makes a gift to his superior, such as a branch family to its main family or tenants to the landlord. In cities, the counterpart would be for employees to present gifts to their superior at work. While this custom does prevail widely, there are also a large number of city people who no longer practice it. In some business firms it has become an established practice not to give gifts to superiors at *o-bon;* in others certain superiors have explicitly prohibited the practice.

City dwellers, however, have not merely let old customs fall into disuse. They have added new practices or at least elaborated on existing customs and made them popular. One such practice is gift-giving between individuals *qua* individuals, without encumbering their households. This is not likely to occur in one's neighborhood, between relatives, etc., where households are already the interacting units. It is more likely to occur at work or at school, where individuals have opportunities to interact as individuals. School friends and work mates give gifts on birthdays, at weddings, and on other occasions. In marked contrast to the traditional type of gift-giving, in which social obligation *(giri)* is the prime mover of gifts, the motivating force in individual-to-individual gift-giving tends to be one's personal affection for the receiver. It is *ninjō,* if you like, rather than *giri,* which is the basis (although few modern urbanites would want their personal motivation identified with such a traditional, and therefore feudalistic, concept as *ninjō*).

In this personal type of gift-giving, in contrast to the *giri*-based type, the giver cares a great deal about what he gives because he is not simply meeting an unpleasant obligation. Much thought goes into the choice of the gift; he does not simply buy something of proper monetary value or resort to *taraimawashi,* as mentioned above. Moreover, the concept of balanced reciprocity, so important in *giri*-based gift-giving, here breaks down. In *giri*-based gift-giving, it is extremely important to consider the value of the gift in relation to what it is a return for, if it is a return gift, or in relation to the relative social status of giver and receiver and the specific occasion for which the gift is intended. In the personal gift, one may choose to give very little, or something of great value. Since mutual trust is already established between the giver and the receiver, it is not necessary to regard gift-giving as an indication of the giver's social character, whereas in *giri*-based gift-giving, it may be recalled, one's character was judged to a considerable degree by the extent to which one observed gift-giving etiquette. Thus the personal type of gift-giving is associated with a whole complex of different attitudes. These attitudes have come into being as a result of the process of individuation that modern city life encourages (Dore 1958:387–389).

Another innovation associated more with urban than rural Japan is what I might call "collective" gift-giving. It occurs most often in situations in which personal gift-giving described above is likely to occur (such as school or work), but it may also be seen in the neighborhood, since the basic unit of "collective" giving may be either the individual or the household. Whichever the unit may be, givers in this type are either already organized into a group—such as clubs at school or neighborhood associations—or organize themselves into a group on an *ad hoc* basis. Each member of the group contributes an equal amount of money, and the total collection is then given as a cash present to the recipient, or a gift is purchased with the collected money and given him. This type of gift-giving is suitable when the giver does not feel very close to the receiver and does not wish to spend much money or time in buying a gift, but he nonetheless feels the obligation to give. In short, "collective" giving occurs as a response to the dilemma in which urbanites are often caught between the lack of personal motivation to give and the persistent social obligation—*giri*—to give.

A third type of gift-giving practice more characteristic of the harsh competitive world of cities than of the corporate community of rural Japan is one based on ulterior motives (Wakamori 1947:198; Takagi 1954). Since a gift traditionally comes wrapped, since the giver, according to etiquette, belittles the content of the gift, and since a gift should not be opened in front of the giver, it is impossible to foresee the value of the gift, which may far exceed the amount deemed proper by the normal measure of balanced reciprocity. In addition, the obligation to accept, once a gift is presented, is as binding as the obligation to give and to return. These norms governing the ritual of gift-giving provide the giver with a vast advantage—unfair though it is—in furthering his objectives. The social obligation thus created by an expensive gift requires in return a special favor for the giver which the receiver would not perform under normal circumstances. It is possible to cancel the debt incurred by the expensive gift by returning an equally expensive gift. But ordinarily the circumstances make it evident that the giver wants a special favor in return. For example, a teacher who receives a very expensive gift from his student's father is fully aware that the father wants to have his son's grade improved.

We regard this type of gift-giving as bribery in America. But because gift-giving is so pervasive in Japan, and the obligations to give, to receive, and to reciprocate are so strongly entrenched in the traditional social system, it is extremely difficult, if not impossible, to discern whether a gift is legitimate or illegitimate. As Dore notes, "only a hairline separates the mere token of gratitude from the bribe" (Dore 1958:262). Because the term "bribery" has a narrow legalistic tinge and because it is difficult to tell when gift-giving is bribery, we shall use the term "ulteriorly motivated" gift-giving. This type of gift-giving is an expression of urban conditions where anomie prevails; that is, emphasis on goals has taken precedence over the culturally approved means of achieving the goal (Merton 1949:125–150).

One final type of gift-giving should be mentioned briefly. I refer to altruistic donation. Donation as such is nothing new in Japan. It is collected in the village association, in the neighborhood association, in the PTA, etc., for constructing a community hall, a school gymnasium, or recreation facilities for children. Such a donation, however, is not usually based on true altruism. Instead, it is a way of expressing one's loyalty to the group, of demonstrating one's economic affluence, or of impressing other members of the group with the important contribution one is making for the group. In short, most Japanese make donations in order to fulfill their social obligations or social ambition. This type of giving is not an expression of altruism, since the motivation is based on considerations of the psychological reward one receives from others through their approval, esteem, or even envy.

True altruism, on the other hand, is based strictly on the satisfaction derived from the simple act of giving. No one has to know one has given, or how much one has given. True, such altruistic giving is not unknown in Japan. Even before the war, for example, commuters saw students standing in front of train stations asking for donations to help starving farmers of Tōhoku, where severe cold had destroyed crops. In the postwar years, we see other kinds of street-corner donation drives, such as the "red feather" or "green feather" donations, copied after the American Community Chest. Although no one knows how much such strictly altruistic donation amounts to in Japan every year, the amount probably is not very large. For such donation is based on a universalistic orientation, in which one does not seek through the donation the approval of "meaningful others," such as kinsmen, friends, and neighbors who "count" in one's social life. To the extent that Japanese are highly interdependent in their emotional patterning (Caudill and Doi 1963; Caudill and Plath 1966; Caudill and Scarr 1962:53–91), they find meaningful social life in particularistic relationships with others. Altruistic donation is not likely to be very successful in this sort of social context.

Conclusion

Let us now enumerate the significant cultural features of traditional Japan that are discernible in gift-giving practices:

1. The supernatural significance of magical contagion through communion and commensality as well as through gifts of food.
2. The household as a basic social institution.
3. *Giri* as a central motivational value in maintaining the custom.
4. Reciprocity as a principle of interaction.

While all these features except the first are still prevalent in modern Japan, there are new trends and changes that are discernible, particularly in urban areas. Let us list these:

1. Secularization, or a gradual loss of religious and magical meanings in gift-giving.
2. Individuation—the opportunity of individuals to interact as individuals and to express personal affect.
3. Instrumentalism, or ulterior-motivated behavior.
4. Weakly developed altruism.

These old and new elements of Japanese culture revealed in gift-giving practices indicate something of the general trend in the modernization of Japan. First, secularization—the decreasing reliance on religion and magic for solving worldly problems—is a natural evolutionary process (White 1959, chap. 15). Along with the secularization of the society in general, it is to be expected that gift-giving would have less and less religious and magical significance. Second, as Dore has observed, the complex city life of industrialized society encourages individuation; as social interaction is conducted on an individual basis rather than on the traditional household basis, it is natural for gift-giving to express this changing social pattern.

Third, I have alluded to the concept of *ninjō*—a concept as old as kabuki—in reference to the increasing tendency for expression of individual affect in modern Japan. But there is a basic difference between *ninjō* and the modern expression of personal affect—not so much in their contents as in their social contexts. In traditional Japan *ninjō* was placed in opposition to *giri,* as Benedict elucidated years ago (Benedict 1946; Furukawa 1952). The concept of *giri* defined proper conduct, whereas *ninjō* implied human failure to carry out *giri.* Society thus had no legitimate place for *ninjō.* Expression of personal affect, on the other hand, is now beginning to win a legitimate status in the modern social order side by side with *giri.*

Fourth, while the society is changing in a secular and individuated direction, it has also retained certain traditional features, such as the concepts of household and *giri.* What is important to note here is that these features are not simply anachronisms, the cuff buttons of modern Japan. Instead, they have played a crucial role in effectuating the process of modernization in Japan.

Lastly, the weak development of altruism also points to the strength of such traditional values as *giri,* which emphasize one's obligation in a particularistic setting. Since the roles of individuals are by and large defined in particularistic terms even in modern Japan, the most effective way to get things done is to take advantage of traditional motivational values. Basing social roles on universalistic criteria, on which altruism is ultimately dependent, is correspondingly rare in Japan. Altruistic gift-giving therefore will probably remain insignificant in Japan as long as the basic value orientation of the people does not change from particularism to universalism.

These observations lead us to consider Japan's modernization from the theoretical standpoint. There are two possible positions one might take. On the one hand, one may argue that in spite of an outstanding performance in the economic sphere, Japan lags behind in its social and cultural modernization, since it retains many traditional elements. On the other hand, one may argue (and many scholars have) that Japan's spectacular economic achievement has been accomplished by exploiting its traditional social and cultural patterns. The former position is based on the assumption that modernization as an end-state ultimately implies a uniform cultural manifestation, disregarding the heterogeneity cultures may display in the process of arriving at the end-state. The second position, which has been advocated by, among others, Ichirō Nakayama (1965:86–87), argues for a parallel development, namely, that although modernization may denote technological efficiency, for which all modernizing nations strive, there are different avenues by which to arrive at it, and moreover that in its social and cultural spheres a modernized nation can retain its traditional patterns.

Although the future is anyone's guess, the "uniform end-state" theory takes a position which has not been empirically demonstrated. The parallel development theory, on the other hand, is based on the widely substantiated position that each modernizing culture, while striving toward a common goal of more efficient integration and organization of its cultural legacy, attempts to achieve this goal through its unique set of cultural "equipment." In conclusion, then, those cultural patterns of Japan that are adaptable to and facilitate modernization will probably remain, and gift-giving as a medium for expressing these patterns will similarly be found in Japan for years to come.

Notes

1. In most statistics, figures for expenditure of gifts are included in the category of "social expenses" (kōsai hi) along with expenditures for entertaining guests. Data published by the Japanese government (Japan, Office of the Prime Minister 1964:24–25, 58–59, 280–281) show that figures in this category range from about 1 percent to 3 percent of the total household expenditure, the percentage increasing as the income level rises. R. P. Dore's City Life in Japan (1958:400–403) is probably the only publication to provide a separate category for gift items in the analysis of household expenditures in Japan. His table shows 17 households in Tokyo, spending 0.8 percent to 19.4 percent of the total household expenditure on gifts. (Dore's definition of "total household expenditure" is, however, slightly different from that of the government in the publication cited above.) Unfortunately Dore's sample does not reflect a larger population of which it is a part, since the sample was not randomly selected.

2. I wish to express my gratitude to the Center for Japanese Studies, University of Michigan, for providing financial aid in carrying out interviews on gift-giving with Japanese nationals resident in Ann Arbor in 1965–1966. I wish to thank Mr. Makio Matsuzono for conducting the interviews and making initial analysis of the data. Thanks are also due Professor Takashi Nakano, who served as a teacher, consultant, and informant for the writer.

3. For an overall discussion of old beliefs surrounding food and food production and consumption, see Segawa 1964:208–246.

4. This token gift does not cancel the debt created by the gift brought. It simply symbolizes the good wishes of the receiver, who is in effect saying through the token return gift, "Please accept the supernatural power inherent in me which I hope will help you in some way." To reciprocate the gift and cancel the debt, the receiver must

let some time elapse and then return a gift of appropriate value. A sick patient generally cancels his gift-debt by holding a feast when he recovers, to which he invites all those who paid him a visit during his illness.

5. The social framework of gift-giving, especially in relation to the concept of reciprocity, has been discussed in my paper, Gift-giving and Social Reciprocity in Japan, an Exploratory Statement, *France/Asie,* 1966/1967, 21:161–168.

6. Incidentally, *kōden,* which is now given in cash (hence the translation "incense money") and is used to supplement the cost of the funeral, originated as an offering of the new crop of rice to the dead. Cf. Kurata 1944:457–463.

12

Criteria of Group Formation

CHIE NAKANE

Attribute and Frame

THE analysis uses two basic contrasting criteria or concepts, namely *attribute* and *frame*, which are newly formulated by myself, assuming them to be most effective in the analysis of Japanese society in comparison with other societies. These two terms, with the manner in which the distinction is employed, might lead the reader to that of the customary European thought, but they are used in a quite different way, and the resemblance is merely superficial.

According to my view, groups may be identified by applying the two criteria: one is based on the individual's common *attribute*, the other on situational position in a given *frame*. I use *frame* as a technical term with a particular significance, as opposed to the criterion of *attribute*, which, again, is used specifically and in a broader sense than it normally carries. *Frame* may be a locality, an institution, or a particular relationship which binds a set of individuals into one group; in all cases it indicates a criterion which sets a boundary and gives a common basis to a set of individuals who are located or involved in it. In fact, my term *frame* is the English translation of the Japanese *ba,* the concept from which I originally evolved my theory, but for which it is hard to find the exact English counterpart. *Ba* means "location," but the normal usage of the term connotes a special base on which something is placed according to a given purpose. The term *ba* is also used in physics for "field" in English.

Let me indicate how these two technical terms can be applied to various actual contexts. "Attribute" may mean, for instance, being a member of a definite descent group or caste. In contrast, being a member of

Reprinted from *Japanese Society,* C. Nakane (Berkeley: University of California Press, 1970). Copyright by George Weidenfeld & Nicholson, Ltd.

X village expresses the commonality of "frame." Attribute may be acquired not only by birth but by achievement. Frame is more circumstantial. These criteria serve to identify the individuals in a certain group, which can then in its turn be classified within the whole society, even though the group may or may not have a particular function of its own as a collective body. Classifications such as landlord and tenant are based on attribute, while such a unit as a landlord and his tenants is a group formed by situational position. Taking industry as an example, "lathe operator" or "executive" refers to attribute, but "the members of Y Company" refers to frame. In the same way, "professor," "office clerk" and "student" are attributes, whereas "men of Z University" is a frame.

In any society, individuals are gathered into social groups or social strata on the bases of attributes and frame. There may be some cases where the two factors coincide in the formation of a group, but usually they overlap each other, with individuals belonging to different groups at the same time. The primary concern in this discussion is the relative degree of function of each criterion. There are some cases where either the attribute or the frame factor functions alone, and some where the two are mutually competitive. The way in which the factors are commonly weighted bears a close reciprocal relationship to the values which develop in the social consciousness of the people in the society. For example, the group consciousness of the Japanese depends considerably on this immediate social context, frame, whereas in India it lies in attribute (most symbolically expressed in caste, which is fundamentally a social group based on the ideology of occupation and kinship). On this point, perhaps, the societies of Japan and India show the sharpest contrast, as will be discussed later in greater detail.

The ready tendency of the Japanese to stress situational position in a particular frame, rather than universal attribute, can be seen in the following example: when a Japanese "faces the outside" (confronts another person) and affixes some position to himself socially, he is inclined to give precedence to institution over kind of occupation. Rather than saying, "I am a type-setter" or "I am a filing clerk," he is likely to say, "I am from B Publishing Group" or "I belong to S Company." Much depends on context, of course, but where a choice exists, he will use this latter form. (I will discuss later the more significant implications for Japanese social life indicated by this preference.) The listener would rather hear first about the connection with B Publishing Group or S Company; that he is a journalist or printer, engineer or office worker is of secondary importance. When a man says he is from X Television one may imagine him to be a producer or cameraman, though he may in fact be a chauffeur. (The universal business suit makes it hard to judge by appearances.) In group identification, a frame such as a "company" or "association" is of primary importance; the attribute of the individual is a secondary matter. The same tendency is to be found among intellectuals; among university graduates, what matters most, and functions the strongest socially, is not whether a man holds or does not hold a Ph.D. but, rather, from which university he graduated. Thus, the criterion by which Japanese classify individuals socially tends to be that of particular institution rather than of universal attribute. Such group consciousness and orientation fosters the strength of an institution, and the institutional unit (such as school or company) is in fact the basis of Japanese social organization.

The manner in which this group consciousness works is also revealed in the way the Japanese uses the expression *uchi* (my house) to mean the place of work, organization, office or school to which he belongs; and *otaku* (your house) to mean a second person's place of work and so on. The term *kaisha* symbolizes the expression of group consciousness. *Kaisha* does not mean that individuals are bound by contractual relationships into a corporate enterprise while still thinking of themselves as separate entities; rather, *kaisha* is "my" or "our" company, the community to which one belongs primarily, and which is all-important in one's life. Thus, in most cases the company provides the whole social existence of a person and has authority over all aspects of his life; he is deeply emotionally involved in the association.[1] That Company A belongs not to its shareholders but rather belongs to "us," is the sort of reasoning involved here, which is carried to such a point that even the modern legal arrangement must compromise in the face of this strong native orientation. I would not wish to deny that in other societies an employee may have a kind of emotional attachment to the company or his employer; what distinguishes this relation in Japan is the exceedingly high degree of this emotional involvement. It is openly and frequently expressed in speech and behaviour in public as well as in private, and such expressions always receive social and moral appreciation and approbation.

The essence of this firmly rooted, latent group consciousness in Japanese society is expressed in the traditional and ubiquitous concept of *ie,* the household, a concept which penetrates every nook and cranny of Japanese society. The Japanese usage *uchi no* referring to one's work place indeed derives from the basic concept of *ie.* The term *ie* also has implications beyond those to be found in the English words "household" or "family."

The concept of *ie,* in the guise of the term "family system," has been the subject of lengthy dispute and discussion by Japanese legal scholars and sociologists. The general consensus is that, as a consequence of modernization, particularly because of the new post-war civil code, the *ie* institution is dying. In this ideological approach the *ie* is regarded as being linked particularly with feudal moral precepts; its use as a fundamental unit of social structure has not been fully explored.

In my view, the most basic element of the *ie* institution is not that form whereby the eldest son and his wife live together with the old parents, nor an authority structure in which the household head holds the power, and so on. Rather, the *ie* is a corporate residential group and, in the case of agriculture or other similar enterprises, *ie* is a managing body. The *ie* comprises household members (in most cases the family members of the household head, but others in addition to family members may be included), who thus make up the units of a distinguishable social group. In other words, the *ie* is a social group constructed on the basis of an established frame of residence and often of management organization. What is important here is that the human relationships within this household group are thought of as more important than all other human relationships. Thus the wife and daughter-in-law who have come from outside have incomparably greater importance than one's own sisters and daughters, who have married and gone into other households. A brother, when he has built a separate house, is thought of as belonging to another unit or household; on the other hand, the son-in-law, who was once a complete outsider, takes the position of a household member and becomes more important than the brother living in another household. This is remarkably different from societies such as that of India, where the weighty factor of sibling relationship (a relationship based on commonality of attribute, that of being born of the same parents) continues paramount until death, regardless of residential circumstances; theoretically, the stronger the factor of sibling relationship, the weaker the social independence of a household (as a residence unit). (It goes without saying, of course, that customs such as the adopted son-in-law system prevalent in Japan are nonexistent in Hindu society. The same is true of Europe.) These facts support the theory that group-forming criteria based on functioning by attribute oppose group-forming criteria based on functioning by frame.

Naturally, the function of forming groups on the basis of the element of the frame, as demonstrated in the formation of the household, involves the possibility of including members with a differing attribute, and at the same time expelling a member who has the same attribute. This is a regular occurrence, particularly among traditional agricultural and merchant households. Not only may outsiders with not the remotest kinship tie be invited to be heirs and successors, but servants and clerks are usually incorporated as members of the household and treated as family members by the head of the household. This inclusion must be accepted without reservation to ensure that when a clerk is married to the daughter of the household and becomes an adopted son-in-law, the household succession will continue without disruption.

Such a principle contributes to the weakening of kinship ties. Kinship, the core of which lies in the sibling relation, is a criterion based on attribute. Japan gives less weight to kinship than do other societies, even England and America; in fact, the function of kinship is comparatively weak outside the household. The saying "the sibling is the beginning of the stranger" accurately reflects Japanese ideas on kinship. A married sibling who lives in another household is considered a kind of outsider. Towards such kin, duties and obligations are limited to the level of the seasonal exchange of greetings and presents, attendance at wedding and funeral ceremonies, and the minimum help in case of accident or poverty. There are often instances where siblings differ widely in social and economic status; the elder brother may be the mayor, while his younger brother is a postman in the same city; or a brother might be a lawyer or businessman, while his widowed sister works as a domestic servant in another household. The wealthy brother normally does not help the poor brother or sister who has set up a separate household, as long as the latter can somehow support his or her existence; by the same token, the latter will not dare to ask for help until the last grain of rice is gone. Society takes this for granted, for it gives prime importance to the individual household rather than to the kin group as a whole.

This is indeed radically different from the attitudes to kin found in India and other Southeast Asian countries, where individual wealth tends to be distributed among relatives; there, the kin group as a whole takes precedence over the individual household, and nepotism plays an important role. I have been surprised to discover that even in England and America brothers and sisters meet much more frequently than is required by Japanese standards, and that there exists such a high degree of attachment to kinfolk. Christmas is one of the great occasions when these kinfolk gather together; New Year's Day is Japan's equivalent to the Western Christmas, everyone busy with preparations for visits from subordinate staff, and then, in turn, calling on superiors. There is little time and scope to spare for collateral kin—married brothers, sisters, cousins, uncles and aunts, and so on—though parents and grandparents will certainly be visited if they do not live in the same house. Even in rural areas, people say, "One's neighbour is of more importance than one's relatives" or "You can carry on your life without cousins, but not without your neighbours."

The kinship which is normally regarded as the primary and basic human attachment seems to be compensated in Japan by a personalized relation to a corporate group based on work, in which the major aspects of social and economic life are involved. Here again we meet the vitally important unit in Japanese society of the corporate group based on frame. In my view, this is the basic principle on which Japanese society is built.

To sum up, the principles of Japanese social group structure can be seen clearly portrayed in the household structure. The concept of this traditional household institution, *ie,* still persists in the various group identities which are termed *uchi,* a colloquial form of *ie.* These facts demonstrate that the formation of social groups on the basis of fixed frames remains characteristic of Japanese social structure.

Among groups larger than the household, there is that described by the medieval concept *ichizoku rōtō* (one family group and its retainers). The idea of group structure as revealed in this expression is an excellent example of the frame-based social group. This is indeed the concept of one household, in which family members and retainers are not separated but form an integrated corporate group. There are often marriage ties between the two sides of this corporate group, and all lines of distinction between them become blurred. The relationship is the same as that between family members and clerks or servants in a household. This is a theoretical antithesis to a group formed exclusively on lineage or kin.

The equivalent in modern society of *ie* and *ichizoku rōtō* is a group such as "One Railway Family" *(kokutetsu ikka),* which signifies the Japanese National Railways. A union, incorporating both workers and management, calls this "management-labour harmony." Though it is often said that the traditional family *(ie)* institution has disappeared, the concept of the *ie* still persists in modern contexts. A company is conceived as an *ie,* all its employees qualifying as members of the household, with the employer at its head. Again, this "family" envelops the employee's personal family; it "engages" him "totally" *(marugakae* in Japanese). The employer readily takes responsibility for his employee's family, for which, in turn, the primary concern is the company, rather than relatives who reside elsewhere. (The features relating the company with its employees' families will be discussed later.) In this modern context, the employee's family, which normally comprises the employee himself, his wife and children, is a unit which can no longer be conceived as an *ie,* but simply a family. The unit is comparable to the family of a servant or clerk who worked in the master's *ie,* the managing body of the pre-modern enterprise. The role of the *ie* institution as the distinguished unit in society in pre-modern times is now played by the company. This social group consciousness symbolized in the concept of the *ie,* of being one unit within a frame, has been achievable at any time, has been promoted by slogans and justified in the traditional morality.

This analysis calls for a reconsideration of the stereotyped view that modernization or urbanization weakens kinship ties and creates a new type of social organization on entirely different bases. Certainly industrialization produces a new type of organization, the formal structure of which may be closely akin to that found in modern Western societies. However, this does not necessarily accord with changes in the informal structure, in which, as in the case of Japan, the traditional structure persists in large measure. This demonstrates that the basic social structure continues in spite of great changes in social organization.[2]

Emotional Participation and One-to-One Relationships

It is clear from the previous section that social groups constructed with particular reference to situation, i.e. frame, include members with differing attributes. A group formed on the basis of commonality of attribute can possess a strong sense of exclusiveness, based on this homogeneity, even without recourse to any form of law. Naturally, the relative strength of this factor depends on a variety of conditional circumstances, but in the fundamentals of group formation this homogeneity among group members stands largely by its own strength, and conditions are secondary. When a group develops on the situational basis of frame, the primary form is a simple herd, which in itself does not possess internal positive elements which can constitute a social group. Constituent elements of the group in terms of their attributes may be heterogenous but may not be complementary. (The discussion here does not link to Durkheimian theory as such; the distinction is between societies where people stick together because they are similar and those where they stick together because they are complementary.) For example, a group of houses built in the same area may form a village simply by virtue of physical demarcation from other houses. But in order to create a functional corporate group, there is need of an internal organization which will link these independent households. In such a situation some sort of law must be evolved to guide group coherence.

In addition to the initial requirement of a strong, enduring frame, there is need to strengthen the frame even further and to make the group element tougher. Theoretically, this can be done in two ways. One is to influence the members within the frame in such a way that they have a feeling of "one-ness"; the second method is to create an internal organization which will tie the individuals in the group to each other and then to strengthen this organization. In practice, both these modes occur together, are bound together, and progress together. They become, in fact, one common rule of action, but for the sake of convenience I shall discuss them separately. In this section I discuss the feeling of unity.

People with different attributes can be led to feel that they are members of the same group, and that this feeling is justified, by stressing the group consciousness of "us" against "them," i.e. the external, and by fostering a feeling of rivalry against other similar groups. In this way there develops internally the sentimental tie of "members of the same troop."

Since disparity of attribute is a rational thing, an emotional approach is used to overcome it. This emotional approach is facilitated by continual human contact of the kind that can often intrude on those human relations which belong to the completely private and personal sphere. Consequently, the power and influence of the group not only affects and enters into the individual's actions; it alters even his ideas and ways of thinking. Individual autonomy is minimized. When this happens, the point where group or public life ends and where private life begins no longer can be distinguished. There are those who perceive this as a danger, an encroachment on their dignity as individuals; on the other hand, others feel safer in total-group consciousness. There seems little doubt that the latter group is in the majority. Their sphere of living is usually concentrated solely within the village community or the place of work. The Japanese regularly talk about their homes and love affairs with co-workers; marriage within the village community or place of work is prevalent; the family frequently participates in company pleasure trips. The provision of company housing, a regular practice among Japan's leading enterprises, is a good case in point. Such company houses are usually concentrated in a single area and form a distinct entity within, say a suburb of a large city. In such circumstances employees' wives come into close contact with and are well informed about their husbands' activities. Thus, even in terms of physical arrangements, a company with its employees and their families forms a distinct social group. In an extreme case, a company may have a common grave for its employees, similar to the household grave. With group-consciousness so highly developed, there is almost no social life outside the particular group on which an individual's major economic life depends. The individual's every problem must be solved within this frame. Thus, group participation is simple and unitary. It follows then that each group or institution develops a high degree of independence and closeness, with its own internal law which is totally binding on members.

The archetype of this kind of group is the Japanese "household" *(ie)* as we have described it in the previous section. In Japan, for example, the mother-in-law and daughter-in-law problem is preferably solved inside the household, and the luckless bride has to struggle through in isolation, without help from her own family, relatives, or neighbours. By comparison, in agricultural villages in India, not only can the bride make long visits to her parental home but her brother may frequently visit her and help out in various ways. Mother-in-law and daughter-in-law quarrels are conducted in raised voices that can be heard all over the neighbourhood, and when such shouting is heard, all the women (of the same caste) in the neighbourhood come over to help out. The mutual assistance among the wives who come from other villages is a quite enviable factor completely unimaginable among Japanese women. Here again the function of the social factor of attribute (wife) is demonstrated; it supersedes the function of the frame of the household. In Japan, by contrast, "the parents step in when their children quarrel" and, as I shall explain in detail later, the structure is the complete opposite to that in India.

Moral ideas such as "the husband leads and the wife obeys" or "man and wife are one flesh" embody the Japanese emphasis on integration. Among Indians, however, I have often observed husband and wife expressing quite contradictory opinions without the slightest hesitation. This is indeed rare in front of others in Japan. The traditional authority of the Japanese household head, once regarded as the prime characteristic of the family system, extended over the conduct, ideas, and ways of thought of the household's members, and on this score the household head could be said to wield a far greater power than his Indian counterpart. In Indian family life there are all kinds of rules that apply in accordance with the status of the individual family member; the wife, for instance, must not speak directly to her husband's elder brothers, father, etc. These rules all relate to individual behaviour, but in the sphere of ideas and ways of thought the freedom and strong individuality permitted even among members of the same family is surprising to a Japanese. The rules, moreover, do not differ from household to household but are common to the whole community, especially among the members of the same caste community. In other words, the rules are of universal character, rather than being situational or particular to each household, as is the case in Japan.[3] Compared with traditional Japanese family life, the extent to which members of an Indian household are bound by the individual household's traditional practices is very small.

An Indian who had been studying in Japan for many years once compared Japanese and Indian practice in the following terms:

> Why does a Japanese have to consult his companions over even the most trivial matter? The Japanese always call a conference about the slightest thing, and hold frequent meetings, though these are mostly informal, to decide everything. In India, we have definite rules as family members (and this is also true of other social groups), so that when one wants to do something one knows whether it is all right by instantaneous reflection on those rules—it is not necessary to consult with the head or with other members of the family. Outside these rules, you are largely free to act as an individual;

whatever you do, you have only to ask whether or not it will run counter to the rules.

As this clearly shows, in India "rules" are regarded as a definite but abstract social form, not as a concrete and individualized form particular to each family/social group, as is the case in Japan. The individuality of the Indian family unit is not strong, nor is there group participation by family members of the order of the emotional participation in the Japanese household; nor is the family as a living unit (or as a group holding communal property) a closed society, as in the case of the Japanese household. Again, in contrast to Japanese practice, the individual in India is strongly tied to the social network outside his household.

In contrast to the Japanese system, the Indian system allows freedom in respect of ideas and ways of thought as opposed to conduct. I believe for this reason, even though there are economic and ethical restrictions on the modernization of society, the Indian does not see his traditional family system as an enemy of progress to such a degree as the Japanese does. This view may contradict that conventionally held by many people on Indian family. It is important to note that the comparison here is made between Japanese and Hindu systems focused on actual interpersonal relationships within the family or household, rather than between Western and Indian family patterns in a general outlook. I do not intend here to present the structure and workings of actual personal relations in Japanese and Hindu families in detail, but the following point would be some help to indicate my point. In the ideal traditional household in Japan, for example, opinions of the members of the household should always be held unanimously regardless of the issue, and this normally meant that all members accepted the opinion of the household head, without even discussing the issue. An expression of a contradictory opinion to that of the head was considered a sign of misbehaviour, disturbing the harmony of the group order. Contrasted to such a unilateral process of decision-making in the Japanese household, the Indian counterpart allows much room for discussion between its members; they, whether sons, wife, or even daughters, are able to express their views much more freely, and they in fact can enjoy a discussion, although the final decision may be taken by the head. Hindu family structure is similar hierarchically to the Japanese family, but the individual's rights are well preserved in it. In the Japanese system all members of the household are in one group under the head, with no specific rights according to the status of individuals within the family. The Japanese family system differs from that of the Chinese system, where family ethics are always based on relationships between particular individuals such as father and son, brothers and sisters, parent and child, husband and wife, while in Japan they are always based on the collective group, i.e., members of a household, not on the relationships between individuals.

The Japanese system naturally produces much more frustration in the members of lower status in the hierarchy and allows the head to abuse the group or an individual member. In Japan, especially immediately after the Second World War, the idea has gained ground that the family system *(ie)* was an evil, feudalistic growth obstructing modernization, and on this premise one could point out the evil uses to which the unlimited infiltration of the household head's authority were put. It should be noticed here, however, that although the power of each individual household head is often regarded as exclusively his own, in fact it is the social group, the "household," which has the ultimate integrating power, a power which restricts each member's behaviour and thought, including that of the household head himself.

Another group characteristic portrayed in the Japanese household can be seen when a business enterprise is viewed as a social group. In this instance a closed social group has been organized on the basis of the "life-time employment system" and the work made central to the employees' lives. The new employee is in just about the same position, and is in fact received by the company in much the same spirit, as if he were a newly born family member, a newly adopted son-in-law, or a bride come into the husband's household. A number of well-known features peculiar to the Japanese employment system illustrate this characteristic, for example, company housing, hospital benefits, family-recreation groups for employees, monetary gifts from the company on the occasion of marriage, birth, or death, and even advice from the company's consultant on family planning. What's interesting here is that this tendency is very obvious, even in the most forward-looking, large enterprises or in supposedly modern, advanced management. The concept is even more evident in Japan's basic payment system, used by every industrial enterprise and government organization, in which the family allowance is the essential element. This is also echoed in the principle of the seniority payment system.

The relationship between employer and employee is not to be explained in contractual terms. The attitude of the employer is expressed by the spirit of the common saying, "the enterprise is the people." This affirms the belief that employer and employee are bound as one by fate in conditions which produce a tie between man and man often as firm and close as that between husband and wife. Such a relationship is manifestly not a purely contractual one between employer and employee; the employee is already a member of his own family, and all members of his family are naturally included in the larger company "family."

Employers do not employ only a man's labour itself but really employ the total man, as is shown in the expression *marugakae* (completely enveloped). This trend can be traced consistently in Japanese management from the Meiji period to the present.

The life-time employment system, characterized by the integral and lasting commitment between employee and employer, contrasts sharply with the high mobility of the worker in the United States. It has been suggested that this system develops from Japan's economic situation and is closely related to the surplus of labour. However, as J. C. Abegglen (1958, chap. 2) has suggested in his penetrating analysis, the immobility of Japanese labour is not merely an economic problem. That it is also closely related to the nature of Japanese social structure will become evident from my discussion. In fact, Japanese labour relations, in terms of surplus and shortage of labour, have least affected the life-time employment system. In fact, these contradictory situations have together contributed to the development of the system.

It might be appropriate at this point to give a brief description of the history of the development of the life-time employment system in Japan. In the early days of Japan's industrialization, there was a fairly high rate of movement of factory workers from company to company, just as some specific type of workmen or artisans of pre-industrial urban Japan had moved freely from job to job. Such mobility in some workers in pre-industrial and early industrial Japan seems to be attributed to the following reasons: a specific type of an occupation, the members of which consisted of a rather small percentage of the total working population and the demand for them was considerably high; these workers were located in a situation outside well-established institutionalized systems. The mobility of factory workers caused uncertainty and inconvenience to employers in their efforts to retain a constant labour force. To counteract this fluidity, management policy gradually moved in the direction of keeping workers in the company for their entire working lives, rather than towards developing a system based on contractual arrangements. By the beginning of this century, larger enterprises were already starting to develop management policies based on this principle; they took the form of various welfare benefits, company houses at nominal rent, commissary purchasing facilities, and the like. This trend became particularly marked after the First World War, when the shortage of labour was acute.

It was also at the end of the First World War that there came into practice among large companies the regular employment system by which a company takes on, each spring, a considerable number of boys who have just left school. This development arose from the demand for company-trained personnel adapted to the mechanized production systems that followed the introduction of new types of machinery from Germany and the United States. Boys fresh from school were the best potential labour force for mechanized industry because they were more easily moulded to suit a company's requirements. They were trained by the company not only technically but also morally. In Japan it has always been believed that individual moral and mental attitudes have an important bearing on productive power. Loyalty towards the company has been highly regarded. A man may be an excellent technician, but if his way of thought and his moral attitudes do not accord with the company's ideal, the company does not hesitate to dismiss him. Men who move in from another company at a comparatively advanced stage in their working life tend to be considered difficult to mould or suspect in their loyalties. Ease of training, then, was the major reason why recruitment of workers was directed more and more towards boys fresh from school. (There is an excellent statement of conditions in Abegglen 1958, chap. 1.)

Recruitment methods thus paved the way for the development of the life-employment system. An additional device was evolved to hold workers to a company, for example, the seniority payment system based on duration of service, age, and educational qualifications, with the added lure of a handsome payment on retirement. The principle behind this seniority system had the advantage of being closely akin to the traditional pattern of commercial and agricultural management in pre-industrial Japan. In these old-style enterprises, operational size had been relatively small—one household or a group of affiliated households centred on one particular household, the head of which acted as employer while his family members and affiliated members or servants acted as permanent employees. Thus, the pattern of employment in modern industrial enterprise has close structural and ideological links with traditional household management.

The shift towards life-employment was assisted in the second and third decades of this century by developments in the bureaucratic structure of business enterprises; a proliferation of sections was accompanied by finer gradings in official rank. During these twenty years there appeared uniforms for workers, badges (lapel buttons) worn as company insignia, and stripes on the uniform cap to indicate section and rank. Workers thus came under a more rigid institutional hierarchy, but they were also given greater incentives by the expectation of climbing the delicately subdivided ladder of rank.

During the war, this system was strengthened further by the adoption of a military pattern. Labour immobility was reinforced by government policy, which cut short the trend to increased mobility that had been the result of the acute shortage of labour. The prohibition on movement of labour between factories was bolstered by the moral argument that it was through concentrated service to his own factory that a worker could best serve the nation. The factory was to be considered as a household or family, in which the employer would and should care for both the material and mental life of his worker and the latter's family. According to the "Draft of Labour Regulations" (Munitions Public Welfare Ministry publication, February 1945):

> The factory, by its production, becomes the arena for putting into practice the true aims of Imperial labour. The people who preserve these aims become the unifiers of labour. Superior and inferior should help each other, those who are of the same rank should co-operate and with a fellowship as of one family, we shall combine labour and management.

Thus, the factory's household-like function came about, in part, at the behest of state authority. In this context, a moral and patriotic attitude was regarded as more important than technical proficiency. Against shortages in the commodity market, the factory undertook to supply rice, vegetables, clothing, lodging accommodation, medical care, etc.

Familialism, welfare services, and extra payments supplied by the company were thus fully developed under the peculiar circumstances of war, and they have been retained as the institutional pattern in the post-war years. It is also to be noted that the process was further encouraged by post-war union activity. Unions mushroomed after the war, when 48,000 unions enrolled 9,000,000 members. These unions were formed primarily within a single company and encompassed members of different types of occupation and qualification, both staff and line workers. It is said that, in some aspects, a union is like the wartime Industrial Patriotism Club *(Sangyō-hōkoku-kai)*, lacking only the company president. Thus it can serve as part of the basis of familialism. The establishment of welfare facilities, company housing schemes, recreation centers at seaside or hill resorts, etc., are all items demanded by the unions along with wage increases. Above all, the single most important union success was the gaining of the right of appeal against summary dismissal or lay-off. In the period immediately after the war, dismissal meant starvation; this, together with the swiftly increasing power of the union movement, accounts for the unions' success in acquiring this tremendous privilege. Thus, life employment, a policy initiated by management, has reached its perfected form through the effect of post-war unionism. Again, to combat the shortage of younger workers and highly trained engineers which is felt so acutely today, management policy is moving further towards attempts at retaining labour by the offer of more beneficial provisions.

As it has shown in the course of its development, life-time employment has advantages for both employer and employee. For the employer it serves to retain the services of skilled workers against times of labour shortage. For the employee it gives security against surplus labour conditions; whatever the market circumstances, there is little likelihood of the employee finding better employment if he once leaves his job. This system has, in fact, been encouraged by contradictory situations—shortage and surplus of labour. Here is demonstrated a radical divergence between Japan and America in management employment policy; a Japanese employer buys future potential labour and an American employer buys labour immediately required. According to the Japanese reasoning, any deficiencies in the current labour force will be compensated by the development of maximum power in the labour force of the future; the employer buys his labour material and shapes it until it best fits his production need. In America, management buys ready-made labour.

Familialism, another offspring of the operational mechanism of modern industrial enterprise, is the twin to life employment. Attention was drawn above to the concept of the "One Railway Family," which was advocated as early as 1909 by the then President of the National Railways, Gotō Shimpei. The concept was strengthened during the war years, and it has appeared in such favourite slogans of post-war management as "the spirit of love for the company" and "the new familialism." According to so-called modern and advanced management theory, a genuinely inspired "spirit of love for the company" is not merely advocated but is indeed an atmosphere resulting from management policy, so that "whether the feeling of love for the company thrives or not is the barometer of the abilities and talents of management staff." Even in the coining of expressions which may seem antithetical—"we must love our company" and "the spirit of love for the company is silly"—the underlying motivation remains the securing of the employee's total emotional participation.

In summary, the characteristics of Japanese enterprise as a social group are, first, that the group is itself family-like and, second, that it pervades even the private lives of its employees, for each family joins extensively in the enterprise. These characteristics have been cautiously encouraged by managers and administrators consistently from the Meiji period. And the truth is that this encouragement has always succeeded and reaped rewards.

A cohesive sense of group unity, as demonstrated in the operational mechanism of household and enterprise, is essential as the foundation of the individual's total emotional participation in the group; it helps to build a closed world and results in strong group independence or isolation. This inevitably breeds household customs and company traditions. These in turn are emphasized in mottoes which bolster the sense of unity and group solidarity, and strengthen the group even more. At the same time, the independence of the group and the stability of the frame, both cultivated by this sense of unity, create a gulf between the group and others with similar attributes but outside the frame; meanwhile, the distance between people with differing attributes within the frame is narrowed, and the functioning of any group formed on the base of similar attributes is paralyzed. Employees in an enterprise must remain in the group, whether they like it or not. Not only do they not want to change to another company; even if they desire a change, they lack the means to accomplish it. Because there is no tie between workers of the same kind, as in a "horizontal" craft union, they get neither information nor assistance from their counterparts. (This situation is identical with that of the Japanese married-in bride as described above.) Thus, in this type of social organization, as society grows more stable, the consciousness of similar qualities becomes weaker and, conversely, the consciousness of the difference between "our people" and "outsiders" is sharpened.

The consciousness of "them" and "us" is strengthened and aggravated to the point that extreme contrasts in human relations can develop in the same society, and anyone outside "our" people ceases to be considered human. Ridiculous situations occur, such as that of the man who will shove a stranger out of the way to take an empty seat, but will then, no matter how tired he is, give up the seat to someone he knows, particularly if that someone is a superior in his company.

An extreme example of this attitude in group behaviour is the Japanese people's amazing coldness (which is not a matter just of indifference, but rather of active hostility), the contempt and neglect they will show for the people of an outlying island or for those living in the "special" *buraku* (formerly a segregated social group, now legally equal but still discriminated against). Here the complete estrangement of people outside "our" world is institutionalized. In India there is a lower-class group known as "untouchables," but although at first glance the Indian attitude towards a different caste appears to resemble Japanese behaviour, it is not really so. The Indian does not have the sharp distinction of "them" and "us" between two different groups. Among the various Indian groups, A, B, C, etc., one man happens to belong to A, while another is of B; A, B, C, and so forth together form one society. His group A constitutes part of the whole, while, to the Japanese, "our" is opposed to the whole world. The Indian's attitude towards people of other groups stems from indifference rather than hostility.

These characteristics of group formation reveal that Japanese group affiliations and human relations are exclusively one-to-one; a single loyalty stands uppermost and firm. There are many cases of membership of more than one group, of course, but in these cases there is always one group that is clearly preferred while the others are considered secondary. By contrast, the Chinese, for example, find it impossible to decide which group is the most important of several. So long as the groups differ in nature, the Chinese see no contradiction and think it perfectly natural to belong to several groups at once. But a Japanese would say of such a case, "That man is sticking his nose into something else," and this saying carries with it moral censure. The fact that Japanese pride themselves on this viewpoint and call it fastidiousness is once again very Japanese. The saying "No man can serve two masters" is wholeheartedly subscribed to by the Japanese. In body-and-soul emotional participation there is no room for serving two masters. Thus, an individual or a group has always one single distinctive relation to the other. This kind of ideal is also manifested in the relationship between the master and his disciple, including the teacher and student today. For a Japanese scholar, what he calls his teacher (master) is always one particular senior scholar, and he is recognized as belonging linearly to that scholar. For him to approach another scholar in competition with his teacher is felt as a betrayal of his teacher and is particularly unbearable for his teacher. In contrast, for the Chinese it is the traditional norm to have several teachers in one's life, and one can learn freely from all of them in spite of the fact that they are in competition.

Thus, in Japanese society not only is the individual's group affiliation one-to-one but, in addition, the ties binding individuals together are also one-to-one. This characteristic single bond in social relationships is basic to the ideals of the various groups within the whole society.

Notes

1. I find it difficult to choose an English equivalent for *kaisha;* though "company" or "enterprise" corresponds etymologically, they do not have the social implications that the word *kaisha* has for a Japanese.

2. I think that, in this analysis, it is effective and convenient to employ the differentiated concepts *social structure* and *social organization,* as proposed by Raymond Firth (1954; the same paper appears as chap. 3 of his *Essays on Social Organization and Values,* 1964).

3. Certainly there exists what may be called a standard norm or commonality which is shared by Japanese households as a whole (or, more precisely, by a local community or different strata), but within this context each individual household normally has its own ways to regulate the behaviour and speech of individual members.

13

Skiing Cross-Culturally

Vincent S. R. Brandt

While on a skiing trip to the mountains of eastern Korea last winter, I stumbled accidently into a situation that permitted the simultaneous observation of comparable behavior among a small sample of Japanese, Koreans, and Americans. In the course of several years of anthropological fieldwork in the Far East I have tried to maintain an aggressively suspicious attitude towards the concept of "national character," emphasizing instead the variation and complexity that exists within each specific cultural context. In this case, however, observed actions on and off the ski hill seemed to support some popular stereotypes and cultural generalizations of American, Korean, and Japanese behavior to an almost ludicrous degree; the consistency of typical behavior in both formal and informal contexts was so marked that I began to neglect my own skiing, spending more and more time watching the fascinating performances around me.

In Korea there are perhaps only 300–400 skiers, a small but dedicated group that is now growing rapidly as higher living standards and improved transportation facilities permit more people from Seoul to take vacations and travel eight or nine hours to the mountains. Also, in the last few years local mountain boys have for the first time been able to acquire modern equipment, and many of them have become first-class skiers. A few have even been able to attend international skiing events, where they absorbed as much of the current racing techniques as possible, passing these on to friends and admirers when they returned home. A few privileged Koreans such as doctors and university professors have travelled to resorts in Japan and Europe where they could obtain instruction in ski schools and buy books containing detailed directions for mastering the latest complexities of technique. Such people have gathered groups of disciples around them who have the

Reprinted from *Current Anthropology* 15, no. 1 (1974): 64–66.

fanatical dedication to the sport that seems to be characteristic every-where.

Japan—in terms of percentage of the total population that skis, num-ber of resorts and lifts, and size of the domestic industry manufacturing ski equipment—probably leads the world as a skiing nation. Group par-ticipation through clubs, tours, and ski schools is highly organized.

Last February at the "research site," a mountainous area in Kang-won Province called Taegwalyong, there were, in addition to some 40 to 50 Korean skiers, 12 members of a Japanese ski club from Nagano City, who had come to Korea as part of a larger group on a sightseeing tour of the foreign country closest to home. Another, lone Japanese was there coaching the Kangnung city high-school team. He had been sent as part of a "sister province" exchange program between Gumma Prefecture in Japan and Kangwon Province. There was no connection between this person and the Japanese club. The period of observation included Washington's Birthday weekend, and for two days some 35 Americans —civilian men and women working for the U.S. Government in Seoul, a few military personnel, and some American high-school students— were at Taegwalyong on a special group tour. All three national groups used the same hill, a relatively modest one about 250 yds. long that would be labelled a "school slope" at most resorts. My own qualifica-tions for studying the sport cross-culturally include some 25 years of ski-ing in America and Europe, four years of intensive skiing in Japan, and Korean ski trips during the years 1954, 1965, 1969, and 1972. I speak a fair amount of both Korean and Japanese.

The Japanese club members were in stylish uniform with bright red matching hats and sweaters and dark ski pants. They advanced on the slope in a solid phalanx and took up positions in a formal pattern for warming-up exercises with a leader out in front giving commands. Nos-talgic memories came back of my years in Japan, where I had even par-ticipated in this kind of thing. The Koreans were apparently astonished. All action on the hill came to a halt as we watched in silent awe, rein-forced perhaps by the fact that one of the Japanese was an extremely good-looking and well-built girl. After calisthenics the Japanese went into a school formation and began practicing on their skis a series of fundamental, stylized turns and running positions. The instructor was again out in front, while his pupils lined up in formation opposite him, each individual skiing down a short distance on command and then lis-tening at the bottom to criticism of his performance. The only thing exceptional about these standard ski-school procedures was the fact that they were carried out with more than ordinary precision by a club.[1] What *was* sensational was the technique being taught—a Japanized ver-sion of the latest Austrian variant of Jean-Claude Killy's *avalement* or "swallowing" technique, which is now in the process of revolutionizing skiing all over the world. Only the instructor and (to a lesser extent) one other Japanese had mastered the new style, while the rest struggled to imitate them with various degrees of failure. Eventually the class split into an advanced and a beginners' section. The leader then made a short speech in Japanese inviting any Korean on the hill who was interested to participate. About 20 Koreans joined the classes.

Meanwhile, the Japanese coach from Gumma Prefecture and his group of high-school students were carrying out a somewhat similar procedure on a higher and steeper part of the hill. The coach had reached the hill, breathless, a little before ten o'clock without having had any breakfast. His hotel was some distance away, and he had been afraid of being late for the morning session, which was to start at ten. The high-school team arrived an hour later. Two of its members having overslept, the whole group had decided to take a later bus. A Korean Marine Corps major was interpreting, so the instruction, given in ordinary Japanese, came through as sharp military commands in Korean, inducing a nervous, apprehensive mood among the boys. The coach, a competent skier, was teaching the modified Austrian, reverse-shoulder, short-swing technique that with numerous regional variations has been pretty much standard internationally for the last 10–12 years. The boys, with one eye on the fascinating new maneuvers going on among the other Japanese down below, went through the motions of following their coach, but as far as I could tell, they (quite sensibly) made little effort to change their own natural, relaxed style. At no time was a greeting or any conversation exchanged between the Gumma coach and the members of the Nagano club. Their roles as purveyors of different skiing styles to (from their point of view) a backward area made for a sort of built-in rivalry between them. The Japanese club was self-sufficient socially, while the lone instructor was surrounded by his Korean hosts and pupils. Still, the lack of contact seemed odd.

The Koreans who had joined the Japanese classes dropped out one by one, as they became bored and impatient with the unaccustomed constraints and long waits that the system required.

About a dozen Seoul college boys of varying ability were energetically climbing the hill and hurling themselves down it in what appeared to be a frantic effort to achieve instant expertise. They were succeeding. If the falls were spectacular, their progress was sensational. One could literally watch the improvement taking place with each additional run. Other Koreans from Seoul were grouped here and there, usually in informal, noisy instruction sessions. If one person considered himself a better skier than someone else, he felt free to give instruction; the result was a chaotic hubbub with some bewildered beginners getting contradictory coaching from three or four people. Everyone knew, or soon got to know, everyone else, and the skiing went on in an atmosphere not unlike that of a ripe cocktail party with different groups constantly forming and dissolving as part of a process of intense social interaction.

Only four or five of the Americans seemed to have skied before, but the group had brought along an enormous amount of miscellaneous equipment including aluminum sliding saucers, Flexible Flyer sleds, and ancient skis. In addition there were rental skis at the lodge, so there were usually 10–20 Americans doing something on the hill at any one time. The most noticeable feature of their behavior, in addition to the lack of winter-sports ability and outlandish costumes, was the fact that they either challenged fate on their own or paired off into couples. Occasionally groups of two or three men would try some sensational new feat on a sled together, but individuals and couples predominated. In terms of recklessness, many of the Americans were fully the equal of the Korean college students. The difference was that they were looking for immediate thrills while the Koreans were striving to achieve a cherished long-term goal. In this sense the samples are not really comparable, since a group of genuine American skiers would have probably behaved quite differently, trying to improve their technique as conscientiously as the Japanese or the Koreans. But the Americans' tendency to ski as individuals or in small groups, often as couples, is characteristic of ski resorts in the United States as well. Both the Korean and American groups presented a startling contrast to the quiet precision and orderliness of the Japanese club members.

Off the ski hill, all of the Americans, many of whom had never met before the trip, formed one big, informal, easy-going group, the only clear internal division being that between the adults and the high-school students, who formed an uninhibited, noisy, self-sufficient clique of their own. In the lodge the Americans tended to group themselves in constantly changing combinations according to such activities as singing, drinking, eating, playing cards, or initiating sexual advances. Those who sat up late around a big stove drinking and talking far into the night formed one group, while other clusters developed on the basis of private cooking parties.[2] There seemed to be no rank order or formal status differences among any of the Americans at any time, but they soon began to distinguish themselves as individuals through such insistent characteristics as extroversion, garrulity, shyness, popularity, or stupidity.

The Koreans, off the hill, were very active socially. The general boundaries of groups that had arrived together or had arranged to stay together at the ski resort continued to be discernible, although individuals circulated freely, coming and going between different inns, hotels, or farmhouses on numerous visits. Some individuals changed their rooms, moving in with other friends as the result of spur-of-the-moment decisions based on convivial feelings. Often bands of five or six from one university or another wandered around together in the evening looking for excitement. Among age-mates, hierarchical prestige differences theoretically don't exist, but they are clearly defined when students of different classes are together. In the context of a ski holiday it seemed to me that such formal, structured differences tended to be mitigated by other factors such as individual personality or skiing ability. On the occasions when I joined groups comprising both students and older acquaintances from Seoul, the atmosphere was fairly informal and relaxed, but status differences were readily apparent. Such differences were emphasized not only by honorific and plain speech forms, but also by the fact that the warmest place in the room, the first glass of whiskey, and the right to dominate the conversation all went to the senior individuals in any gathering. Conversely, those who ran errands, washed the glasses, and put smoked oysters on crackers were invariably the most junior.

Such a system of ranking is also characteristic—perhaps even more intensely so—of Japanese groups. On this occasion the Japanese ski club kept almost entirely to itself off the ski hill, so there was little chance to observe relationships among its members, but years of participation in and observation of such informal groups in Japan have given me some understanding of the social dynamics involved. Also, they have been well described by Nakane (1970, chap. 2). Despite the subtlety of the ranking, it seems to me that their internal structure is more clearly defined than in Korea. Still a greater contrast exists with regard to the decisiveness of group boundaries and the demands made on the loyalty of individual members. In this case the Japanese club members appeared on the ski hill as a group, skied together as a group, and left at the end of the day as a group. They also entertained themselves in the evening, so that an appearance of overwhelming solidarity was presented to the outside world. In Japan this same sort of self-contained exclusiveness exists among most ski clubs. Individuals are known by their organizations, and it is expected that they will always ski in one and only one social context. I was accused more than once in Japan of being fickle—with intimations of disloyalty—for going skiing with members of different groups on successive weekends. Nevertheless, members of the Japanese ski club with whom I talked on the hill were certainly friendly. They appeared delighted to find an outsider who could speak Japanese and expressed regret that they could not communicate with Koreans of their own age, so some of their separateness must also be attributed to the language barrier.

The reader may draw whatever cross-cultural generalizations he wishes (or his lack of caution permits) from this brief behavioral description. Except for the comments on group structure and cohesion, I have tried to avoid analytical statements in the interest of providing an opportunity for do-it-yourself ethnology. I would like to point out, however, that there is plenty of fertile ground here for drawing parallels between skiing behavior and, for example, economic entrepreneurship. Korean economic development has been often characterized by reckless risk-taking, bursts of enormous self-confidence and enthusiasm, a concern with personal relationships and feelings, and a certain transient approach to group loyalties. There is an almost heroic element to both triumph and failure. In Japan, where the concern with human relationships is also great, the emphasis has been more on combining the latest research and innovation with discipline, control, and restraint. Do such correlations seem too pat, reflecting speculative imagination rather than sober reflection? The reader might try his own.

The fact that striking patterned contrasts were observable is possibly of greater interest than their specific nature. There has been considerable criticism in recent years of the anthropologist's obstinate tendency to insist on cultural differences where it is alleged that they are, in fact, trivial. Some sociologists and political scientists, in particular, who now seem to be riding a wave of grandiose generalization that covers the entire range of human experience, get very impatient with our passion for hunting down and describing the unique. They emphasize (usually from the academic armchair) the increasing social convergence in industrialized or industrializing societies and come up with statements such as the following: "The logic of industrialism inevitably leads to a convergence which cuts through and undermines tradition, regardless of culture, history, and values" (Cole and Karsh 1968:46).

Most of the persons observed in this instance on the ski hill were educated, middle-class representatives of modern industrial society. It seems evident from even superficial and brief observation, however, that cultural differences remain crucial at fundamental levels of human association and interaction, moulding the supposedly universal effects of modernization to fit a more congenial local pattern.

Notes

1. In Japan this kind of formal, club-centered instruction, whereby the more skilled members teach the rest (usually without compensation), is routine. In the United States and Europe, ski schools are organized as money-making concerns, staffed with paid professionals. While professional schools exist in Japan they serve only a tiny portion of the skiing public.

2. Although the lodge served adequate (by U.S. Eighth Army standards, actually rather good) Western-style food which the Americans had already paid for as part of the package tour, several of them refused to eat it, cooking up nasty (but doubtless sanitary) messes of canned spaghetti in their rooms over gasoline-fueled camp stoves. The danger of fire in the crowded wooden building as a result was probably 10 times as great as that of any possible amoebic contamination from eating the Korean food, but military obsessions die hard.

Development and Socialization

Editorial Note to Part Three

PART 3 views the individual person longitudinally as he or she grows from infancy through childhood. Interlaced with this developmental transformation is the process of socialization or enculturation whereby a newborn child is moulded into a Japanese through interaction with adult caretakers and educators. The underlying assumption is that early-childhood socialization is essential to the formation of the adult personality, and that Japanization begins on the very day of the child's birth, if not earlier.

Chapter 14 by William Caudill and Helen Weinstein is an observation-based comparative study of infant-caretaker interaction, drawing upon matched samples of baby-mother pairs (thirty cases each) from Japan and the United States. Following a carefully constructed procedure, the observed sequences of behavior were quantified to be amenable to statistical tests of significance. Remarkable and intriguing differences emerged between the two cultural groups in the behavior of three-to-four-month-old infants and, correspondingly, that of their mothers. Notable differences were detected in the patterns of mother-infant communication. The findings here, in our view, offer a persuasive explanation for the psychological and behavioral differences between Japanese and American adults, such as Japanese reticence versus American open expression.

Another collaborative work is presented in chapter 15. Co-sleeping among Japanese, thus far understood impressionistically, is described and characterized by Caudill and David W. Plath with quantitative data. It is with confidence, therefore, that the authors come to conclude that the Japanese family tends to sleep together even when there is enough space to disperse. The main question they raise is with whom a Japanese sleeper shares the bedroom or the bed. In their answers, the reader will find characteristically Japanese types of relationships between child and parent, husband and wife, and siblings. How sex does and does not interfere with sleeping arrangements will be a revelation to the American reader for whom co-sleeping is usually associated with conjugal or sexual pairs. Also instructive is the change of co-sleeping arrangements over the life cycle course, which the authors trace with singular ingenuity.

It should be noted that co-sleeping arrangements have been changing since the early 1960s, when the data for this chapter was gathered. The Western-style house or apartment and furniture have been replacing the old tatami-floored dwelling partitioned by thin sliding doors; the Western bed is displacing the old futon bedding, particularly for children. This transformation in residential architecture and furnishings, along with a changing sex ideology, is separating children from parents in sleeping as well as in other aspects of life. In other words, this chapter may not reflect the sleeping pattern of urban middle-class Japanese today, insofar as some of the specific findings are concerned. Nevertheless it should be remembered that sleeping side by side in the same room is still a common way of maximizing the pleasure of reunion between close friends or kin of the same sex.

As the child grows up, he or she is initiated into school life, which is to absorb the student's entire time and energy for the next twelve or more years until the last entrance examination. It is common knowledge that there is a wide discrepency between Japanese and American students in their attitudes toward learning and in their academic performances. In an unpublished paper Hiroshi Azuma (1984) has suggested an answer for this difference. While American children must be motivated "intrinsically" to perform a task, Japanese children are ready to persist through task completion, irrespective of whether they are instrinsically interested or not. Azuma terms this persistence "receptive diligence," which is not a product of school education but has already been internalized by the child through family socialization, especially through the mother's identification with the child. From this perspective one might comprehend why the Japanese child, seemingly so unruly and spoiled in the family setting, is transformed into a disciplined, compliant student. For a related study of differences between Japanese and American mothers in the modes of child discipline see Conroy et al. 1980.

Betty B. Lanham, in chapter 16, deals with the moral education of schoolchildren as inferred from textbooks. Analysis is made of "ethics" (the term the author uses interchangeably with "morality," although she thinks the latter implies sexual behavior for Americans) in two aspects: how it has changed from the prewar to postwar era, and what differences are found between Japanese and American ethics. The content of *Dōtoku,* a moral education textbook series used for postwar school children, is analyzed in comparison with a prewar equivalent *(Shūshin)* and American readers (McGuffey and Golden Rules). Some moral values have persisted, and among them perseverance stands out. We also learn about radical changes from *Shūshin* to *Dōtoku*, the latter divested of Confucian tenets, Shintoism, emperor worship, war heroes, and the like. This does not surprise us in view of the postwar abolition and denigration of the *Shūshin* lessons and the controversial nature of the reinstatement of moral education in democratic Japan.

It is interesting to note the subtle difference in the "manner of presenting ethical tenets" by the American and Japanese texts. The *Dōtoku* narratives, Lanham states, are characterized by their open-endedness, involving less rewards and punishments than the American. A greater emphasis is put on the complexity of inner feelings of self and others by the Japanese, and hence stories tend to end with apologies and forgiveness. The adult appears less authoritarian and more subject to the child's disapproval in the Japanese text.

We are tempted to suggest that the lack of dogmatic morality is compensated for by the autonomy or immunity of the individual's inner world. This then explains two points of Lanham's finding which are seemingly paradoxical: the Japanese texts stress the individual's integrity against group pressures while American texts refer more to the misery of isolation; Japanese teachings are more cosmopolitan compared with the ethnocentric tendencies of the American counterpart. It may be that the Japanese moral lessons reflect the autonomy of the individual's inner feelings and ideations from social pressures, whereas group conformity and parochialism loom larger when morality is acted out in social situations.

The child, going through the kind of socialization in the family and school that has been characterized in the foregoing chapters, may or may not turn out to be a normal Japanese. There are deviants as well as conformists, losers as well as winners. While Japanese in general are regarded as academic achievers on a worldwide scale, many of them are sources of parents' and teachers' worry and despair as "dropped-out" *(ochikobore)*, hopelessly unable to follow class instructions and thus prone to delinquency. Such problems are not necessarily unique to the Japanese, but chapter 17 by Hayao Kawai reveals a type of deviant behavior of schoolchildren which is quite distinct from our notions of deviancy and which says something about contemporary Japan.

This chapter takes up the child's violence against his or her family, particularly mother, as a new phenomenon which has shocked the nation. Out of a scatter of psychiatric and correctional cases there emerges a pattern: a "good," compliant child suddenly refuses to attend school and goes out of the way to abuse and torment mother physically and mentally. Kawai attempts to explain this by contending that Japan is a society governed by the maternal principle, one of embracement and containment. Trapped by this, the child has no chance to develop a separate self-identity and at puberty feels that there is no option but to break away by revolting violently.

Part 3 concludes with Thomas Rohlen's case study (chap. 18) of socialization, or rather resocialization, of young adults. A detailed account is given of the spiritual training that new recruits of a commercial bank undergo to be transformed into qualified employees (for a complete enthnographic study of the bank, see Rohlen 1974). The bank administration apparently denies any attempt to brainwash its employees. But quite obviously these young men, fresh from college, are viewed as somewhat deficient and requiring three months of extensive spiritual education, although ostensibly this is offered to familiarize them with the bank's perspective. Rohlen describes five of the principal training events—*zazen* meditation, training at a military camp, performing free manual labor for strangers, farm work and contact sports in the country, and finally an endurance hike of twenty-five miles. The implicit emphasis throughout is on development of spiritual strengths—composure, endurance, acceptance (especially of unpleasant or difficult tasks), social responsibility, and self-reflection, among others. Interestingly, bank administrators regard these educational tasks as properly falling within the province of the family and schools, but feel the institutions have failed to perform these functions in the postwar era. It should be noted that this kind of employee resocialization is, far from being unique to this particular organization, an example of widespread practices.

14

Maternal Care and Infant Behavior in Japan and America

WILLIAM CAUDILL

HELEN WEINSTEIN

HUMAN behavior can be distinguished, in one sense, from that of other animals in the degree to which it is influenced by culture—that is, influenced by shared patterns of action, belief, feeling, and thinking that are transmitted knowingly and unknowingly from one generation to the next through learning. The influence of culture is universal in that in some respects a man learns to become like all men; and it is particular in that a man who is reared in one society learns to become in some respects like all men of his society and not like those of others. A general question underlying the investigation reported here concerns the degree of importance of particular cultural differences, as a variable in the understanding of human behavior.

We began the present longitudinal study of children over the first six years of life in Japan and America because we wished to explore how early in the lives of infants, and in what ways, cultural differences become manifest in behavior. Our focus on culture as a variable is in no way meant to deny the great, and interrelated, importance of other major sources of variation, such as genetic endowment and physiological functioning of the infant, psychological characteristics of the parents, and position of the family in the social structure. Rather, by either controlling for or randomizing the effect of these other sources of variation, we wished to estimate more clearly the amount of the total variance in our sample of human behavior which may be attributed to cultural differences.

In the present study, we selected a matched sample of 30 Japanese and 30 American three-to-four-month-old infants—equally divided by sex, all firstborn, and all from intact middle-class families living in urban settings—and carried out an observational study in the homes of these infants during 1961–64. This article gives the results of that study. Subsequently, we made observations in the homes of the first 20 of these same children in each culture at the time they became two-and-a-half

Reprinted from *Psychiatry* 32 (1969): 12–43.

years of age, and again when they became six years of age, but these data have not as yet been analyzed.

Earlier studies by ourselves and others in Japan and America have indicated meaningful cultural differences in values, interpersonal relations, and personality characteristics. On the basis of this previous work we predicted that our Japanese mothers would spend more time with their infants, would emphasize physical contact over verbal interaction, and would have as a goal a passive and contented baby. We predicted that our American mothers would spend less time with their infants, would emphasize verbal interaction rather than physical contact, and would have as a goal an active and self-assertive baby. Underlying these predictions is the assumption that much cultural learning takes place out of the awareness of the participants, and although the Japanese mother does not consciously teach her infant specifically to become a Japanese baby, nor does the American mother specifically teach her infant to become an American baby, such a process does take place. We therefore also expected that by three-to-four months of age, infants in the two cultures would behave differently in certain important ways.

Our hypotheses were generally confirmed, although there were some surprises, and we conclude that, largely because of different patterns of interaction with their mothers in the two countries, infants have learned to behave in different and culturally appropriate ways by three-to-four months of age. Moreover, these differences in infant behavior are in line with preferred patterns of social interaction at later ages as the child grows to be an adult in Japan and America.

Background and Hypotheses

Before we began our study we thought a good deal, in a conceptual and theoretical sense, about the sources of the wide variation that we expected to find in any of the dependent variables in our observations of the behavior of Japanese and American infants and their caretakers.

We planned to do our observations in the natural setting of the home and because of this we knew, of course, that chance events would contribute to the variation in the data. The main systematic sources of variation, however, we believed would arise from biological, psychological, social, and cultural dimensions of human behavior. Although all of these dimensions are interrelated in actual behavior, each is sufficiently distinct to be thought of as a separate system (Caudill 1958). In the biological dimension we decided to control on birth order, age, and sex of our infants. We expected that the influence on behavior of *individual* differences in genetic endowment and physiological functioning among the Japanese and American infants would be randomly distributed in the two samples. We do not, however, know of any *group* genetic or physiological differences between Japanese and American populations that would meaningfully exert an influence on the behavior of infants. In the psychological dimension, also, we expected the influence of individual differences in the personalities of the mothers and the infants to be randomly distributed in the two samples.

There is a tendency in scientific writing to blur the distinction between social and cultural dimensions of behavior by the use of such combined terms as "sociocultural"; or by subsuming one dimension under the other, as in the work of many anthropologists who think of social structure solely as a part of culture; or by simply ignoring one dimension while concentrating on the other, as in the work of many sociologists who emphasize the effect of position in the social structure to the exclusion of culture. We think of the cultural dimension as particularly referring to those historically derived patterns of thinking, feeling, and behaving that are shared in large part by all members of a society—for example, those qualities that make Englishmen differ from Frenchmen. We think of the social dimension as particularly referring to the occupational and industrial structure that has developed along similar lines in many societies in accompaniment with technological advancement. This process is usually called "modernization" and results in a society that is stratified into social classes (or levels of responsibility) which are closely tied to position in the occupational structure. In this sense, middle-class managerial personnel in England and France may have more in common than either group has with working-class machine operators in its own country.

In the world at present, we believe that each of these dimensions—the cultural and the social—exerts a relatively independent influence on human behavior, and that both dimensions need serious consideration in any cross-national study. There is considerable empirical evidence in the literature, from our own work and that of others, to support these ideas.[1]

For the foregoing reasons we decided in our study to control on social class in the selection of the sample of infants, and thus reduce the variation in our data that might be expected if the families came from differing positions in the social structure. As noted, all families in our sample are middle-class, but we did divide the sample in each country into two groups: (1) the father is the owner or employee of a small, established, independent business; (2) the father is a white-collar, salaried employee in a large business or in government. This distinction between an entrepreneurial and a bureaucratic occupation, and its ramifications in family life, is an important one in Japan, and we expected to find some differences in the behavior of mothers and infants in the two types of families.[2] Despite the work of Miller and Swanson (1958), who did find differences in child rearing in terms of this occupational distinction in their study of families in Detroit, we felt that this distinction would not be very meaningful in our American data.[3]

In the light of the sources of variation we expected, and the controls we decided to use, in the biological, psychological, and social dimensions of infant and caretaker behavior, we emerged, by design, with the cultural dimension as the main independent variable.

On the basis of our previous work in Japan over the past fourteen years, coupled with a study of the literature, we have come to feel that the following differing emphases on what is valued in behavior are important when life in Japan is compared with life in America. These differing emphases seem to be particularly sharp in the areas of family life and general interpersonal relations with which we are most directly concerned here, and perhaps to be somewhat less evident in other areas of life such as business, the professions, or politics.[4] Japanese are more "group" oriented and interdependent in their relations with others, while Americans are more "individual" oriented and independent.[5] Going along with this, Japanese are more self-effacing and passive in contrast to Americans, who appear more self-assertive and aggressive. In matters requiring a decision, Japanese are more likely to rely on emotional feeling and intuition, whereas Americans will go to some pains to emphasize what they believe are the rational reasons for their action.[6] And finally, Japanese are more sensitive to, and make conscious use of, many forms of nonverbal communication in human relations through the medium of gestures and physical proximity in comparison with Americans, who predominantly use verbal communication within a context of physical separateness.[7] One particularly pertinent example of the latter point is that a Japanese child can expect to co-sleep with his parents until he is ten years of age, and that in general a person in Japan can expect to co-sleep in a two-generation group, first as a child and later as a parent and grandparent, over half of his life span; to sleep alone is considered somewhat pitiful because a person would, therefore, be lonely.[8] In this regard, things are quite different in America, and the generations are usually separated in sleeping arrangements shortly after birth and remain so throughout the life cycle of the individual.[9]

In summary, in normal family life in Japan there is an emphasis on interdependence and reliance on others, while in America the emphasis is on independence and self-assertion. The conception of the infant would seem to be somewhat different in the two cultures. In Japan, the infant is seen more as a separate biological organism who from the beginning, in order to develop, needs to be drawn into increasingly interdependent relations with others. In America, the infant is seen more as a dependent biological organism who, in order to develop, needs to be made increasingly independent of others. Our more specific hypotheses in this study came from this general background of family life and interpersonal relations in the two cultures.

As indicated earlier, we expected that our Japanese mothers would spend more time with their infants, would emphasize physical contact over verbal interaction, and would treat them as objects to be acted upon rather than as objects to be interacted with. But, more than this, we expected the quality of the interaction to be differently patterned in the two cultures, and in Japan for it to be a mutually dependent, even symbiotic, relation in which there was a blurring of the boundaries between mother and child.[10] In contrast, we expected that our American mothers would spend less time with their infants, would encourage their physical activity and chat with them more, and would treat them more as separate objects to be interacted with. And we expected the interaction in America to give evidence of the self-assertion of the child and his budding awareness of separateness from his mother.

By focusing on the contrasts in the behavior of mothers and infants in the cultural dimension, we do not mean to imply that we thought of child rearing as completely different in the two countries; we anticipated that we would find many similarities centering around the basic biological needs of the infant and the necessity for the mother to care for these needs. The differences we expected refer more to the "style" of caretaking and its effect upon the child. Equally, we do not mean to imply that one style of caretaking is "better" or "worse" than the other. An individual mother can do a good or a poor job of caretaking within either style. Our emphasis, rather, is upon the effect of differences in behavior as these are repeated day after day in the simple routine of life.

If we find that by three-to-four months of age Japanese and American infants have learned in some ways to behave differently in response to the culturally patterned behavior of their mothers, then this is a fact of great practical and theoretical importance. It means that, out of the direct awareness of mother or child, the precursors of certain ways of behaving, thinking, and feeling that are characteristic of a given culture have become part of an infant's approach to his environment well before the development of language and hence are not easily accessible to consciousness or to change.

Design and Method

The design of our study called for 30 Japanese and 30 American normal infants, who at the time of observation would be between three and four months of age and would be matched as previously described. Our plan was to gather data on the Japanese infants during 1961–62, and then to match the Japanese sample as closely as possible on all characteristics with an American sample that was to be studied during 1962–64. We were able to carry out this plan, although with some variation in the number of cases in each cell. The number and distribution of cases in the final sample used in the analysis of data are given in Table 1.

The Japanese families are of solely Japanese ancestry, and the American families are white and at least second-generation families of European ancestry. All of the Japanese families are nominally Buddhist, and the American families are divided among Protestant (18 cases), Catholic (9 cases), and Jewish (3 cases) affiliation.

In both cultures we checked carefully with the infant's pediatrician and mother concerning any anomalies at birth or special developmental problems during the first three months of life. We decided to use first-born infants not only to control on birth order, but also because the observational situation would be simpler if there was only one child in the home. Thus, strictly speaking, our results are applicable primarily to firstborn infants, and to mothers who are caring for their first child. We chose the age level of three-to-four months because we felt the relationship between mother and infant would have settled into a pattern by that time, and also because the observational method we planned to use had been worked out with infants of that age in mind. The age in days of the infants is quite close in both samples—a Japanese median age of 103 days, and an American median age of 109 days—and a comparison of the two samples in a rank-ordered distribution is not significant. There are more males (18 cases) than females (12 cases) in the Japanese sample because of the limited time we had for research in Japan coupled with the immediate availability of families who met our criteria in other respects.

Japanese mothers in the sample are somewhat older on the average (26.6 years) at the time of birth of their first child than the American mothers (23.7 years). Similarly, Japanese fathers are somewhat older on the average (29.7 years) than American fathers (26.7 years). These differences are in line with the reality in the middle class in the two countries concerning the age of marriage.[11]

All of our families are intact, and the largest number of households (15 Japanese and 25 American) in both samples consists of father, mother, and new baby—that is, the nuclear family. For the Japanese, those households with additional members (usually the father's parents) are mainly independent business families.

All of the families are residents of large cities. In the Japanese sample, we selected 20 cases from Tokyo and 10 from Kyoto because we

Table 1. Distribution of Cases in Terms of Independent Variables

Sex of infant	Japanese (30 cases) Father's Occupation		American (30 cases) Father's Occupation	
	Salaried	Independent	Salaried	Independent
Male	9	9	10	5
Female	6	6	10	5

wished also to take a look at the differences, if any, in child rearing in the two cities. The general way of life in Tokyo is thought of as more modern, and in Kyoto as more traditional. We did not find any significant differences between the two cities as measured by the dependent variables for infant and caretaker behavior, and have combined the cases from the two cities. In the American sample, all cases were selected from the metropolitan area of Washington, D.C.

All of the families are middle class as measured by the occupation and education of the father, and the education of the mother.[12] Although the Japanese sample is equally divided into 15 salaried and 15 independent business families, the American sample contains 20 salaried families and 10 independent business families because we had trouble in locating American cases in which the father was engaged in a small independent business.

The Japanese sample was obtained through pediatricians at St. Luke's International Hospital and at Tsukiji Maternity Hospital in Tokyo, and at Kyoto Prefectural Hospital in Kyoto. In Japan, middle-class mothers, in general, take their babies back to the hospital in which they were born for check-ups, so that the hospital is a normal channel for obtaining cases. Since the normal procedure for American middle-class mothers is to take their babies to the pediatrician's office for routine check-ups, the American cases were obtained from pediatricians in private practice.[13] In both cultures, the pediatricians selected cases from their practice which met our criteria, and they explained our work to the mothers by telling them that we were interested in studying the ordinary daily life of babies in different countries. If the mother agreed to participate in the study, the pediatrician introduced us to the mother and we carried on from there. In addition, in a few cases in both cultures, a mother with whom we had already worked would refer us to a mother who was a friend of hers and who met our criteria for inclusion in the study.[14] We did not pay our families for their time, but in each case we did give a present at the end of the observations.[15]

The data on the Japanese cases were gathered by Mrs. Seiko Notsu-ki, a psychologist; the data on the American cases were gathered by Mrs. Helen Weinstein, an anthropologist and the junior author of this article. Both are married and citizens of the country in which they worked. These circumstances were helpful in establishing easy and friendly relations with all of our families.

Before beginning the collection of data, the senior author trained his colleague in each country in the observational method used in the research. This was done by discussion of the variables, and by jointly conducting observations in a few pilot cases in each culture. After this training period, the senior author, in company respectively with his colleague in Japan and America, gathered actual data on several cases in order to involve himself directly in the collection of research material, and also to obtain duplicate records to be used in a check on the reliability of observations.

At the time of the initial contact with a mother we further explained our study, and told her that we wished to observe the ordinary daily life of her baby. We requested that during our observations she go about her normal routine in the home, including leaving the house if this was her usual activity. We received excellent cooperation from the mothers in both cultures, and in this regard it is important to note that we stressed that our focus was on the life of the baby, and not directly on the behavior of the mother. As explained to the mothers, our method of observation calls for the observer to be near the infant at all times, and if a mother (or other caretaker) leaves the room, the observer stays with the infant.

Upon completion of our observations in the home, we also interviewed the mother for several hours to obtain information on the course of her pregnancy, the birth and subsequent development of the infant, and the general background of the family. A second purpose of the interview was to gather material on those aspects of the current life of the baby that we were not likely to observe because of the particular hours during which we were in the home.

We worked with each family for two days; usually these were consecutive days, and they were never separated by more than a few days. In general we spent about four hours on each day with a family, starting at nine in the morning on the first day, and at one in the afternoon on the second day. In planning our visits, we avoided days on which the mother or baby was ill, and in both cultures we spaced our work throughout all seasons of the year.

In making the observations we used a time-sampling procedure adapted from that originally developed by Rheingold. In this method, one observation of approximately one second in duration is made every fifteenth second in terms of a set of predetermined variables concerning the behavior of the infant and the caretaker. We designed an observation sheet that listed the variables down the side of the page, and provided columns for 40 observations across the page.[16] For each observation, a decision was made for all variables as to their occurrence or non-occurrence, although only occurrences received a check mark on the observation sheet. Four observations were made each minute, and thus a single observation sheet covered a period of ten minutes, or 40 observations. Upon completion of an observation sheet, the observer took a five-minute break during which she clarified, if necessary, the data recorded on the completed sheet, and also wrote descriptive notes concerning the context of the behavior that had just occurred. At the end of this five-minute break, another sheet of 40 observations was begun.

On the first day, observations were made from 9:30 A.M. until noon, and on the second day, from 1:30 P.M. until 4:00 P.M. Thus, 10 sheets, or 400 observations are available for each day, resulting in a total of 800 observations per case for the two days. This is a key number to be kept in mind because it forms the basis upon which the statistical analysis of the data is carried out.

In making the observations, the observer used a simple clipboard with a stopwatch mounted on the top. She sat in a convenient corner of the room and participated minimally in the ongoing situation. The observer would look for one second, and then would check what she had seen in terms of the predefined variables on the observation sheet during the next fourteen seconds. At various points in the observations the mother would carry the baby from one room to another, or into the yard, or onto the street. At these points, the observer followed along and continued to make her observations. Such transition points were naturally more "busy," but things usually settled down within a few observations once the new situation was established.

After a few training sessions this method proved to be very simple to use and to produce reliable data. For example, the simplest situation is that in which the baby is alone, in bed, and asleep. In this case, the same observation concerning the sleeping baby merely moves across the sheet. A more complicated situation is exemplified by the following: At the beginning of a sheet the baby is alone and asleep; he awakens and cries; the mother comes into the room, looks at and talks to the baby; she begins to diaper the baby, with the baby shifting from crying to being happily vocal. Despite the general sequential nature of the observations, it must be remembered that the period of 14 seconds between observations is unrecorded. In this article, therefore, we will only present data on the behavior of the infant and the caretaker in terms of frequency of occurrence within a time-sample of 800 observations made over a five-hour span.

Definition of Dependent Variables

On the original observation sheet the 40 dependent variables were grouped under four headings: (1) Who is the caretaker (4 variables)? (2) Where is the baby (7 variables)? (3) What is the baby doing (14 variables)? (4) What is the caretaker doing (15 variables)? A detailed definition for each variable was established prior to the collection of data. In the process of analysis we have omitted, collapsed, or subdivided some of the variables. Results are presented here predominately in terms of 12 variables for infant behavior and 15 variables for caretaker behavior (see Tables 3 and 4). The definitions for the variables used in this analysis, and how we arrived at them, are as follows.

The basic problem under the heading of "Who is the caretaker?" is how to define a caretaker. Excluding the observer, a caretaker is any adult who is able, at a moment's notice, both to see and to hear the baby.[17] Usually this means that the caretaker is in the same room, but we also define a caretaker as present if the adult is in an adjoining room and can still both see and hear the baby. If the observation is made outside of the house, the same rule of being able both to see and hear the baby is applicable.[18] In all other situations, the baby is considered to be alone. Since the two variables, *caretaker present* and *infant alone,* are reciprocal, only the first is used in this analysis, and is placed under caretaker behavior (see Table 4).

When present, a caretaker can be actively caretaking (doing one or more of the caretaker behaviors listed in Table 4), or can be merely present. When several adults are present, the one who is actively caretaking is considered to be the caretaker. In those rare situations when two adults are equally active, the person who is closer in biological relationship to the infant is considered the caretaker (e.g., the mother rather than the grandmother, or, in the one possibly ambiguous case, the mother rather than the father). When several adults are merely passively present, again the person closer in biological relationship is considered the caretaker.

In recording, we always identified the caretaker by means of a simple code ("M" for mother, "F" for father, "GM" for grandmother, etc.). Empirically, the caretaker is the mother in over 90 percent of such observations in both cultures. In this paper, therefore, we will use the terms "caretaker" and "mother" as equivalent, and will not make any further distinction as to who is the caretaker.

The basic question for us under the heading of "Where is the baby?" finally became whether or not the infant was in close physical contact with the caretaker. An infant is defined as in close physical contact if he is being held in the caretaker's arms or lap, or is being carried by the caretaker; otherwise he is not in close physical contact. In this analysis the variable *in arms* is placed under caretaker behavior (see Table 4) and means close physical contact by being held in arms or lap, or being carried in any fashion. Since the variable is reciprocal with *not in arms,* it is only analyzed here in its positive sense.[19]

Under the heading of "What is the baby doing?" the basic distinction is whether the baby is *awake* or *asleep.* We define these two states largely in terms of whether the infant's eyes are open or closed, coupled with the degree of relaxation of the body. Since the two variables are reciprocal, we only present the results for *infant awake* (see Table 3). If the infant is awake, then he can also be engaged in one or more of the other behaviors.

Breast or bottle must be in the infant's mouth at the time of observation in order to be scored. On the observation sheet these were separate variables, but they are combined here into a single category meaning "attempting intake of liquid nourishment" because there was so little breast feeding in the American cases.[20] When we discuss our results we will give the findings for breast and bottle both separately and in combination. In addition to milk, mothers also gave water, fruit juice, and (in Japan) weak tea by bottle. The attempted intake of these liquids is also scored under the variable of *bottle.*

In America it is usual to start babies on semi-solid food at about the end of the first month of life, but in Japan this type of feeding is delayed much longer and is not typical until about the fourth month. On the observation sheet we had a separate variable labeled "food," under which we scored semi-solid food, or any harder food such as a cracker, when it was in the mouth of the infant at the time of observation. We will later give our findings for this variable separately. Since the data from the Japanese cases are rather scanty,[21] we made a composite variable called *all food* in which we combine the observations of breast, bottle, and food. This variable may be thought of as "attempting intake of any nourishment."[22]

All infants (and adults too) do a certain amount of sucking on "non-nutritive" objects. The variable of *finger or pacifier* denotes this behavior and includes all such actions as sucking on a finger or hand, or sucking on other objects, like a pacifier or the edge of a blanket.

In the area of infant vocalization, it is important to note that we mean any expressively voiced sound, and we did not include hiccups, coughs, and so on, in any of the definitions. *Unhappy vocal* means any negatively voiced sound, and was initially divided into "protest" (a weak negative vocal) and "cry" (a strong negative vocal). *Happy vocal* means any positively voiced sound, and was initially divided into "vocal to caretaker" if the caretaker was in close proximity, and "vocal" if the caretaker was at some distance from the infant or absent. Since the categories of infant vocalization are additive, we also use a composite variable of *total vocal,* which is defined as any vocalization by the infant.

Active means gross bodily movements, usually of the arms and legs, and does not include minor movements such as twitches or startles.

Toy, hand, and *other object* are all categories in which the baby is playing with an object. "Toy" means an actual toy; "hand" means playing with a part of the body, such as the hands, arms, legs, or toes; and "other object" means playing with another object, which must be specified— such as a blanket or the edge of the crib. These variables are mutually exclusive for a single observation, and hence may be added together to form a composite variable called *baby plays,* which may be thought of more conceptually as "baby explores his physical environment."

Under the heading of "What is the caretaker doing?" we have omitted "talks" and "bathes," which were on the original observation sheet. "Talks" was defined as talking to a person other than the infant, and is omitted here because it is not a direct caretaking action.[23] "Bathes" is omitted because the customary time for the Japanese infant to be given a bath is in the evening, whereas the American infant is usually given a bath in the daytime. Since our hours of observation were restricted to the morning and afternoon, we saw only a few Japanese babies being bathed.[24] In designing our study we had to make a choice between (1) standardizing our periods of observation and concentrating on studying simple events which would frequently occur in both cultures (e.g., the infant's vocalization and the caretaker's talking to the baby), or (2) letting our periods of observation vary while studying fewer and more dramatic events (e.g., how the baby was bathed or put to sleep at night) at whatever time they happened. We chose the former course.[25]

The caretaker variables of *feeds, diapers, dresses,* and *positions* are all reasonably self-explanatory. The caretaker is scored as feeding the infant whenever she is offering him the breast, bottle, or food at the time of observation. Diapering is restricted to the checking for wetness and the taking off and putting on of the diaper and its cover, plus assisting the baby to urinate or defecate, and the cleaning, powdering, and oiling of the baby's body. All other removal, putting on, or rearranging of clothing is scored as "dresses." "Positions" is the manipulation of the baby's body to make him more comfortable and can occur whether the infant is "in arms" (e.g., shifting the baby from one shoulder to the other) or not "in arms" (e.g., shifting the position of the baby in an infant seat).

Pats or touches is another combined variable. "Pats" can occur whether the infant is "in arms" or not, and consists of a rhythmic stroking or gentle striking of any part of the baby's body with the apparent intent of soothing or burping. "Touches" can occur only when the infant is not "in arms," and means that the caretaker's hand is resting on the baby's body, again with the apparent intent of soothing.

Other care is a general category under which are scored other caretaking acts which must be specified in writing on the observation sheet— such as "wipes baby's face" or "takes baby's temperature."

Plays with means that the caretaker is in direct interaction with the baby and is attempting to amuse or entertain him by such acts as playing peek-a-boo or pat-a-cake, bouncing him on her knee, or showing him how a toy works. The somewhat related variable of *affections* is sharply delimited and means that the caretaker kisses the baby, or snuggles her face against the baby's body.

Looks at is combined from two mutually exclusive variables, "looks" and "looks at," on the observation sheet. "Looks" means that the caretaker glances at, or directs her visual attention to, the infant from a distance of more than six feet. "Looks at" means that the caretaker is within six feet of the infant or is holding the infant "in arms" and looks directly at the baby's face.

Talks to means that the caretaker is talking, or otherwise vocalizing, directly to the infant. We have subdivided this variable, making use of the descriptive notes on the observation sheets, into *chats* and *lulls*. "Lulls" is a very delimited variable and means that the caretaker is softly singing or humming a lullaby, or making repetitive comforting noises, with the apparent intent of soothing and quieting the baby or getting him to go to sleep. "Chats" includes all other vocalization to the infant, such as talking to him, singing to him in a lively fashion, and playing word games ("boo," "goo," etc.) with him.

Rocks includes all conscious acts of the caretaker to cause the baby to sway rhythmically back and forth. Rocking usually occurs when the infant is "in arms," but can occur when he is not "in arms"—as when the mother rocks a cradle or a baby carriage. "Rocks" is not scored when the infant is "in arms" and is merely being moved up and down by the normal walking motion of the caretaker.

Reliability and Standardization of Data

Reliability was checked between two observers in 7 Japanese cases, using every other case among the first 14 cases completed, and in 3 American cases, using the first 3 cases completed. The senior author was the "constant" observer in the reliability check, being paired with Mrs. Notsuki in Japan and with Mrs. Weinstein in America.

In our approach to the question of reliability, we chose to use severe criteria, and to look at agreement between observers at the level of the individual observation. In assessing reliability we made both an "exact check" and what we call a "contiguous check." In an exact check, the two observers must agree about the presence of a category of behavior in exactly the same observation. In a contiguous check, the two observers must agree about the presence of a category of behavior within the limits of two observations.[26] The contiguous check seems to us to be a reasonable procedure because of the difficulty of keeping stopwatches synchronized, and because of the visual difficulty in picking the correct column in which to place an observation while moving across the sheet. In some places in the raw data, the observers have obviously recorded the same behavior for the infant and the caretaker over a ten-minute sheet, but are consistently off one column across the entire 40 observations. In Table 2, therefore, the percentage agreement between observers is given in terms of the contiguous check. In general, the reliability of the dependent variables is satisfactory in both cultures. There are only two instances in which reliability is poor, both in the Japanese data —a level of 49 percent agreement on "positions," and of 61 percent on "affections."

As we checked reliability, we also became aware that a variable could be satisfactorily reliable and still be "biased." By this we mean that compared to the scores of a constant observer (Caudill), the observers in the two cultures (Notsuki and Weinstein) might differ in the same direction (that is, both observers would have proportionately greater or fewer observations on a variable than the constant observer, but the proportions would be meaningfully different); or, what is worse, the observers in the two cultures might differ in opposite directions (that is, one observer would have proportionately greater and the other proportionately fewer observations than the constant observer). For example, on the variable of "active" in the Japanese cases Caudill had 91 percent as many presence scores as Notsuki, but he had only 75 percent as many presence scores as Weinstein in the American cases; on the variable of "total vocal" Caudill had 104 percent as many presence scores as Notsuki, but only 86 percent as many presence scores as Weinstein.

Because of these differences in proportions, we computed a weight for each variable which would standardize the scores to those of the constant observer. Thus, for example, on the variable of "active," we reduced Notsuki's scores by applying a weight of 0.91, and reduced Weinstein's scores by a weight of 0.75. Similarly, in the variable of "total vocal," we increased Notsuki's scores by a weight of 1.04, and decreased Weinstein's scores by a weight of 0.86. The weights used to standardize all of the dependent variables are given in Table 2. The use of this method effectively eliminates the error introduced by the other

Table 2. Observer Reliability and Weights Used for Standardization of Frequencies of Observations across Cultures

Dependent Variables	Japanese (7 cases)			American (3 cases)		
	Average Frequency per Case	Average Percent Agreement per Case†	Weight Used for Standard-ization‡	Average Frequency per Case	Average Percent Agreement per Case†	Weight Used for Standard-ization‡
Infant Behavior						
Awake	497	98	—	430	100	—
Breast or Bottle	56	99	—	16	100	—
All Food	56	99	—	25	99	.98
Finger or Pacifier	105	92	—	253	84	.94
Total Vocal	111	91	1.04	126	80	.86
Unhappy	63	89	1.05	70	88	1.07
Happy	56	70	1.10	58	70	.64
Active	87	69	.91	104	74	.75
Baby Plays	145	85	.96	115	93	1.07
Toy	72	90	.94	83	95	1.05
Hand	29	79	1.04	11	87	1.12
Other Object	43	84	—	26	94	—
Caretaker Behavior						
Presence of	574	99	—	275	100	—
Feeds	64	99	—	37	100	—
Diapers	17	95	.98	25	96	.93
Dresses	13	84	1.06	15	99	1.03
Positions	12	49	1.75	12	77	.71
Pats or Touches	44	78	.82	39	87	.84
Other Care	29	85	.97	19	85	.86
Plays with	26	67	1.34	34	86	1.16
Affections	9	61	1.44	6	74	1.11
Looks at	233	94	—	170	90	1.06
Talks to	120	90	—	85	83	.83
Chats	91	90	—	82	83	.83
Lulls	29	94	—	3	100	—
In Arms	158	100	—	91	99	—
Rocks	66	90	.95	3	88	—

† Agreement between two observers as to the presence (Yes) or absence (No) of a behavior is classified within four cells: (a) Yes/Yes, (b)Yes/No, (c) No/Yes, (d) No/No. Percent agreement is computed as the ratio of (2a) to (2a + b + c), thus avoiding the use of the somewhat spurious agreement on absence of behavior.

‡ Weight used to standardize frequencies across cultures is computed as the ratio of (Sum of Caudill's Presence Scores) to (Sum of Other Observer's Presence Scores).

observers' being "off" in differing proportions (and directions) from the constant observer, and permits a more accurate comparison of scores across cultures.

We believe that, as a general methodological point, the issue of standardizing scores has great importance; and, so far as we know, this is the first time it has been met directly in cross-cultural research. Without standardization, it is quite possible to have satisfactory reliability among observers within several cultures, but not to know whether the general perception or "set" of the observers is the same or different across cultures.

Techniques Used in Analysis of Data

The major results reported here (see Tables 3–10) were arrived at through use of multivariate analysis of variance.[27] The collection of the data over 800 equally spaced observations in each case makes the use of this technique of analysis very appropriate. In the analysis, the dependent variables were divided into two groups, 12 infant behaviors and 15 caretaker behaviors. Within each group, dependent variables were analyzed singly, and in combination (by means of canonical correlation as discussed later), in relation to three independent variables—culture, father's occupation, and sex of infant. The results for any one independent variable were always controlled in terms of the effect of the other two independent variables. In Tables 3–10, all means given for an independent variable are adjusted (that is, they are co-varied) for the effects of the other two independent variables.[28]

In addition to the analysis of the data over the total sample of 60 cases, we always also split the sample by culture into two groups of 30 cases each and ran duplicate intra-cultural analyses on all dependent variables in relation to the two independent variables (and their interaction) of father's occupation and sex of infant. We do not present the results of these intra-cultural analyses in tabular form in this article, but we will refer to these further analyses as they become important for the development of our argument.

In evaluating results we give two measures of the effect of an independent variable upon a dependent variable. The first measure is a correlation, and is an estimate of the magnitude of the effect (the proportion of the variance of the dependent variable attributable to the independent variable). The definition of the correlation coefficient used in this analysis is given in the footnotes to Table 3.[29] The second measure is an estimate of the significance of the effect (the likelihood that the null hypothesis can be rejected), and is derived from the F ratio obtained in an analysis of variance. All tests of significance reported in this paper are "two-tailed," meaning that for statistical purposes we take the conservative position that we have not predicted the direction of the finding.

The canonical correlation which is given at the bottom of Tables 3–10 is a very useful summarizing statistic. In descriptive language, the computer is programmed to develop what is, in effect, a composite dependent variable from the set of dependent variables through a process of discriminate function analysis.[30] Thus, in Tables 3–10, the composite dependent variables corresponding to the canonical correlations may be thought of as "infant behavior in general" and "caretaker behavior in general."

A few words need to be said about the use of percentages in the analyses that led to the development of Tables 6–10. After finishing work with the total frequencies (see Tables 3 and 4), we classified the 800 observations in each case in terms of their occurrence in six "states," which were defined by the infant's being either asleep or awake, and by the caretaker's doing caretaking, merely being present, or being absent (see Table 5). Because each case varies in the frequency with which its observations occur in the various states, we converted the frequency of occurrence of the dependent variables to percentages (that is, the frequency of occurrence of a dependent variable in a given state relative to total observations in that state).[31]

Finally, we ran a correlation matrix (Pearsonian r) over the frequency tabulations within each culture for the 12 infant and 15 caretaker variables for all of our analyses both in terms of total frequencies, and in terms of the frequencies in each of the states. We are not presenting these correlation matrices in tabular form in this article, but we will refer to pertinent patterns of correlations as they relate to our results.

Results

Total Observations

The results of the analyses of the main effects of the independent variables over the total 800 observations in each case are given in Tables 3 and 4.[32] A general inspection of the tables will quickly indicate that culture is by far the most important variable in accounting for the differences in infant and caretaker behavior. Before turning to a detailed examination of the results by culture, however, let us dispose of the findings for the other two independent variables.

As can be seen in Tables 3 and 4, there are no findings by sex of infant for the behavior of either the infant or the caretaker. Equally, an examination of the intra-Japanese and intra-American analyses reveals no significant findings by sex of infant.

Father's occupation does not produce any findings for infant behav-

Table 3. Adjusted Mean Frequencies, in Total Observations, of Infant Behavior: By Culture, Father's Occupation, and Sex of Infant

Categories of Infant Behavior	Adjusted Mean Frequencies								
	Culture			Father's Occupation			Sex of Infant		
	Japanese	American	Correlation†	Salaried	Independent	Correlation	Male	Female	Correlation†
Infant Awake	494	493	.01	474	521	.20	498	488	.04
Breast or Bottle	66	55	.11	59	62	.03	63	57	.06
All Food	68	74	.06	71	71	.00	74	68	.06
Finger or Pacifier	**69**	**172**	**.44****	116	127	.06	124	116	.04
Total Vocal	94	116	.25	100	112	.13	108	102	.07
Unhappy	66	45	.33	50	64	.21	55	57	.03
Happy	**30**	**59**	**.51****	45	44	.02	48	41	.14
Active	**51**	**95**	**.45****	73	74	.02	73	73	.00
Baby Plays	**83**	**170**	**.50****	129	124	.03	133	119	.09
Toy	48	82	.28	66	64	.01	76	52	.21
Hand	**14**	**27**	.33	21	20	.01	21	20	.01
Other Object	**22**	**57**	**.47****	41	38	.04	34	46	.18
Canonical Correlation‡			**.80****			.24			.38
Total Cases	30	30		35	25		33	27	

† This partial correlation is the square root of the ratio of (a) the sum of the squared deviations from the mean attributable to the independent variable in question, to (b) the total sum of the squared deviations minus the sum of the squared deviations attributable to the control variables and their interactions. When this partial correlation is squared, the result is a measure of the proportion of variance attributable to the independent variable in question. The means and partial correlations for all findings significant at $p < 0.05$ are printed in boldface. One asterisk (*) indicates $p < 0.01$, two asterisks (**) indicate $p < 0.001$.

‡ The variables of "Total Vocal" and "Baby Plays" are not included in the canonical correlations because of linear dependency with their constituent variables "Unhappy" and "Happy," and "Toy," "Hand," and "Other Object." The means for the constituent variables do not, however, add exactly to the mean for the corresponding total variable because of rounding and the weights used to standardize frequencies of observations across cultures as indicated in Table 2. The variable of "Infant Awake" is also omitted from the canonical correlations in this table to make them comparable with the canonical correlations in Tables 6, 8, and 9.

Table 4. Adjusted Mean Frequencies, in Total Observations, of Caretaker Behavior: By Culture, Father's Occupation, and Sex of Infant

| | Adjusted Mean Frequencies | | | | | | | | |
| | Culture | | | Father's Occupation | | | Sex of Infant | | |
Categories of Caretaker Behavior	Japanese	American	Correlation†	Salaried	Independent	Correlation†	Male	Female	Correlation†
Caretaker Present	**541**	**421**	**.37***	**437**	**543**	**.33**	471	494	.08
Feeds	74	71	.03	71	74	.04	78	65	.13
Diapers	23	17	.24	19	21	.08	20	20	.02
Dresses	12	13	.03	12	14	.11	13	12	.05
Positions	**8**	**19**	**.49****	13	14	.02	15	12	.17
Pats or Touches	34	47	.23	38	43	.08	41	39	.04
Other Care	17	23	.15	21	19	.05	19	22	.10
Plays with	39	24	.25	29	35	.10	34	28	.10
Affections	7	9	.09	7	10	.17	9	7	.20
Looks at	**242**	**299**	**.27**	247	302	.26	278	260	.09
Talks to	101	123	.21	101	127	.24	116	107	.09
Chats	**79**	**120**	**.42****	94	108	.25	102	96	.06
Lulls	**22**	**3**	**.44****	**8**	**20**	**.28***	14	11	.09
In Arms	**197**	**139**	**.27**	**133**	**217**	**.36***	163	175	.06
Rocks	**46**	**20**	**.35***	22	47	.34	39	25	.19
Canonical Correlation‡			**.79****			.52			.51
Total Cases	30	30		35	25		33	27	

† See footnote in Table 3 for explanation of this partial correlation. The means and correlations for all findings significant at p < 0.05 are printed in boldface. One asterisk (*) indicates p < 0.01, two asterisks (**) indicate p < 0.001.

‡ Canonical correlations do not include the variable of "Talks to" because of linear dependency with the constituent variables "Chats" and "Lulls"; the means of the constituent variables do not, however, add exactly to the mean for the total variable because of rounding and the weights used to standardize frequencies of observations across cultures as indicated in Table 2. In addition, the variable of "Caretaker Present" is omitted to make the canonical correlations in this table comparable with those in Tables 7 and 10.

ior, but it does produce an interesting pattern of findings for caretaker behavior. As can be seen in Table 4, mothers in small independent business families are present more, and lull, carry, and rock their infants more than mothers in salaried families. When, however, we look at the separate intra-cultural analyses, there are no significant findings by father's occupation in the American data. In the Japanese data, on the other hand, all of the findings in Table 4 are significant in the same manner, and in addition there are two further findings in the same direction on "infant awake" and caretaker "talks to" baby. Thus, the pattern of findings in the intra-Japanese analysis is that in the small independent business family the baby is awake more, and the caretaker is present more and doing more talking to, lulling, carrying, and rocking of the baby than is the case in the salaried family. It seems evident, therefore, that as a minor theme, occupational style of life does make a difference in Japanese culture, but not—at least in our data—in American culture.

Let us look now at the results of the analyses by culture in more detail. We will consider the areas of similarity in behavior before turning to the areas of difference.

As can be seen in Table 3, the types of infant behavior in which there are no differences between the two cultures are those clearly concerned with biological needs. Thus, there are no significant differences in the amount of time awake, sucking on breast or bottle, or intake of all food.[33] Technically, there also is no difference in the amount of total vocalization, but the correlation is .25, which is just short of being significant ($F = 3.7$, $df = 1/52$, $p < 0.058$).

For the caretakers in the two cultures, most of the areas of similarity indicated in Table 4 are concerned with basic functions involved in caring for the infant's biological needs for nutrition, elimination, and physical comfort. Thus, there are no significant differences in "feeds," "diapers," "dresses," "pats or touches," and "other care." Also, there is no difference in the overall amount of talking to the infant, but the manner in which this talking is done is clearly different. Affectionate behavior toward the infant may or may not be a requirement of basic caretaking, depending on one's point of view, but, in any event, there is no difference in such behavior between the two cultures. Finally, playing with the baby, which is not a requirement of basic caretaking, shows no difference in a technical sense, but the finding has a correlation of .25, on the borderline of significance ($F = 3.8$, $df = 1/52$, $p < 0.058$).

To generalize, the areas of similarity in both cultures point to the expression of biological needs by all of the infants, and the necessity for all of the mothers to care for these needs. Beyond this, however, the differences lie in the styles in which infants and mothers behave in the two cultures.

The American baby appears to be more physically active and happily vocal, and more involved in the exploration of his body and his environment than is the Japanese baby, who, in contrast, seems more subdued in all these respects. These differences can be seen in Table 3, which shows the American infant as more active,[34] more happily vocal (and quite possibly more totally vocal, as indicated earlier), more exploring of his body by greater sucking on his fingers (or by putting other parts of his body and objects into his mouth),[35] and more exploring of his environment in playing with toys, hands, and other objects. The Japanese infant, on the other hand, is only greater in unhappy vocalization.

These differences, moreover, do not just occur singly, variable by variable, but appear to be interconnected. For example, the physical activity of the American baby is negatively correlated with "finger or pacifier" ($-.42$), and positively correlated with "total vocal" ($.71$), "happy vocal" ($.80$), "baby plays" ($.64$), "toy" ($.56$), "hand" ($.45$), and "caretaker present" ($.38$). On the other hand, the physical activity of the Japanese baby shows much less patterning, and is only correlated with "total vocal" ($.59$), "unhappy vocal" ($.39$), and "happy vocal" ($.43$).[36]

The differences in styles of caretaking in the two cultures appear to be equally pronounced. The American mother seems to have a more lively and stimulating approach to her baby, as indicated in Table 4, which shows the American caretaker as positioning the infant's body more, and looking at and chatting to the infant more. The Japanese mother, in contrast, is present more with the baby, in general, and seems to have a more soothing and quieting approach, as indicated by greater lulling, and by more carrying in arms, and rocking.

It may also be that the Japanese mother plays with her baby more, but of even greater interest is the very different pattern of intercorrelations for this variable in the two cultures. The Japanese mother's playing with baby is negatively correlated with "hand" ($-.39$), and "other object" ($-.36$), and positively correlated with "caretaker present" ($.48$), "affections" ($.63$), "looks at" ($.53$), "talks to" ($.77$), "chats" ($.65$), "lulls" ($.66$), "in arms" ($.76$), and "rocks" ($.61$). At the least, this pattern means that those Japanese mothers who play more with their babies also do more soothing of their babies. In contrast, the American mother's playing with baby is correlated with "positions" ($.36$), "pats or touches" ($.57$), "talks to" ($.47$), and "chats" ($.47$). There is no suggestion in the American pattern that a mother who plays more with her baby is also likely to do more soothing.

The key link between the infant and mother in the American culture seems to us to show up in the pattern of correlations with infant's "happy vocal." For the American infant, "happy vocal" is correlated negatively with "finger or pacifier" ($-.41$), and is positively correlated with "total vocal" ($.92$), "active" ($.80$), "baby plays" ($.55$), "toy"

(.48), "hand" (.39), "caretaker present" (.48), "affections" (.37), "looks at" (.39), "talks to" (.39), "chats" (.39), and "rocks" (.38). We feel that the link between baby's happy vocalizations and caretaker's chatting with baby is especially important, as it indicates a major type of communication between the American infant and his mother that is not found in the Japanese data. For the Japanese infant, "happy vocal" is correlated only with the following: negatively with "rocks" ($-.36$), and positively with "active" (.43) and "other care" (.48).

In summary, then, of the analyses by culture of the total observations, the expression of the infant's biological needs, and the mother's basic caretaking of these needs, are the same in both cultures; but beyond this, the styles of the infant's behavior and the mother's care are different. The Japanese baby seems passive, and he lies quietly with occasional unhappy vocalizations, while his mother, in her care, does more lulling, carrying, and rocking of her baby. She seems to try to soothe and quiet the child, and to communicate with him physically rather than verbally. On the other hand, the American infant is more active, happily vocal, and exploring of his environment, and his mother in her care does more looking at and chatting to her baby. She seems to stimulate the baby to activity and to vocal response. It is as if the American mother wanted to have a vocal, active baby, and the Japanese mother wanted to have a quiet, contented baby. In terms of the styles of caretaking of the mothers in the two cultures, they seem to get what they apparently want. That these two patterns do, indeed, discriminate between the cultures is indicated by the significant canonical correlations for infant behavior (.80) and for caretaker behavior (.79).

Division of the Data into States

Our next step was further to refine the data by grouping them into what we call states. The six states are made up of the combination of the infant's being either awake or asleep in relation to the caretaker's doing active caretaking, being present but not doing caretaking, or being absent. We divided the 800 observations in each case into these six states. The results of an analysis of variance for "time in state" in terms of culture can be seen in Table 5.[37]

The first thing to note in Table 5 is that the amount of time spent in doing caretaking when the baby is awake (State One) is not significantly different in the two cultures. Thus, the styles of caretaking and of infant behavior are different, but the mothers in both cultures do caretaking about the same amount of time during the daytime hours. This finding contradicts the popular notion that the Japanese mother is more attentive to her baby. What is true, however, is that the Japanese mother does seem to spend more time simply being with her baby when he is

Table 5. Cultural Comparison of Adjusted Mean Frequencies for Time in Six States

Culture	Infant Awake			Infant Asleep		
	Caretaker Present and Caretaking (State One)	Caretaker Present but Not Caretaking (State Two)	Caretaker Absent (State Three)	Caretaker Present and Caretaking (State Four)	Caretaker Present but Not Caretaking (State Five)	Caretaker Absent (State Six)
Japanese (30 cases)	**286**	**103**	106	**52**	**100**	153
American (30 cases)	321	53	119	16	32	**259**
Correlation†	.16	.34	.08	.37*	.45**	.42**
Canonical Correlation‡	.37			.58**		

† See foot note in Table 3 for explanation of this partial correlation. The means and correlations for all findings significant at $p < 0.05$ are printed in boldface. One asterisk (*) indicates $p < 0.01$, two asterisks (**) indicate $p < 0.001$.

‡ It is not possible to obtain a canonical correlation over the six states because of linear dependency. Canonical correlations are given, however, for States One, Two, and Three in which the infant is awake, and for States Four, Five, and Six in which the infant is asleep.

awake as indicated by the finding in State Two. And yet, in State Three, when the infant is awake and alone, again there is no significant difference between the two cultures. The canonical correlation over the three states in which the baby is awake is not significant, and perhaps the best general statement we can make is that there is not a significant difference between the cultures in the amount of time a mother is present or absent during the time that her baby is awake.

The three states in which the baby is asleep, however, show a sharper contrast between the cultures. In State Four, the Japanese mother is clearly doing more caretaking for the sleeping baby, and we will return later to this question of what it is that Japanese mothers do to sleeping babies. In State Five (as in State Two) the Japanese mother is again simply present more. It follows, therefore, that in State Six, the American infant is alone more when asleep than is the Japanese infant. The overall pattern of cultural difference for the three states in which the baby is asleep is confirmed by the significant canonical correlation (.58).

A further insight into the patterns of behavior represented in Table 5 comes from a different type of analysis that we are in the process of applying to the basic data. Because the 800 observations follow along in regular sequence over the data sheets, it is possible to define various kinds of "episodes" that have a definite beginning and ending. From this type of analysis, we know that caretaking for the American mother is largely an "in" and "out" affair. When she is in the room with the infant she is usually doing active caretaking, and upon finishing this she goes out of the room. The Japanese mother, although not engaged in active caretaking any greater amount of the time, is passively present in the room with the infant to a greater extent. This behavior of the Japanese mothers in our sample is not due to a shortage of other rooms into which to go (see footnote 18), but is again more a matter of style of caretaking.

We turn now to a consideration of what is going on in the various states, as measured by the dependent variables for infant and caretaker behavior. By definition, nothing is happening in States Five and Six beyond their occurrence, and we will, therefore, confine the discussion to States One through Four.

Analyses by States

As can be seen in Tables 6 and 7, which give the results for infant and caretaker behaviors in State One, when the baby is awake and the mother is doing caretaking, the general picture is mainly a more sharply focused version of that obtained from the analysis of the total observations. Once again, culture proves to be the most interesting independent variable, although there are a few findings by sex of infant, an

Table 6. Adjusted Mean Percentages, in State One, of Infant Behavior: By Culture, Father's Occupation, and Sex of Infant

| | Adjusted Mean Percentages | | | | | | | | |
| | Culture | | | Father's Occupation | | | Sex of Infant | | |
Categories of Infant Behavior	Japanese	American	Correlation†	Salaried	Independent	Correlation†	Male	Female	Correlation†
Breast or Bottle	**24**	**14**	**.31**	20	18	.08	19	18	.04
All Food	**24**	20	.14	24	20	.13	23	22	.02
Finger or Pacifier	6	9	.17	7	9	.15	7	8	.13
Total Vocal	**14**	**22**	**.45****	18	18	.03	18	19	.07
Unhappy	10	8	.17	9	10	.09	9	10	.13
Happy	5	**11**	**.62****	8	7	.13	8	8	.03
Active	5	**15**	**.60****	11	10	.08	10	10	.03
Baby Plays	**11**	**25**	**.65****	17	19	.14	19	17	.13
Toy	7	9	.10	7	9	.12	**10**	**6**	**.35***
Hand	1	**4**	**.51****	2	3	.18	3	3	.01
Other Object	3	**11**	**.63****	7	7	.01	6	8	.20
Canonical Correlation‡			**.84*****			.34			.49
Total Cases	30	30		35	25		33	27	

† See footnote in Table 3 for explanation of this partial correlation. The means and correlations for all findings significant at $p < 0.05$ are printed in boldface. One asterisk (*) indicates $p < 0.01$, two asterisks (**) indicate $p < 0.001$.
‡ See footnote in Table 3.

Table 7. Adjusted Mean Percentages, in State One, of Caretaker Behavior: By Culture, Father's Occupation, and Sex of Infant

Categories of Caretaker Behavior	Culture			Father's Occupation			Sex of Infant		
	Japanese	American	Correlation†	Salaried	Independent	Correlation†	Male	Female	Correlation†
Feeds	26	21	.16	26	21	.15	24	24	.01
Diapers	9	6	.25	8	6	.16	7	8	.01
Dresses	4	4	.05	4	4	.07	4	4	.01
Positions	**2**	6	**.62****	4	4	.12	4	4	.09
Pats or Touches	11	14	.25	13	12	.10	12	13	.03
Other Care	5	7	.18	6	5	.20	5	6	.15
Plays with	12	7	**.34***	10	9	.07	10	9	.06
Affections	2	3	.14	2	3	.09	3	2	.21
Looks at	77	89	**.42****	84	81	.11	83	83	.03
Talks to	33	39	.22	36	36	.01	36	36	.02
Chats	28	**39**	**.45****	34	31	.13	32	34	.09
Lulls	6	**1**	**.46****	2	5	.24	4	3	.10
In Arms	**55**	42	**.35***	46	53	.20	45	52	.20
Rocks	**12**	**5**	**.38***	7	**11**	**.28**	10	7	.19
Canonical Correlation‡			**.85****			.57			.49
Total Cases	30	30		35	25		33	27	

† See footnote in Table 3 for explanation of this partial correlation. The means and correlations for all findings significant at $p < 0.05$ are printed in boldface. One asterisk (*) indicates $p < 0.01$, two asterisks (**) indicate $p < 0.001$.

‡ See footnote in Table 4.

occupation of father.[38] Let us discuss the latter findings before turning to the analysis by culture.

In Tables 6 and 7 there is only one finding by sex of infant, and this is that boy babies play with toys more than girl babies. Upon inspection of the intra-cultural analyses, however, this turns out to be solely an American finding. In the intra-American analysis, boy babies play significantly more with toys, and, in addition, American mothers show significantly more affection to boy babies. These findings hint at the possibility that the American mother does, in some ways, treat her boy baby differently from her girl baby. In the Japanese data this is clearly not the case, and there are no findings by sex of infant in the intra-Japanese analysis.

By father's occupation there is one finding in Tables 6 and 7: Caretakers in independent business families rock their infants more than caretakers in salaried families. This finding proves to be solely an intra-Japanese finding, and there are no findings for infant or caretaker behaviors by father's occupation in the intra-American analysis. The intra-Japanese analysis shows that mothers in independent business families rock their babies more, but that mothers in salaried families look at their babies more and perform other care for them more. This contrast by type of family between rocking and looking at suggests that the mother in the salaried family is beginning to give up some aspects of traditional Japanese child care, and is moving toward what she considers a "modern" kind of care.

Turning to the analysis by culture in State One, the similarities and differences in behavior for Japanese and American infants and mothers are much the same as those described earlier for the total observations. For infants in State One, it can be seen in Table 6 that there is no difference in the variable of all food—that is, in the total intake of nutritive substances. In contrast to the analysis by total observations, however, Japanese babies in State One suck more on breast or bottle than do American babies.[39] Also in contrast to the total observations, there are no significant differences in "finger or pacifier" and "unhappy vocal" in State One, probably because mothers in both cultures are, by definition in this state, present and doing caretaking.

As can be seen in Table 7, the findings on similarities in caretaker behavior in State One are almost a duplicate of those for total observations. There are no significant differences in the proportion of time that mothers in both cultures devote to the following activities: "feeds," "diapers," "dresses," "pats or touches," "other care," "affections," and "talks to." Thus, in the more sharply focused situation in State One, where the mother is doing caretaking for an awake infant, once again the similarities in the behavior of the infants in the two cultures are centered on biological needs, and the similarities for the mothers lie in basic caretaking for these needs.

The differences in the behavior of infants and caretakers in State One are also quite clear and in line with the results from the total observations. As can be seen in Table 6, the American infant is more happily vocal (as well as definitely more totally vocal) and is more active, and more engaged in play—specifically with his hand or other object. In State One the Japanese infant is greater only in sucking on breast or bottle. And, as can be seen in Table 7, the American mother is doing more positioning of, looking at, and chatting with her infant, while the Japanese mother is doing more playing with, lulling, carrying, and rocking of her infant.

A particularly interesting and suggestive finding concerning cultural differences in the style of communication between mother and baby emerges from the correlational analyses of the data in State One. In each culture, the caretaker's chatting to infant shows a strong patterning of correlations with other variables,[40] but the key difference is that the American mother's "chats" is significantly correlated with the infant's "happy vocal" (.66) and not with his "unhappy vocal" (.29), whereas the opposite is true for the Japanese mother's "chats," which is significantly correlated with the infant's "unhappy vocal" (.44) and not with his "happy vocal" (.30). Apparently, the mother's chatting to infant serves a different purpose in each culture, and probably also serves to reinforce the happy vocalization of the American infant, and the unhappy vocalization of the Japanese infant. The American mother would appear to be using chatting as a means of stimulating, and responding to, her infant's happy vocals. The Japanese mother, however, would appear to be using chatting to soothe and quiet her infant, and to decrease his unhappy vocals. In support of the latter point, it should be noted that the Japanese mother's chatting is significantly correlated with "lulls" (.40), but this is not so for the American mother (where the correlation is only .14).

The preceding line of thought receives further confirmation from the patterning of the correlations associated with "lulls" in each culture. The American mother's lulling is only significantly correlated with one other variable—"rocks" (.42). On the other hand, the Japanese mother's lulling shows a strong pattern, and is significantly correlated with "total vocal" (.61), "unhappy vocal" (.65), "active" (.38), "baby plays" (.64), "toy" (.63), "pats or touches" (.44), "plays with" (.67), "affections" (.57), "looks at" (.49), "talks to" (.74), "chats" (.40), "in arms" (.68), and "rocks" (.57). At the least, this pattern suggests that those Japanese mothers who do more lulling, carrying, and rocking, have babies who are more vocal, active, and playing. In future work with the data, we plan to explore further the context of communication between caretakers and infants in the two cultures by making use of the sequential nature of our observations in an analysis of "vocal episodes."

In conclusion of the discussion of State One, it should be noted that the canonical correlations in Tables 6 and 7 for the effect of culture on infant and caretaker behavior are significant, whereas those for father's occupation and sex of infant are not.

States Two and Three, in which the infant is awake and the caretaker is either passively present (Table 8) or absent (Table 9), can be discussed more summarily because the major results are variations on an already familiar pattern of infant behavior. In both states, culture is the most meaningful independent variable, and sex of infant and father's occupation are of minor importance. Both of these states are of particular interest because the infant is behaving in them without direct stimulation from the caretaker. Because the patterns of behavior are so familiar, however, we believe the infants are behaving the way they do in each culture on the basis of what they have already learned from their caretakers.

In State Two (see Table 8),[41] in which the infant is awake and the caretaker is passively present, the effect of culture on infant behavior shows the familiar pattern: The American infant is more active and more engaged in play, whereas the Japanese infant is more unhappily vocal. The canonical correlation is significant for culture, but not for the other two independent variables.[42]

In State Three (see Table 9),[43] in which the infant is awake and alone, the effect of culture on infant behavior shows the same pattern: The American infant is more happily vocal and active, and plays more, whereas the Japanese infant is only more unhappily vocal. And again, the canonical correlation is significant only for culture.[44]

State Four, as indicated in Table 10, presents us with the interesting question of what mothers are doing to sleeping babies.[45] There are no general findings by sex of infant or father's occupation.[46] The effect of culture, however, is strong, and in Table 10 it can be seen that American mothers are proportionately greater in looking at sleeping babies, but Japanese mothers are greater in the feeding, dressing, giving other care, carrying, and rocking of sleeping babies. From our beginning analysis by "episodes" over the observation sheets, we know that the pace of the Japanese mother is more leisurely. She tends to continue her caretaking activities after her baby has fallen asleep more than does the American mother. The proportionately greater amount of time spent looking at the baby for the American mother occurs because she has left her sleeping baby alone, and then return periodically to the door of the room to glance at him.

Specifically with reference to feeding, the Japanese mother is more content to continue sitting, holding the baby who has fallen asleep with

Table 8. Adjusted Mean Percentages, in State Two, of Infant Behavior: By Culture, Father's Occupation, and Sex of Infant

Categories of Infant Behavior	Adjusted Mean Percentages								
	Culture			Father's Occupation			Sex of Infant		
	Japanese	American	Correlation†	Salaried	Independent	Correlation†	Male	Female	Correlation†
Breast or Bottle	0	0	.14	0	0	.14	0	0	.11
All Food	0	0	.09	0	0	.11	0	0	.12
Finger or Pacifier	17	20	.08	**14**	**24**	**.29**	15	22	.19
Total Vocal	22	20	.05	19	23	.15	21	20	.02
Unhappy	**14**	7	.28	7	**16**	**.32**	10	12	.12
Happy	8	11	.21	10	8	.18	11	7	.22
Active	**15**	23	.31	19	18	.06	18	19	.02
Baby Plays	**23**	45	**.40***	39	28	.20	37	31	.13
Toy	12	26	.31	22	15	.16	22	15	.16
Hand	6	8	.06	9	5	.12	7	7	.01
Other Object	6	11	.26	8	8	.00	8	9	.04
Canonical Correlation‡			**.67****			.46			.40
Total Cases	30	30		35	25		33	27	

† See footnote in Table 3 for explanation of this partial correlation. The means and correlations for all findings significant at $p < 0.05$ are printed in boldface. One asterisk (*) indicates $p < 0.01$, two asterisks (**) indicate $p < 0.001$. Mean percentages of less than one-half of a percent are indicated as zero.

‡ See footnote in Table 3.

Table 9. Adjusted Mean Percentages, in State Three, of Infant Behavior: By Culture, Father's Occupation, and Sex of Infant

	Adjusted Mean Percentages								
	Culture			Father's Occupation			Sex of Infant		
Categories of Infant Behavior	Japanese	American	Correlation†	Salaried	Independent	Correlation†	Male	Female	Correlation†
Breast or Bottle	0	1	.10	1	0	.09	0	1	.14
All Food	0	1	.16	0	0	.03	0	1	.08
Finger or Pacifier	26	23	.09	26	22	.11	**20**	**30**	**.27**
Total Vocal	30	29	.02	27	33	.19	33	25	.26
Unhappy	**24**	**14**	**.31***	17	21	.15	20	17	.12
Happy	7	**13**	**.39***	10	11	.07	**12**	**8**	**.27**
Active	**18**	**30**	.34	22	28	.21	26	22	.10
Baby Plays	**21**	**50**	**.53****	37	33	.21	40	30	.22
Toy	**10**	**32**	**.46****	22	21	.08	26	15	.26
Hand	6	6	.01	7	4	.03	6	5	.07
Other Object	**5**	**11**	.29	8	8	.01	7	9	.07
Canonical Correlation‡			**.60**			.39			.47
Total Cases§	29	30		35	24		33	26	

† See footnote in Table 3 for explanation of this partial correlation. The means and correlations for all findings significant at $p < 0.05$ are printed in boldface. One asterisk (*) indicates $p < 0.01$, two asterisks (**) indicate $p < 0.001$. Mean percentages of less than one-half of a percent are indicated as zero.

‡ See footnote in Table 3.

§ One infant (Japanese, Independent, Female) was never in the condition of State Three.

Table 10. Adjusted Mean Percentages, in State Four, of Caretaker Behavior: By Culture, Father's Occupation, and Sex of Infant

| | Adjusted Mean Percentages | | | | | | | | |
| | Culture | | | Father's Occupation | | | Sex of Infant | | |
Categories of Caretaker Behavior	Japanese	American	Correlation†	Salaried	Independent	Correlation†	Male	Female	Correlation†
Feeds	13	0	**.44***	6	6	.02	7	6	.04
Diapers	1	0	.19	0	0	.16	0	0	.03
Dresses	1	0	**.34**	1	1	.03	0	1	.11
Positions	5	2	.18	5	2	.20	4	4	.03
Pats or Touches	12	6	.21	10	7	.11	10	7	.09
Other Care	14	6	**.31**	10	9	.05	9	11	.11
Plays with	0	0	.01	0	0	.18	0	0	.18
Affections	0	0	.01	0	0	.06	0	0	.13
Looks at	68	98	**.53****	87	79	.18	84	83	.01
Talks to	4	5	.04	5	3	.11	7	1	.23
Chats	1	5	.17	4	1	.14	5	0	.18
Lulls	3	0	.25	1	2	.01	2	0	.16
In Arms	46	9	**.52****	26	29	.06	24	31	.11
Rocks	11	3	**.28**	7	6	.03	9	4	.20
Canonical Correlation§			**.78****			.49			.47
Total Cases	26	28		32	22		30	24	

† See footnote in Table 3 for explanation of this partial correlation. The means and correlations for all findings significant at $p < 0.05$ are printed in boldface. One asterisk (*) indicates $p < 0.01$, two asterisks (**) indicate $p < 0.001$. Mean percentages of less than one-half of a percent are indicated as zero.

‡ See footnote in Table 4.

§ Six caretakers were never in the condition of State Four. Using the obvious abbreviations, these 6 cases have the following classification: JSF, JSM, JIF, JIM, ASM, AIF.

the nipple of the breast or bottle in his mouth. By definition then, in this situation, the mother is still scored as feeding. The American mother, in contrast to the "slow motion" feeling in the Japanese situation, is more brisk, and usually gets up and leaves once her baby has fallen asleep.[47]

A comparison of the canonical correlations for States One through Four is an illuminating way of summarizing the results of the analyses in this section. As indicated earlier, the canonical correlation shows the magnitude of the effect of the independent variables on the entire set of dependent variables for infant behavior (Tables 6, 8, and 9) and caretaker behavior (Tables 7 and 10). In States One through Four none of the canonical correlations is significant for sex of infant or father's occupation, and all of the canonical correlations are significant for culture.

We have three chances to examine the effect of culture on the behavior of awake infants—in State One, when the infants are in interaction with their mothers, and in States Two and Three, when the mothers are either passively present or absent. Although all three of the canonical correlations are significant, the effect of culture is greater when the infants are in interaction with their mothers than when they are not. The highest correlation (.84) occurs in State One, when the mothers are doing caretaking, and accounts for 71 percent of the variance in the general behavior of the infants; when the mothers are only passively present, in State Two, the correlation (.67) is lower and accounts for 45 percent of the variance in the behavior of the infants; when the infants are alone in State Three, the correlation (.60) drops a bit more and accounts for 36 percent of the variance in behavior. Thus, it would seem that culture definitely does make a difference in the behavior of infants, and it makes more of a difference, as would be expected, when the mothers are directly engaged with their babies.

Since the mothers are adult members of their cultures, while the babies are only very junior members of theirs, it seems sensible that the canonical correlations for the effect of culture on caretaker behavior in States One (when the baby is awake) and Four (when he is asleep) should be more similar. The correlation (.85) in State One accounts for 72 percent of the variance in caretaker behavior, and the correlation (.78) in State Four accounts for 61 percent of the variance.

Discussion

We feel that the most parsimonious explanation of our findings is that a great deal of cultural learning has taken place by three-to-four months of age, and that our babies have learned by this time to be Japanese and American babies in relation to the expectations of their mothers concerning their behavior. Nevertheless, we are aware that some of our findings might be thought of as due to group genetic differences, or to group differences in rates of physiological development. These questions cannot be answered with finality within the limits of our sample, but we did what checking we could on biological dimensions in our data that might be related to the infant's physical activity and total vocalization, as these are two central areas of difference between the cultures. A thorough check of the data (by Spearman's rank-order correlation) for the variables of "active" and "total vocal," both in terms of all 60 cases and of the 30 cases in each culture considered separately, did not reveal any significant differences in the relation of either variable to the independent variables of birth weight of infant, age in days of infant at time of observation, age of mother at time of birth of infant, or type of feeding of infant (in terms of breast, bottle, or mixed feeding).[48]

There is considerable experimental and observational evidence, on the other hand, that supports our conclusion that infants have learned by three-to-four months of age to respond in culturally appropriate ways. For example, Weisberg (1967) has shown experimentally that the vocalizing rate of three-month-old American infants can be increased (operantly conditioned) by the social consequences provided by the experimenter (briefly touching the infant's chin, smiling, and talking to him), but not by nonsocial consequences (the ringing of a door chime), nor by the mere presence of an inactive adult. This experimental result closely approximates the results obtained in the comparison of the observed behavior of American and Japanese caretakers in our study.

Our results on activity, playing, and vocalizing are also reflected in a study by Rubenstein (1967) of maternal attentiveness and exploratory behavior in American infants. In her study, maternal attentiveness (as defined by the number of times the mother was observed to look at, touch, hold, or talk to her baby) was time-sampled in the homes of 44 five-month-old infants who were later examined at six months for exploratory behavior. Three groups of babies were distinguished at five months of age as receiving high, low, or medium attentiveness. At six months of age, the high-attentiveness group significantly exceeded the low-attentiveness group in looking at, manipulating, and vocalizing to a novel stimulus presented alone, and the high-attentiveness group exceeded both other groups in looking at and manipulating novel stimuli in preference to familiar ones. Rubenstein interprets her data as suggesting that maternal attentiveness facilitates exploratory behavior in the infant. We would agree on the basis of our results, if we conceive of attentiveness mainly in terms of stimulating the infant to activity, play, and vocalization, as appears to be the pattern for the American mothers in contrast to the Japanese mothers.

The observational study by Moss (1967) in the homes of 30 firstborn

American infants equally divided by sex, at one and three months of age, is, in its latter phase, almost exactly the same as ours. Using a series of dependent variables for infant and caretaker behaviors, he made observations by a time-sampling procedure, using a unit of one minute in which behavior could occur or not occur, over eight hours, resulting in a total of 480 observations per case. Many of the variables used by Moss were defined in almost exactly the same way as ours, and by converting his data and our American data to percentages of total observations, a direct comparison is possible. When this is done, either for the total samples, or separately by sex, the results of the comparisons (by means of a Mann-Whitney U test) show no significant differences for the infant behaviors of "awake," "finger or pacifier," "active," or "unhappy vocal." The data for the infants in the Moss study on his variable of "vocalizes" (which includes our variable of "happy vocal" plus "neutral" vocalizations such as grunts) significantly exceed those for our variable of "happy vocal." Equally, for caretaker behaviors, there are no differences in the two studies on the variables of "feeds," "looks at," "talks to," "in arms," and "rocks." It is therefore fairly obvious that much the same results would be achieved in a comparison of infant or caretaker behaviors in America and Japan, whether we used our American data or used the data from the Moss study.

Finally, we wish to draw attention to the detailed study by Arai, Ishikawa, and Toshima (1958) of the development of Japanese children from one month to 36 months of age, as measured by the Gesell norms established on American children.[49] The Japanese investigators used a sample of 776 children in the Tōhoku area (the northern part of the main island of Japan near the city of Sendai), equally divided across the age range of one to 36 months. In the areas of motor development and language development, which are closest to the variables in our study of physical activity and total vocalization, the findings of the Japanese study were that the Japanese infants matched the American norms in both respects in the age period from 4 to 16 weeks, but after that there was a steady decline from the norms in the Japanese scores for both motor and language development from 4 months to 36 months of age. In general across the entire age range, Arai, Ishikawa, and Toshima say: "For children having a developmental quotient between 90–119, . . . motor behavior is 71.5 percent of the norms, social behavior is 70.4 percent, and language aptitude (the weakest behavior) is 66.0 percent."[50]

It seems likely from the results of this study in the Tōhoku area of Japan that there are no differences in motor or verbal behavior of Japanese and American infants during the first several months of life. If this is so, it strongly supports our contention that these are learned more than genetic or maturational differences.

Conclusion

In this report of work with Japanese and American middle-class mothers and their firstborn, three-to-four-month-old infants, our analysis quickly revealed that of the three independent variables considered, culture is by far the most important source of difference in the behavior of these infants and caretakers. This is followed by father's occupation, which is important in the Japanese situation but not in the American. Sex of infant, at least at three-to-four months of age, is of little relevance.

Reviewing our findings in reverse order of importance, there is a hint, stemming from the intra-cultural analyses, that American mothers may give somewhat more attention, particularly of an affectionate sort, to their boy babies, but this is a tenuous finding in the American data, and there are no findings by sex of infant in the Japanese data.

The analysis by father's occupation produced more results, but all of these, upon further examination, proved to be important only for the Japanese data. In the Japanese independent business families the infant is awake more, and the caretaker is present more, and talks to, lulls, carries, and rocks the infant more than in the salaried families. In contrast, the caretaker in the salaried families is only greater in looking at the infant when compared with the caretaker in the independent business families.

In the single matter of looking at her infant more frequently, the mother in the salaried Japanese family seems more like the American mother, who, in the general cross-cultural analysis, looks at her infant more often. But the American mother also chats with her infant frequently, whereas the Japanese salaried mother is more silent than the Japanese independent business mother. If, as is reasonable, we consider the salaried mother in Japan to be more "modern," then, in her move toward modernity, she seems to have subtracted from traditional ways of caretaking rather than to have added anything new. If anything, the independent business mother in Japan is closer to the American mother in the extent of her direct involvement with her infant. Thus, with regard to the relation of child care to social change, there would not seem to be any simple connection between a move toward modernity for the family in general and a shift toward Western patterns of child care.

The preceding findings, although of interest, become pale in the light of the strong findings of cultural differences. American infants are more happily vocal, more active, and more exploratory of their bodies and their physical environment than are Japanese infants. Directly related to these findings, the American mother is in greater vocal interaction with her infant and stimulates him to greater physical activity and exploration. The Japanese mother, in contrast, is in greater bodily contact with her infant and soothes him toward physical quiescence and passivity with regard to his environment. Moreover, these patterns of behavior, so early learned by the infant, are in line with the differing expectations for later behavior in the two cultures as the child grows to be an adult.

For now, we believe we have arrived at distinctive patterns of learned behavior for infants in Japan and America. Analysis of our data for the first 20 of the same cases in each culture at two-and-a-half and six years of age will establish whether these patterns persist and jell in the behavior of the children we are studying. Our prediction is that this will happen, because of the strong external pressures for conformity and the strong internal pressures toward being accepted favorably by one's fellows, in any culture.

If these distinctive patterns of behavior are well on the way to being learned by three-to-four months of age, and if they continue over the life span of the person, then there are very likely to be important areas of difference in emotional response in people in one culture when compared with those in another. Such differences are not easily subject to conscious control and, largely out of awareness, they accent and color human behavior. These differences add a zest to life and interpersonal encounters, but they can also add to bewilderment and antagonism when people try to communicate across the emotional barriers of cultures.

We hope that our analysis helps to illuminate the reasons for some of these difficulties in cross-cultural communication despite the seeming increase in similarity between countries in the modern world. One may wish, on moral and practical grounds, for greater real understanding by people of each other across cultures, but it is a moot point whether the world would be a better place in which to live if such cultural differences were to be obliterated.

Notes

1. In work with our colleagues on the symptoms of Japanese and American psychiatric patients, we find both social-class similarities and cultural differences in the characteristics of patients in the two countries. See Schooler and Caudill 1964, and Caudill and Schooler 1969. An especially pertinent example also comes from the work of Pearlin and Kohn 1966; in a comparative study in Italy and the U.S. of parents' values concerning their children's behavior, they demonstrate that middle-class parents in both countries are more likely to value the child's self-direction, while working-class parents in both countries place a greater emphasis on the

child's conformity to external proscription; but equally, and from the same data, they show that regardless of social class, American parents are more likely than Italian parents to value happiness, popularity, and consideration, while Italian parents more than American parents tend to value manners, obedience, and seriousness.

2. We predicted that the Japanese mother in the small-business family would spend more time with her infant, would carry him more, and in general would be more attentive than the Japanese mother in the salaried family; and, because of the greater attention, we believed that the infant in the small-business family would be more responsive than the infant in the salaried family. Detailed information on the differences between these two occupational ways of life can be found in Dore 1958, Vogel 1963, and Plath 1964.

3. The work of Miller and Swanson is very suggestive as to differences in child rearing in entrepreneurial and bureaucratic families, but their study is subject to some criticism on methodological grounds.

4. Even in the latter areas, however, the differences in emphasis are still evident. See Nakane 1965.

5. See Caudill and Scarr 1962, and Caudill and Doi 1962.

6. See Reischauer 1957, esp. pt. 3, "The Japanese Character"; and Nakamura 1964, esp. chaps. 35 and 36.

7. See Caudill 1962. Specifically with reference to Japanese reticence, Fisher and Yoshida (1968) comment upon their analysis of the nature of speech according to Japanese proverbs as follows: "Basically, the most ubiquitous lesson about speech in Japanese proverbs is, 'Shut up' " (p. 36). For example, they cite the following proverbs: *Kuchi o mamoru kame no gotoku su* ("One treats one's mouth like a guarded jar"); *Kuchi wa motte kuubeshi, motte iu bekarazu* ("Mouths are to eat with, not to speak with").

8. These patterns of sleeping are not a function of "overcrowding" in the Japanese home, but rather are a matter of choice, as is shown in Caudill and Plath 1966. Much the same point can be made concerning bathing. Starting at approximately the beginning of the second month of life, the Japanese infant is held in the arms of the mother or another adult while they bathe together in the deep bathtub *(furo)* at home or at the neighborhood public bath *(sentō)*, and this pattern of shared bathing will continue for a Japanese child until he is about ten years of age, and often much longer (see Vogel 1963:229–232). In contrast, the American mother seldom bathes with an infant; rather, she gives him a bath from outside of the tub, and she communicates with him verbally and by positioning his body.

9. Although Japan is at one extreme in the length of time spent co-sleeping in a two-generation group, America is probably at the other extreme in this, and in many matters concerned with child rearing. Indeed, compared with the rest of the world, family life in the United States is in many ways rather peculiar. See Stephens 1963, esp. chap. 8.

10. This hypothesis concerning the greater mutual dependency of mother and child in Japan will become more pertinent as we analyze in the future our great wealth of data on children in the two countries at $2\frac{1}{2}$ and 6 years of age. But it is symbolized at birth by the widespread custom in Japan for the hospital to present the infant's navel cord *(heso no o)* to the mother upon discharge. The cord is sprinkled with preservative powder, and placed in a neat wooden box which is tied with ribbon. This is, of course, not too different from the custom of some American parents of saving locks of hair, baby shoes, and other objects as momentos of their child's infancy. The difference lies in the "directness" of the relation of the symbol to its meaning in Japan, and to the history of the symbolic object thereafter. In

Japan the cord of the new infant is only one of many such cords of other family members that may be kept in the home, either in the household Buddhist altar or in a safe place in a bureau drawer. Custom varies from region to region, and household to household, as to the subsequent disposition of the cord. If the infant is a girl, she may be given the cord to take with her to her husband's household upon marriage; or the mother may retain the cords of all of her children, and these may be placed with her body in the coffin upon her death. In our interviews with the 20 Japanese mothers whose children we followed up at $2\frac{1}{2}$ years of age, we inquired about whether they had received their first child's navel cord and what meaning this had for them. We did not ask similar questions of our American mothers as it seemed inappropriate to do so. Of the 19 Japanese mothers from whom we have relevant information, 17 had received their cords from the hospital. Of the two mothers who had not, one was sad about this as she was keeping her own cord with that of her second child, which she had received since the second child was born in a different hospital. All of the 17 mothers who had received the cords kept them safely, and 8 mothers said the cord had real meaning for them; the other 9 mothers said that the cord only represented an old custom, but they usually added, ". . . but you can't just throw it away."

11. The age of marriage in Japan is increasing, and has been consistently later than that in the United States for at least the past 35 years. See Blood 1967; Taeuber 1958:227; and Japan, Office of the Prime Minister, 1962a, table 3, 72–73.

12. In the Japanese sample, 12 of the fathers are college graduates in professional or managerial positions (8 are salaried, and 4 are independent), and 18 of the fathers are college or high school graduates in white-collar or highly skilled trade jobs (7 are salaried and 11 are independent). In the American sample, 14 of the fathers are college graduates in professional or managerial positions (10 are salaried, 4 are independent), and 16 of the fathers are college or high school graduates in white-collar or highly skilled trade jobs (10 are salaried and 6 are independent). Of the Japanese mothers, 7 are college graduates, 19 are high school or technical school graduates, and 4 have less than a high school education. Of the American mothers, 9 are college graduates, 20 are high school or technical school graduates, and 1 has less than a high school education. In devising procedures for estimating social-class position, we made use of the work of Hollingshead on American populations and modified it to approximate the Japanese situation along lines suggested by the work of Odaka. See Hollingshead and Redlich 1958, esp. app. 2, "The Index of Social Position," 387–397; Nihon Shakai Gakkai Chōsa Iinkai 1958; Odaka and Nishihira 1965; Odaka 1964–1965; and Ramsey and Smith 1960.

13. We wish to thank Dr. Hirotoshi Hashimoto, Dr. L. Takeo Doi, and Dr. Takajiro Yamamoto at St. Luke's International Hospital; Dr. Shigeki Takeuchi at Tsukiji Maternity Hospital; Dr. Fumio Nakamura, Dr. Tsuneo Nakamura, and Dr. Shigeo Imagi at the Kyoto Prefectural Hospital; and Dr. Emilie Black, Dr. Carol Pincock, Dr. Morris I. Michael, and Dr. Stanley I. Wolf in the Washington, D.C. area. We are indebted to Mrs. Seiko Notsuki of the St. Luke's International Hospital for carrying out the interviews and observations with the Japanese cases, and to Mrs. Mieko I. Caudill for her constant help in all stages of the research.

14. Because the pediatricians selected the bulk of our cases for us and had already received a positive response from the mothers before we met them, there were no refusals to participate in the study after we had made our contact with the mothers. It seems likely, however, that our mothers were a bit more adventuresome than most, but this would be true in both countries. In general, the mothers were pleased that their babies had been chosen for observation, and that they could be of help in

a scientific way; on the whole, however, the mothers did not show any particular intellectual interest in our work. After the observations were completed, we invited the mothers to ask questions about the research, but if there were any questions, these usually simply concerned the mothers' wish to know how the behavior of her child compared with that of other children in our study.

15. In both cultures we gave the families copies of the best pictures we had taken of the infant and the mother during our work, and also often brought a toy for the infant. In addition in Japan, as is customary, we gave a modest amount of money in a white envelope suitably inscribed with the message that it be used in some way for the child's enjoyment.

16. An illustration of the original observation sheet may be found in a preliminary report of this research, given at the Ninth International Seminar on Family Research in Tokyo in 1965. See Caudill and Weinstein 1970.

17. We are not saying that only adults can be caretakers of infants, but we did not expect to find many older children acting as caretakers of young babies in our study because all of the infants are firstborn and do not have older siblings. In the actual observations on the 60 cases, there were only a few times when an infant was with older neighborhood children without an adult caretaker also being present. In these few situations we scored the infant as alone—that is, without adult supervision.

18. The rule that a caretaker is present even if in an adjoining room was made because of the nature of housing in the two countries. In Japan, the interior walls separating most rooms are usually made of sliding doors (fusuma) that are frequently kept in the open position (resulting in an opening which is half of the total wall space for the most usual four-door wall) during the day. In America, there frequently is no wall at all in the L-shaped living room and dining area. In either country, an ordinary door can, of course, be left open between rooms. In Japan it is easier for a caretaker to be outside and still "present," even though the baby is inside because the exterior walls of much of the standard Japanese house are made of sliding latticed panels covered with paper (shōji) which are frequently kept open during the day. At night these panels are closed, and in addition sliding solid wood doors on separate tracks (amado) are locked into place just beyond the shōji. In our judgment, based on the floor plans we drew of the housing of each family, the American families probably had on the average more total floor space, but the Japanese families had on the average more rooms. This is because in the two samples of fairly recently married couples, the Americans tend to live in apartments (21 of the 30 families), and the Japanese, in houses (22 of the 30 families).

19. On the original observation sheet this variable was represented by two additive variables: (1) being carried on the caretaker's back, and (2) being in the caretaker's arms or lap. The specific variable "on caretaker's back" was initially included because, in general, young Japanese children are often carried there. As we found out, somewhat belatedly, the Japanese infant at three-to-four months is not very frequently carried on the back because the mother feels the infant's neck muscles are not yet strong enough, although this becomes common a month or so later and varies by social class and occupational style of life. The infant was carried on the back during observations in only 3 of our Japanese cases, and we have therefore recorded these data as "in arms or lap." When the infant was not on the caretaker's back or in arms or lap, we originally recorded what sort of receptacle he was in (in bed, in bath, in infant seat, and in other places—such as playpen or on a zabuton, that is, a flat cushion on the floor). These variables did not prove to be very useful. As a subclassification of "in bed" and "in other place" we scored whether the baby was lying on his stomach or back. It is of interest that the Japanese babies

were almost always on their backs, whereas the opposite tended to be true for the American babies. The reason for the difference, especially when the baby is asleep, is that the Japanese mother has been told that the baby might smother if placed on his stomach, and the American mother has been told that he might choke if left on his back.

20. At the time of our observations, 18 Japanese and only 5 American mothers were continuing breast feeding. In many of these cases, particularly among Japanese mothers, there was a combination of breast and bottle feeding.

21. Only 6 of the Japanese mothers gave their infants semi-solid or harder food during the observations, whereas 21 of the American mothers did so.

22. Although it is a minor matter in terms of number of observations, the giving of liquid vitamins to the infant is scored under bottle if the vitamins are given by dropper, and under food if the vitamins are given by spoon. The action of the caretaker in giving the vitamins is always scored under "feeds."

23. All of the mothers in both cultures did some talking to other persons, including the observer, during the observations. The amount of this is almost the same in each culture. Using an analysis of variance, the mean number of observations of talking to other persons is 53 for Japanese caretakers and 55 for American caretakers ($F = 0.7$, $df = 1/52$, not significant). The targets of the talk, however, were in some respects different: Japanese mothers did more talking to tradesmen coming to the door, and American mothers did more talking on the telephone to friends and to their husbands at the office.

24. During the observations, 4 of the Japanese and 16 of the American mothers bathed their infants, with an average of 22 observations in the Japanese cases, and 17 observations in the American cases. Using these data in an analysis of variance over the total sample of 60 cases, the mean number of observations is 3 for the Japanese and 9 for the American cases ($F = 5.6$, $df = 1/52$, $p < 0.05$). These numbers, however, have little meaning considering the difference in the customary time of day for bathing, and the qualitative difference in the context in which bathing takes place (see notes 8 and 25).

25. We believe this was a wise choice, particularly because the differences between Japanese and American family life in such more dramatic events as bathing and sleeping (see note 8) are so pronounced as scarcely to require detailed observational study. Specifically in our samples, as determined from the interviews with the mothers, all of the Japanese infants bathed together with their mother or another caretaker (usually the father or the father's mother if she was living in the household); and all of the Japanese infants co-slept with both parents, who had no intention of terminating this arrangement for several years. All of the American infants were bathed from the outside of the tub or bathinette by their mothers; 17 of the American infants slept alone in a separate room, while 13 infants slept in a crib in the parents' bedroom. In the latter cases, the young couple was living in an apartment with one bedroom, and without exception, each couple planned to move to a dwelling with two bedrooms so that the infant could have a separate room by the time he was one year old.

26. To illustrate, using the exact check the observers must agree, for example, that the caretaker looks at the infant in observation 24; using the contiguous check, there must be agreement by the observers either within observations 23 and 24 or within observations 24 and 25. The limits of the contiguous check are, obviously, foreshortened in observation 1 and in observation 40 of an observation sheet.

27. The computer program we used is called MANOVA, and is described in Dean J. Clyde, Elliot M. Cramer, and Richard J. Sherin, *Multivariate Statistical Pro-*

grams, Coral Gables, Fla., Biometric Laboratory, Univ. of Miami, 1966 (revisions issued Dec., 1967). On analysis of variance in general, see Blalock 1960. We earlier did a separate and complete analysis of the data by use of a nonparametric statistical technique, the Mann-Whitney U test. Such a technique does not, however, easily allow for the testing of one independent variable while controlling for the effect of others, and the testing of interactions is not feasible. The results of the earlier analysis were essentially similar to those presented here, but much less controlled and refined. See Caudill and Weinstein 1970.

28. We also tested for all possible three- and two-way interactions of the independent variables. Two-way interactions were controlled in terms of the effect of the three independent variables considered separately and the effect of all other two-way interactions. Three-way interactions were controlled in terms of the effect of the three independent variables considered separately and the effect of all two-way interactions.

29. The correlation coefficient used here has the utility that it can be determined by computer through use of an option in the MANOVA program (see note 27). Elliot M. Cramer has suggested another correlation coefficient which is the square root of the ratio of (a) the sum of the squared deviations from the mean attributable to the independent variable in question, to (b) the total sum of the squared deviations. Two other correlation coefficients, *eta* and *epsilon,* might be used. Both are derived from the *F* ratio in conjunction with the degrees of freedom between and within cells. *Epsilon* is the more conservative of the two measures, and is to be used in evaluating the results obtained from small samples, such as are used in the present research. The formulas for these measures, and an excellent discussion of the need for an estimate of the magnitude as well as the significance of an effect, can be found in Cohen 1965. In practical terms, if an effect is a strong one, there is little difference between the four measures in our data. For example, in Table 3 for the dependent variable of "baby plays," the effect of culture results in a correlation of .50; Cramer's measure also gives a correlation of .50; the formula for *eta* gives a correlation of .51; and the formula for *epsilon,* a correlation of .49. In all of these cases, when the correlation is squared, the amount of variance attributable to culture is about 25 percent of the total variance.

30. In technical language, the canonical correlation is a multiple correlation of one or a set of independent variables to a set of dependent variables. More precisely, it is the maximum correlation between linear functions of the two sets of variables. See Cooley and Lohnes 1962.

31. In all of our analyses by states, we did an analysis of variance both of frequencies (ignoring time in state) and percentages. Obviously, however, the percentage analysis provides more pertinent information for this article because it answers the question of, relative to time in state, what the infant or caretaker is doing in terms of the dependent variables. One difficulty that may arise in doing analysis of variance with percentages is that the mean and variance for such binomial data are not independent. To meet this situation, especially in the case of percentages derived from small frequencies, it is appropriate to use an arc-sine transformation to gain independence of mean and variance. We did a thorough check of our data by comparing the results when using the arc-sine transformation with the results when using straight percentages. In no case did the use of the arc-sine transformation result in making a significant finding become not significant or vice versa. We have therefore presented our results (in Tables 6–10) in terms of straight percentage analyses because this procedure involves less manipulation of the basic data. See Snedecor 1946:445–448.

32. An examination of the interactions of the independent variables in the analyses of total observations produced very little of interest. There are no significant three-way interactions for the 12 infant or 15 caretaker dependent variables. There is one significant two-way interaction out of 36 tests for the infant variables, and there are two significant two-way interactions out of 45 tests for the caretaker variables. Because of the large number of tests, these findings could easily be due to chance alone. We have no ready explanation for the two-way finding on "unhappy vocal," which shows an interaction between father's occupation (S or I) and sex of infant (M or F):SM 56, SF 40, IM 56, IF 77 ($F = 4.8$, $df = 1/52$, $p < 0.05$). The finding on "lulls," which shows an interaction between culture (J or A) and father's occupation (S or I) is obviously an artifact that is better explained by a one-way finding in the intra-Japanese analysis, as indicated later in the text. The interaction is: JS 15, JI 34, AS 2, AI 3 ($F = 4.1$, $df = 1/52$, $p < 0.05$). The finding on "plays with" infant, which shows an interaction of culture and father's occupation, strikes us as more pertinent to the argument of this paper because it suggests that an independent occupational style of family life has a different meaning for child care in the two cultures, and is particularly distinctive in Japan, as will become evident from other results. The interaction on plays with infant is: JS 29, JI 51, AS 27, AI 15 ($F = 5.0$, $df = 1/52$, $p < 0.05$).

33. As indicated earlier, there was very little breast feeding among the American mothers, and, hence, "breast" and "bottle" were combined. As is to be expected, the finding on the variable of "breast" considered separately shows the Japanese infant to be greater, with a mean of 30, compared to the American infant with a mean of 3 ($F = 10.1$, $df = 1/52$, $p < 0.01$). On the other hand, "bottle" considered separately is not significantly different, although the Japanese mean of 37 is lower than the American mean of 51 ($F = 1.0$, $df = 1/52$, $p < 0.32$). When semi-solid food is considered as a separate variable (see note 21), the American infant is greater, with a mean of 19 compared to a Japanese mean of 2 ($F = 16.2$, $df = 1/52$, $p < 0.001$).

34. We are particularly interested in the category of "active," and we thought that the greater occurrence of gross bodily movements among the American infants might be related to the difference in temperature in the homes, especially in the winter, in the two cultures. In general, we avoided doing observations during particularly hot or cold days—when the outside temperature was above 85 or below 45 degrees Fahrenheit. The temperature inside of the homes in Tokyo, Kyoto, and Washington, D.C., is about the same during the warmer months of May-October, but during the cooler months of November-April the temperature in the Japanese homes probably averages about five to ten degrees less than that maintained in the American homes. During the cooler months, Japanese infants wear more clothing and are under more covers than American infants. Fortunately, roughly half of the cases in each culture were observed during the warmer months. For the American infants, there is no difference between the active behavior of the cases observed during the cooler (a mean of 125 observations) and warmer (a mean of 128 observations) months (using a Mann-Whitney U test of the rank-order of the frequencies, $z = 0.18$, n.s.). For the Japanese infants, however, the cases observed during the warmer months (a mean of 65) are more active than those in the cooler months (a mean of 34) ($z = 2.1$, $p < 0.05$). Nevertheless, in the cross-cultural comparison of the infants observed only during the warmer months the American babies are still the more active ($z = 3.0$, $p < 0.01$). Naturally, then, the American infants are also the more active ($z = 3.8$, $p = 0.001$) in the comparison of cases observed during the cooler months. It appears, therefore, that temperature of the home and heavier

clothing make some difference, but not enough to account for the greater activity of the American infant.

35. The occurrence of behavior in the category of "finger or pacifier" appears to be related to breast versus bottle feeding in both cultures, although the Japanese infants are in general much lower in any sort of comparison. The clearest data on this question come from the comparison of those mothers who never breast fed versus those mothers who were feeding entirely by breast (no use of the bottle at all) at the time of observation. The 9 American infants who were never breast fed have an average of 196 observations in the category of "finger or pacifier," while the 4 American infants being fed entirely by breast have an average of 97 observations in this category. Among the Japanese cases, the 4 infants who were never breast fed have an average of 88 observations in the category of "finger or pacifier," while the 6 infants being entirely breast fed have an average of 42 observations in this category. Thus, there is roughly twice as much finger sucking by babies who have never been breast fed in both cultures, but the average for the Japanese babies fed entirely by bottle is lower than the average for the American babies fed entirely by breast. It seems unlikely, therefore, that the greater average number of observations for the American infant in the variable of "finger or pacifier" is due to differences in methods of feeding. It may be due, however, to the greater use of a pacifier by the American mother, who often puts this device into her child's mouth as she leaves the room. The Japanese mother, in contrast, makes very little use of a pacifier.

36. As indicated earlier, these are Pearsonian r correlations, and a correlation matrix using the 12 infant and 15 caretaker variables was made separately for each culture. With an N of 30, using a two-tailed test, a correlation of .361 is significant at less than 0.05, and a correlation of .463 is significant at less than 0.01.

37. We did a complete analysis of main effects and interactions for the three independent variables of culture, father's occupation, and sex of infant. There are no significant three- or two-way interactions. There are no findings for the main effects of sex of infant, and also there are no findings for sex in either of the intra-cultural analyses. There are several findings of main effects by father's occupation, but all of these are explained by the intra-Japanese analysis, and there are no findings in the intra-American analysis. The intra-Japanese findings by father's occupation are that caretakers in independent business families spend a greater amount of time in State One (doing caretaking when baby is awake) than do caretakers in salaried families; and that with regard to State Six (baby asleep, caretaker absent), caretakers in salaried families are absent more than those in independent business families.

38. An examination of the interactions in the analyses of the data for State One provided little of interest. No three-way interactions are significant for either infant or caretaker behaviors. Of the 33 possible two-way interactions for infant behaviors, only one is significant. This is a finding on "toy" showing an interaction between culture and sex: JM 8%, JF 7%, AM 12%, AF 4% ($F = 5.2$, $df = 1/52$, $p < 0.05$). Obviously, this is not a meaningful interaction since the difference occurs only in the American data as discussed in the text. Of the 42 possible two-way interactions for caretaker behaviors, only one is significant. This is a finding on "looks at" showing an interaction between culture and father's occupation: JS 82%, JI 72%, AS 87%, AI 92% ($F = 4.7$, $df = 1/52$, $p < 0.05$). In the intra-Japanese analysis of "looks at" by father's occupation, caretakers in salaried families look at their infants significantly more than do caretakers in independent families; the comparable test in the intra-American analysis is not significant.

39. The separate analyses of variance on the component parts of the variable of "all food" in State One are as follows: On "breast," which, of course, is greater

among the Japanese, the Japanese mean is 9% and the American mean is 1% ($F = 8.6$, $df = 1/52$, $p < 0.01$). On "bottle" there is no difference, just as there is not in the total observations. The Japanese mean in State One on "bottle" is 14% and the American mean is 13% ($F = 0.4$, $df = 1/52$, $p < 0.55$). On the variable of "food," where, of course, American babies are given more semi-solid food, the Japanese mean is 1% and the American mean is 6% ($F = 12.4$, $df = 1/52$, $p < 0.01$).

40. The complete pattern of significant correlations (see note 36) for each culture is as follows: The American caretaker's "chats" is correlated with "finger or pacifier" (.57), "total vocal" (.64), "happy vocal" (.66), "active" (.58), "baby plays" (.57), "toy" (.40), "other object" (.41), "dresses" (.52), "positions" (.46), "pats or touches" (.55), "other care" (.43), "plays with" (.47), "affections" (.44), "looks at" (.73), "talks to" (.99), "in arms" (.43), and "rocks" (.37). The Japanese caretaker's "chats" is correlated with "total vocal" (.50), "unhappy vocal" (.44), "baby plays" (.57), "toy" (.58), "diapers" (.41), "positions" (.37), "plays with" (.65), "affections" (.63), "looks at" (.69), "talks to" (.91), "lulls" (.40), "in arms" (.76), and "rocks" (.66).

41. In State Two, no three-way interactions are significant. Of the 33 possible two-way interactions, two are significant, but both of these are explained by the intra-cultural analyses. "Total vocal" shows an interaction between culture and father's occupation: JS 16%, JI 28%, AS 21%, AI 17% ($F = 4.8$, $df = 1/52$, $p < 0.05$). The intra-Japanese analysis for "total vocal" by father's occupation is significant; the comparable test in the intra-American analysis is not significant. "Hand" shows an interaction between culture and sex of infant: JM 2%, JF 12%, AM 14%, AF 3% ($F = 7.8$, $df = 1/52$, $p < 0.01$). The intra-Japanese analysis for "hand" by sex of infant is not significant ($p < 0.14$); the comparable test in the intra-American analysis is significant ($p < 0.01$).

42. There are no findings in Table 8 by sex of infant for State Two. The intra-Japanese analysis has no findings by sex of infant. The intra-American analysis shows a single finding—male infants are greater on "hand" than are female infants (see note 41), but this could well be a chance finding. The two findings in Table 8 by father's occupation are better explained by the intra-Japanese analysis, and there are no findings by father's occupation in the intra-American analysis. In the intra-Japanese analysis, infants in independent business families suck more on finger or pacifier, and are more unhappily vocal; in addition, they also are greater in "total vocal." Quite possibly this is due to the passive presence of their mothers, because we know from the intra-Japanese analysis of the total observations that the mother in the independent family does more lulling, carrying, and rocking than the mother in the salaried family, and the infant in the independent family in State Two may be more aware of his mother's passive presence and may be seeking attention by his greater unhappy vocals. Further evidence for this line of thought is that in the intra-Japanese analysis in State Two, the infant from the salaried family shows up as playing more by himself, which would indicate that he is more self-absorbed.

43. In State Three there are no significant three- or two-way interactions.

44. By sex of infant, the finding in Table 9 for "finger or pacifier" is better explained in terms of the intra-Japanese analysis, where female infants are doing more nonnutritive sucking than male infants; the comparison is not significant in the intra-American analysis. There are no other significant findings in the intra-Japanese analysis. The other finding by sex of infant in Table 9 shows male infants as more happily vocal when alone; in the intra-cultural analyses, this finding is of borderline significance ($p < 0.07$) in the Japanese data, where male infants may be more happily vocal, and is not significant ($p < 0.36$) in the intra-American data. The one significant finding in the intra-American analysis by sex of infant is that

male infants are greater in "total vocal." There are no findings in Table 9 by father's occupation, and none in the intra-Japanese analysis. There is one finding in the intra-American analysis, which could be merely a chance finding—infants in salaried families play with their hands more than infants in independent business families.

45. In State Four, there are no significant three-way interactions. Of the 42 possible two-way interactions, one is significant but is explained by the intra-cultural analyses. "Looks at" shows an interaction between culture and father's occupation: JS 80%, JI 55%, AS 96%, AI 100% ($F = 61$, $df = 1/46$, $p < 0.05$). In the intra-Japanese analysis, "looks at" by father's occupation is significant; the comparable test in the intra-American analysis is not significant.

46. In the intra-cultural analyses for State Four, there are no findings in either culture by sex of infant. By father's occupation, there are no findings in the intra-American analysis, and only one finding in the intra-Japanese analysis. Japanese mothers in salaried families do proportionately more looking at sleeping babies than do Japanese mothers in independent business families (see note 45). This finding also occurs in the intra-Japanese analysis for State One (see note 38), and it does indicate, that in this regard, Japanese mothers in salaried families are closer to American mothers.

47. For further information on this general topic derived from our data, see Windle 1968.

48. A further important source of evidence, although the research is only currently being developed, comes from the comparison of infants in Japan and America from birth through the first month of life. This work is being carried out by Dr. Peter Wolff of the Judge Baker Guidance Center in Boston, and by Dr. Yukio Okada of Kobe Medical College in Kobe. The data being gathered by these two workers are incomplete at present, and hence Dr. Wolff has strong reservations about any general statements, but his preliminary impression is, ". . . nothing in my data or the data that Dr. Okada and I put together would indicate essential differences between Japanese and American one-month-old infants" (personal communication). In addition, because obstetrical techniques vary somewhat between Japan and the United States, an additional indirect source of evidence indicates that "minimal brain damage" at birth is no more prevalent among normal elementary school children in Japan than in the United States. See Wolff and Hurwitz 1966.

49. See also Toshima 1958.

50. See Arai, Ishikawa, and Toshima 1958:269. (We are indebted to Miss Frederica M. Levin for her translation of this article from the French.) The authors of this study seem, in the discussion of their results, somewhat distressed that the Japanese mothers were so bound up in the lives of their infants that they interfered with the development of their infants in ways which made it difficult to meet the American norms. Our results agree in general with those of this Japanese study, but we do not agree with the concern over the lack of matching the American norms. We do not believe that the differences which we find are necessarily indications of a better or a worse approach to human life, but rather that such differences are a part of an individual's adjustment to his culture.

15

Who Sleeps by Whom?
Parent-Child Involvement in
Urban Japanese Families

WILLIAM CAUDILL
DAVID W. PLATH

IF a third of life is passed in bed, with whom this time is spent is not a trivial matter. As ethnologists, we expect co-sleeping customs to be consonant with major interpersonal and emotional patterns of family life in a culture, and at the same time to reflect cross-cultural differences.[1] Westerners viewing Japanese sleeping arrangements usually sense a high degree of "overcrowding," which they say results from lack of space in "densely populated" Japan. We argue that this apparent "overcrowding" in the bedroom is only in part a function of lack of space: It derives more directly from the strength of family bonds. We argue further that the frequency with which children co-sleep with parents expresses a strong cultural emphasis upon the nurturant aspects of family life and a correlative deemphasis of its sexual aspects. We support our arguments by asking, of data from urban families, who sleeps by whom?

Selection and Characteristics of the Sample

Co-sleeping in Japan usually occurs behind closed shutters and is not open to easy observation. Participant observation has its limits, and an ethnographer who asked to sleep all around town probably would not be welcomed. But both of us found that Japanese would willingly sketch their dwelling spaces and indicate where each person slept. We happened upon this independently and for different purposes, but have combined our data in a joint report.

The sketches were drawn in the course of individual interviews. The interviews in Caudill's research were conducted in 1962 at three hospitals, two of them in Tokyo and one in Kyoto. At each hospital, information was obtained from the first 100 mothers coming to the well-baby

Reprinted from *Psychiatry* 29 (1966): 344–366.

clinic who had, at the time of interview, a three- to four-month-old infant.[2] The interviews in Plath's research were conducted in 1960 in Matsumoto City, and information was obtained from fathers or mothers in 30 households in two neighborhoods.[3]

Discarding seven cases with inadequate data, we have a total sample of 323 households—198 in Tokyo, 99 in Kyoto, and 26 in Matsumoto. Each household consists of at least an unmarried child and both of his parents; and in many cases there are additional children, extended kin, and unrelated persons (maids, roomers, and employees in the family business). We examined household sleeping arrangements in terms of city of residence, size of household, number of generations living together, style of life, social class, and density. Statistically, density proved to be the most important single variable. Several of the other variables, however, were of minor importance in influencing co-sleeping patterns, and these results will be given at the appropriate points in the analysis. The meaning we assign to these variables is discussed in the following paragraphs, and the distribution of the sample in terms of them is given in Table 1.

In designing the research, our aim was to clarify parent-child co-sleeping patterns, and we chose our sample of households accordingly. We wished to obtain a sufficient number and spread of households on each variable to permit comparative analysis rather than trying to collect a sample that would be statistically representative of the general population. Thus, in contrast to the general population, our sample contains no one-person or two-person households, a greater proportion of three-generation households, more households whose main income is from a family business, and more upper middle-class and lower middle-class households.[4]

City of Residence

Japanese tend to think of life in Tokyo as being more modern than that in other parts of Japan, and to think of life in Kyoto as being especially traditional. The image of life in Matsumoto falls between the two, and carries an aura of provincialism. From city to city there are minor variations in sleeping arrangements—notably in central Kyoto, with its older and larger houses, where families are somewhat more spread out in their sleeping arrangements than in Tokyo or Matsumoto. But if the data by city are controlled by any other variable, these differences vanish.

Household Size

The total sample has an average of 4.8 persons per household, and city-to-city differences are minor—5.0 for Tokyo, 4.6 for Kyoto, and 4.5 for

Table 1. Distribution of Households in the Sample by Number of Generations, Style of Life, Social Class, and Density

Category	Tokyo (N = 198)	Kyoto (N = 99)	Matsumoto (N = 26)	Total Households (N = 323)
Number of generations in household				
Two	128	60	23	211
Three	70	39	3	112*
Style of life: main source of income				
Salary and wages	104	71	11	186
Family business	94	28	15	137
Social class				
Upper middle	65	60	6	131
Lower middle	71	29	8	108
Working	62	10	12	84
Density				
High	155	43	17	215
Low	43	56	9	108

* Includes 4 four-generation households.

Matsumoto. In this regard the sample is close to the 1960 census, which found (for households of like composition) an average of 4.8 persons per household for all urban areas, 4.9 for Tokyo, and 4.8 for Kyoto. Census figures for Matsumoto are not available to us.[5] As will be seen, size of household does prove to be a useful variable in certain respects.

Number of Generations

In line with the patrilineal emphasis in Japanese culture, 79 percent of the three-generation households in the sample include one or both of the husband's parents, while only 21 percent include one or both of the wife's parents. No household contains grandparents from both paternal and maternal sides.

Style of Life

The distinction concerning the main source of income for a household is related more to a "style of life" than to economic matters. Following World War II, the role of the "salaryman" has become more important and desirable, and is seen as a modern way of life free from some of the traditional constraints associated with working in a small family business. It should be noted that style of life is conceptually separate from social class.[6] And, as will be seen, style of life does play a minor role as a meaningful variable in sleeping arrangements.

Social Class

To determine social class, we first separated our households into five logical groups based on the occupation and education of the head of the household. Because there were so few cases in groups one and five, we combined the first two groups into an "upper middle class," we retained the third group and labeled it "lower middle class," and we combined the last two groups under the heading of "working class." We did not, however, find any important differences by social class in sleeping arrangements.[7]

Density

We define density as the ratio between the number of rooms available to a household for sleeping purposes, and the number of persons residing in the household. When there are fewer available sleeping rooms than persons, we call this *high density;* when there are as many or more sleeping rooms than persons, we call it *low density.*

It should be noted that we define density in terms of space available, not space actually used. In tabulating rooms available for sleeping, we excluded kitchens, baths, toilets, halls, porches, storage areas, and rooms used predominately for business purposes (that is, the "shop"). We counted all other rooms as available for sleeping, including a room that a household might reserve for visitors during the daytime. Because of the ordinary construction of the Japanese dwelling, almost all of the rooms counted as available are mat-floored *(tatami)* rooms; people sleep in such rooms on quilts *(futon),* which are spread out each evening and taken up during the day. Ninety percent of the adults in the sample sleep in this manner, while 10 percent use Western-style beds. We shall return later to this question of bedding.[8]

As can be seen in Table 1, density varies by city, being highest in Tokyo. In this regard, the sample seems to reflect the fact that Tokyo's population has been increasing two to three times faster than that of Kyoto or Matsumoto; in addition, both of these latter cities have a larger proportion of old multiple-room houses because they were not bombed during World War II, whereas Tokyo was gutted by fire-bomb raids in 1945. Japan, in general, continues to suffer from a shortage of housing. Conditions probably have improved since 1955, the latest year for which we have reliable figures, but at that time in cities over 200,000 population the average dwelling space per person was still 10 percent below what it had been in 1941.[9] And the average Japanese urban household in 1955 had nearly twice as many persons per room as did its

American counterpart—1.22 persons in Japan to 0.67 persons in the United States.[10] But if there is need for more living space in general in Japan, the need for more sleeping space in particular is less apparent.

Availability and Use of Sleeping Space

Our first question is: How much available sleeping space do the households in the sample have, and how much of it do they regularly use? Table 2 shows the distribution of the 323 households in the sample by number of persons in a household and number of rooms it has available for sleeping. The households to the left of the step-line have less than one sleeping room available per person, and these 215 households (67 percent) have a high density. The households to the right of the step-line have one or more rooms available per person, and these 108 households (33 percent) have a low density. These latter households could provide a separate room for each member if they chose to do so.

In contrast, Table 3 shows the distribution of all households by number of persons and number of rooms actually used for sleeping. There is a dramatic shift to the left of the step-line, and of the 108 households in Table 2 that could provide each member with a separate room, only one remains to the right of the line in Table 3.

A more detailed comparison of Tables 2 and 3 will show that three-person households in our sample prefer to sleep in one room, whereas four-person households are more likely to divide into two rooms. Given the household composition of our sample, this is perhaps not so surprising, but if one continues to look in Table 3 for the modal frequency in terms of size of household relative to number of rooms used for sleeping, the idea begins to dawn that Japanese prefer to sleep in clusters of two or three persons, and prefer not to sleep alone.

We do not, of course, expect every person in a household, even if this were possible, to sleep in a separate room. It would be highly unusual even among privacy-minded American households. Each of the households in the sample contains at least one married couple, and most of them also contain an infant. Presumably most of the married couples, and some of the mothers and infants, will co-sleep. This in itself makes it unlikely that many households will exhaust their available sleeping rooms.

But if some amount of co-sleeping seems likely a priori, the next question we ask is: To what extent does the amount of available space influence the degree of co-sleeping? If, for example, Japanese parents and children co-sleep simply because they lack space, then they should tend to disperse as more rooms become available. We can begin to test this as follows.

Table 2. Number of Persons in Household by Number of Rooms Available for Sleeping

Number of Persons in Household	Number of Rooms Available for Sleeping										Total Households
	1	2	3	4	5	6	7	8	9	10+	
3	31	45	17	8	10	3			1	2	117
4	6	20	15	17	3	2	2	1			66
5		8	4	13	9	4	3			1	42
6	1	1	3	7	7	8		2	1	2	32
7		1	1	7	6	2	3		1	2	23
8				7	4	2	4	4		1	22
9			1	3	3		1				8
10				1		1	1			1	4
11+				2		2	1		1	3	9
Total Households	38	75	41	65	42	24	15	7	4	12	323

Table 3. Number of Persons in Household by Number of Rooms Used for Sleeping

Number of Persons in Household	Number of Rooms Used for Sleeping										Total Households
	1	2	3	4	5	6	7	8	9	10+	
3	102	14	1								117
4	23	41	2								66
5	5	25	11	1							42
6	1	8	17	6							32
7		2	11	10							23
8			8	11	3						22
9			3	3	2						8
10			1	3							4
11+				2	5		2				9
Total Households	131	90	54	36	10		2				323

First, we exclude 38 households that have only one sleeping room available.[11] We assume that they have no opportunity to disperse, save that of bedding down members in kitchens or hallways. The remaining 285 households, however, have some freedom of choice in sleeping arrangements, since each of them has at least two sleeping rooms available.

Next, for each of these 285 households we compute two indexes. The first we call *use density*. To obtain this we divide the number of persons in a household by the number of rooms they now use for sleeping. For example, a four-person household sleeping in two rooms has a use density of two persons per room. The second index we call *available-space density*. To obtain this we divide the number of persons in a household by the number of available rooms, up to the point where the ratio equals one. For example, a four-person household with four available rooms has an available-space density of one person per room. A household with more available rooms than members would have a theoretical available-space density of less than one person per room, but we have set a lower limit of one for this index because it seems a bit unrealistic to expect a person regularly to use more than one sleeping room.

Finally, we examine the correlation (by the Pearson r method) between use density and available-space density for each group of households having the same number of members. There are nine such groups, ranging from three-person to eleven-or-more-person households (see Tables 2 and 3). The results of this analysis are: (1) the correlation is not significant ($r = -.05$) for three-person households; (2) the correlations are significant ($r = .25$, n.s.; $r = .29$ to $.89$, $p < .05$) for seven of the eight groups of households having four to eleven or more members; and (3) the correlation is significant ($r = .47$, $p < .01$) when all households having four or more members are considered together.

These results mean that three-person households do not tend to disperse for sleep even when rooms are available, but larger households do tend to disperse to some extent. For the larger households, the correlation tells us that the availability of space accounts for 22 percent (r^2) of the variance in the actual use of space. In other words, lack of space does make a difference in co-sleeping arrangements in our urban Japanese households having more than three members, but space alone tells only about one-fifth of the story. To fill out the story, we must ask, Who sleeps by whom?

Sleep and Social Structure

Our question now becomes: Which kinship roles are most likely to co-sleep, and which to disperse? Once again we exclude the 38 households having only one sleeping room available; and, for the households having at least two sleeping rooms, we consider separately the 86 three-person households and the 199 four-or-more-person households.

Each of the three-person households consists of a child with both parents—and in 79 of the cases the child is an infant of three to four months. Thus it is perhaps not too unusual that all members sleep together in one room in 71 (86 percent) of the households. Another 14 (16 percent) use two rooms; in 9 of these cases it is the child who is alone, but in 5 cases it is the father. In one household the three members each sleep alone.

Given the high number of infants in these three-person households, one might argue that the "instrumental need" to look after the infant at night would favor keeping him in the parental bedroom. But if convenience were the only consideration, the infant would probably be excluded from the room a few months to a year after birth. This tends to happen in American households but is much less true for Japanese households,[12] as will be seen in detail at a later point.

The next question we must ask is: What happens when a household becomes larger? We turn now to 199 four-or-more-person households in which density does make a difference. Remember that each of these households contains a father, mother, and child, plus some combination of additional children, extended kin, and unrelated persons. Table 4 presents data on sleeping arrangements by kinship category for all persons in these households. The table should be read horizontally: for example, of the 132 fathers in high-density households, 3 percent sleep alone; 97 percent sleep in nuclear family groupings, of two (15 percent), three (44 percent), and four-or-more (38 percent) persons; and one percent sleep with an extended kinsman. Complex-mixed sleeping groups are composed of three or more persons with at least one representative from each of the three categories—nuclear family, extended kin, and nonrelated persons.

The first point to be made from Table 4 concerns the effect of household social structure on who sleeps by whom. As indicated by the percentages within the heavy lines, to a striking extent nuclear kin co-sleep with nuclear kin, extended kin with extended kin, and nonrelated persons with nonrelated persons. For the father, mother, and infant, the exceptions to this generalization are trivial; and for the child, extended kin, and nonrelated persons, the exceptions occur somewhat more often in high-density households. We did not fully anticipate this result, and it shows a highly regular sorting by social roles within the general tendency to cluster into co-sleeping groups.[13]

The second point to be made from Table 4 concerns the size of co-sleeping groups. Within the nuclear family, regardless of density, the three-person group is most common for the father, mother, and infant. This pattern is particularly apparent in low-density households, whereas high-density households have a substantial percentage of four-or-more-person groups. A child is found most often in a four-or-more-person group in high-density households, but in a two- or three-person group in low-density households. If anyone sleeps alone in the nuclear family, it is most likely to be an infant in a low-density household.

Table 4. Percentage Distribution of Participation in Various Types of Co-Sleeping Groups by Kinship Category and Density of Household for All Persons in 199 Households Having Four or More Members

Types of Co-Sleeping Groups by Number of Persons Co-Sleeping

Kinship Category	Density	Sleeping Alone	Nuclear Family			Extended Kin			Nonrelated			Complex-Mixed		Total Percent*	Total Persons
			2	3	4+	2	3	4+	2	3	4+	3	4+		
Father	High	3	15	44	38	1								101	132
	Low	9	19	64	8									100	67
Mother	High		15	47	37								1	101	132
	Low		23	70	8									101	67
Infant	High	3	10	50	36								1	101	125
	Low	14	10	68	8									100	55
Child	High	2	19	13	53	6	4						3	100	120
	Low	8	40	30	17	6								101	34
Extended kin	High	22	3	*	*	44	18	3	2	*	*	5	1	98	231
	Low	35	2			52	6	4						99	92
Nonrelated persons	High	28				4		4	21	27	12	2	3	101	112
	Low	63				7			20	10				100	30

* Totals do not add to 100 percent because of rounding; an asterisk indicates less than .5 of a percent.

Among extended kin, regardless of density, the most frequent pattern is to co-sleep in a two-person group, and the next most frequent is to sleep alone. Nonrelated persons are most frequently found alone, and this is especially true in low-density households.

The manner in which data are presented in Table 4 obscures two dimensions that require examination. First, the table does not fully indicate which persons are co-sleeping in terms of social roles. For example, it tells us that about one father in five co-sleeps with some one other person; it does not tell us who that other person may be. American common sense might suggest that it is his wife—but here American common sense is not the best predictor. Second, the table combines information from families that are at different stages in their life cycle. Let us re-sort the data with these points in mind.

Co-Sleeping and the Life Cycle of the Nuclear Family

From the point of view of the parents, the life cycle of a nuclear family begins at marriage; continues through the birth, rearing, and subsequent marriage of the children, until toward the end only the spouses remain; they are separated by the death of one; and finally the family ceases to exist upon the death of the other. We shall focus upon the intermediate stages of this cycle, since our data are inadequate for generalizations about the beginning and ending stages.[14]

Once again we exclude the 38 households with only one sleeping room. The remaining 285 households all contain a "primary" nuclear family that is in almost all cases a younger family in one of the early stages of the cycle. In addition, 110 households contain a "secondary" nuclear family, or the remnants thereof, which is in almost all cases in the later stages of the cycle. These older nuclear families make up the great bulk of the extended kin in Table 4.[15] Since we have already shown that there is little co-sleeping between extended kin and other groupings, let us also in a sense "stand the sample on its head" and look at sleeping arrangements from the point of view of these older nuclear families, being careful to note those situations in which older nuclears occur in the sleeping ranks of younger nuclears, and vice versa.

We have, then, 285 primary and 110 secondary nuclear families to consider across the stages of the nuclear family cycle. The sample can be divided readily into seven stages, of which the first three occur among younger nuclear families and the last four among older ones. These stages are: (1) both parents and an infant, (2) both parents and an infant plus one or more young children, (3) both parents and one or more older children, (4) both parents and one or more adult children, (5) both parents only, (6) one parent and one or more adult children, and (7) one parent only.

These stages are logically exclusive except for the line to be drawn between "older children" and "adult children" in stages 3 and 4. We decided this empirically by looking at sleeping arrangements in terms of the age of the child among the total 535 children in the 285 primary and 110 secondary nuclear families.

As can be seen in Table 5, the sharpest break in sleeping arrangements comes between the children who are 11 to 15 years old and those who are 16 to 20 years old. The former have a 50 percent chance of co-sleeping in a two-generation group (with a parent or extended kin member), whereas the latter have only a 17 percent chance of so doing. Moreover, although the numbers involved are smaller, the break clearly seems to fall between children who are 13 to 15 years old and children who are 16 to 18 years old. The implication here is rather strong that puberty for the boy and the onset of menstruation for the girl set the stage for a withdrawal from co-sleeping with parents or extended kin. For these reasons we draw the line between stages 3 and 4 at 15 years of age. That is, we place a nuclear family in stage 3 if they have at least one child who is 15 years or younger. And we place a family in stage 4 if all of their children are 16 years or more.

Looking across the early years of life in a more general sense, it is apparent in Table 5 that from the point of view of a child he can expect to co-sleep with an adult until he is 10 years old. The period from 11 to 15 years is one of transition, with the greatest increase being in the co-sleeping with a sibling. After the age of 16, a child is more likely to co-sleep with a sibling or to be alone, but there always remains a fair chance (at about the 20 percent level) that he will co-sleep with a parent. As for sex differences, which are not shown in Table 5, there are none until after the 11 to 15 years old period. From 16 years on, there is a tendency for daughters more than sons to co-sleep with a parent. In these later periods both daughters and sons are about equally likely to co-sleep with a sibling, but sons are more likely to sleep alone than are daughters.[16]

Having established a reasonable cutting point between stages 3 and 4 in the nuclear family cycle, we show, in Table 6, the frequency distribution of the families across the seven stages. The table also gives the median ages of the parents and children at each stage. In these stages where data are drawn from several sources (that is, stages 1, 3, and 4), we first checked to see if the pattern of sleeping arrangements differed significantly according to the source. There were no differences, so we combined the cases to obtain the total families indicated in each stage.

The importance of the median ages given in the table will be explained more fully later. For now, we point out only that the median ages of the mother (26 years) and father (29 years) in stage 1 are in close agreement with findings in other studies. Since the infants in these fam-

Table 5. Percentage Distribution of Sleeping Arrangements by Age for 535 Children from Primary and Secondary Nuclear Families

Sleeping Arrangements	Age of Child						
	3–4 Months (N = 259)	1–5 Years (N = 103)	6–10 Years (N = 28)	11–15 Years (N = 28)	16–20 Years (N = 46)	21–25 Years (N = 38)	26+ Years (N = 33)
Two-Generations	90	91	79	50	17	24	18
With parent(s)	90	79	68	46	15	24	15
With extended kin	—	12	11	4	2	—	3
One-Generation	2	7	11	36	46	40	33
With sibling(s)	2	7	11	36	46	37	21
With nonrelated person(s)	—	—	—	—	—	3	12
Alone	8	2	11	14	37	37	49
Total Percent*	100	100	101	100	100	101	100

* Totals do not add to 100 percent because of rounding.

Table 6. Source of Data on Nuclear Families across the Stages of the Nuclear Family Cycle

Source of Data	Younger Nuclear Families			Older Nuclear Families				Total Families
	1 Both Parents, Infant Only	2 Both Parents, Infant, Child(ren)	3 Both Parents, Older Child(ren)	4 Both Parents, Adult Child(ren)	5 Both Parents Only	6 One Parent, Adult Child(ren)	7 One Parent Only	
Primary Nuclear Families								
From 86 three-person households..........	79	—	5	2	—	—	—	86
From 199 four-or-more-person households..........	92	88	16	3	—	—	—	199
Secondary Nuclear Families								
From 199 four-or-more-person households..........	—	—	10	36	32	13	19	110
Total Families	171	88	31	41	32	13	19	395
Median Age:								
Mother..........	26	29	40	56	58	55	63	
Father..........	29	33	45	61	63	66	68	
Child	3–4 mos.	3–4 mos., 3	13	24	—	22	—	

ilies are three to four months old, it is likely that the parents were married one to two years earlier, on the average. At that time, the wife would have been about 24 or 25, and the husband about 27 or 28. In a study conducted in 1959, Blood found the median age of marriage to be 24 for wives and 28 for husbands among 444 young married couples living in three government apartment houses in Tokyo; and Taeuber cites data for 1935 on Japan as a whole giving an average age of first marriage of 24 for women and 28 for men. It is also apparent from the 1960 census in Japan that the average age of marriage is increasing, particularly in densely populated urban areas.[17]

Parental Sleeping Arrangements in the Early Stages

Table 7 presents the data for sleeping arrangements from the point of view of the parents in stages 1 through 3. Four broad categories of sleeping arrangements are used, and these need a word of explanation. In the first category, *Two Generations: Together,* both parents and at least one child are co-sleeping. This category is subdivided into those families in which all nuclear members are literally together, in that both parents and all children share a sleeping room; and those families which are more symbolically together, in that at least one of the children co-sleeps with both parents. In the second category, *Two Generations: Consanguineous,* the parents separate in order to provide parental co-sleeping partners for the children. This category is also subdivided into those situations where each parent takes one or more children as a co-sleeping partner, and those situations where the father sleeps alone while the mother co-sleeps with one or more children. The third category, *One Generation: Conjugal,* is the usual "American" pattern where the parents are co-sleeping as a couple, and the children are elsewhere. Finally, in the fourth category, *One Generation: Separate,* the parents separate, each sleeping alone, and the children are elsewhere.

In stage 1 the overwhelming proportion (86 percent) of parents co-sleep with their infant. In 10 percent of the cases, the parents sleep conjugally, but we found no variable that distinguishes this group. And in a few cases, the father sleeps alone.

In stage 2 the most important change is the substantial increase (to 22 percent) in the *Two Generations: Consanguineous* pattern, even though the *Two Generations: Together* pattern remains high (73 percent). Remember that in stage 2 each family has two or more children—an infant and at least one young child whose median age is three years. The amount of two-generation co-sleeping actually increases from stage 1 to stage 2 if the first two categories are added together (from 90 percent to 95 percent). It is as if the Japanese parents, wanting to provide a parental sleeping partner for all children at this stage and faced with the issue of

Table 7. Percentage Distribution of Parental Sleeping Arrangements by Stage in Family Cycle for Younger Nuclear Families

	Stages in Family Cycle		
	1	2	3
	Both Parents, Infant Only (3–4 mos.)* (N = 171 families)	Both Parents, Infant, Child(ren) (3–4 mos. and 3 yrs.)* (N = 88 families)	Both Parents, Older Child(ren) (13 yrs.)* (N = 31 families)
Parental Sleeping Arrangements			
Two Generations: Together	**86**	**73**	**52**
Both parents and all children	86	53	29
Both parents and child(ren) — another child elsewhere	n.a.†	19	23
Two Generations: Consanguineous	**4**	**22**	**10**
Separation of parents, each with child(ren)	n.a.	15	3
Exclusion of father, mother with child(ren)	4	7	7
One Generation: Conjugal	**10**	**6**	**35**
Parents together, all children elsewhere			
One Generation: Separate	—	—	**3**
Parents sleep separately, and children sleep separately from parents			
Total Percent‡	**100**	**101**	**100**

* Median ages for infants and children.
† n.a. = not applicable.
‡ Totals do not add to 100 percent because of rounding.

sleeping four or more to a room, which they dislike (possibly because of the size of the room, as indicated in note 8), have, in about one-fifth of the cases, decided to separate in order to meet the problem.

We have some evidence that spouses are not likely to separate if they have an alternative. And the preferred alternative is to send one or more children to co-sleep with a kinswoman. Of the 88 families in stage 2, 40 households include extended kin and 48 do not. Parents in the latter households are significantly more likely to separate than those in the former. This tendency can be seen even more sharply when we focus on the 30 families in stage 2 that are included in the sleeping patterns of both parents and one or more children (19 percent, or 17 families), and separation of parents (15 percent, or 13 families). Among the 17 families where both parents are together, 13 households contain extended kin, and four do not; on the other hand, among the 13 families where the parents are separated, only one household contains extended kin, and 12 do not (chi square = 13.6, 1 df, $p < .001$). Clearly, in households where there are extended kin, the parents have decided to remain together; when there are no extended kin available, the parents have decided to sleep separately.

We can explore this question further by asking where the "other" child sleeps among the 17 families in which both parents are together with one or more children. Four of these households do not include extended kin, and in all four the "other" child sleeps alone. But, in the 13 households that include extended kin, the "other" child co-sleeps with a kinswoman in 11 instances, and is alone only in two. Two points stand out here. First, it is always a child who goes to sleep with extended kin; the infant (and sometimes other children) remains with the parents. Second, it is usually an older kinswoman who takes the child (the husband's mother in six cases, the wife's mother in two, the husband's unmarried sister in three). In short, if an older kinswoman is present during stage 2, she is likely to become a mother surrogate for co-sleeping.

Among the 13 families in which the parents are separated, the one household containing extended kin includes a husband's father who sleeps alone. Since in this pattern each parent is co-sleeping with one or more children, it is of interest to know how the children are distributed. The fathers in these families always co-sleep with a child and never with an infant, and the sex of the child apparently does not matter—in eight cases it is a son, and in five cases it is a daughter. The mothers always co-sleep with the infant, who is joined by a child in four cases (the additional child being a son in three cases and a daughter in one case).

In stage 2, the remaining sleeping patterns are not proportionately very important, but when the father sleeps separately (7 percent), he is most often alone, and the mother is with all of the children. Finally, in the few families in which the parents sleep conjugally (6 percent), the infant and a sibling usually share another room.

In stage 3, in which there are only older children and no infants, the total proportion of two-generation co-sleeping declines but remains high (62 percent). The decrease occurs primarily in the categories of parents co-sleeping with all children, and of parents sleeping separately —each with one or more children. The proportion of parents sleeping conjugally, however, rises nearly sixfold, although at 35 percent this still seems well below American norms.

In stage 3, if the nuclear family is not co-sleeping all together (29 percent), the parents usually keep the youngest child with them (23 percent). There are seven families in this latter pattern, and although there is no difference by density, it is informative to look at the three low-density families (which could provide, if they chose to do so, a separate room for each member). In the first case, the parents share a room with a 15-year-old son, while a 23-year-old daughter and a 19-year-old son share another room. In the second case, the parents co-sleep with a 10-year-old daughter, and two older daughters (15 and 13 years of age) share another room. And in the third case, the parents are with a 14-year-old daughter, and a 20-year-old daughter is alone.

In the consanguineous patterns (10 percent) there are only three cases. In two of these the father sleeps alone while the mother co-sleeps with all of the children, and in one case the father co-sleeps with a 10-year-old daughter and the mother with two other daughters (13 and 9 years of age).

Where the parents sleep conjugally (35 percent), the children also most often all share another room—about half of the time with a sibling of the opposite sex. Most of these cases are high-density families and are crowded for space as, for example, the family in which the parents share one room and the other room is occupied by four children (two sons, 23 and 16 years of age, and two daughters, 20 and 14 years of age). Still, the one low-density family arranges itself with the parents in one room and the two children (an 8-year-old daughter and a 14-year-old son) in another.

Finally, there is one individualistic family with three members, each of whom sleeps alone (father, mother, and 14-year-old daughter).

Parents' Sleeping Arrangements in the Later Stages

The data for parental sleeping arrangements in the later stages of the nuclear family cycle are given in Table 8. Remember that each of these 105 older families is living in the same household with a married child. This is a common—and preferred—situation in Japan. For example, a

national survey on aged persons (65 years and over) conducted by the
Ministry of Health and Welfare in 1960 found that in Japan's six largest
cities, 51 percent of the households containing aged persons also contained a married child; in smaller cities the proportion rose to 64 percent.[18] It seems probable, therefore, that our findings should be valid
for about half of the older nuclear families in urban areas.

In stage 4, in which the adult children have a median age of 24, for
the first time the proportion of parents sleeping conjugally rises above
the proportion of two-generation co-sleeping. There would seem to be
three types of parents at this stage. The most numerous are those who
have decided to sleep conjugally (68 percent), now that their children
have become adults. A second group continues two-generation sleeping
habits, either with an adult child or a grandchild (22 percent). And
third, a small proportion separate and sleep alone (10 percent).

More in detail, among the 28 cases (68 percent) in which the parents
sleep conjugally, the children sleep alone in 20 cases, with siblings of the
same sex in four cases, and with cross-sex siblings in three cases; in one
case a son co-sleeps with a male employee. Among the nine cases (22
percent) in which the parents sleep in some two-generation combination, seven cases involve children and two cases involve grandchildren.
For example, the parents in a low-density family choose to co-sleep with
a 24-year-old son; and the mother in a low-density family co-sleep with
her unmarried 35-year-old eldest son while the father sleeps alone (a
younger son is married, and his family forms the younger nuclear family in this household). Finally, among the four cases (10 percent) in
which the parents sleep separately, in one case three sons share a room
together, and there are three rather peculiar cases in which not only the
mother and father but also each of the children sleeps alone.

In stage 5 both older parents remain, but there are no unmarried
adult children. In this stage, conjugal sleeping reaches its highest proportion (75 percent), followed by two-generation co-sleeping with a
grandchild (19 percent), and with a small proportion sleeping separately and alone (6 percent). It would seem that there are always about
one-fifth of the grandparents in this kind of household who volunteer, or
who are pressed into service, to care for the needs of a grandchild at
night.

Stages 6 and 7 represent the fragmented remains of the nuclear family at the end of its cycle. The situations in these two stages appear to be
reciprocal: In stage 6, where there is an unmarried child, the widowed
parent tends to co-sleep with the child or with a grandchild (62 percent
of the time); in stage 7, where there is no unmarried child, the widowed
parent tends to sleep, at the end, alone (68 percent of the time) unless a
grandchild is available.

Table 8. Percentage Distribution of Parental Sleeping Arrangements by Stage in Family Cycle for Older Nuclear Families

Parental Sleeping Arrangements	Stages in Family Cycle			
	4 Both Parents, Adult Child(ren)* (24 years)* (N = 41 families)	5 Both Parents Only (N = 32 families)	6 One Parent, Adult Child(ren)* (22 years)* (N = 13 families)	7 One Parent Only (N = 19 families)
Two Generations: Together.	15	16	n.a.	n.a.
Both parents and child(ren)	10	n.a.	n.a.	n.a.
Both parents and grandchild(ren)	5	16	n.a.	n.a.
Two Generations: Consanguineous	7	3	62	32
Separation of parents, each with child(ren) or grandchild(ren)	—	—		
Exclusion of father, mother with child(ren) or grandchild(ren)	7	3		n.a.
Widowed parent with child(ren) or grand-child(ren)	n.a.†	n.a.	n.a.	n.a.
One Generation: Conjugal.	68	75	62	32
Parents together, child(ren) or grandchild(ren) elsewhere				
One Generation: Separate	10	6	39	68
Parents, or widowed parent, sleep separately and alone				
Total Percent‡	100	100	101	100

* Median age for children.
† n.a. = not applicable.
‡ Totals do not add to 100 percent because of rounding.

In support of the above generalization, the 13 cases in stage 6 are made up of 10 widowed mothers and three widowed fathers who do have an unmarried child living in the household. Among the 10 mothers, six co-sleep with a child (four with daughters and two with sons), one co-sleeps in a cluster with three grandchildren, and three sleep alone. Among the three fathers, one co-sleeps with a daughter, and the other two sleep alone.

The 19 cases in stage 7 are made up of 16 widowed mothers and three widowed fathers who do not, of course, have an unmarried child living in the household, and must co-sleep with a grandchild if they are not to sleep alone. Among the 16 mothers, five co-sleep with a grandchild; and among the three fathers, one co-sleeps with a grandchild.

There is a further point of interest. If we combine the cases in stages 4 and 6, and the cases in stages 5 and 7, we have two types of older nuclear families—those that contain older parents and adult unmarried children (54 cases), and those that contain only older parents (51 cases). Here style of family life does make a difference. Households with a "small family business" style of life contain more older nuclear families having parents and adult unmarried children, whereas households with a "salaryman" style of life contain more older nuclear families having only parents.[19] It would seem that young married salarymen are willing to assume responsibility for their parents, but are less willing to have their adult unmarried siblings living with them. In contrast, adult unmarried siblings seem to be more welcome in small business households where they may more directly contribute to the work of the family.

Co-Sleeping and the Life Cycle of the Individual

So far we have considered co-sleeping mostly in terms of the life cycle of the nuclear family. What about the co-sleeping career of an individual from birth to death? What are his co-sleeping "chances" at different ages? We have already seen (Table 5) that until the age of 15 a child has about a 50 percent chance of sleeping with one or both parents. From birth to age 15, a child's chances of co-sleeping with a sibling gradually increase; and before age 15 only a few children are likely to sleep alone.

In these early years of life, co-sleeping bears importantly upon questions of socialization and identity.[20] We have shown that, in general, when a family has more than one child, the parents may separate and each co-sleep with a child, or sometimes a child may be sent to co-sleep with an older kinswoman. On the whole we would expect that the older a child, the more likely he is to be removed from the parental bedroom. One way to test this is to contrast the treatment of infants and young children. Of the 88 families in stage 2, 73 have exactly two children—in each case an infant of three to four months, and a child with a median age of three years (see Table 7). We constructed a five-point scale of physical closeness to a parent in sleeping arrangements, and then asked of the data for each family: Who is closer, the infant or the child? The results are given in Table 9.

In each family, the infant and child are assigned a position on the five-point scale, and a tie occurs where both occupy the same position. The scale is as follows: (1) *Alone* means sleeping in a room by oneself. (2) *Other Person's Room* means co-sleeping in a room with a person other than a parent. This can occur when the infant and child are sharing a room (in which case it is a tie), or it can occur when the infant or child is co-sleeping with an adult (usually a grandmother). (3) *Parent's Room in Own Bed* means that the infant or child is sleeping in his own Western-style bed or crib in the same room with both parents, or with either the mother or father separately. (4) *Parent's Room in Own Futon* means that the infant or child is sleeping in his own individual *futon* (quilts spread on the floor) with both parents, or with either the mother or father separately. (5) *In Parent's Bedding* means that the infant is sleeping in the same bedding (either in a Western-style bed or in Japanese *futon*) with both parents, or with either the mother or father separately.

We consider sleeping in one's own *futon* to be closer in access to a parent than sleeping in one's own bed or crib for this reason: the Japanese quilts of the several co-sleepers are usually laid out next to each other with the edges almost touching. This means that a parent need only reach over to care for an infant or child, without the necessity of getting up. In contrast, a bed or crib is a more distinctly separate "container," and a parent needs to get up in order to care for an infant or child. In fact, cribs are mainly used only during the first year of life; after this the crib is put away, and the young child is given his own *futon*. Even during the first year, the crib may be used only as a daytime container, and the infant will be brought down on the mats to sleep in *futon* during the night. Therefore, we scored beds and *futon* differently, but these points on the scale may be collapsed into a single category of *In a Parent's Room in Own Bedding*. We will give the results in both ways.[21]

In Table 9, cases falling on the diagonal represent ties between infant and child in closeness of access to a parent. Cases above the diagonal represent situations in which the infant is closer, and cases below the diagonal represent situations in which the child is closer.

Using the full five-point scale, it is clear that the child is closer to a parent than is the infant. There are 20 ties; the infant is closer in 16 cases; and the child is closer in 37 cases (chi square = 10.0, 2 *df*, $p <$ .01). There is no significant difference in this pattern by density, social class, or style of life. There is a difference, however, by whether or not

Table 9. Comparison of Closeness of Access to Parents in Sleeping Arrangements for Infant and Child in 73 Families Having One Infant and One Child

		Infant's Access to Parents					
Scale of Access to Parents		Alone	Other Person's Room	Parent's Room in Own Bed	Parent's Room in Own *Futon*	In Parent's Bedding	Total Cases
Child's Access to Parents	Alone	1		2		1	4
	Other Person's Room		4	5	4	2	15
	Parent's Room in Own Bed	1		1			2
	Parent's Room in Own *Futon*	1		18	12	2	33
	In Parent's Bedding	1		8	8	2	19
Total Cases		4	4	34	24	7	73

there are extended kin living in the household—a result which we have previously seen in the more general analysis of the data for stage 2.

In the data in Table 9 there are 33 families in which extended kin are present, and 40 families in which they are not. In the extended-kin families, the infant and child are equal in access to a parent (9 ties, 12 infant closer, and 12 child closer) because the child is frequently provided with a "substitute mother" and is sleeping in another person's room while the infant is with the mother (or with both parents). In the families with only nuclear members, the child is closer to a parent (11 ties, 4 infant closer, and 25 child closer). The comparison of closeness to a parent in these two types of families is significant (chi square = 8.2, 2 df, $p < .02$).

If the distinction between sleeping in own bed and in own *futon* is collapsed into a broader category of sleeping in own bedding, then the infant and child become equidistant in access to a parent (38 ties, 16 infant closer, and 19 child closer).

We conclude that, at the very least, there is little change in access to a parent in sleeping arrangements during the transition from infancy to childhood. In contrast, there is a sharp physical separation from the parents during this transition in the urban American family, if indeed such a separation had not already been made in infancy.[22] The relative conception of the path to be followed in the socialization of the young child would seem to be different in the two cultures. In Japan, the path seems to lead toward increasing interdependence with other persons, whereas in America the path seems to lead toward increasing independence from others. As we have shown, even in stage 3, at a time when the median age of the child is 13 years, the proportion of two-generation co-sleeping remains very high (see Table 7).

From the age of 16 to 26 or more (see Table 5), roughly 20 percent of the children continue to co-sleep in a two-generation group, mainly with a parent; and about 40 percent co-sleep in a one-generation group, mostly with a sibling. At this older age sleeping alone rises significantly, to 37 percent from age 16 to 25, and to 40 percent by age 26 or more. If our data included children living away from home,[23] then the total proportion of children sleeping alone between the ages of 16 and 26 and older would probably be over 50 percent.

As we have seen, however, daughters tend to marry in urban Japan around the age of 24 to 26, and sons a few years later around the age of 27 to 30. Presumably, after marriage the young couple sleeps conjugally for a year or two until the birth of their first child. But, from that point on, for at least the following 15 years the parents will usually co-sleep in a two-generation group containing one or more of their children. This repeats, of course, their own childhood experience, as can be seen in

Table 10. Summary Percentage Distribution of Parental Sleeping Arrangements across Stages in the Nuclear Family Cycle

Parental Sleeping Arrangement	Stages in Family Cycle						
	1 Both Parents, Infant Only (N = 171 families)	2 Both Parents, Infant, Child(ren) (N = 88 families)	3 Both Parents, Older Child(ren) (N = 31 families)	4 Both Parents, Adult Child(ren) (N = 41 families)	5 Both Parents Only (N = 32 families)	6 One Parent, Adult Child(ren) (N = 13 families)	7 One Parent Only (N = 19 families)
Two Generations: Together	86	73	52	15	16	n.a.*	n.a.
Two Generations: Consanguineous	4	22	10	7	3	62	32
One Generation: Conjugal	10	6	35	68	75	n.a.	n.a.
One Generation: Separate	—	—	3	10	6	39	68
Total Percent†	100	101	100	100	100	101	100
Median Age of Parents:							
Mother	26	29	40	56	58	55	63
Father	29	33	45	61	63	66	68

* n.a. = not applicable.
† Totals do not add to 100 percent because of rounding.

Table 10, which summarizes the data on sleeping arrangements across our seven stages in the nuclear family cycle.

Somewhere between stages 3 and 4, when the mother is in her middle to late forties and the father is in his late forties to early fifties, the balance shifts for the parents in favor of conjugal sleeping. This pattern persists through stage 5 and until one of the parents dies. Then, if there is an unmarried child available, the widowed parent tends to "revert" to the earlier pattern of co-sleeping with a child in stage 6. Finally, in stage 7, when there is only the widowed parent, the proportion of sleeping alone rises steeply.

In summary, then, an individual in urban Japan can expect to co-sleep in a two-generation group, first as a child and then as a parent, over approximately half of his life. This starts at birth and continues until puberty; it resumes after the birth of the first child and continues until about the time of menopause for the mother; and it reoccurs for a few years in old age. In the interim years the individual can expect to co-sleep in a one-generation group with a sibling after puberty, with a spouse for a few years after marriage, and again with a spouse in late middle age. Sleeping alone appears to be an alternative most commonly found in the years between puberty and marriage, and to be a reluctantly accepted necessity for the widowed parent toward the end.

We wish to make one broad generalization, and one speculation. The generalization is that sleeping arrangements in Japanese families tend to blur the distinctions between generations and between the sexes, to emphasize the interdependence more than the separateness of individuals, and to underplay (or largely ignore) the potentiality for the growth of conjugal intimacy between husband and wife in sexual and other matters in favor of a more general familial cohesion.[24]

The speculation concerns the coincidence of those age periods when sleeping alone is most likely to occur, with the age periods when suicide is most likely to occur in Japan. The rates for both types of behavior are highest in adolescence and young adulthood, and again in old age.[25] It might be that sleeping alone in these two periods contributes to a sense of isolation and alienation for an individual who, throughout the rest of his life cycle, seems to derive a significant part of his sense of being a meaningful person from his sleeping physically close by other family members. We are not suggesting that sleeping alone "causes" suicide, but rather that this type of separation is an added increment in the unusually difficult problems that Japanese young people seem to have in making the transition from youth to early adulthood as they shift from high school to college, enter the occupational world, and get married. Such transitions do involve the establishment of an identity more separate from one's natal family, and this is made harder by the long period of very close involvement in family life. Similarly, in old age, after a second long period of close familial involvement, to come finally to sleep alone probably carries with it a greater sense of separation than it does in the West.

Culture and Co-Sleeping

Others before us have hinted in a general way at the importance of co-sleeping in Japanese family life. But we believe that our work documents this with a degree of precision not achieved before, and at the same time demonstrates the wider relevance of what might otherwise appear to be only an offbeat sort of sociometry.

Dore, for example, writes of life in a Tokyo ward as follows: "Beyond the limits of actual cramped discomfort, crowded sleeping seems to be considered to be more pleasant than isolation in separate rooms. The individual gains a comforting security, and it is a sign that a spirit of happy intimacy pervades the family" (Dore 1958:49). The co-sleeping-as-intimacy theme also occurs frequently in Japanese fiction and biography. For example, the twentieth-century social reformer, Toyohiko Kagawa, as a child prized—and later vividly remembered—opportunities to sleep by his elder brother. As a seminarian he was deeply impressed when a missionary offered to share his bed even though Kagawa was tubercular. When he recovered, Kagawa in turn shared his bed in the Kobe slums with criminals, alcoholics, the ill, and the destitute. And throughout his adult life he enjoyed praying in bed but was embarrassed because he feared the Almighty might take this as a sign of disrespectful familiarity.[26]

Evidence of a negative sort comes from "collective" societies that attempt to weaken parent-child bonds by requiring children to sleep away from the home. The Israeli kibbutzim are usually cited in this regard; two Japanese collectives tried this method but abandoned it after a period. For example, the Yamagishi community in Mie prefecture once had all children sleep in a dormitory from the age of three months, but now the children move to the dormitory in the third year of primary school (at about age 8). Also at the Yamagishi community, co-sleeping among adults is self-consciously used as a means of weakening interpersonal barriers. During training sessions for prospective members, they live together in one room and are expected to sleep in same-sex pairs. Trainees are told that co-sleeping will help reduce the strength of selfish desires.[27]

In another collective, Shinkyō village in Nara prefecture, a children's sleeping room was also tried, but at present children generally co-sleep with their parents. The following comment by one member is revealing:

During the first stages of collective living, our plan to give the same love to every child led us at times to deliberately separate bawling children from their parents and make them sleep with other parents, and at times we had all the children sleep together. But lately we have not been particularly concerned about it either way; we are letting matters take their natural course. That is, a younger child sleeps with its parents, an older child sleeps with some other adult. Thus, there are couples who sleep by themselves even though they have children, and there are childless couples who sleep with other peoples' children. . . . Since we are all part of one family, these things can be arranged according to need. . . . Adults and children share their joys and sorrows alike, whatever their ages; so it is simply unthinkable that the emotional foundations of our collective life could shake over whether adults and children sleep together or not. (Sugihara 1962:214–215)

Vogel's work is perhaps closest to our own, and we have earlier cited his data on sleeping arrangements for infants and young children.[28] He goes on to note: "When a second child is born, and the mother must sleep with the baby, the eldest child ordinarily stops sleeping with the mother and begins sleeping with the father or a grandparent. While elementary-school-age children often sleep in a separate room . . . it is not unusual for grown children to sleep next to their parents" (Vogel 1963: 231). These observations are in general in line with the results of our analysis, although we believe we have defined the alternative patterns of sleeping arrangements more clearly, and shown that the separation of parents, each with a child, is an important variant pattern at the stage when there is an infant and one or more young children in the family.

Vogel stresses the "mutual dependency" of mother and child and relates it to what he feels is the basic alignment in the family: "mother and children versus father" (Vogel 1963:211). This alignment is not usually hostile, but refers to a real psychological and behavioral division within the family despite (or in some sense because of) the predominance of all-together sleeping arrangements. The relative lack of husband-wife intimacy in sexual and other matters is related to this division, as is the elaborate world of pleasure for males outside the home. This world of bars, restaurants, and clubs is, however, a great deal less sexual than Americans like to imagine. True, sex is available if a man has the money and time, and the motivation and energy, to invest in the relationship; but for the most part this world is a "play-acting" one which is entered for a few hours after work and then left for the long ride home to family and to bed.

Thus, our analysis of sleeping arrangements has ramifications beyond the confines of the family, and is related to the patterning of values and emotions in Japan in general. Japanese place great emphasis on collaterality (group interrelatedness) not only in the family but in many spheres of activity. They also find much of their enjoyment in the simple physical pleasures of bathing, eating, and sleeping in the company of others. Given these emphases in values and emotions, it is not surprising that individual assertiveness and the open indication of sexual feelings have negative connotations.[29]

A certain proportion of Japanese, however, as would be true among people in any society, have difficulty in behaving, thinking, and feeling according to the norm. Such variant persons may have good or poor adjustments to life. Among the latter, it is interesting that schizophrenic patients in Japan show more sleep disturbance and greater physical assaultiveness (especially toward their mothers) than do comparable American patients in the year prior to hospitalization.[30] There may, therefore, be something mildly ironic in the fact that it is usual to provide patients in small private psychiatric hospitals (which make up the bulk of psychiatric hospitals in Japan) with a personal female attendant who as a matter of routine care is with the patient throughout the day and sleeps in the room with him at night.[31]

In Western eyes, Japanese co-sleeping patterns may appear pathogenic, or at least be taken as a denial of maturation and individuation. And yet, there is no evidence that on the whole people are not as happy and productive in Japan as in America, and there does not seem to be more grief in one country than in the other. It is true that the rhythm of life across the years is different in the two countries, and we have shown this particularly for sleeping arrangements. But two cautions are necessary here. First, we have little information about sleeping arrangements in America, but what we do have suggests more variation than might be supposed.[32] Because a child in middle-class America is given a separate room in which to sleep does not mean that he stays in it throughout the night; and how do the parents handle this situation? Secondly, the comparison of Japan with America results in sharp differences, but if the comparison were made between Japan and other Eastern or even European countries, the differences might be minor.

Finally, it seems that at least for the first few years of life, the tendency for mother and child to co-sleep is a "natural" one that human beings share in a general way with other mammals. Only recently has Western society tried to interfere. As Peiper notes:

> As late as in the eighteenth century the child slept with his mother. . . . The custom was so widespread—especially because it had such ancient origins—and the conditions so bad that legislators many times had to take measures against it. For example, as late as 1817 the general law for the Prussian States decreed, under threat of imprisonment or physical punishment: "Mothers and wet nurses are not allowed to take children under two years of age into their beds at night or to let them sleep with them or others."[33]

If the pattern of sleeping together was so common in the West as late as the eighteenth century, then we need more information about these matters over the years up to the present. Social change has been rapid in both Japan and America in recent decades, but it is likely that such changes have been greater in technological and occupational sectors than in patterns of family life.

In both cultures, in the flow of events across days and nights and years, as evening descends and the focus of the family turns from contact with the outside to the ordering of life within the house, who sleeps by whom is an issue with serious implications that warrant further study.

Notes

1. See Whiting, Kluckhohn, and Anthony 1958; Burton and Whiting 1961.

2. The three hospitals used were St. Luke's International Hospital and Tsukiji Metropolitan Maternity Hospital in Tokyo, and Kyoto Metropolitan Medical School Hospital in Kyoto. In addition to having a three- to four-month-old infant, a mother selected for interview could, and frequently did, have other children as well. The several hospitals were picked so as to insure a good spread of cases by social class and style of life. The reason for focusing on mothers with infants was to provide background on various aspects of family life, not only sleeping arrangements, from a fairly large sample of such cases in order to supplement Caudill's intensive study in the homes of 30 Japanese and 30 American infants and their mothers. On this, see Caudill and Weinstein 1970.

3. Matsumoto City, and life in it, is described in Plath 1964, see chap. 2 in particular. Concerning sleeping arrangements in the Matsumoto area, Plath read a preliminary report, including 20 rural cases omitted here, at the 1964 annual meeting of the American Anthropological Association in Detroit.

4. The proportion of two-generation to three-generation households is roughly 2 to 1 in our sample, whereas it is roughly 4 to 1 in comparable households (census household types 4, 5, and 11, 12) for all urban areas (that is, "densely inhabited districts of all *shi*") in Japan. The proportion of salary and wage households to family business households is 1.4 to 1 in our sample, whereas it is 3.0 to 1 for all urban areas in Japan. There is no easy way to estimate accurately the distribution of households by social class from census data, but we are certain that our sample has more households in higher social classes than is true in the general population. See Japan, Office of the Prime Minister 1962a, table 5, p. 137, and table 13, p. 428.

5. The 1960 census data were recomputed, omitting households of two persons or less, so as to be in line with the household composition of our sample. See Japan, Office of the Prime Minister 1962a, table 1, pp. 20–21.

6. A person may at the top of the social system working in a family business or an individual enterprise—for example, a well-known physician in private practice—or he may be at the bottom as the owner of a cigarette stand. Similarly, he may work for salary or wages as an executive, or as a janitor in a large company. In research in Japan, a useful operational break can be made between these two ways of life by classifying businesses having less than 30 employees as "small independent businesses," and by considering owners or employees of such businesses as participating in a way of life that is meaningfully different, in occupational and familial terms,

from that of owners or employees in "large businesses." Such a cut-off point is, of course, arbitrary to a degree, and the distinction is more readily apparent between businesses having less than 10 employees and those having more than 100 employees—and this latter classification would still cover the great bulk of cases. We have followed this sort of reasoning in our classification in this research, although our data on occupation of the head of the household are not sufficient for such precise placement. More generally, concerning the meaning of these two styles of life, see Plath 1964, note 3; Caudill and Weinstein 1970, note 2; and particularly Vogel 1963.

7. In devising these procedures for estimating social-class position, we made use of the work of Hollingshead on American populations, and modified it to approximate the Japanese situation along lines suggested by the work of Odaka. See Hollingshead and Redlich 1958, particularly app. 2, "The Index of Social Position," 387–397. Nihon Shakai Gakkai Chōsa Iinkai 1958. Odaka and Nishihira 1965. Odaka 1964–1965. See also Inkeles and Rossi 1956; Ramsey and Smith 1960.

Our final three social-class groups may be described as follows. The upper middle class consists mainly of heads of households who are college graduates, and who are in professional or supervisory positions or are owners of substantial businesses. The lower middle class consists mainly of heads of households who are high-school graduates, and who are white-collar workers or owners of small businesses with paid employees. The working class is equally divided between heads of households who are high-school graduates and those who have less than a high-school education, and who are technicians, skilled or unskilled workers, paid employees of small businesses, or owners of small family shops with no paid employees.

8. Mat-floored rooms in Japanese dwellings lack the "specificity of purpose" usually assigned to rooms in Western dwellings. Thus, the oridinary Japanese house is not sharply divided into living rooms, bedrooms, dining rooms, recreation rooms, and so on. In part this reflects the relative sparsity of furniture in the Japanese house. Nevertheless, household members do tend to divide the space among themselves and to assign the use of a particular room to one or several persons. In addition, a household with multiple rooms is likely to set aside one of them as a "living room" or "guest room." The size of a room is usually given in terms of the number of mats it contains. One mat is roughly six by three feet in size and two inches in thickness, and it is made of packed rice straw covered with a finely woven rush. The edges of better quality mats are bound in cloth. The most common sizes for rooms in Japan are six mats (roughly 9 by 12 feet) and four and one-half mats (roughly 9 by 9 feet). On these matters of use and construction of rooms see Dore 1958; Beardsley, Hall, and Ward 1959; Taut 1958.

9. See Gleason 1964.

10. See Gleason 1964, table 1 and note 3, p. 28.

11. Two of these households include extended kin; the other 36 are composed of nuclear kin only.

12. For example, in the observational study of 60 three-to-four-month-old infants by Caudill and Weinstein (1970), 17 of the 30 American infants slept alone, and the parents of the remaining 13 infants planned to move to a larger apartment by the end of the first year so as to provide a separate bedroom for the baby. All of the 30 Japanese infants co-slept with their parents, while the idea of moving to provide more space for the baby never occurred. In other reports, Pease found that in one Tokyo suburb a child co-sleeps with his mother for an average of 92 months; and Vogel found that the interval varies from 35 months among Tokyo shopkeeping

families to 130 months in a deep-sea fishing village in Miyagi prefecture. See Pease 1961:179–181; and Vogel 1963:229–230. In contrast, the only fairly large-scale study for the United States that we have found reports data on sleeping arrangements for children in Baltimore who were patients at a psychiatric outpatient clinic, and for a control group, in answer to the question: "Did your child ever sleep in the same room with you and his/her father?" This question assumes that co-sleeping may be an unusual and infrequent event (and at times of sickness), and thus the answers are not strictly comparable with our Japanese data, which are reported in terms of habitual sleeping arrangements. The Baltimore study found no differences between children who were patients and those who were controls. Of the total group of 370 children, 61 percent either had never co-slept with parents (39 percent) or had stopped by the end of the first year (22 percent). Of the remainder, 21 percent had stopped by the end of the fourth year, and 17 percent had continued beyond the end of the fourth year. These results are from unpublished data supplied by Martha S. Oleinick, Office of Biometry, National Institute of Mental Health. See also Martha S. Oleinick, Anita K. Bahn, Leon Eisenberg, and Abraham M. Lilienfeld, "A Retrospective Study of the Early Socialization Experiences and Intrafamilial Environment of Psychiatric Out-Patient Clinic Children and Control Group Children," unpublished manuscript.

13. Discussions of Japanese family life often stress the role played by the grandparents when they are present in the household—particularly the grandmother—in the rearing of children. Table 4 shows that 13 percent of the children in high-density families and 6 percent in low-density families co-sleep in some combination with an extended kin member who is, in fact, most often a grandmother. These percentages do not seem to represent a "considerable influence" in this regard on the lives of our group of children, but we defer discussion of this issue until the next section of the paper. It is also not unusual to find reference to the importance of the role of a family servant in the rearing of children. And yet, in our data, no nonrelated person co-sleeps exclusively with a nuclear family member; and the likelihood of a nonrelated person co-sleeping at all with a nuclear family member is at most 5 percent in complex, mixed groups in high-density households.

14. We are indebted to Koyama (1962) for pointing out the necessity to consider the various stages in the family life cycle when analyzing social characteristics of the Japanese family. We have not made use of all of his stages here, and have made finer subdivisions in others.

15. Within the 199 households represented in Table 4, there are 323 extended kin members (231 in high-density and 92 in low-density households). These members live in 123 households. Of these, 13 households contain only adult unmarried brothers or sisters of the husband or wife in the younger nuclear family. These unmarried brothers or sisters sleep alone, or co-sleep in same-sex groups of two. Our concern here is with the remaining 110 households that contain at least one parent of the husband or wife in the younger nuclear family, and may contain the other parent plus the parents' grown unmarried children.

16. In considering these data for children who are 16 years of age or more, remember that these show the sleeping arrangements of older children who are *living at home*. If they have left the home, and are living in company dormitories, rooming houses, apartments, and so on, their sleeping arrangements most likely would show higher proportions of co-sleeping with nonrelated persons, or alone. A survey conducted in October 1965, by the Economic Planning Agency concerning the patterns of life of 2,500 young unmarried workers between 15 and 29 years of age in large companies in Tokyo and Osaka, found that 76 percent of the young

women, and 44 percent of the young men, were living with their parents. See Japan Information Service 1966:5–7.

17. See Blood 1967; Taeuber 1958:227; Japan, Office of the Prime Minister 1962a, table 3, pp. 72–73.

18. Percentages for other types of households that include aged persons are: (1) In the six largest cities an additional 25 percent of the aged lived with adult unmarried children, and 18 percent lived with a spouse only or alone; (2) in the smaller cities an additional 17 percent lived with adult unmarried children, and 13 percent lived with a spouse or alone. The remaining percentages for the two kinds of cities include miscellaneous types of households in which the aged lived with grandchildren, with other aged persons, in institutions, and so on. All of these data are cited by Watanabe from The National Survey on the Aged published by the Ministry of Health and Welfare in 1961. See Watanabe 1963:6–7.

19. The data are as follows: Small business households contain 34 cases of parents and adult unmarried children, and 20 cases of only parents; salaryman households contain 20 cases of parents and adult unmarried children, and 31 cases of only parents. This fourfold comparison is significant (chi square = 5.9, 1 df, $p < .02$).

20. See note 1.

21. The main reason given by Japanese mothers for the use of cribs during the first year is that they are easier to clean than $futon$ if the infant should soil his bedding. A secondary reason is the fear of rolling on the infant while asleep, although this applies mostly to the situation where the infant is sleeping in a parent's $futon$ rather than in his own $futon$. The types of bedding used by individuals in our sample present some interesting contrasts. Restricting the analysis to the 259 households which include an infant and have two or more sleeping rooms, the following results are found. Among the 259 infants, 172 use cribs and 87 use $futon$; whereas among the 105 children in these households, only 10 use beds and 95 use $futon$. Thus, only 34 percent of the infants use $futon$, but 91 percent of the children do so. Among infants, the use of cribs is linked to higher social class ($p < .001$), to a salaryman style of life ($p < .01$), and to residence in Tokyo ($p < .05$). There are, of course, 518 parents of the infants in the 259 households, and the overwhelming proportion, 85 percent, of these parents sleep in $futon$ (439 $futon$ to 79 beds). Variations in parental use of beds or $futon$ are influenced by several variables. First of all, beds are found in Tokyo more than Kyoto ($p < .05$), in low-density households ($p < .01$), among salarymen rather than small businessmen ($p < .001$), and are concentrated at upper social levels ($p < .001$). Secondly, double beds, in contrast to single beds, are used in high-density households ($p < .001$); and, equally, double $futon$, in contrast to single $futon$, are used in high-density households ($p < .02$). So it would seem that when things are crowded people adjust by using a container in which they can double up, whether they choose a bed or a $futon$.

22. See note 12.

23. See note 16.

24. To be sure, sexual relations between parents take place, but in what is reported as a brief and "businesslike" manner (for example, see Beardsley, Hall, and Ward 1959:333). Vogel, citing his own data and that of Shinozaki in a larger study, indicates that, compared to American couples, Japanese couples have intercourse less frequently, and have less foreplay and afterplay (see Vogel 1963:220–222). As might be presumed from the sleeping arrangements shown in our data, sexual intercourse in Japan frequently takes place in the presence of sleeping children. The most usual answer given by the 30 Japanese mothers in an intensive case study of mother-child relations (see Caudill and Weinstein 1970) was that the par-

ents wait until they think the child is sound asleep and then have intercourse. In addition, as Table 4 shows, the parents are usually the only *adults* in the bedroom, at least until they are in late middle age, and hence have a certain degree of privacy. In more traditional Japan, however, it was not too unusual for a young married couple to co-sleep with the husband's parents even though other rooms were available. In this regard, the famous Meiji reformer Fukuzawa urged that young married couples have a room apart from the husband's parents. Apparently Fukuzawa was not concerned about sex so much as he was with providing the young wife with at least a nocturnal sanctuary away from her carping mother-in-law. However, Fukuzawa did not practice his own precepts. See Blacker 1964:88, 157–158.

25. In our data, as indicated, sleeping alone is most likely during the ages of 16–26 and after approximately age 65. Suicide in Japan, as De Vos and others have pointed out, is of special interest because of its sex and age distribution. The ratio of women to men is higher than in any other country, and the concentration of suicide in early life (15-24 years) and old age (60 years and over) is unique in having this U-shaped pattern. Moreover, these phenomena have occurred yearly as far back as reliable Japanese statistics have been kept. For example, in terms of the rates in Japan per 100,000 population for 1952–1954: for ages 15–19 the rate among males is 26.1, and among females is 18.7; for ages 20–24 the rate among males is 60.0, and among females is 35.5. In the United States, the comparable rates are: for ages 15–19, males 1.7 and females 1.6; and for ages 20–24, males 7.8 and females 2.8. In old age in Japan the rates for ages 60–69 are 58.1 for males and 34.6 for females; whereas in the United states the rates are 42.4 for males and 8.9 for females. See De Vos 1966:13–17; and De Vos 1962:153–171.

26. On these aspects of the life of Kagawa see: Ayling 1932:22, 41–42; Bradshaw 1952:84; and Topping 1935:4.

27. See Plath 1967.

28. See note 12.

29. On these broader issues see: Caudill and Scarr 1962:53–91; Caudill 1962; and Caudill and Doi 1963.

30. See Schooler and Caudill 1964:172–178.

31. See Caudill 1961:204–214.

32. See note 12.

33. Peiper 1963:611. For further information on this topic see also Ariès 1962.

16

Ethics and Moral Precepts Taught in Schools of Japan and the United States

Betty B. Lanham

In the United States, little attention has been given to the subjects of ethics and morality, except in the fields of religion and philosophy. This lack of concern is surprising if one is to assume the achievements and well-being of a society are dependent upon the adequacy with which these precepts are conveyed to the young. It is true that professional organizations and Congress have undertaken the setting of standards for their own members; also, university students have demonstrated against foreign policy that they have found unacceptable; still, in the mundane affairs of daily conversation, the subject of ethics is rarely mentioned.

The lack of attention, in part, arises from there being an indeterminate source from which instruction should derive. Presumably, it is the parent who assumes major responsibility; however, this situation is generally unrealized in the United States, where an American in all seriousness will ask how children in Japan learn ethics if there are no Sunday schools. Some responsibility for instruction would seem to be shared by teachers; however, expectations are unclear. Teachers are chastised both for their effort and lack of effort along these lines. The decentralized American system of education enables the biases of parents and community to intrude in the educative process. Teachers must be on guard. Sometimes it is simpler to delete instruction than face possible dissent and contention. Ambiguity within the American ethos itself does not simplify the instructive process; that is, individualism, ambition, and success are highly extolled along with the conflicting precepts of cooperation, kindliness, and humility. Still, whatever the deficiencies in verbalized attention to the subject of ethics, the basics of expected behavior are communicated to the growing child in the United States, as well as in other countries.

In Japan, unlike the United States, there has been no dearth of aca-

Adapted, by permission of the Society for Psychological Anthropology, a section of the AAA, from *Ethos* 7, no. 1 (1979): 1–18. Not for further reproduction.

demic interest in the teaching of ethics. A compulsory course was introduced, from France, into the schools in early Meiji (1868–1912) and was continued up until 1945. A more recent course, *Dōtoku* (ethics), is currently in the curriculum. It first appeared after World War II. There are many articles written on these courses. Oshiba (1961) and Kaigo (1963) discuss the history of courses on ethics, and Karasawa (1965) presents a detailed analysis of teacher's manuals accompanying the course. Passin (1970), in a bibliography on education in Japan, includes an extensive section on moral instruction.

The political and social outlook of the Japanese people changed radically in the era following World War II. It occurred to me that a comparative examination of books used in the teaching of ethics during the two periods might prove fruitful. A further advantage of this potential inquiry was the existence of two sets of books in Japan and in the United States covering both the pre- and post-World War II periods. Of course, the best source of information on moral instruction given to children would be an intensive and extended observation of children in the two countries; the near impossibility of such a task enhances the value of such documentary evidence as is available.

The validity of the comparative study that follows is that the books were adopted by schools of the respective countries. Stories that appear in the texts may reasonably be said to represent the feelings, attitudes, and innovations that parents, teachers, administrators, and government officials found acceptable. Only the *Shūshin* books (prewar moral education textbooks) required the limited approval of one source—the government of Japan. The contents of stories and the nature of their presentation, within limits, can be assumed to represent the culture—the religion, ethos, prejudices—from which they emanate.

An analysis of the readers could be both complex and extensive, since it is possible to examine the contents for both subject matter and method of instruction. An additional historical inquiry would shed light on social change of the past and in the future. Given the limitations of space, the following discussion concentrates on: (1) instances of considerable variation with respect to either nationality or historical period and (2) analytical interpretations that are descriptive of the respective cultures. The findings are examined in the light of research on child rearing in Japan undertaken in 1951–1952, 1960, and 1965 (Lanham 1956, 1966).

Materials for the following analysis are drawn from the four readers and teacher's manuals, each covering grade levels one through six:

1. the Ministry of Education's *Jinjō shōgaku shūshin sho* (1935–1939). These books have been examined in translation as they appear in Robert King Hall's *Shūshin: The Ethics of a Defeated Nation* (1949)

2. the *Shōgaku dōtoku* readers by Kumura, Amano, and Uchimi (1965) and the *Shōgaku dōtoku shidōsho* (guidance manuals) by Uchimi and Amano (n.d.)
3. *McGuffey's Eclectic Readers* (1879)
4. the *Golden Rule Series* by Laevell and Friebele (1961) and Laevell, Friebele, and Cushman (1964) and *Teacher's Guide Book* by Laevell (1961).[1]

(Reference to these books will be as follows: *Shūshin, Dōtoku,* McGuffey, and Golden Rule.)

Ordinarily there is some distinction between the terms *ethics* and *morality.* The writer would prefer restricting the use of ethics to behavior which, by intent, is beneficial to the person or persons with whom ego is interacting. The term morality would more appropriately include the above as well as admirable character and personality traits. Unfortunately, in the United States, this latter term often has reference to sexual behavior only. In this paper, the two terms have been used synonymously to include the broader definition of both.

A course on morality, titled *Shūshin,* was taught in Japan before World War II. The importance it gave to nationalism, militarism, and emperor worship led to its discontinuance by the United States Occupation Forces. After the peace treaty, it was not reinstated—in agreement with the Japanese themselves, who feared a return to militarism. On the other hand, some mothers did worry lest their children mature without proper training. They were concerned about a lack of proper respect for the elderly and feared that an increase in juvenile delinquency was related to the absence of this instruction.

An entirely new course, titled *Dōtoku,* was introduced in 1958 and made compulsory in 1962. A special period of one hour once a week was set aside for teaching the subject. There was strong initial resistance by the Teachers' Union to any course in ethics over which a conservative, centralized educational system would have control. Modifications and safeguards were introduced; the books are not in universal use. They have been approved, but not written, by the Ministry of Education. The editors seemingly have paid close attention to public opinion. Controversy has been settled through deletion. There are no lessons on respect for the elderly. Local school boards in consultation with administrators and teachers decide which of a number of publications on *Dōtoku* will be adopted, or that none at all will be used. When without a text, a course curriculum may include classics, biographies, literary writings, essays, slides, recorded tapes, photos, charts, and movies. The particular *Dōtoku* books examined for this study have been used in the Kansai area (a plains area of southwest Japan on which Osaka lies).

McGuffey's Eclectic Readers included many stories with ethical themes. They were widely used in the American schools for some sixty years— up until the early twentieth century. The *Golden Rule Series,* published in 1961 and 1964, contains stories exclusively devoted to the teaching of ethics. They had been intended as supplementary readers and as such were widely used. Currently, they are out of print.

An itemized analysis has been made of the *Dōtoku* readers, to which primary attention will be given. The other three sources are used mainly for comparative purposes. Less attention has been given to the McGuffey readers grades four through six, since they mostly include advanced materials written by someone other than the author and editor for an initial purpose unrelated to the texts. Major emphasis is given to readers of the post- rather than pre-war period.

Certain cautions are to be observed in evaluating the presented materials. The study is of reading matter used in the schools, not of the number of children subject to specific teachings. There exists no perfect match between the frequency with which instruction appears in the text and the extent of impact. Actually, an admonishment may be strongly emphasized or frequently repeated for the very reason that an adult initially fails to enforce compliance; on the other hand, an admonishment may receive little or no attention because the initial strength of emphasis renders further instruction unnecessary. It should be noted that the values of the two cultures are basically similar. Differences are found (1) in the extent of emphasis given an instruction and (2) in the method of presentation.

References to stories in the *Shūshin, Dōtoku,* and McGuffey readers will be by roman numerals indicating grade level and arabic numbers indicating the lesson. A small *i* is inserted where a reference is to the teacher's manual instead of to one of the readers. The Golden Rule books do not provide lesson numbers. In this case, the page is given instead.

The following discussion is divided into two parts. The first describes the content of the four sets of books. The second discusses the potential significance of findings with respect to culture and personality. Here, attention will be directed toward the subjects of restraint and freedom; self-discipline as opposed to external control; and to the nature of social isolation in each culture.

Part 1

Dōtoku *Compared with* Shūshin

A major contrast in the two sets of books of pre- and post-war Japan is to be realized by their respective titles. *Shūshin* (pre-war) is derived from a Confucian expression that contends the proper regulation of self enables the maintenance of harmony within one's family. This in turn paves the way for the proper governing of the nation and ultimately the world. *Dōtoku* (post-war) is an agglutinated term that renders the meaning "way or path to goodness, virtue, and/or respectability." Both terms may be translated as "morality."

A glance at similarities between the *Shūshin* and *Dōtoku* readers reveals sufficient continuity to confirm that one is still in the same culture. Instruction in the basics of proper behavior is included in both sets of readers at the first and second grade levels, for example, "don't give others trouble," "take care of your health," "return a lost possession to its owner," and "report an injury to another's property, even though an inadvertent act." These teachings are reinforced in the home. Both *Shūshin* and *Dōtoku* stress character development in the forms of planning ahead and orderliness. Patience, perseverance, diligence, and hard work continue to be of major importance. Attention in both readers is given to those forms of ethics that involve the interpersonal relationships of forgiveness, gratitude, kindliness, and benevolence. The virtues of humility and modesty are emphasized to a minimal extent.

Differences between the two sets of books, however, would appear to be greater than similarities. Lessons encouraging ancestor worship, esteem for the teacher, loyalty,[2] and etiquette are absent from the *Dōtoku* texts. The traditional Confucian treatment of sibling relationships and filial piety have been deleted although there are stories that encourage gratitude to parents and to national leaders of the past. Instruction manuals would have pupils understand the affection their parents hold for them. In narrative accounts children express their feelings about specific situations, as in the case of a boy who reports his disturbance over his mother's going from door to door loudly calling "fish for sale." Other children react, interpret, and respond with sympathy (VI-8).

The *Dōtoku* books place a high emphasis upon the kind of courage that involves opposition to the group in deference to a morally just position. (This admonishment is somewhat strange in a Japanese setting, where strong social pressures are not only present but felt to be justifiable.) The fact that such behavior acts to oppose a militaristic, imperialistic, and authoritarian regime may have encouraged its inclusion. Actually, commendation for courage in opposition to the group or higher authority is not new. During the feudal period a peasant could petition a person of high rank for correction of the abuses of a lesser official if he were willing to pay the death penalty. The commoner was highly admired for his bravery and courage, as is any present-day or historical figure who embarks upon a course of action in a conscientious, determined, and sincere manner.

American Stories

Certain ethical tenets that figure prominently in the American stories are given less attention in Japan. Benevolence is strongly advocated in the readers of both countries, but the idea of helping the poor and unfortunate is more prevalent in the American narratives, particularly in the McGuffey readers, where the recipient of aid may or may not have been previously known to the giver. A second common theme of American stories is friendship and the misery of a child who is shunned by others. (American mothers threaten, "People won't like you." Foreigners sometimes comment upon a high preoccupation of Americans with whether or not they are liked. A number of stories in the Golden Rule books describe the misery of an isolated child. A happy ending is reached when he is later accepted by his peers.) The Golden Rule books are concerned with matters of kindliness but not politeness. "Selflessness" and "fairness" are given more attention in the Golden Rule than the *Dōtoku* books. Here in particular the instructional emphasis should not be equated with actual practice. In Japan, the percentage of one's income spent on friends and acquaintances usually far exceeds that of the United States.

Nationalism

The post-war *Dōtoku* are remarkably different from the prewar *Shūshin* books in that they do not mention soldiers, war, Shintoism, or the Emperor. The heroes of these books are persons who have contributed in the fields of science, technology, and the humanities. Stories illustrating bravery are rarely found in the *Dōtoku* books. Perhaps they were deleted in the process of removing those relevant to war. A story that is included comments upon the bravery of an airline hostess who displays calmness in the face of danger and lives to tell about it afterwards (VI-7). The *Shūshin* books, by contrast, contain a number of stories about soldiers and generals who either commit suicide for a noble cause or die on the front lines. In the Golden Rule books, patriotism, war heroes, and nationalism continue to be of importance. As might be expected, the McGuffey readers contain a large number of stories on the subject.

The subject of internationalism affords subtle and significant contrasts between Japan and the United States. Lessons on the American flag in the McGuffey and the Golden Rule readers do not mention foreign countries. The *Dōtoku* readers on the same subject picture flags of other countries. The instruction manual for teachers advises "create an interest in the flags of other countries . . . and encourage a sense of friendship" with children of other nations (Ii-12). The *Shūshin* readers also advise respect for the flags of other nations (III-17). An outstanding effort has been made by the Golden Rule readers to encourage friendship with children of diverse racial and national origin; however, careful scrutiny of the writings reveals the subtle manner in which ethnocentrism is still maintained. An immigrant boy is glad to be in the United States, even though attacked without provocation by a boy on the street, because afterwards the defeated adversary and his gang were friendly. "In his own country, all of the boys would have jumped on him at once. It seemed as though, even when it came to fighting, things were better in this America!" (V-p. 290). The daughter of an immigrant worker from Mexico says, "Oh, the beautiful desk! We have no desks at my school. Like parrots we sit on benches all around the teacher" (V-p. 31). Jane Addams of Hull House is made to comment, " 'Sam . . . things are different, here in America, from the way they are in other countries. We do not call a person bad unless we can prove he has done something wrong. We don't decide who is at fault until we know all the facts' " (IV-p. 171).

An American Sunday school pamphlet presents other religions in a favorable light and advocates neighborliness at the same time it unintentionally reinforces earlier held opinions with the comment that other religions may seem difficult to understand and strange in their approach to God (Alysworth 1946). The *Dōtoku* teacher's manual renders an anthropological interpretation:

> There are parallel efforts in seeking the right way to life even in nations and races of different life patterns or histories. From early days, every nationality has fought against difficulties, sought studies from foreign countries for improvement of culture, and thus today's world wide culture has developed. We must always study the culture of our own country and cultures of other peoples abroad, in order to acquire a better way of living. (VIi-9)

Foreign heroes are included in both the *Shūshin* and *Dōtoku* readers, six in the former and nine in the latter. On a questionnaire circulated by the writer in the United States and Japan, children of ages ten and eleven were asked, "If given a choice, who of the past would you most like to be?" The percentage of persons mentioned who were foreign was sixty for Japan and nine for the United States. Lincoln fared three times as well outside his native land. (The questionnaire was circulated in 1965 in Japan. In the United States it was distributed to a school in the northern section of the country among a predominantly white population in 1966.)

Perseverance

One of the major differences in the American and Japanese books lies in reference to "perseverance," the English translation for *gaman* or *shinbō*. Dependent upon context, both terms may also mean "patience." In the

Dōtoku books perseverance in the face of adversity appears more often than any other precept. The first-grade reader contains the story of a small boy who remains in the bitter cold, though exhausted, to help his father complete his farming chores (I-20). The third-grade text includes an account of a boy who replants his strawberries each day after unkindly children have made sport of continually pulling them up (III-5). Finally he is rewarded with some plants that mature and bear beautiful fruit. For the fourth, fifth, and sixth grades, there are stories of scientists, great men, or others who succeed in spite of adversity or an infirmity. When the hero has undertaken an insurmountable task, narratives frequently describe the laughter and ridicule of bystanders. In Japan, people are particularly sensitive to the "loss of face." The insertion of this statement in a story acts to enhance the difficulty of achievement. Generally, when the hero was near success and onlookers realized the sincerity of his purpose, they relented, admired, and sometimes helped him. In other lessons children are encouraged to choose a task that no one has yet undertaken and pursue it to the point of accomplishment in spite of adversity. The emphasis given to self-discipline and the need for leading a well-organized life enhance the potential for success. Teacher's manuals instruct in the encouragement of perseverance even when irrelevant to the subject matter of the accompanying lesson. Teachers are advised to stress ambition and resourcefulness. The rapid development of Japan in the scientific, economic, and industrial spheres may in part be explained by the emphasis upon instruction in perseverance both at an earlier period and at present.

The American educational system runs somewhat counter to the beneficial effects of encouraging perseverance, resourcefulness, and self-discipline. In an effort to build self-confidence, the teacher avoids confronting pupils with potentially "frustrating" situations. The challenge to create, innovate, and succeed through patience, diligence, and perseverance is partially erased from the potential of his full development. In effect, it is assumed that the child will not succeed, so it is best not to try. (I encountered resistance in two of three schools in the United States to the display of paintings done by Japanese children. The acknowledged explanation in one case was that the quality of the work would discourage the American children.) The Japanese, in turn, do not face up to what happens if the individual is unsuccessful. Unfortunately, in extreme cases, the answer is sometimes suicide. The rate among Japanese youth, though currently down somewhat, remains relatively high.

Training in Democratic Processes

One of the most striking features of the *Dōtoku* books is the application of democracy to situations that arise daily in the classroom and during other school activities. Students in Japan are responsible for the janitorial services of their school. Narratives in the texts describe events and procedures. Tasks are assigned by groups. It is expected that friction will arise and that disputes will be handled through discussion in the classroom or in smaller groups. Disputes are not settled by intervention of the teacher. When the subject of fairness arises, for example, when a child reports that he has been victimized by another who cheats or is not doing his proper share of the work, he is encouraged to ignore others and act in a way that is proper for himself—even to the extent of doing the work required of another in addition to his own (IV-1). Although the child is encouraged to stand out against the group for that which is right, other lessons strongly encourage cooperation and joint decisions. The instruction manuals accompanying the *Dōtoku* books advise teachers to aim at democratic attitudes in the classroom and, in addition, to discourage impulsive thoughts, emotional opinions, and ideas that are strictly for fun. Pupils instead should present that which has been thought through carefully and which is based on a wide scope of knowledge. They should try to be open minded for the sake of creativity. Children should not exclude a person from their group because of prejudice or because they might personally benefit by so doing. They should listen to and respect the opinions of others, freely make their own decisions, express them unhesitatingly, and put them into action. Further, in making decisions, pupils should not be too easily influenced by their peers (IIIi-13, 14, 19; Vi-1). Instructions mentioned more than once were the necessity of stating one's own point of view and of respecting the opinions of others.

Manner of Presenting Ethical Tenets

The manner of presenting ethics used by the recent writers of Japan and the United States departs dramatically from that of their counterparts of the pre-war days. An introductory passage in the teacher's manuals of the Golden Rule books describes the modern trend. In substance it says that comic book villians and "goody-goody" heroes do not appear. Instead the stories include boys and girls who solve the kinds of personal, emotional, and social problems that confront them in daily life or in the classroom. The moral in a story is often implied rather than stated. It is never preached. Stories are oriented around an individual rather than events. They are more concerned with how the hero is covertly affected than with the situation that confronts him (Ii-p. 5).

Stories in the modern readers of both countries tend to focus on a single individual and give a continuous running account of his reactions and feelings in various situations. Other characters in the narratives are seen through the eyes of this one person; thus, the reader is more easily able to understand, empathize, and identify with the hero of the story.

The manner of presenting the narratives can be differentiated in the following ways: (1) the extent of realism, that is, whether or not the events and their outcomes are similar to what happens in real life; (2) the extent of psychological awareness in interpreting the feelings of others; and (3) the degree of freedom accorded a pupil in acceptance of a given moral precept.

Stories of the *Dōtoku* books are more realistic than those of their American counterpart. Many tell of the unkindliness, lack of consideration, and meanness of one or more children to another. Situations generally center around school and home events. Writers do not feel the need for an ending that punishes or rewards. A story is often culminated without the solution to a dilemma. Maximum contrast with this kind of presentation is found in the McGuffey readers, where stories bear heavily the stereotype of the period in which they were written. Upon occasion, the necessity for providing an appropriate ending is carried to ridiculous lengths, as for example in the story of a barber who, in yielding to his conscience, refuses to shave customers on Sunday. The consequent years of misery, poverty, and hardships are ameliorated when a lawyer happens in for a shave who is very surprised to find the barber a nephew of a client who had died in India—of course, leaving a fortune to his next of kin (V-13).

The psychological astuteness of the Japanese writers is particularly evident in the *Dōtoku* books. There are accounts in which children orally or through letters criticize their parents or an adult.[3] An apology is the expected response where parents fail to measure up, that is, set an appropriate example. Narratives in the *Dōtoku* books relate the misery of children faced with situations that are severely disturbing. In a letter to the class, one girl speaks of her unhappiness at being unsuccessful when performing an athletic feat easily accomplished by others. A reply by another child evidences sympathy, understanding, and encouargement (VI-12). Another story relates the disturbance of a boy who weighs potential loneliness and isolation against going with his gang to rob an apricot tree. The money gained from the sale of the fruit was to be used to buy baseball gloves, and the decision to rob had been reached through the democratic process of a majority vote. The manner in which the child was tantalized, ridiculed, and teased for his hesitancy is fully described (IV-6). As related in the *Dōtoku* readers and as described to the researcher in Japan, children in the classroom are encouraged to express both their positive and negative inner feelings fully, for example, their reactions when presenting someone with a gift which they would really prefer to keep for themselves. In the *Dōtoku* books, a girl is critical of herself for having earlier misjudged a male peer who later voluntarily carried her books when she had a broken arm (II-10). In another situation, a child who was criticized for failing to help with the cleaning at school later was discovered to be too poor to afford a scrub rag (III-6). When a child in a narrative is victimized by his peers, the teacher's manuals advise that children think back over their past for similar experiences in which they may have acted in an unkindly manner, "help them to criticize their daily lives." If disliked by a former friend, the child should explore the reasons why, and if he himself is to blame, he should have the fortitude to change (IIIi-19). In class, not only is a pupil encouraged to express his opinion, failure to do so is just cause for criticism. Students may also discuss their feelings toward members of the opposite sex. In a story of the *Dōtoku* readers a boy is made to say:

> When there is cleaning to be done, girls immediately pick up a broom. They leave for boys the carrying of water and moving of desks. When boys lift something heavy, girls, even when in the vicinity, pretend not to see and go elsewhere. . . . When there is a class discussion and girls disagree, usually instead of expressing an opinion before the group, they afterwards talk individually among themselves.

A girl contends:

> Boys are always boasting. When we warn them of something wrong they are doing, they do not listen. They use rude words when calling us. At times when displeased, they are rowdy. When we ask them to help, they say, "Girls and boys are equal, do it yourself."

And a girl concludes:

> Why do boys boast? Is it because of tradition? If it is because of physical strength, this is a primitive trait. It is not true that boys are superior in every way to girls. I don't think that a boy's life is more important than a girl's. The human value is the same for both and I know that the boys in our class know this fact very well. It is wrong to depend on boys to do all the heavy work. Girls are also capable. Together we should decide who does the cleaning tasks. Girls should talk and participate more in discussions thus sharpening our mental processes. It is for the very reason that girls are quiet that boys think they are stupid. For both boys and girls there are good points. Boys are strong, healthy, and active. Girls are gentle, quiet in movement, and skillful at minute tasks. This being true, why don't we strive together and make use of each other's good points? (V-5)

A common ending for a story in the *Dōtoku* books is a request for forgiveness or an apology. This is not a new phenomenon with these readers. In Japan, folklore intended for children has occasionally been altered to encompass this ethical precept; for instance, a translated version of *Little Red Riding-Hood* (Shōgakukan 1965) portrays the fox with tears in his eyes asking for forgiveness. Such a request provides the means for reinstatement within the group; acceptance of the apology is expected.[4] In the United States, the "loss of face" accompanying an apology appears to prevent its use and thus also the potential readjustment that may be possible.

The extent of freedom allowed pupils in making their own decisions differs from one set of books to the next. The Golden Rule teacher's manuals for grades one through six, in contrast to the *Dōtoku*, present questions to be asked in class after the story has been read. At the end of each appears the proper answer. For the lower grades, it is sometimes simply "yes" or "no." Jules Henry (1955) has spoken of a procedure in American schools whereby children become psychologically dependent upon the teacher's continuous approval. This is partly achieved by the pupil's providing the one "correct" answer to a question. Contingent upon success, elation or dismay follows.

Some prefatory remarks concerning variation in the nature of child rearing in the United States and Japan help to clarify instructions contained in the texts of the two countries. Earlier investigations (Lanham 1966) show a strong Japanese emphasis on getting the child to understand; that is, having him want of his own volition to do that which is acceptable and proper. Force is rarely used. When the child resists, parental response is more like the way an American relates to another adult rather than to his or her child. In Japan, for instance, a child's request is generally granted when a parent is unable to change his mind. The parent's ultimate concern is the importance to the child of his desire, not who should have authority in the situation. By contrast, in the United States, some degree of denial and restraint is felt necessary in order to teach the child self-control. The American parent engages in an unrecognized assumption that restraints imposed forcibly from without automatically lead to the child's imposition of discipline upon himself at some later day—a hypothesis that as yet has not been adequately tested. Use of the term "obedience" in the Western world ordinarily attributes virtue to the child who complies for compliance' sake—irrespective of whether an explanation is given or, in fact, actually exists. The McGuffey readers contain many stories admonishing obedience. Some are still to be found in the Golden Rule books.

Confusion in parental instruction frequently arises (particularly in the United States) from the failure to differentiate precept from method. The adult's rights and privileges become entangled with the tenets he is endeavoring to teach. An analysis of method of presentation used in the conveying of precepts clarifies this issue. The following terms and techniques are differentiated by degree of compulsion, beginning with the most severe. (The extent of involvement by the admonisher is implied.)

1. Statements inclusive of the word "must." Implied are dire consequences and retribution from an unknown source for failure to
   comply.
2. Statements inclusive of the words "do" and "don't" where used
   for forcefulness rather than as a form of instruction. Use of the
   term carries the threat that punishment will follow defiance.
3. Statements inclusive of the terms "should" and "shouldn't"; here
   the listener is simply informed that a moral is involved and for this
   reason he should comply.
4. Stories in which the main character is confronted with temptation
   but resists and makes the proper decision, and is then rewarded.
   Divine sanction is implied.
5. Stories in which the final outcome or interpretation is not given.
   Sometimes they end before a decision is carried out. The offending
   individuals are not punished. The reader is free of intervening
   threats and of the opinions of others; thus he is able to define the
   situation for himself.
6. Stories that take for granted that proper behavior has already been
   established. The account is only for reinforcement. Here decision
   making is probably on a subconscious level and is influenced by
   identity mechanisms.

Intervention by the writer of a story, a parent, or an adult into the
child's decision-making process interferes with self-sufficiency and the
developing of confidence. The child, instead of making an evaluation of
the situation, is compelled to accept or reject the admonisher and is thus
forced into a decision of identity with good or bad, evil or virtue, propriety or impropriety. The terms "must" and "do" are common in the
McGuffey readers. The former is often used in the *Shūshin* books. In
both the Golden Rule and McGuffey readers wrong behavior is normally followed by retribution. In the *Dōtoku* books both reward and
punishment are rare; satisfaction derives from having done that which
is right. Stories in which the final outcome is not given are common in
the *Dōtoku* books, rare in the Golden Rule series. The objective in the
latter situation is to have the reader ponder the pros and cons as well as
the potential ramifications of possible solutions.

Roughly equivalent kinds of instruction are found in the early writings of both Japan and the United States. The McGuffey readers, grade
one, contain the following:

> Your parents are very kind to send you to school. If you are good, and if you
> try to learn, your teacher will love you, and you will please your parents. Be
> kind to all, and do not waste your time in school. (I-63)

The *Shūshin* book for grade two reads:

. . . he did his own work by himself; he took care of his health. . . . He doesn't forget favors bestowed by others. His father and mother have become very happy. They say, "Please from here on, listen carefully to the teacher's instruction, as before; and become an even better child." (II-27)[5]

Observations I made in Japan reiterate the character of instruction found in the *Dōtoku* books, that is, freedom in the making of one's own decisions, training in democracy, and the restraint of parents in making decisions for their children. At one of the elementary schools of Kainan, Japan, an elected group of students met with teachers and parents. They discussed and decided upon matters that had been troublesome to all, such as the amount of spending money a parent should provide at specific ages and what time children should be home at night. An assumption that students interviewed in the presence of the principal would feel restrained proved to be in error. Confirmation of this observation was in the offing when a group of students who had gone to the music room for instruments lingered too long. The assistant principal's request that they hurry was answered with *"iya,"* perhaps best translated in this context as "uh uh, not yet."

Two situations dramatically contrast the extent to which adults are controlling in their interaction with children. In an American school, a principal abruptly stopped a conversation with me to strongly reprimand a boy for hurriedly coming down the stairs, even though the halls and stairs were empty. In a school of Japan, pupils, occupied with the yearly cleaning, were conspiciously about. They prepared to leave the principal's office because a foreign visitor had arrived. One boy who had sprawled out on a chair refused to move. Others of the group were disturbed by his unusual and improper behavior; the principal took no notice of the situation. Finally other children bodily carried him off.

A film presented by Ray Birdwhistell at the American Anthropological Association meeting of 1966 was designed to show how children and adults of different cultures relate to an elephant. It unintentionally revealed at the same time parent-child relations. The American mother put her hands on each side of her child's face and moved it into position for seeing what she deemed desirable. The Japanese father lowered a peanut to the visual level of the child and from this location threw it to the mouth of the elephant.

Part 2

Conclusion

A consideration of the texts raises the question of how personality is molded. One aspect of this subject, "social isolation," deserves special attention since it is the opposite of the "warm and cordial relationships" sought in both Japan and the United States. Explanation would seem to lie in forms of restraint and interpretations of propriety that vary, contingent upon the culture. Reference to the specifics of what is either included or excluded in the stories of each country illuminate distinctions. Presentation is in question form to dramatize contingencies that may produce social isolation.

1. Is the re-gluing of a broken relationship more important than the potential adverse effects that might result from an apology? The texts and folktales told in Japan give merit to the offering of an apology. In the United States, resistance seems to lie in the fear of "loss of face."

2. Is the expression of spontaneous feelings encouraged or discouraged? Is the rapport and shared emotional responses occurring with a continuous flow of uninhibited communication facilitated or restrained? Japanese teachers are advised to discourage students from expressing impulsive thoughts and emotional opinions; thus the potential for eradicating negative feelings through this means is lost. The result may be the establishing of two identities, one functioning on the communicative level and the other known only to ego. A damper is placed on the potential for shared excitement. There are, of course, inhibitors in the United States. The difference is a matter of degree.

3. At what point does an emphasis upon "fairness" distract from the potential for effective communication? In Japan, harmony and feelings of cordiality of all members of a group is considered more important than is "fairness," that is, having all parties to a decision happy with the outcome is given precedence over who is in the right and deserving in a specific situation. This does not diminish the importance of "fairness" (strongly emphasized in the American stories); it rather indicates the order of priority.

4. At what point does increased cordiality become an intrusion on privacy? "Friendliness" (stressed in the American stories) does not imply the depth of a relationship indicated by a cognizance of the feelings of self and others, by expressing gratitude, and by unspoken subtle communication—more common in the Japanese stories.

5. Where do the boundaries of cordiality lie with respect to group affiliation? Are the limits set with respect to one's family and/or clan as in the case of China before 1949; with respect to friends and acquaintances—to some extent evident in France and Japan; or with respect to one's country? The American texts make a definite effort to reduce prejudice toward ethnic groups. The Japanese do little to enhance cordiality toward the stranger; but on the other hand, they do stress more egalitarian relationships with foreign nations. Ethnocentrism is still evident in the American writings.

To an extent at least, cultural differences are realized in varying reactions to the term "individualism," which to the Japanese implies egotism and a lack of concern for others. The American, on the other hand, legitimizes spontaniety, freedom of expression, and creative individuality. When carried to the extreme, either of the interpretations can be productive of social isolation.

In one sense "freedom" is greater in Japan than in the United States. This statement, however, must immediately be followed by a qualification. Reference is not to freedom of action in interpersonal relationships but rather to freedom from the control of others. This would then mean for both the child and adult the encouragement of internal rather than external controls. In Japan, the parent strives to get the child to want to do what is right. The strong emphasis given to perseverence, diligence, and patience reinforces "self" discipline. Decision making is by the child. Both the Buddhism and Confucianism strongly emphasize internal discipline. This admonishment is not prominent in the Judeo-Christian tradition except in cases where rigidity becomes intense. The Puritans emphasized internal control, but the external also was equally enforced. In this sense, the individual is freer in Japan; however, it should be mentioned that control of a different order is maintained by the development of delicate sensitivity to and concern for social acceptance.

In spite of the above general differences between Japan and the United States, there are changes predictive of the future that both countries share in common. The texts indicate a movement away from an imaginary world of virtuous extremes. Militarism, war, and the sacrifice of one's life for country are deemphasized. In the past, the McGuffey readers dichotomized individuals as villians or as paragons of virtue. The current trend is toward realism—acceptable humans who possess both negative and positive feelings which can be acknowledged, considered, evaluated, and effectively handled. More choice in decision making is given children in both cultures. The reduction in popularity of Western films in the United States may be a by-product of this trend. In Japan, the older generation complains about the freedom of contemporary youth—a descriptive statement that would seem to be born out in reality. This may well mean that parallel developments which speak for similarity are occurring in both countries rather than there being a westernization of Japan or an orientalization of the United States.

Notes

1. The purpose of this paper has been to compare ethics taught in the schools of Japan and the United States. A review of the quality of the various books cited is

not intended. Contrary to what might seem to be the case and in spite of shortcomings, I regard highly the *Golden Rule Series,* which includes Laevell and Friebele (1961); Laevell, Friebele, and Cushman (1964); and Laevell (1961). (The Golden Rule books for teachers include the manual in the same binding with the readers. Pages are separately numbered.)

2. For an extensive discussion of the subject of "loyalty" see Redekop (1964).

3. On a questionnaire circulated among Japanese mothers in 1960 and fathers in 1965, parents were asked to record a day's conversation between themselves and their youngest child of at least three. Mothers and fathers both frequently mentioned the criticisms their children made of them. Since Confucian ethics specifies that parents should set an example, failure to do so would be just cause for complaint.

4. For a more extensive commentary on comparative ethics in Japanese and American folktales see Lanham and Shimura (1967).

5. Translated directly from Japan, Mombushō 1935–1939.

17

Violence in the Home: Conflict between Two Principles— Maternal and Paternal

HAYAO KAWAI

RECENTLY, there has been a sharp upsurge throughout Japan in incidents of violence perpetuated by children in their homes. As a result, violence in the home is attracting attention as a social problem of major dimensions. The problem is taken up in this article because the writer believes violence in the home and the circumstances behind it throw into relief many of the problems affecting Japanese society today. Child violence is also a serious problem in the United States. The issue in Japan, however, is of an entirely different nature than that in the United States. It would be no exaggeration to say that, by throwing light on the problem of violence in the home, we can get a clearer picture of the important characteristics which mark individuality, the household, and society in Japan.

Revenge of the "Good Child"

Incidents of violence in the home are most common among children during the age of puberty. This writer, from his position as a psychotherapist involved in the treatment of such children, would like to take some typical examples based on his experiences in treating such cases. First, a distinctive feature of violent children is that prior to the time when they give way to violent outbursts they are actually extremely "good children." They are obedient toward their parents and perform well in school. Such children, however, will suddenly develop a strong aversion to attending school. The child will reach a state where he or she is unable to go to school even before his parents, let alone the child, have discovered a clear reason for this. After this state has continued for a while, the child begins to break furniture and use abusive language which previously he or she would never have used. When this stage reaches a serious level, the child begins to act violently within the

Reprinted from *Japan Quarterly* 28 (1981): 370–377.

home. For the boy, the object of his violence is in most cases his mother. The level of injury inflicted is almost beyond belief. The victims suffer broken bones, whiplash, or in more serious cases have their lives threatened. Most parents, upon seeing the unusual acts of their children, think the children have "gone crazy." Indeed, in early times before the phenomenon of violence in the home was properly understood, it was not uncommon for even experts to diagnose such cases as schizophrenia. There are examples of attacks made by children not only on the mother but also on the father, or brothers and sisters. These acts are not confined to physical violence. There are instances of children ordering family members to take a bath with their clothes on or to get down on the ground and bow 100 times, or of scattering soy sauce or seasoning around the room and demanding family members clean it up.

A further characteristic of children who exercise violence in the home is that outside the home they fully maintain their guise as the "good child." Neighbors, unless they are able to hear the sounds of breaking or screaming at the time of violence, have trouble believing that such violent acts actually take place. In instances when the parents, no longer able to endure their children's violence, have called the police, it is not unknown that the very children who have been running wild will receive the police with courtesy and tell them, "This is a domestic squabble. There is no need for you to stay." The police see the excited state of the parents, and, deciding it must be a quarrel between the husband and wife, withdraw. Such cases are not rare.

According to recently announced National Police Agency (NPA) figures, in the year 1980 the police were consulted a total of 1,025 times for incidents of violence in the home. Considering that the police alone handled that many cases during the year, the total number of such incidents throughout the nation must have been extremely high. Of the cases recorded by the NPA, boys were responsible for an overwhelming number, with 902 out of the total of 1,025 involving boys and 123 involving girls. However, one reason for this is that parents are more likely to report the violence of sons, because in the case of a boy they are not strong enough to control the child's physical behavior. From the writer's own experience, it may be supposed that the ratio of cases involving girls is somewhat higher than the NPA figures indicate, probably around 30 percent of the total. According to NPA statistics, the assailants included 360 middle school students, 252 high school students, and 32 elementary school pupils. Mothers were the victims 61.3 percent of the time, and fathers 15.9 percent. On the cases of violence, the same report says, "Violence in the home is occurring in one out of five households, even those seemingly normal households where there does not appear to be any particular problem." This statement is worthy of note.

The question is why violence in the home has increased so rapidly in recent years and whether this phenomenon is in any way related to the behavior of Japanese people in general. As a key to solving these questions, let us first focus on the point that violent children are "good children."

Society Controlled by the Maternal Principle

When we make distinctions between the "good child" and the "bad child," it can be assumed that some kind of value standards exist. It should be noted that there is a difference in the value standards found in Europe and the United States and those found in Japan. Whereas Japan follows the maternal principle, it is the paternal principle that is more adhered to in Europe and the United States. The words "maternal principle" and "paternal principle" are used in this paper in the context of standards of judgment in respect to the social behavior of people, and should in this case be considered separately from terminology such as paternal and maternal rights, or paternal and maternal lines, as used in discussing family systems and social structures.

The paternal and maternal principles used here can be distinguished by whether their chief function is to cut or to contain. The maternal aspect contains everything. The most important thing for the child is whether he or she is included in this total containment. As long as a child is his mother's child everything he does is permitted and forgiven. What is not permitted is for the child to arbitrarily leave the mother's side. In contrast to this, the paternal aspect cuts and separates all things. It classifies everything into the subjective and objective, good and bad, top and bottom, and so on. Accordingly, the paternal aspect includes the strictness to discipline the child. The difference between the two aspects is clear. In contrast to the mother, who says "my child is a good child," the father says "only the good child is my child." What is important here is that in the case of the father judgments concerning right and wrong take precedence and clear standards come into being, but in the case of the mother what comes first is the feeling that this is "my child."

Many misunderstandings arise between Japanese and the people of Europe and the United States as a result of this difference in principles. To state the matter simply, Europeans and Americans, brought up on the basis of the paternal principle, criticize Japanese for being too tolerant toward "evil." On the other hand, Japanese, raised on the maternal principle, censure the Westerner for being "too cold."

Societies based on the paternal principle place a high value on the establishment of individuality. A society based on the maternal principle, however, accords priority to the maintenance of a condition of equilibrium with regard to "space." In the latter case, the individual restrains personal self-assertiveness and everyone acts in concert so as not to disturb the condition of equilibrium in which every person has his or her given "space." In these circumstances "space" and "condition of equilibrium" are words without a clear conceptual framework. However, Japanese people, unconsciously and non-verbally, have a "feeling" for these concepts.

In accordance with the maternal principle as explained above, when parents raise a "good child" that child becomes an entity totally divorced from any expression of "independence" or "individuality." Children, to an extreme degree, suppress their own will and live submissively at the orders of adults. However, if the desire to attain self-dependence, inherent in all humans, is muzzled too much, when the child reaches puberty this desire may explode forth in the warped shape of violence toward the mother. Hidden in the violent acts of the child is the desire to break away from the all-enveloping mother and seek self-dependence. Seen from this angle we can understand the causes of violence in the home in Japan. This still leaves the question, however, of why such acts of violence did not exist in Japan to any conspicuous degree in the past.

Thus far we have analyzed the causes of violence in the home by pointing out the contrasts between the paternal and the maternal principles. The belief of this writer is that in any culture, even if one of these two principles gains a position of dominance, invariably it is compensated for by the other principle. Japan before World War II was as today controlled by the maternal principle. However, at that time paternal rights held a powerful position in the social fabric and were sufficient to compensate for the maternal tendencies of society. There is no question that the father in prewar Japan was a frightening existence and his presence was strongly felt in the household. The Japanese father held power supported by the traditional social system without having power as an "individual." In a process of oversimplification, however, Japan was misunderstood by some foreign countries as being "a nation where the father is strong," and it was in relating to this image that the United States, as victor in the Pacific War, took away paternal rights in Japan "for the sake of achieving democracy in Japan." In this way, postwar Japanese society has come to be troubled by the reign of an unrestricted maternal principle. Before the war, the father was an image to be feared. Even so, however, in teaching his children the father always stressed the lesson that "one should act so as not to be laughed at by others." In other words, he gave importance to the maternal principle by suppressing self-assertiveness and encouraging the maintenance of the conditions of equilibrium of "space." Put in a different way, the prewar father stressed the paternal principle but within bounds that were defined by the maternal principle.

Japanese society after the war has seen a rapid strengthening of maternal control. Lighter housework duties and a reduction in the number of children per family must also be cited as elements in this. Japanese mothers of the past clung to their children to the same extent or even more than mothers do today, and it was their hope, too, to raise "good children." But because they were so occupied by housework and child-raising, the actual extent of their control over the child's upbringing stopped naturally at a moderate level. In other words, as a result of the harsh natural conditions into which many children were born, the child was forced to fend for himself, and, unlike today, there was little opportunity for fostering the existence of the artificial "good child" raised by the overly protective mother.

Traditionally, Japanese society has centered on the parent-child relationship rather than on relations between husband and wife. Regrettably, the Japanese wife's excess energy, an outcome of the advent of electrical appliances and a consequent reduction of household chores, is not readily absorbed by the Japanese husband. Accordingly, a woman's energy is turned not toward her husband but to her children. Not only that, it is now not rare for fathers even to follow along with the maternal principle, thus furthering the tendency for "good children," highly regarded by their school friends and neighbors, to turn into tyrants within the home.

For the Japanese today who still live in a traditional society, achieving self-dependence is not an easy matter. Japanese-style self-dependence is established through the delicate balance of not denying the maternal principle but at the same time avoiding being buried by that principle. Japanese children, while gradually experiencing what is considered "bad" from the standpoint of the maternal principle, must grapple with that "bad" within their own selves in forming a composite personality. Children, by their very nature, are prone to go against the instructions of their parents and act "independently." The child disobeys the orders of his mother and climbs a tall tree. With the thrill of climbing to a high spot and the danger of falling on his way up, the child remembers the injunctions of his parents. Children in their growth period naturally learn within the natural environment the meaning of "bad" prohibited by their parents and come to know the meaning of "self-dependence." In Japan in the past, even if parents were not aware of their respective roles in the household, the natural environment raised and disciplined children. The destruction of the natural environment, resulting from the accelerated urbanization of society through scientific and technological development and high economic growth, has exerted a bad influence on the personality formation of young men and women.

Violence within the Affluent Society

Human relations and social behavior derived from the dominance of the maternal principle can be counted among the reasons for the remarkable development achieved by the Japanese economy. As many writers have pointed out previously, Japanese-style human relations are very effective in concentrating the personnel makeup of an organization into a single force. Yet it should be noted that the concept of Japan giving priority to the maternal principle is made as a point of comparison with Europe and America; our conclusions would differ if comparisons were made with other Asian and African nations. In the past, the paternal and maternal principles mutually compensated each other and functioned together well in Japan. It has only been in the last 20 years or so, with the advent of the period of high economic growth, that the balance between the two principles has crumbled.

First, as life in the Japanese home has become materially more affluent, there has been a growing tendency for mothers to interfere excessively in their children's lives. At the same time, Japanese parents have lost the capacity to decide by themselves what and how much they should give their children. In seeking to maintain conditions of equilibrium of "space," parents have inevitably come to be overly conscious of "other people." They have become excessively competitive and express this competition, for example, by buying too many toys for their children. Children are thus raised to be self-indulgent and to think that demands made upon their parents will always be met. In the past, when Japan was not materially affluent, economic reasons placed an effective restraint even on those parents who were inclined to buy everything for their children. Many of today's parents, however, coming from a background of postwar material poverty during their own childhoods, do not want to subject their own children to the same straitened circumstances, and they have come to believe, naively, that the road to happiness for children is to be found by amply providing them with everything they want. Contrary to their intentions, though, the high-level growth of the Japanese economy has meant that these parental aspirations have now been overfulfilled, and, far from becoming happier, children have been forced into distressing circumstances. Realities have taken precedence before the parents have established their outlook on human life and a method of child-raising appropriate to a materially affluent society.

The Japanese are today being paid back for their pursuit of material affluence from high economic growth in the unexpected form of violence in the home. The concentration of population in urban areas in the period of high economic growth has hastened the shift from the extended to the nuclear family. There is nothing intrinsically wrong with the nuclear family. In the 35 years since the war, Japan has moved toward the nuclear family, taking as its model the family structures of the industrialized West. However, as a result of the rapid economic development, the transformation from the Japanese-style extended family to the nuclear family has been carried out at an inordinately fast pace, and there has been inadequate time to make the necessary psychological preparations.

A father and mother are essential elements in a family. Nevertheless, in a strict sense, it is enough that there is someone in the household to fulfill the paternal and maternal functions, and these roles need not always be performed by the biological father or mother. In the Japanese-style extended family system of the past, persons variously responsible within the family for carrying out the father role or the mother role might be the grandfather or male group within the house or again the grandmother or female group. Accordingly, when a young couple married, they were not necessarily faced with an immediate demand to show the mental maturity which would qualify them as parents.

It has been pointed out by many people that in comparison to the discipline and training toward becoming self-dependent that is given children in Europe and the United States, the Japanese are very loose in this area. This difference can probably best be understood if we consider the lifestyles engendered by Japan's extended family system.

If, in the Western sense of the term, a young man and woman become "self-dependent" and fully assert their own self-identities, they no longer fit within the extended family. In Japan in the past, the absence of training in mental self-dependence was replaced by an emphasis on the necessity of possessing the strength of "endurance" within the extended family. Fundamentally, there has been no change in this traditional way of thinking in Japanese society. As a result of the rapid shift to the nuclear family, young men and women become parents without possessing the discipline of self-dependent adults, which would allow them to make their own decisions and thus able to confront a chaotic situation.

It would seem that Japanese parents today do not have a clear perspective as to how they should raise their children. In the bottom of their hearts they hope their children grow up to be "good children," following the maternal principle. On the other hand, though, they emphasize the importance of self-dependence and individuality. Since the logical standards by which parents should judge right and wrong in the actions of their children are not spelled out in the minds of the adults, parents inevitably give weight to school records and other achievements which can be defined clearly in terms of points. For that reason, from the time children enter first grade, parents show an abnormal interest in school records. As a consequence, the education industry outside the regular school system flourishes in the form of "juku" preparatory schools, and from an early age children's minds are crammed with as much knowledge as they can possibly absorb.

A comparison of the scholastic ability of the first-grader in Europe or the United States with that in Japan would probably show that Japan has an overwhelming lead in this area. But this attitude of parents toward the upbringing of their children actually works to destroy the creativity of the child. Even if a Japanese person achieves an excellent school record in his childhood, it is possible he will lose his creative powers upon becoming an adult. As proof of this, the Japanese scholar is often criticized for his lack of creativity.

Because parents evaluate their children's performance by school records alone and because the children must win out in the fierce competitive battle with their friends, they end up being relieved of all work within the household. Inside the framework of the strong maternal principle, fathers, acting under the orders of their wives, even clean their children's rooms and shine their shoes while the children devote their time to studying. This comical scene is played out in the homes of Japanese intellectuals. That the "good child" artificially cast in this way suddenly revolts at a certain point of time—regardless of how wrong the methods of his resistance might be—seems to be a rather natural course of events.

Until 20 or 30 years ago, Japanese children helped out in the house a great deal. A child's chores were linked closely to the four seasons. Through work like watering the garden in summer and shoveling snow in the winter, the child was surrounded and trained by his natural environment. The child also had the chance to observe nature by raising chickens or rabbits and stood in wonder at the mysteries of life. Parents in the past did not raise their children to have any particular philosophy. The unwritten sense of unity which existed in society and the family, and the natural environment, were the forces which raised them. High economic growth has broken down not only traditional society and the extended family, but the natural environment as well. The cry in Japan that "nature is dead" can be compared to the cry once heard in the West that "God is dead."

Questioning the Origins of Human Existence

Let us here turn our attention to the "abusive language" of the children who act violently. Children turn to their parents and scream "Why did

you give birth to me?" or "It's your fault I was born." This writer sees
fundamental questions about humanity behind such language. By the
act of violence, the child is desperately trying to answer the question,
"Where did I come from?" These children feel anxiety about the origins of their own existence and physically hurl this anxiety at their parents.

Many of these children turn on their parents and yell "You're not my
real parents." The intensity of the shock to the parents assaulted with
this language by their beloved child, denying the parent-child relationship, is probably difficult for people in Europe and the United States to
understand. Parent and child in Japan, however, are linked not only by
blood but also by the formation of a fate-like communal body. This
blood-related communal body is expanded to include the natural environment. The Japanese formerly found peace of mind in living with a
sense of unity with the natural environment. For the Japanese, nature
itself is God. Although the Japanese are not clearly conscious of this,
this concept envelops all things in a nebulous totality.

Yet children will ask their parents "Why was I born?" and they utter
statements such as "I am not your child." This is an entirely new phenomenon, never seen before in Japan. These children intuitively recognize the death of nature, the subliminal god of Japan, and they are seeking verbally from their parents a clear answer to their doubts about
their origins.

The Japanese have worshipped nature as a great mother-deity, the
possessor of unlimited love. But with the period of high economic
growth, the rampant exploitation of the land has destroyed the natural
environment. In Japan, the mother-deity of nature has died. Japanese
have sought a new deity in the affluent society which has replaced traditional society. In the process they have ended up denying the bonds and
blood-related communal body which hold parent and child together.
From this, the artificially cast "good child" one day suddenly under-
goes a transformation and revolts against his parents, seeking revenge.
The causes for revolt by these children cannot simply be attributed to
the individual attitudes of the father and mother toward life and child-
raising. These causes are deeply related to the rapid changes that have
taken place in Japanese society and to the death of the mother-deity,
nature. Thus, incidents of violence occur even in normal homes where
previously there seemed to be no problems at all. This is not the tragedy
of a particular type of family but a tragedy for all Japan. This writer
believes that the problem of violence among children in the United
States is rooted in the weakness of the maternal principle. In Japan, by
contrast, the major problem is how to re-establish the paternal principle.

Those children who revolt are unconsciously feeling the need for a father. By appealing to "strength" in the form of brute force, these children would appear to be trying to reinject "strength" and "strictness" into a home overly dominated by the mother. This "strength," however, is not to be found only in the physical force of the father. The function should originate in the masculine strengths of thinking and judgment. While these children unconsciously feel the need for a father, because they lack the power to call up a "high" father they end up calling for a "low" father, a chthonic father. One violent youth ordered his father to get into the bathtub with his clothes on and to apologize by bowing to the ground 100 times. When investigating this case, the writer was reminded of the now defunct Japanese Imperial Army in the period after Japan's surrender and how the army was disarmed by the Allied Forces. In those camps the newer soldiers were often subject to individual punishment from the more veteran soldiers, and, as in the child violence cases, were required to carry out unreasonable tasks. The Japanese military was perhaps strong in that it displayed the paternal principle. But in a spiritual sense was it not a maternal-type group in which men indiscriminately obeyed the authority wielded by their superiors?

Recently, many people have pointed to the weakness of the father in Japan. What worries this writer is that such opinions will simply be short-circuited toward the restoration of paternal rights and lead to the revival of the old-time "tough old man" or the return of the military draft system. Before we appeal for the "restoration of paternal rights," we need to fully understand the reasons why the Japanese father is weak. Establishment of the paternal principle in Japanese society will by no means be easy, and it will be necessary to remain constantly aware of the dangerous side-effects, such as the revival of militaristic tendencies, that such a course could produce. Yet it is essential that we discover what these "good children" who revolt are looking for, deep in their hearts, and that adults respond to their wishes by laying the foundation of a new paternal principle in Japanese society.

18

"Spiritual Education" in a Japanese Bank

Thomas P. Rohlen

Many Japanese companies train their new employees according to a philosophy of "spiritualism," a set of ideas about human psychology and character development that inspired much of the country's pre-war education. "Spiritualism's" debts to the Zen, Confucian, and samurai traditions are quite apparent. It emphasizes social cooperation and responsibility, an acceptance of reality, and perseverance. Its educational methods emphasize specially constructed training experiences. As a case study in the anthropology of education, Japanese company spiritual education points to the value of (1) studying educational processes outside formal school systems; (2) considering native concepts of psychology in analyzing educational processes; (3) finding relationships between educational techniques and techniques found in religious conversion, psychological therapy, and social initiation; and (4) discovering avenues of education that proceed by non-verbal means.

During the last few years Japanese media have given considerable attention to the startling increase of company training programs devoted at least in part to *seishin kyooiku,* a manner of training commonly translated as "spiritual education." As many as one-third of all medium and large Japanese companies may now conduct such programs as part of their regular in-company training.[1] The accounts of these in the media have been impressionistic and generally critical, with journalists in particular labelling company "spiritual education" practices as unwanted and unwarranted echoes of Japan's pre-war educational philosophy, universally condemned in the early post-war period as militaristic and stultifying to individualism and the democratic impulse. This harsh judgment is entirely predictable and not without some validity, but a

Reproduced by permission of the American Anthropological Association from *American Anthropologist* 75, no. 5 (1973): 1542–1562. Not for further reproduction.

closer examination of the phenomenon of company *seishin kyooiku* is in order before any reasonable conclusions as to its nature and political implications may be made.[2] Furthermore, spiritualism *(seishin-shugi)* is much more than a sensitive public issue in Japan; it is a key to much that Japanese now regard as traditional and foreigners regard as Japanese in the nation's ongoing cultural pattern. Spiritualism provides a very definite philosophy of socialization and human development, one that underlies such well known pursuits as flower arranging, judo, and the study of the tea ceremony. At one time it inspired the training of the country's samurai and, more recently, her pre-war youth.[3] Spiritualism offers a perspective by which individual character continues to be widely judged today. Company spiritual education is, in summary, but the most recent manifestation of a very long and still quite vital Japanese orientation to issues of human psychology and education and for this reason the subject is of far greater interest than the matter of resurgent nationalism alone would imply.

In this article I wish to describe a company spiritual training program in which I was a participant for its three-month duration in 1969.[4] The full scope of the program is too varied to permit a complete account and consequently only the major activities that are focal events of the instruction and a few themes of training life will be described in detail. The patterns underlying these activities will be discussed as they provide something of a definition of the concept *seishin* and as they indicate the methods by which individual spiritual strength is fostered. Finally, a few observations about the implications of this material for the anthropology of education are presented. In a previous paper (Rohlen 1970b), I have considered Japanese company training from the point of view of theories about initiation rituals and consequently this topic will not be taken up here.

The training program studied is conducted by a bank located in one of Japan's large regional centers. The bank has three thousand employees, two thousand men and one thousand women. *Seishin* education is given routinely to all new men and to many others in the course of their mid-career training. The program described here involved 120 new men, all recent graduates of high schools and universities. It began within several weeks after their graduation and lasted for three months. During that time they lived together in a modern five-story training institute located near the bank's home office. Training sessions lasted between ten and sixteen hours per day, six days a week. The time devoted to *seishin* education was estimated by the training staff to be about one-third of the entire introductory program. The remaining two-thirds is devoted to training new bank members in the numerous technical skills expected of them in their job. This estimate of the division of time between spiritual training and technical training, however, ignores the fact that individual performance in the task of learning banking skills is commonly interpreted according to *seishin* concepts and even many aspects of recreation, such as the songs taught the trainees are, in fact, vehicles for *seishin* messages.

While unquestionably this bank's program varies in many details from the *seishin* training of other companies, the goals and methods involved are essentially the same according to my experience and inquiry. The similarities among all of them are to be found in the underlying patterns and concepts of *seishin kyooiku*. It is the purpose of this paper to clarify and document what these are.

Japanese who have had no personal contact with company spiritual education tend to associate it with the moral education *(shuushin kyooiku* or *dootoku kyooiku)*[5] practiced in the public schools before the war. This was essentially education in nationalism and social propriety based in the teaching of parables and reverence for national symbols. In a very much altered form, moral education does survive in the bank's training program, but the morality is considerably altered in content and presentation. Today, the institution sponsoring the training is the prime focus of morality, whereas before, the nation, in the person of the emperor, was central. Instead of rituals of nationalism, the bank today draws attention primarily to its own symbols. Through such daily actions as singing the bank song, reciting its motto, learning of its history, saluting its flag, being told of the "company spirit," and hearing inspirational messages from its leaders, the trainees are taught pride and respect for their bank. The nation is not ignored, but rather the company stresses the service given to Japan by the bank and urges its trainees to fulfill their responsibilities to the nation through loyalty to their company. It is not uncommon that service to the bank even be characterized as service to the entire world and to world peace, so organic is the model of social life taught by the bank. No matter what the ultimate benefit, however, the message is that the moral man is the man who works hard for his own company. The bank and all other institutions, according to this view, serve as intermediaries between individual intentions to aid the greater society and the actual realization of national well being. By virtue of its intermediary position, the bank is properly an interpreter and defender of social morality and its practice of moral and spiritual education is done not only for the good of the bank, but also for the entire society.

It is an oversimplification, however, to describe the moral education of the bank exclusively in terms of a narrow focus on loyal role fulfillment. The content of the program includes many elements borrowed from the pool of inspirational stories of other countries. The diary of a missionary's medical work in Vietnam, the pronouncements of President Kennedy, and the opinions of the Ethiopian olympic marathon champion are among the instructional materials drawn from international sources. "Foreigners do this," or "abroad the custom is such and such" are common and powerful arguments in the bank's moral instruction program.

In addition to foreign influence, the bank's program utilizes the prestige of scholarship and science whenever convenient. Writings of famous professors that are consistent with the bank's message are found on the required reading lists and scholars from the regional university lecture occasionally on inspirational topics at the bank's institute.

Yet the overall aim of the moral instruction program is not to "brainwash" or greatly manipulate the thinking of the trainees. This, it is agreed, would be an impossibility. What is intended is that the trainees become familiar with the point of view of the bank, its competitive circumstances, and its intention to contribute to the social good. This moral perspective will hopefully strengthen their will to perform their work properly in the future. In this way, moral education, which is almost exclusively verbal in nature, fits into the spiritual training program in which the emphasis is primarily on learning through experience.

The more dramatic means for teaching the company's values are a series of special training events. The five reported here—*zazen,* military training, *rotoo,* a weekend in the country, and an endurance walk—are the most fascinating of a larger group of such activities. They constitute an important part of the introductory training program and find occasional application in mid-career courses. Because individual experience is the key element in these lessons, I have occasionally inserted observations of my own reaction to the events in the course of the following description.

Zen Meditation

During the three months of training, Zen meditation *(zazen)* was practiced on three different occasions.[6] The longest and most thorough of the three sessions took place during the second month of training, when the trainees, in three separate groups, visited a large and well known Zen temple several hours bus trip from the training institute. This temple, with its many fine buildings and lovely gardens, has long been supported by the leading industries of the area. It has a tradition of being the foremost institution in the region for the training of new Zen priests and, although the number of new priests has diminished somewhat from earlier days, the temple has become extremely busy providing brief Zen training sessions for sports teams, student groups, and business trainees. One priest mentioned that because the calendar for such training was very crowded, requests had to be made long in advance.

On arrival the trainees were lined up and marched into the temple to a small room where they deposited their shoes and baggage. They were then conducted to a hall large enough to accommodate the entire group of forty. A priest, the instructor, asked them to sit formally on their knees. Once seated, he informed them of the temple's rules and procedures and explained in detail the special manner of eating meals in a Zen temple. He left and the group sat for some time in silence. When he returned, he brought with him the head priest. The trainees were instructed to bow their heads to the floor, and to stay in that position until the head priest's greeting was ended. For about three minutes, they bowed in this manner while he spoke of the tradition, rigors, and purpose of Zen. When the head priest finished all sat up and silently accompanied him in drinking tea before he left.

The instructor next asked the group to try to sit in the lotus position, and while they struggled with this, he went on to explain the procedures of *zazen*. He emphasized that it was very important to sit up straight. "This will bring one's 'spirit' [*kokoro*] and body together in harmony," he said. "Sit up straight and you won't waver, either in spirit or in body. If you don't waver, you won't go astray or become confused." Next he explained the method of counting breaths, telling them to breathe in and out very slowly, taking as long as possible without becoming uncomfortable. "This serves to preserve the unity of spirit and body. It may be quite helpful for you in your work, since it will teach you the power of spiritual concentration. When you are bothered or worried, you can overcome such interferences and perform more efficiently," he added.

Next the long wooden paddle, the *kyoosaku,* was explained. "You are struck by the *kyoosaku* or more literally given the *kyoosaku* for the purpose of supporting your determination." He then demonstrated how he would walk up and down the room carrying the pole across his shoulder. Stopping before someone he demonstrated how the person was to bring his hands together in a praying position in front of him, bow, and receive two blows across the back between the base of the neck and the top of the shoulder blade. Before assuming the regular *zazen* position, the person was to bow once again to the *kyoosaku,* this time with gratitude.

With the conclusion of the priest's introduction, we underwent two half-hour sessions of Zen meditation. There was no tranquility or concentration, however. Everyone was obviously uncomfortable and throughout the group there was constant movement. The priest walked up and down, stopping frequently to apply the *kyoosaku* to individual backs. The loud "wack, wack" as it struck created considerable anxiety. I tried to concentrate on adjusting my breathing and maintaining the proper count and rhythm, but the noise and motion and the recurring thought that perhaps the priest would stop and strike me made the simple task of mentally counting up to ten over and over very difficult. The more I tried to forget my concern with the progress of the priest the worse my anxiety grew. When I was finally struck by the priest, the pain was inconsequential compared to the relief and physical release I experienced. Afterwards for a few minutes at least I could relax and begin to concentrate. Others told me of having the same response to the *kyoosaku.*

In between the two half-hour sessions, the trainees were instructed to stand and walk in single file around the hall. Keeping their hands in a praying position and their eyes slightly lowered, they were to maintain concentration on breathing and counting as they walked. These brief walking sessions are designed to provide respite from the pain and discomfort of sitting, yet it seemed that just as the circulation in my legs began to return we were instructed to begin another half-hour of painful sitting. The moments when these walking sessions ended were poignantly described as ones of regret and resignation.

After the first full hour of *zazen,* the group was marched single file into the adjoining mess room where all again sat in the lotus position along low, narrow tables. Hymnals were passed out and for five minutes the trainees chanted Buddhist hymns following the lead of the priest. Eating utensils were then passed out, and first soup and then an unappetizing rice gruel were dished out by younger priests running in a squatting position along the line of tables. The recipients were told to bow as the priests passed. Without a word everyone ate these offerings. There was an opportunity for seconds, but most, hungry as they were, refused. Next, hot water was poured and, using it, each cleaned his bowls in turn until only the final one contained warm water and residue. This awful stuff we were told to drink in one gulp. Nothing was left over, and all the utensils were ready for use at the next meal. The entire proceedings had not taken twenty minutes. During the short break after lunch everyone complained bitterly about the food.

With the end of the break we returned to the large hall for another hour and a half of *zazen.* Although tranquility was the goal, most trainees continued to struggle with the uncomfortable sitting position. A few stealthily glanced at their watches to find out how much time remained before the next opportunity to stand and walk around. Yet, most were seriously attempting to breathe and concentrate as the priest instructed. This was the best way to survive the endless discomfort. At the end of this session the priest explained that it was quite natural to feel pain and impatience. Just to learn to sit correctly takes considerable practice and enduring the pain was just the beginning. He repeated that a straight back, counting, the half opened eyes, and a position of weightlessness for the shoulders are the keys to learning to sit without discomfort. This, he said, was the first step in really learning to concentrate one's spirit.

When the group was told that for the next ninety minutes they were to work silently clearing the gardens and other buildings there was considerable relief. Some went to clean the outhouse and others helped clean up around the kitchen. One detail raked leaves and pulled grass along a path. The priest instructor was unbelievably meticulous in his pursuit of even the smallest weed and leaf, but his example was ignored by many of the trainees who, forgetting their joy at being relieved from the trials of *zazen*, lazily wandered about with rakes over their shoulders.

After work in the garden, the group did another hour of *zazen* and then had dinner exactly on the pattern of the previous meal. From six to seven they were given free time to wander about the temple. Some trainees found a small snack stand in a park adjoining the temple grounds and, against instructions, purchased snacks which they greedily consumed. All agreed the temple food was terrible. Without exception, they observed that all one could possibly think about was enduring each half-hour session until the bell rang and the walking session began. Their discomfort and distraction were so great they said that little or nothing of Zen as a religious experience or as a methodology for anxiety reduction could be appreciated.

From seven until nine that night, the *zazen* practice continued. The temple hall by that time had become quite cold, but there was no relief for the seated trainees. At nine we went to sleep. There was some talk and some illicit eating of food bought at the snack stand, but very soon everyone was asleep.

It was pitch dark and bitterly cold at 3:00 a.m. when the trainees were awakened and brusquely told to get up, to fold up their sleeping gear, and to assume the *zazen* position. Soon after, they were marched to the main hall where, once more sitting, they joined fourteen priests of the temple in an hour long ceremony involving the chanting of prayers, occasional prostrations, and long passages when only the priests chanted. There were no cushions in this hall and the floor was excruciatingly hard. My stomach was empty, and it was very cold. The high point of my difficulties during the two-day session was reached.

Breakfast, served at 5:30, was no different from the two previous meals, and yet many more asked for seconds. By that time some were famished, and the hot soup tasted good on such a cold morning. From six to seven, there was another free period. Most trainees tried to sleep covering themselves with the cushions as best they could. Most were too tired, shocked, and unhappy to talk with one another. I recalled the treatment of prisoners of war a number of times, and found it quite easy to understand the breakdown of morale and social cohesiveness among them. All I wished to do was escape into sleep.

The next hour was spent again sitting and chanting in the main hall of the temple. The head priest gave a half-hour lecture. My outline of his talk, written afterwards, is as follows:

(1) A brief history of Zen Buddhism.

(2) An explanation of the concept that according to Zen teaching each is to find the answers for his own problems within himself and not from the explanations of others.

(3) Temptations, such as the desire to eat, drink, have sex, and be loved, cause people to become confused and disoriented in life.

(4) The purpose of Zen is to assist individuals in perfecting (literally "polishing") their own character. This is a process which must last throughout one's life.

(5) Self improvement involves learning to become less selfish and to be of greater benefit to one's company and to others. Improvements in the ability to serve others inevitably mean greater benefit for the individual himself.

(6) A company or any group of people working together requires cooperation and good relations. These things can only be attained when people are not selfish.

(7) Just as the temple has rules to benefit its priests and guests, so any company has rules that must be supported by its members.

(8) Concerning labor-management relations, there should be no strikes, but rather the two parties should work in harmony together to improve production. The profits of this cooperation should be shared alike between both parties.

(9) Training of any kind must be painful and difficult for only in this way can the improvement of character be accomplished.

(10) He admonished the trainees to be firm of heart and steadfast in spirit. Think for yourself and don't be swayed or silenced by others.

For the rest of the morning we practiced *zazen* for a final time. No one seemed any more comfortable or adapted to the sitting position, and the squirming continued. My legs continued quickly to become numb and often I could not stand in order to walk around at the end of the half-hour sessions. The only consolation during the last two and a half hours was the knowledge that with each minute we were getting nearer the end.

During the ride back there was much comment about the pain, and the terrible food, and how one of the hardest events of the three-month training was passed. While very few of the trainees were impressed by what they had learned of themselves or the nature of Zen experience, many were deeply impressed by the strict discipline and dedication of the younger Zen priests training at the temple. Some indicated that in the future, when they felt depressed or sorry for themselves, they would remember the stern, simple lives of those priests. *Satori* ("enlightenment"), *mushin* ("selflessness"), and other Zen concepts were no more comprehensible after the two days than they had been previously, but the Spartan ways of Zen living had become tangible realities for the trainees.

Visits to Military Bases

The first trip to a Japanese military installation for training came in the second week of the program. The trainees, sixty at a time, went to an army base not far from the city. The purpose, they were told, was to learn to maintain group order. This was the first activity outside of the training institute and the first organized *seishin* event. The young men were noticeably nervous on the bus going to the base. Most of them rode silently looking out the window. After arrival, they were assigned to several barracks and given army fatigues to wear. These were cast-off uniforms that gave them an appearance more like guerrillas than members of a regular army.

In the afternoon of the first day, after a lunch in the enlisted men's mess, the trainees were run through an obstacle course and then given the Japanese army physical fitness test. Nothing particularly frightening occurred and people grew more relaxed. During the occasional breaks, there was much joking about being in military uniforms. In particular they took great pleasure in saluting one another. A respectful appreciation for the precision of passing regular army units also developed.

The following morning everyone sat through a two hour program of military history concluded by an explanation of why Japan's Self-Defense Forces needed strengthening. The talk was skillfully presented and illustrated with many anecdotes which the trainees found interesting. While this was obviously propaganda and out of place in a bank's training program, no one seemed offended. Later, the bank's instructors explained that listening to this lecture was one of the conditions for the use of base facilities and the services of the drill sergeants. The director of training in the bank commented that he would much prefer not to use military facilities, but no other source for teaching military drill was available.

The mood on the bus home was in marked contrast to the gloomy atmosphere going out. There was much ebullient yelling back and forth and noisy rubbernecking at girls along the way. Everyone gaily saluted the driver and his assistant as we descended from the bus.

Near the end of the three months, we again went to a military base, this time the former Naval Officer Candidate School at Edajima— "Japan's Annapolis."[7] Today it is still in use as a school for the Self-Defense Force Navy. Some years after the war, a museum for the various personal effects, diaries, reminiscences, and other illustrations of the brief days of Japan's suicide pilots was established on the base. The director of this museum is a man who began collecting these mementos after the war as evidence of the true attitudes and character of the pilots. He has given himself the mission of explaining or reinterpreting the *kamikaze* to a generation of younger Japanese who know very little of their actual lives or character. The day and a half visit to Edajima was made primarily to see the museum and hear the director's explanation.

Our group was prepared for the visit by watching several recent commercial movies that depict the life of midshipmen training there during the war. According to the movies, only the cream of Japan's young men could enter Edajima after having passed the most rigorous academic and physical tests. In one movie it was described as the most difficult school to enter in Japan. The movies emphasized the character strength and camaraderie of the young men, qualities making more tragic the fact that most were destined to die shortly after graduation. Having seen these dramatic portrayals of Edajima, the young bankers were duly impressed with its tradition and its almost sacred quality for pre-war generations.

In an hour lecture, the director of the museum told of his impressions of the suicide pilots and the lessons their example might hold for young people in a peaceful, modern Japan. His lecture, entitled "What is Man's Mission in Life," had a stirring impact on the trainees.

He began by describing the education given at Edajima. In addition to physical and intellectual skill, perfection and alertness were also demanded at all times. Midshipmen arriving at the top of a long flight of stairs might be asked, for example, to say how many steps they had just climbed. Discipline was so strict that many grew to hate their officers and yet they would never complain openly, for to do so was to fail training. Teachers at the school also accepted great personal suffering without complaint, for the spirit of the place was endurance and sacrifice for the nation. Newcomers gradually acquired this spirit and passed it on. The epitome of this was that after 1941, young men coming to Edajima realized that they were in fact volunteering to die. In the classrooms of Edajima, he claimed, there was much discussing of the small possibility Japan had for winning the war. He stressed that preparation to serve one's country up to and including death was not something that began with the suicide pilots. It was the spirit at Edajima long before the war. He told of a pilot of one of the miniature suicide submarines that set off for Hawaii at the time of Pearl Harbor departing with the final words, "We are bound to lose."

Such stories of courage and uprightness continued a while longer and then he observed:

> Nobody wishes to experience unpleasant things, but unpleasant things are part of life and nothing of significance can be achieved without suffering. Today's individualism ignores this fact and easily becomes empty egoism. The men at Edajima had the kinds of individualism and independence that focus on the mission to serve one's country, not on the pursuit of pleasure. The trouble with today's student movement is that they know nothing of the discipline and sacrifice required to change society for the better. Soon enough they are fighting among themselves. There was a young cadet at the academy who, because he opposed a certain rule in the school, sat in the same place for many weeks, fasting and drinking only water to show his opposition. His action was respected by the others because he didn't complain or criticize, but rather demonstrated the sincerity of his objection by personally suffering. How many so-called revolutionaries today are prepared to do that kind of thing?

He told a story about the novelist Kawabata Yasunari. During a visit to a grade school near the end of the war, Kawabata asked the youngsters if there were any in the class willing to die for Japan. One young boy stepped forward and said, "I will." Kawabata asked his reasons with the observation, "If Japan loses, do you think your death will be regarded as a loss? If Japan wins, do you think you will be honored?" The little boy replied, "Mister, aren't you being misleading? I know that Japan is going to lose." Kawabata bowed to the little boy.

Through such anecdotes the courage of Japan's wartime youth, particularly those volunteering to become suicide pilots, was presented. Their spiritual strength, not their zealousness or their naiveté was emphasized. The *kamikaze* were Japan's best, the museum director concluded. They were the best informed about Japan's impending defeat, and yet they volunteered to die without even, in most cases, an opportunity to see family or friends a last time. There is a popular song about the fellowship of the suicide pilots, and the fact that they would never again meet at cherry blossom time. The image of these young men taking off on warm spring afternoons is truly a tragic one, and the museum director at the end recalled this scene. Sitting very straight in their chairs, the trainees, to a man, were weeping silently as he finished.

The visit to the museum proper the next day was made in silent interest with none of the troublemaking spirit that the trainees usually brought to their excursions. Once inside, they were allowed to wander about on their own looking at the many rooms of paintings and other mementos of naval history until they reached the rooms containing the story of the suicide pilots. The trainees were deeply affected by the similarity in age between themselves and the young men who died in 1945. They noticed how beautifully written the pilot's diaries were. According to their own statements, it was a moving experience.

Later, after inspecting the base, teams were assigned to row heavy, cumbersome longboats, traditionally part of Edajima training. The difficulties of developing coordination in the crew were stressed. Later, the group climbed a nearby mountain that is climbed at a run every day by cadets of the school. The ascent was made at a jogging pace, and the trainees were amazed to learn that their speed, which they thought to be fast, was twice as slow as the cadet average.

As in the previous visit to an army base, people were extremely courteous and pleasant, and the group did not taste much of the rigors and hierarchy of military life. They were, however, keenly interested in the memories and past glories of the place and they drank up the mood created by the old buildings. It was July and the sunburnt cadets in their summer whites, the ocean breezes, and the pride of the academy combined to create an almost irresistible spell. Without this atmosphere the explanations of courage and purpose might have had less impact, but being at Edajima removed much of the historical distance between the *kamikaze* and the young bankers their age.

Rotoo

For two days during the latter part of the second month of training, the group stayed at a youth center sponsored by the Japanese government. This center, located on a mountainside, overlooks a large agricultural valley and just below is the market town for the area. Early on the morning after arrival the trainees were instructed to go down into the town and find work from the residents. Instructions were to go singly from house to house offering to work without pay. They were to do whatever their host asked of them. It was strongly emphasized that this was not to be a group operation. Each was to go alone and work alone for the entire day. In addition, the trainees were disallowed from making any explanation for themselves or their reasons for volunteering to work. They could offer no more than their name and their willingness to work.

They dressed for the exercise in white, nondescript athletic uniforms, common throughout Japan. Without benefit of a social identity or a reasonable explanation for themselves, the trainees were sent out to make a most unusual request of strangers. Their reliability would not be vouched for by their relationship to a known institution like the bank. They were thus made dependent on the good will of the people they met.

This form of situation, difficult as it would be anywhere, is of particular difficulty in Japan where, as a rule, strangers ignore one another and social intercourse between them is unusual and suspicious. Approached by an unknown person with a request like this the common response would be a hurried and not very polite refusal. People doing *rotoo* in Japanese cities have met refusals perhaps four times out of five. It was with considerable consternation, therefore, that the trainees left for the town below.

At first they wandered about from street to street. Many were reluctant to leave their friends and go alone to the front gate of some house. In the case of some groups, they walked four or five blocks together before anyone mustered the courage to make his first approach to a house, but gradually the groups dispersed. The common experience was to be refused two or three times before finally locating a house or shop where they would be allowed in and given work. All agreed to having been very anxious about the first approach, but found the second and the third easier to make as long as people were polite. An impolite refusal created considerable upset, but was rare. Those who did take them in were regarded as warm and understanding people for whom they were very happy to work hard. The common pattern was to volunteer to do things that even the host would not have thought to ask. This was partly to avoid going out again seeking another house and partly from a felt desire to be of help.

Boys who had been raised on farms tended to go to the edge of town seeking familiar work with farming families. The majority found work in various small shops. One helped sell toys and another assisted a mat maker, a third delivered groceries, and another pumped gas. One rather clever young man found work in a small roadhouse by the bus station. He quickly established himself as more than just a dishwasher by showing his skill in mixing cocktails. An instructor happened to notice him working there and was angered by the lack of seriousness with which this trainee regarded the day's exercise. The offender was told he had selected an inappropriate place. Instead of doing service for some respectable family, the young man was busy swapping jokes with the customers and waitresses of a roadhouse. He was sent away from the place and told to find other, more appropriate work. Later he was roundly criticized for taking *rotoo* lightly.

When the group had all returned, a general discussion of the day's experience was held in the auditorium. It was soon apparent that com-ments from the floor would not be forthcoming, so the instructor in charge had each squad talk over their impressions of the day and discuss the relevance of the *rotoo* experience to the question, "What is the mean-ing of work?" As usual, a variety of opinions emerged. Some trainees had had such an interesting and pleasant time with their hosts that it had not occurred to them to think of their tasks as work. When this was noticed, it was generally observed that enjoyment of work has less to do with the kind of work performed, and more to do with the attitude the person has toward it. The bank's reasons for utilizing *rotoo* centered on establishing precisely this lesson.

The actual intent of *rotoo,* as it is used by some Buddhist temples, is, however, somewhat different. It is used as a method of shocking people out of spiritual lethargy and complacency. The word *rotoo* actually means something like "bewilderment" and refers to the state of insecu-rity established when the individual is divorced from his comfortable social place and identity. In the course of begging for work, that is, beg-ging for acceptance by others, the subject learns of the superficial nature of much in his daily life. It is expected that his reliance on affiliations, titles, ranks, and a circle of those close to him will be revealed, and, per-haps for the first time, he will begin to ask who he really is. *Rotoo* also provides a unique opportunity for a trusting and compassionate interac-tion between strangers. After a *rotoo* experience it is unlikely that the person will continue to disregard the humanity of others, no matter how strange they are to him in terms of social relationship. It is hoped that this will foster a greater warmth and spontaneity in the individual.

From the point of view of the bank, however, there are additional purposes for this training, ones that help explain why *rotoo* is included in a training program for new bankers. It has been the experience of many people from the bank that the meaning of work and attitudes toward work have been changed by doing *rotoo.* The anxiety of rejection and isolation mounts with each refusal until finally, when some kindly per-son takes the individual in and gives him work, a cathartic sense of grat-itude for being accepted and allowed to help is created. No matter what the work, even cleaning an out-house, the sense of relief makes the work seem pleasant and satisfying. Work that is normally looked down upon is, in this circumstance, enthusiastically welcomed.

After such an experience, it is difficult to deny the assertion that any form of work is intrinsically neither good nor bad, satisfying nor unsatisfying, appropriate nor inappropriate. Pleasure in work, it must be concluded, varies according to the subject's attitude and circum-stances. Failure to enjoy one's work is interpreted in the bank as essen-tially a question of improper attitude, and *rotoo* exemplifies the teaching that any work can be enjoyable with a positive attitude. Since it must assign rather dull and methodical tasks to many of its employees, the bank finds this lesson of obvious value.

Weekend in the Country

One weekend was spent on a small island about an hour's boat ride from the city. The educational purposes for this special session were varied. According to our leaders, we were expected to learn something of self reliance and the kind of ingenuity engendered by simple, rural living conditions. The weekend's activities were also to provide many opportunities to let off steam and be as boisterous, rowdy, and aggressive as we wished. Several activities designed to teach us a greater appreciation for social inter-dependency and social service were also included. Finally, living together in quarters more cramped and primitive than those at the institute was to be part of our general experience in *shuudan seikatsu* (group living). All of these goals were outlined to us upon arrival at the prefectual youth hostel on the island.

The hostel was a large barn-like building of two stories with wooden bunks upstairs and a large open room downstairs. The atmosphere of the hostel was in the boy scout tradition even to the large stone fireplace, and a collection of handicrafts displayed on the walls. The beach was a twenty-minute jog from the place and in the opposite direction on the hillsides were tangerine groves and small vegetable gardens belonging to local farmers.

With the unloading completed we gathered in the main room in our usual squad formations and listened to a short explanation from the head of the training section:

> In the city, in our modern and well equipped training institute, we have no chance to let loose and become rough and tumble, so we have come out here to let you express your energy and youthfulness. While all of you are bankers and therefore are expected to be proper and decorous when working as bankers, we want you to have a more aggressive spirit burning inside. This weekend will be a chance for you to find out just how boisterous and full of fight you can be. So don't hold back. Throw yourself into the activities we have planned as completely as you can. Finally, we are also going to help some farmers in their fields, and we hope that all of you will learn and benefit from this experience.

The leader then divided the room into two groups, had them face each other and instructed everyone to yell out in a loud voice, *"washoo, washoo,"* one group alternating with the other. We then began doing squat jumps thrusting our arms high over our heads yelling *washoo*. The two groups alternated and a piston effect was created, one group jump-ing up and yelling followed by the other. After ten or fifteen minutes of this the room seemed filled with a weird frenzy. The heat, constant rhythmic yelling, and unceasing motion made me feel a bit afraid, as if I had been locked in a boiler room with a monstrous engine. When the exercise ended, and it seemed interminably long, we collapsed with exhaustion. This was our introduction to what the trainers had in mind when they said they wanted us to be full of energy and boisterousness. I was fascinated to realize that our training went from the extremes of silent Zen meditation to this mass explosion of energy and noise.

The first morning before dawn the group ran in formation to a wide, empty stretch of beach facing the open sea. A light rain was falling and the wind off the ocean soaked our thin athletic outfits. After the usual calisthenics we separated into squads arranged in lines facing the wind. Led alternately by each in the squad we screamed commands at the top of our lungs. Most were quite inhibited at first, but eventually all were yelling as loud as possible. Next we practiced swinging wooden swords up and down as one would in practicing Japanese fencing. Intersquad sumo matches, marked by more effort than skill, were the last events held on the beach before breakfast. The run through the rain back to the hostel for breakfast seemed particularly long.

During the morning on both days we went off with various farmers who had agreed to put us to work in their fields. We were provided with scythes and other farm equipment and under the farmers' direction we weeded gardens and cut grass under tangerine trees. Some of the trainees worked strenuously while others loafed. The farmers were not inclined to make the trainees work harder, and the project was much like other work details we had experienced, even though it was ex-plained to us as service *(hooshi)* to the farmers.

When we got back to the hostel that afternoon people were asked to comment on their experience. The general opinion was that being directed to go out and help farmers who had obviously been rounded up by our instructors and persuaded to allow us to work for them provided very little sense of actual service. Some said they enjoyed the work, others said they found it inappropriate to training as bankers. It was agreed that to learn about service to others the work should be volun-tary. The primary lesson for the city boys had little to do with service; they had learned more about farmers and their contribution to society.

Incidentally, the president of the bank would like someday to have all new men spend their entire first year farming together. He feels the long, arduous agricultural cycle is the best education in persistent effort and due reward. He has spoken of this on numerous occasions, and the director of training may have instituted the service to farmers routine as a response to the president's vision.

The second afternoon was spent playing contact sports on the beach. Stripped to our waists and divided into two teams, we played several games popular in the old Japanese navy, *kiba gassen* and *boo-taoshi,* and then held a sumo wrestling tournament. In the first game, each side creates a set of mounted warriors with one man riding on the shoulders of three compatriots. Starting from opposite sides of the field, the two teams charge and the side that forces the other's men to the ground first is the winner. The second game involves the defense of standing poles, one for each team. The object is to attack and tear down the opponents' pole while preserving one's own. At each end of the field the attackers assault the other's defenses by leaping upon the group, surrounding the pole, tearing people away from it, and wrestling with the people who come to reinforce the defenders. Neither of these two games took much over fifteen minutes, but they were fiercely contested and some of the less aggressive trainees were quite evidently frightened to have to fight their fellow trainees. The rest of the afternoon was devoted to a round robin sumo tournament among the squads with contestants from each squad matched by size.

During the time on the island squads were assigned cooking, clean-up, and other chores, and the conditions and organization of life in the hostel followed the usual camp patterns even as far as singing songs around a great bonfire the last night. After the entertainment and singing, the program ended with all standing arm-in-arm in two great circles around the fire swaying back and forth singing the bank's song and the very sentimental song of the *kamikaze* pilots.

Endurance Walk

Ever since the first day, the trainees had heard about the twenty-five mile endurance walk to be held sometime near the end of the training period. The daily morning mile run and the other climbing and hiking activities were explained as preparation for this event. On the morning they were to begin the endurance walk, there seemed to be a high level of anticipation and readiness even among the weaker and less athletic trainees.

The program was simple enough. The trainees were to walk the first nine miles together in a single body. The second nine miles were to be covered with each squad walking as a unit. The last seven miles were to be walked alone and in silence. All twenty-five miles were accomplished by going around and around a large public park in the middle of the city. Each lap was approximately one mile. There were a number of rules established by the instructors. It was forbidden to take any refreshment. During the second stage, each squad was to stay together for the entire nine miles and competition between squads was discouraged.

Finally, it was strictly forbidden to talk with others when walking alone during the last stage. The training staff also walked the twenty-five miles going around in the opposite direction. Some dozen or so young men from the bank, recent graduates of previous training programs, were stationed along the route and instructed to offer the trainees cold drinks which, of course, they had to refuse. This was the program and there was no emphasis at all placed on one person finishing ahead of another. Instructions were to take as much time as needed as long as the entire twenty-five miles was completed. The walk began around 7:30 a.m. and finished around 3:00 p.m. There was no time limit and many had not gone the full twenty-five miles, but the collapse from heat prostration of a few led the instructors to call the event off at a point where most had a lap or two remaining.

On the surface, this program was simple enough, but in retrospect it seems to have been skillfully designed to maximize certain lessons related to *seishin*. When we began, the day was fresh and cool and it seemed as though we were beginning a pleasant stroll. Walking together in one large group, everyone conversed, joked, and paid very little attention to the walk itself. The first nine miles seemed to pass quickly and pleasantly, and the severe physical hardship that we had been expecting seemed remote.

Forming up into squad groups at the beginning of the next nine miles we were reminded again not to compete with other squads. But discovering squads close before and behind, the pace began escalating and resulted in an uproarious competition that involved all but a few of the squads. Each time a team would come up from the rear, the team about to be overtaken would quicken its pace, and before long trainees found themselves walking very fast, so fast that those with shorter legs had to run occasionally to keep up. There was much yelling back and forth within each squad, the slower and more tired people crying out for a reduction in speed, the others urging them to greater efforts. A common solution was to put the slowest person at the head of the squad. This not only slowed the faster ones down, but forced the slow ones to make a greater effort. The competing squads were so fast that within four or five miles they had already begun to lap those squads that stayed out of the competition. By the end of the second nine miles the toll on the fast walkers was obvious. Many, besides suffering from stiff legs and blisters, were beginning to have headaches and show evidence of heat prostration. Some lay under a tree by the finish line sucking salt tablets. It was noon by that time and the park baked under the full heat of a mid-June sun.

Any gratification the leading squad found in their victory was soon forgotten. At the finish line, there was no congratulation and no rest.

Squads were instructed to break up and continue walking, this time in single file and in silence. Soon a long line of trainees stretched over the entire circumference of the course. Having already covered eighteen miles, the last nine at a grueling pace, most were very tired.

At that point everything was transformed. The excitement and clamor of competition was gone. Each individual, alone in a quiet world, was confronted by the sweep of his own thoughts and feelings as he pushed forward.

My own experience was to become acutely aware of every sort of pain. Great blisters had obviously formed on the soles of my feet; my legs, back, and neck ached; and at times I had a sense of delirium. The thirst I had expected to be so severe seemed insignificant compared to these other afflictions. After accomplishing each lap, instead of feeling encouraged, I plunged into despair over those remaining. My awareness of the world around me, including the spectators in the park and the bank employees tempting us with refreshments, dropped almost to zero. Head down I trudged forward. Each step was literally more painful than the one before. The image of an old prospector lost on the desert kept recurring in my mind. The temptation to stop and lie down for a while in the lush grass was tremendous. Near the end I could do no more than walk for a minute or two and then rest for much longer. The others around me seemed to be doing the same thing. It was hard to be aware of them for very long, however. After a rest, it was very difficult to stand and begin again. For some reason it was heartening to discover that six or eight of the trainees had fainted and were prostrate under a shady tree at the finish line where they were receiving some medical attention. I, too, wanted to lie there with them, and yet I felt encouraged by the fact that I had not yet fallen. "I was stronger, I could make it," I thought to myself as I passed by. Other moments brought feverish dreams of somehow sneaking away. I reasoned that no one would notice if I slipped out of the park and returned just when the event was closing. Bushes became places I could hide behind, resting until the group was ready to go home. I kept going, I suppose, because I feared discovery. Although in a feverish state, I was in some sense quite capable of looking objectively at my response to this test of endurance. The content of lectures about *seishin* strength came back to me. I could see that I was spiritually weak, easily tempted, and inclined to quit. Under such stress some aspects of my thoughts were obviously not serving my interest in completing the course. Whatever will power I had arose from pride and an emerging, almost involuntary, belief in the *seishin* approach. If I was to finish, I needed spiritual strength. It angered and amused me to realize how cleverly this exercise had been conceived. I vowed over and over never to get involved in such a situation again, and yet, within days, when the memory of the physical pain had dimmed, I was taking great pride in my accomplishment and viewing my completion of the twenty-five mile course as proof that I could do anything I set my mind to.

These were the most notable activities of the *seishin kyooiku* program during those three months. In addition, there are a number of other aspects of spiritual training that deserve our attention. These efforts are less dramatic and are conducted on a "day in day out" basis.

In order to sponsor an intense group life *(shuudan seikatsu)* for its trainees, the institute staff has devised a number of interesting procedures and episodes. All leadership and direction of daily activities is placed in the hands of the trainees themselves who take turns commanding the various twelve man squads and assuming overall leadership of the entire group. Such things as clean-up, kitchen and service details, the morning and evening assemblies, scheduling, and travel are all directed by the young men on a rotation basis. It was expected that a strong appreciation for the burdens of leadership and the need for cooperation would develop under such conditions. The most poignant illustrations of the necessity for order in group living come whenever the entire retinue of one hundred twenty travelled as a unit. The value of group discipline and coordination learned during the early sessions of military drill was evident at such times, and waiting at stations and elsewhere the young men enjoyed watching other less orderly groups of young people struggle with the problem of keeping together.

Closely related to the matter of group living is the popular theme of teamwork *(chiimu waaku)*. While this is a borrowed term, it is also closely related to the traditionally important value of *wa* (usually translated as "harmony"). The form of organization for most competition is the team, and the regular squads usually serve as the basis for other activities. Studies related to banking, pursuit of hobbies, and other less obviously group oriented pursuits are arranged to require teamwork. While competition between individuals was seldom encouraged, group competition was a major means of motivation throughout the training period. It should be stressed that emphasis on teamwork is so common in Japanese society that none of the young trainees, even those who were critical of other aspects of the program, complained of an overemphasis on subordination of the individual to the group.

Physical conditioning has a definite role in spiritual training. Each morning and evening group exercises were held. On three occasions lectures on physical fitness were delivered, twice by outside specialists. Whenever feasible, the instructors had the trainees hike and even run to their destination. It is not unusual for lectures at the institute to be interrupted by an instructor for the purpose of correcting trainee posture, and the value of good posture, both to health and to mental concentration, is often stressed. Underlying these efforts is the assumption that good physical condition and proper posture are fundamental to the development of spiritual power.

Newcomers who have trouble developing enough skill and speed to pass the bank's standard abacus test find that practicing the abacus is an exercise with strong *seishin* overtones. The practice required is long and tedious, and there are no shortcuts to developing speed. Practice is left entirely up to the individual trainees, but the instructors watch their response to this situation with great interest. Those that do not practice or who give up easily are privately cautioned in *seishin* terms and encouraged to try harder. The moral that dogged persistence will solve the problem is one that lies at the heart of *seishin* oriented thought. Practicing the abacus, like many other aspects of the overall training program, is not officially described as part of spiritual training, but because of the wide applicability of its principles, *seishin* philosophy influences it and most other training activities.

Discussion

As already mentioned, *seishin kyooiku* is commonly translated as "spiritual education," but the meaning of "spiritual" in this case is far from clear to non-Japanese. Certainly, the education described above is quite different than, say, the "spiritual education" of Christian churches. For Japanese the concept *seishin* is sufficiently general and vague to allow many interpretations and variations,[8] yet underlying the diversity are common patterns of thought and practice which may be described.

If we begin by using experience as the groundwork for our explication of Japanese "spiritualism," then perhaps for Westerners it would be useful to keep in mind the parallels between the activities described above and the practices of such quasi-educational organizations in the West as summer camps, Sunday schools, sports teams, boy scouts, and military training. These all claim special qualities and abilities in the socialization of both adults and youth which formal public education, according to the claims, cannot or will not offer. We have no overreaching word for the special kind of education these institutions offer in common, but it is not too difficult to appreciate certain similarities underlying all of them.

In Japan, training in social membership and the cultivation of the individual *(shuuyoo* and *kyooyoo)* have for centuries been very serious enterprises regarded as imperative to the creation of an orderly society, individual character, and personal fulfillment. In the Chinese tradition the properly organized state is believed to depend on leadership by men of outstanding character, and the Japanese, especially during the Toku-gawa period (1600–1868), have also emphasized this perspective. In China, personal development was primarily the concern of the scholar-official and activities and disciplines of a scholarly nature were accord-ingly emphasized, whereas in Tokugawa Japan, the pursuit of the same basic goals was strongly flavored by the fact that the Japanese elite was largely military in outlook and experience. In both China and Japan the social benefit of such training was seldom separated from the acknowl-edged benefits to the individual, and various arts and military skills, such as judo and the tea cult in Japan, were appreciated as important paths of spiritual growth. A point to note is that unlike in the West, there arose no distinctions encouraging the separation of the individual and the social or the sacred and the secular in education.

After the Meiji restoration of 1868, the responsibility for spiritual education in Japan shifted from local governments, private academies, and commercial enterprises to the new national educational system. Until defeat in 1945 the government pursued a policy of spiritual educa-tion for the masses based on a combination of the teachings and methods of Confucian China, the samurai heritage, and the morality of the Tokugawa merchants. What the West has long attempted to accom-plish through religious schools, youth organizations, and sports, the Japanese chose to institutionalize in the public school program proper, a fact the reformers of the American occupation hardly appreciated in their enthusiasm to root out the "totalitarian," "nationalistic," and "militaristic" strains in Japanese education. According to spokesmen for companies now practicing *seishin kyooiku*, this approach was for Japa-nese synonymous with education in good citizenship, and when it was purged from the school system, an educational vacuum was created. Company spiritual training, they explain, is but an attempt to reinsti-tute conventional and necessary socialization practices which, for politi-cal reasons, the government has been reluctant to revive. Does spiritual education mark a revival of Japanese militarism? Companies assert they are experimenting with this form of education for the more imme-diate reason that they wish to produce more highly socialized and effec-tive employees. The fact that spiritual education has deep historical connections with the Japanese military tradition serves to color spiritual training, they say, but it does not mean that it is militaristic in the usual sense of the term. Spiritual training is primarily the product of a reac-tion against both the loosening of social ties in contemporary Japan and the Western influence that is blamed for this trend.

How may we define the term *seishin?* If the frame of reference is a very general one contrasting physical and mental, the concept *seishin* would most likely be placed in the mental column. Attitudes, will power, concentration, and many other "mental" qualities are important aspects of spiritual power. Yet this kind of distinction obscures more than it clarifies, for the physical/mental distinction is not central to the concept. It is true that the "mind over matter," and "power of positive thought" philosophies approach the meaning of *seishin,* but there are differences. In the case of traditional Japanese thought, the mind/body duality (which does exist in Japanese expressions such as *nikutaiteki* "physical or corporal") is overridden by the concept *kokoro,* important in Zen and in many traditional forms of education. *Kokoro,* translated "heart" or "spirit," represents the broad area of individual psychosomatic unity. The state of an individual's *kokoro* may be composed or disturbed, and there are numerous terms for both of these. Composure implies that both the mind and the body operate properly, efficiently, and in harmony; in the state of disturbance, the mind and body are accordingly upset, undependable, and involved in an adverse way with one another. Both of these states may be distinguished as to degree. Learning to achieve composure is one goal of *seishin* training, and a composed *kokoro* is regarded as a major source of *seishin* strength.

Many lessons in bank training are specifically aimed at teaching the trainees how to attain composure, or at least to awaken in them a greater awareness of the interrelationship of the physical and mental aspects of disturbance. Zen meditation and the emphasis on posture are two outstanding examples. Yet, composure is not an end in itself so much as it is a basis for more effective individual action. The standard by which spiritual strength *(seishinryoku)* is measured is performance. The outward manifestations of strength are such things as the ability to endure trouble and pain, a coolness in the face of threat, patience, dependability, persistence, self-reliance, and intense personal motivation; qualities we would associate with "strong personal character." Yet spiritual strength is not measured by performance, no matter how spectacular, that results solely from cleverness or physical power, although these qualities are often interpreted as products of spiritual strength.

Illustrations of *seishin* strength hinge on difficulties that test a man's will, particularly his will to carry on in some social purpose.[9] Most often these difficulties are "psychological" (actually psychosomatic) in nature. They include fear, disillusionment, boredom, loneliness, and failure, as well as the more obvious problems of physical pain and the temptations of easy reward. Any form of stress that tempts a person to resign his effort or to escape a problem is relevant as a test. Similarly, any quality that helps the individual pass such tests is part of his spiritual strength. For this reason verbal education in morality can be regarded as contributing directly to spiritual power, if it provides conviction and strengthens the individual's resolve to carry on.

Education for spiritual strength uses artificially created tests to build up staying power for life's actual tests. The most dramatic examples in the bank's training program are the endurance walk and *zazen*. The designs for tests are usually quite well considered, for there are a number of factors governing their success as educational devices. First they can be neither so easy that they are not really tests, nor so hard that they cannot be passed. Secondly, the experience of passing them must reveal to the individual both the process of temptation and the methods of dispelling it. That is, the trainee must be prepared to experience the test in *seishin* terms, and this often requires considerable teaching, in the normal sense, before the event.

The test must also be of some relevance to the trials of real life either by virtue of imitation or analogy. An endurance walk may not seem very relevant to work in a bank, but the instructors pointed out that the temptation to take a forbidden drink of water "which costs nothing" is like the temptation to steal from one's own bank. An analogy was also made between the arduousness of sitting in *zazen* and the problem of maintaining concentration during mundane clerking in the bank.

No matter what form of test is devised for training purposes, the key element in the whole process is the experience of emotional wavering and the "spiritual" struggle within the individual to carry on until the test is completed. Passing any *seishin* test is not a matter of scoring high, or coming in ahead of others. Competition is within the self, and success is marked by completion of the ordeal. Enduring one test to its conclusion will make completion of subsequent, similar tests less difficult, it is assumed. During the moments of greatest wavering, the individual experiences his own individual weaknesses with heightened awareness and on the basis of this self-knowledge, he is enabled to proceed to overcome such weakness and prepare to endure even greater tests in the future.

According to *seishin* thought, "incorrect" attitudes are often the source of personal difficulty.[10] What is meant by attitudes in this instance is not opinions, such as political opinions, but rather the issue is the person's general attitude toward things around him to which he must personally respond. For example, the bank's purpose in using *rotoo* is to teach a better attitude toward work, one that is positive and enthusiastic. With such an attitude, according to *seishin* theory, the individual could better enjoy working as well as work better. The basis of a proper attitude, in this meaning of the term, begins with acceptance of necessity and responsibility. Instead of fighting life's requirements, such as work, the most satisfactory attitude is to acknowledge and accept necessary difficulties. To regret or attempt to avoid them only leads to frustration, disappointment, and upset. The dimension accepting/resisting, which is consistently important throughout Japanese life, is the key to evaluating the "correctness" of a person's attitudes, and judgments depend less on verbal expression than on other actions. Complaining, criticizing, arguing, and other forms of resistance constitute examples of the kinds of actions that evidence improper attitudes. Ready acceptance of unpleasant or difficult tasks, on the other hand, illustrate a man's correct attitude. Those who complained during training, for example, were asked to reconsider their attitude.

While *seishin kyooiku* seeks to sponsor an accepting attitude[11] toward all of life's necessities, greatest attention is paid to developing the proper attitude toward social responsibilities.[12] The requirements of a social system and the interdependent quality of society, both of which make the diligent performance of every role important, are taught as the basic facts of life. The necessity that individual responsibility to the role assigned by the system be accepted and fulfilled follows from this fact. In the bank's training, improper attitudes toward tasks and exercises were frequently pointed out by the training staff, and much of the morally oriented lectures and reading focused on teaching acceptance of the necessities of social life. One such reality, international economic competition, was an ever-present theme in these discussions.

While social realities are underlined, individual requirements, other than the most elementary necessities, are ignored or treated as unimportant. It is a firm principle that individual needs and desires are properly challenged and controlled as part of the program to develop spiritual strength, and there are numerous historical cases in which the coincidence of a desire to toughen up trainees on the part of the instructors and a desire to demonstrate spiritual strength on the part of the trainees have resulted in endurance tests causing serious injury and even death in extreme cases. In the post-war period the training activities of student outing clubs have produced the only examples of how a *seishin* orientation can produce tragic results when the limits of physical endurance are ignored.

For any person, the correct and most satisfying goals according to *seishin* thought are fulfillment of his social role and achievement in his chosen personal pursuit. These goals are assumed to be self-evident. The spiritually strong man is by definition a contributor to society. He excels in cooperation and service to others because he has mastered the art of self-discipline. The bank's training program strongly emphasizes social values such as cooperation, yet these are regarded by the training staff as rudimentary lessons that, once learned, allow the individual to graduate to more independent kinds of spiritual development. Training to social necessities is also stressed because of its immediate relevance to the trainee's transition from being a student to membership in the bank, and because it is felt that today's young people are not learning in the public school system to subordinate themselves to the group. Executives of the bank state that socialization should not be of such concern to companies; it is more appropriately carried on in the family and the school but, as already mentioned, they feel these other institutions, particularly the new "progressive" schools, have failed to perform this function adequately.

A few more characteristics of the *seishin* approach to education should be noted briefly:

(1) In *seishin* education, emphasis is placed on non-verbal forms of behavior. A well behaved but silent class, for example, is not necessarily an indication of lethargy, stupidity, or the failure of the teacher. It is likely to be interpreted as evidence that students are well disciplined, receptive, and respectful. In some instances, a *seishin* orientation may take a skeptical view of verbal logic and its forms of understanding, favoring experience as the basis of knowledge instead.

(2) Rather than viewing difficulties and hardships the students face as barriers to education and therefore things to be overcome by better facilities or improved methods of instruction, *seishin* based education is liable to regard problems in the educational situation as valuable assets to the training process itself. They are tests and therefore useful. Environmental problems are viewed as opportunities rather than as the source of failure.

(3) A knowledge of self and self-reflection (*jikaku* and *hansei*) are stressed in *seishin* training and the blame for difficulties or failure, individual or social, will be placed most heavily on spiritual weakness rather than on a lack of knowledge or inadequacy of social organization. The *seishin* approach to social betterment gives precedence to spiritual reform over social reform. Schools are viewed as instruments of change and improvement, but their influence should be over individual character rather than over the shape of society.

(4) Rather than encouraging students to consider themselves as different from one another and thus sponsoring individualistic thought and creativity, *seishin* education sponsors outward conformity to teachers' examples and group standards. Nonconformity is viewed as disruptive of group unity and a sign of individual character weakness. It is thought that conformity is made from conviction, not dullness, and that to conform to the group is difficult, rather than easy.

(5) *Seishin* education aims to help the individual achieve contentment through the development of an ordered and stable psyche free from confusion and frustration. This is to be attained through the gradual conquest of *waga* or *ga* (one's primitive self, or id in Freudian terms). The phrase expressing this process, *waga o korosu* (literally "kill the self"), is a common expression related to the *seishin* approach.

(6) Whenever possible in *seishin* education, competition is organized along group rather than individual lines and many events have no obvious competitive quality. This is not because competition hurts feelings, but because it disrupts group unity and because the real competition takes place within each individual.

(7) The unchanging nature of spiritual problems and their solutions is a basic assumption of the *seishin* approach. Teachers, parents, and senior students are, by virtue of greater experience and training, spiritually more advanced and therefore worthy of respect and authority. Age does not become a sign of out-datedness, and intergenerational continuity and concord in the unchanging pursuit of spiritual strength is encouraged.

I would, in conclusion, like to offer a few observations on the significance of this material to the emerging field of the anthropology of education.

(1) The bank example represents a kind of education which to date has received very little attention. It is not centered in a school system; it involves adults; it is not universal for the society; and it is operated by a kind of institution that in other societies may conduct little or no education at all. Such conditions would hardly attract the attention of anthropologists about to study education, and yet, at least in Japan, such forms of education are quite significant. It is my impression that educational anthropologists have devoted relatively far too much attention to studies of schooling, schools, and school systems and not enough to religious education, sports training, military indoctrination, and the countless other ways societies seek to improve and integrate their members.

(2) The manner in which *seishin* concepts regarding human psychology and the methods of *seishin* education interlock indicates that the cross-cultural study of education must take cognizance of the culture's "common sense" psychology in analyzing the intent and methods of any educational endeavor. That is, there is a broad area of overlap between concepts of education and those of psychology in any situation, and the educational anthropologist dealing with a non-Western educational system should be prepared to inquire deeply into the psychological understandings of the people involved. One benefit of a greater attention to ethnopsychology in education would be a greater clarification of how our own native psychology influences the manner in which we pursue educational goals.

(3) The similarity between the bank's program and processes and methods found in certain Japanese forms of psychiatric therapy (see, for example, Reynolds 1969), Zen training, religious rituals of individual reform (Wimberley 1969), and practices of therapy for criminals in Japan illustrates a simple lesson, namely, that educational efforts which seek some kind of character change or improvement are perhaps best

studied within a single theoretical framework, one that will also adequately account for other kinds of psychological transformations. At various points in the training reported here, for example, anxiety or deprivation was artificially intensified and then reduced, creating a strong sense of relief and catharsis which served to strengthen certain intended directions of change in a trainee's view of himself and of his relationship with society. The parallels between education and such processes as initiation, therapy, and conversion would deserve more attention.

(4) Whether the bank's program is to be labelled education, initiation, socialization, conversion, or therapy is not, however, a profitable question to ask, except as it illustrates the pitfalls of viewing education as equivalent with schooling. There is a strong academic inclination to understand education as verbal instruction leading to improved storage and manipulation of symbolic information. This is what explicitly happens in schools between teachers and students. Yet learning and maturation may be sponsored by many means, not just verbal instruction. *Seishin kyooiku* emphasizes experience and the development of spiritual strength. There are, no doubt, many other valued avenues of human growth which are as unlike Japanese spiritual education as they are unlike classroom instruction. The use of various hallucinogenic drugs to educate religious initiates and train practitioners is one widespread example.

Just as the study of kinship began to make notable headway only after considerable skepticism arose about the ethnocentricity of the concerns and impulses which originally gave it momentum, so the anthropology of education could benefit from a reexamination of its implicit understanding of education.

Notes

1. This is my estimate based on (1) correspondence with the Industrial Training Association of Japan concerning the number of their members practicing *seishin kyooiku,* (2) reports reaching me or the bank about other company training programs, and (3) mention in magazines, newspapers, and on television of the increase of *seishin kyooiku* in companies.

2. The material on company *seishin kyooiku* of a descriptive nature in Japanese includes articles in Nakamura (1966), the special issue entitled "Seishin Kyooiku Tokushuu" of the magazine *Sangyoo Kunren* (1968), and Rohlen (1969, 1970a). In English, there is only Rohlen (1970b, 1971) for descriptive information. There are, however, a large number of books in English that describe educational methods in Japan that come under the broad heading of *seishin kyooiku.* They include the writing on sports training, Zen, and pre-war education. Of special interest is Minami (1953:136–167) for his discussion of wartime spiritualism. Benedict (1946) also discusses training and discipline in her analysis of Japanese character.

3. See, for example, Nitobe (1905), Benedict (1946), Suzuki (1959), and Minami (1953). Unfortunately, explanations of Japanese arts and sports in English seldom mention the *seishin* foundations or much of their methodology.

4. This study of the company's training program was part of a general study of the ideology and social organization of the bank which has been reported in Rohlen (1971).

5. For an account of this see Hall (1949).

6. Kapleau (1965) offers a thorough account of the procedures and philosophy of *rinzai* Zen, the same sect as the temple visited by the trainees. Suzuki (1965) describes something of the life in a Zen temple where training is conducted.

7. Toland (1970) mentions the Edajima tradition as it affected Japanese military spirit during World War II.

8. The term *seishin* has many applications, including *seishin no ai* (platonic love), *seishin bunseki* (psychoanalysis), *seishin kagaku* (mental science), and *dokuritsu seishin* (the spirit of independence). Many of these are Japanese translations of foreign concepts and perhaps it is not correct to argue for a single meaning for the word, yet, once the broad, inclusive perspective of human psychology at the foundation of the *seishin* concept is grasped the differences among the various applications recede in significance. My understanding is that *seishin* is a universal, human quality. Its character, strength, and development are relative to such factors as culture, education, experience, and the individual.

9. Many of the most commonly encountered values about personality, such as expressed by *nintai* (fortitude), *gaman* (patience), *shimboo* (endurance), *gambaru* (tenacity), and the like point to this form of behavior. Of course, loyalty is hardly meaningful without the ingredient of persistence.

10. Here I have in mind the expressions *kokoro-gamae, taido, kokoro no mochikata,* and *mono no kangaekata,* all of which translate as attitude.

11. To receive or accept in a *sunao* manner. *Sunao* is translated as gentle, obedient, and honest.

12. In the case of bank training, *sekinin* (responsibility) is frequently used, but the concepts *on* (beneficence), *giri* (obligation), and *gimu* (duty), emphasized by Benedict (1946) are seldom heard. My impression, however, is that *sekinin* is often used to support the same behavioral patterns that *gimu* and *giri* allegedly supported in the pre-war company situation.

Cultural Stress, Psychotherapies, and Resocialization

Editorial Note to Part Four

THE previous parts of this volume referred to dominant, normative patterns of values, behavior, and socialization shared among Japanese. Nonetheless, not all Japanese follow, nor does any individual always follow, the normative model. Furthermore, no person is entirely immune from one or another form of incapacitation detrimental to normative conduct. Part 4 is concerned, first, with some forms of deviation which are considered attributable to cultural stress or inadequacies in training or learning experience. Second, and in conjunction with the first, we are concerned with some of the culturally derived methods of psychotherapy or resocialization employed to straighten out the deviants, to cure mental and somatic illnesses, or more generally to transform the self-identity of the afflicted person.

Some of the common sources of stress and tension in Japanese culture leading to frustration, anxiety, and potential conflict might be surmised by what has been covered so far in the first three parts. Surely one striking feature is the high emphasis placed on achievement. It commences early in life with the *kyōiku* mama (education-obsessed mothers) and with the child being socialized for high achievement. Japan is not alone among the modern industrial (and postindustrial) societies in this respect, but on any comparative basis one must be impressed by the series of "examination hells" facing students and by the many who devote long hours to cram *(juku)* school study. The scores of Japanese students in international testing, especially in math and the sciences, well attest to the outcome. But as we have seen, school phobia and violence toward parents have emerged as part of the price paid for these attainments. De Vos (1978:256) has commented that Japanese are a people "unduly concerned with standards of excellence." This does not end with schooling, but extends to other spheres of life as well. The concept of "Zero Defect" in manufacturing, though an American innovation, appears to have been avidly seized upon by the Japanese, particularly notable in the precise production requirements of memory chips.

High demands for achievement and for observance of excellence in performance are offset by and also conflict with the requirements of the social group. Doi has discussed in chapter 8 the emphasis on mutual dependency in Japanese culture. Viewed from an American perspective the Japanese appear to have much higher affiliative proclivities. Ties with family, classmates, and co-workers appear stronger, more enduring (and more binding). Within the group there are demands for harmony and conformity, and here individual pursuit of self-interest is strongly disvalued. Accepting responsibility and respecting obligations are valued positively. In return the group provides its support and an identity for the individual; a consistent failure to measure up warrants the threat of withdrawal of support, even ostracism. Ideally, as Doi notes, there is a balancing of *on* and *amae* in Japanese society; prolonged frustration of *amae* may lead to neurosis, but unbridled *amae* may result in a weak self-identity.

Lanham (chap. 16) indicates that Japanese teachers attempt to restrain impulsivity in their students, in effect putting a damper on spontaneity. And the outsider living in Japan is repeatedly struck by the numbers and frequency of formulaic, highly stereotypic rituals which apply both in speech and in so many social situations. These may seem, especially at first, onerous and controlling and, of course, to a degree they are, but these also facilitate predictability, certainty, ease, and minimize potential discomfort in social relationships. From any relative perspective the Japanese seem more socially bounded than most Westerners, highly sensitized to even the minor nuances of social relationships.

In the consideration of responses to cultural stress, some reference must be made to the subject of suicide, which has not been separately treated in this volume. Contrary to what frequently appears in the popular press, the Japanese do not have the highest suicide rate in the world, although the rate was high during the early post–World War II period. However, some features of Japanese suicide do stand out. Most notable was the highly ritualized samurai practice of hara-kiri imposed by the authorities for a violation of law, resorted to as a protest against authority, or undertaken in military defeat to avoid the humiliation of capture. Among the members of this class, suicide was an honorable action. Equally noteworthy is the practice of joint suicide (in actuality, usually murder and suicide) involving lovers, mother and child, or a whole family. These receive considerable attention in the popular press. In brief, suicide in Japan has been viewed from a substantially different perspective than in the West. Another distinctive feature of Japanese suicide has been the age pattern, which tends to display peak periods in late teens, early twenties, and again in old age. Caudill and Plath (chap.

15) note that Japanese suicide seems to rise during periods of sleeping alone, after leaving the parental bed and prior to marriage, and again after the decease of a spouse. (We should note, however, that lately the suicide rate has declined among youth and risen among middle-aged men, a pattern similar to the Western one.)

Psychotherapy, a form of treatment for mental, behavioral, and psychosomatic disorders, has many forms, not the least of which is religiotherapy. Indeed, religion is perhaps the oldest of cures. Although contemporary Japan has national health insurance, modern hospitals, and several thousand medical psychiatrists, religious psychotherapies continue to flourish. In chapter 19 Sasaki states that while shamans as traditional folk healers may still be found in many areas, the so-called new religions are clearly the most important of the nonmedical therapies today. He and his colleagues at the Tokyo Metropolitan Mental Health Center found that approximately 44 percent of their patients professed some religious faith, and of these 83 percent were followers of one of the new religions. Their research revealed that many of these patients were taking religious and medical treatments simultaneously. Moreover, it was found that remarkably favorable results could be obtained for neurotics through participation in some of the magicoreligious cults. Surprisingly, even some of the epileptics suffering grand mal attacks had felt themselves improved by this means.

Chapter 20 by Takie Sugiyama Lebra describes the process of psychotherapy in one of these new religious cults which claims a high therapeutic efficacy through "self-reconstruction" of members. A large percentage of the ritual participants were females. Self-reconstruction involved four aspects: self-accusation (I am to blame for whatever ails me), allocentric attribution (I owe you for the benefit I am enjoying), identity interchange (I am you, and you are me), and expurgation (cleansing of self, physically and mentally). Lebra suggests that during spirit possession taking the role of a helpless spirit may gratify the *amae* wish. It is to be noted here and later in the discussion of Morita and Naikan therapies that renunciation of ego appears to be a critical feature.

Munakata in chapter 21 presents a summary overview of Japanese attitudes toward mental illness and mental health treatment. There appears to be a considerable reluctance to acknowledge, let alone accept, mental and/or behavioral factors as causal. Instead, the preference is for physiological explanations. Moreover, society prefers to view mental and behavioral anomalies as departures from the norm which are largely self-corrective by the individual or with help of the family. Consequently, when mental illness occurs, the first inclination is not to seek psychiatric assistance, but to contain the illness within the family and to shore up the afflicted person with encouragement. Needless to say, this may not be the most beneficial course of action for the sick person. Another factor impeding early recognition and treatment of mental illness is the continuing prejudice of the public, which views such illness as hereditary. Therefore, the social position of the family and marriageability of its members may be impaired by this stigma. The net consequence is that the Japanese family not only tends to delay seeking effective treatment and hospitalization for their mentally ill member, but their continued coping efforts often prove futile, resulting in discouragement and frustration. Acceptance of psychotherapy thus often comes as a final act of despair.

Considerable efforts are apparently directed toward selecting a congenial doctor, willing to take over and accept complete responsibility for the patient. The doctor is cast in the role of family head with the family members assuming subordinate positions. Mental hospitals in Japan are relatively small and privately owned, Munakata indicates, so that a near familylike atmosphere can be maintained and the large bureaucratized, prisonlike character of some Western mental hospitals avoided. Once hospitalized for mental illness, Japanese patients tend to remain for much longer periods than their counterparts in Western countries. This may be accounted for by at least two principal factors—the long delay in obtaining treatment may have impeded recovery, and the continuing social prejudice toward the mentally ill may have led to virtual abandonment of the patient by his or her family. Such is the strength of this prejudice that doctors frequently resort to a "disguised diagnosis," giving the disorder a more innocent label and thus sparing the patient and family both psychological shock and social stigma.

The psychiatrist Yomishi Kasahara describes in chapter 22 one type of common neuroses among young people in Japan: the phobia of interpersonal relations. Specifically discussed are the fear of eye-to-eye confrontation and the fear of emitting body odors offensive to others. In this type of neurosis patients feel themselves to be repulsive to others (as well as to themselves). This is in contrast to our common interpretation of phobia as unrealistic fear of something, such as height, the outdoors, cats, and so on. In explanation of the cultural embeddedness of these, Kasahara suggests that the preferred mode of communication among Japanese is nonverbal and indirect, Japanese esteeming vague expressions and avoiding frankness. The concern with bodily odor (while this is surely not unique to Japanese, the frequency of clinical occurrence appears to be so), he speculates, may derive from religious notions of purity and from the general attitude that odorlessness is preferable to fragrance.

In the final section of this chapter, Morita psychotherapy, associated with the treatment of these phobias of interpersonal relations, is briefly described. Morita therapy, like Naikan, is a distinctly Japanese creation, and has two features in the therapeutic process which stand out. The first is the initial confinement of the patient with bed rest, isolation, and without verbal communication (even contact with the physician is by means of a diary). The second feature is that cause of or elimination of symptoms does not figure in the treatment; life history analysis does not take place, and the unconscious is not probed, quite contrastive to Western psychoanalytic thinking. Rather, the patient is enjoined to accommodate, to adjust, and to accept. Parenthetically, it should be noted that Freudian psychoanalysis has found little favor in Japan.

In his conclusion, Kasahara, who has had extensive clinical experience with university students, notes that these symptoms are not decreasing, but he expresses doubt as to the continued acceptance of Morita treatment methods and expects that psychiatry may be facing a critical period in the treatment of phobias of interpersonal relations. Whatever the case may be on the campuses, a recent study (Mori 1985) from the Morita Clinic of Jikei University, a leading center for Morita practice, revealed most patients were young, of high educational background, and predominantly office workers or students.

In chapter 23 Takao Murase gives a view of a uniquely Japanese psychotherapy which has its historical origins in Buddhism. The principal procedure rests upon concentrated meditation, directed toward introspection. The patient is enjoined to look inward, to think of self in terms of the benevolences received from significant others, especially parents, teachers, boss, and the like, and to reflect on how poorly these were repaid. The moral burden is placed fully upon the patient. Attempts to blame a neglectful mother or a self-centered father are brushed aside, and instead the patient is persuaded to acknowledge his or her failure to recognize the benevolence bestowed by others. Not uncommonly, tearful confessions of guilt occur. Ideally, the patient should emerge more selfless, more ready to live for others. Personality change is less an expectable outcome than a correction of attitude, a willingness to accept responsibilities and be accommodative in social relationships. Naikan, according to its adherents, has had its greatest success with delinquents, criminals, alcoholics, drug users, and some neurotics. At least one American therapist (Reynolds 1983) has been experimenting with its use among American patients.

19

Nonmedical Healing in Contemporary Japan: A Psychiatric Study

YUJI SASAKI

IT is well known that Japan, though extensively modernized and Westernized, still retains many practices bequeathed from the past. For instance, modern medicine, which was introduced in the late nineteenth century and which has since grown enormously under official sanction, does not seem to prevent a large number of people from flocking to various nonmedical healers. Moreover, it appears that though nonmedical practices are increasing with modernization rather than diminishing, it is very difficult to obtain proof of this, especially in the field of mental health. The question occurs as to why such methods of healing would flourish with modernization.

On December 9, 1970, a murder case was reported in the Japanese newspapers. The caption was "Mother's faith in shaman killed her son. Superstition never dies out."

> A carpenter's wife, 47 years old, in Aomori Prefecture had worried about her 18-year-old son's headache, which had not improved despite various medical treatments. One day she asked an *itako,* a kind of shaman [Sasaki 1969], to cure his headache. The shaman diagnosed it as possession by an evil spirit. In order to exorcise the evil spirit the family forced him to fast for three consecutive days, and then beat him on the head and face again and again. The son failed to respond to their efforts and died.

I read a newspaper account of such a death, induced by a shaman, at least once or twice a year even now, but unreported incidents may be even more common. In addition, the various sectarian newspapers regularly report many miraculous cures: "Thanks to faith, I am cured of diabetes mellitus . . . schizophrenia . . . gastric cancer" et cetera.

This might suggest that nonmedical healing has reached full bloom in

Reprinted from *Culture-Bound Syndromes, Ethnopsychiatry, and Alternate Therapies,* vol. 4 of *Mental Health Research in Asia and the Pacific,* ed. W. P. Lebra. An East-West Center Book. © 1976 The University Press of Hawaii.

Japan. As a matter of fact, if we add up the number of believers claimed by each sect, the number of sectarian adherents amounts to one and a half times the total population. However, according to a recent sociological field survey (Nishihira et al. 1970), the actual number of present-day participants is perhaps no more than 20 percent of the population, with another 10 percent marginal. Nonetheless, in times of trouble people frequently become religious, and there is an illustrative proverb, "Once on the shore, we pray no more," which probably holds true for about 60 percent of the population, according to Nishihira (1970). Whatever the actual state of affairs may be, there can be no doubt that those who have a psychological problem often turn to religion. My report on this phenomenon derives from a field survey of religious healing on an island community and from a study of healing practices in two new religious sects.

Religious Healing on Hachijo Island

In 1961, my colleagues and I (Akimoto et al. 1964) made an epidemiological and social-psychiatric field survey of Hachijo Island. Hachijo is an island located 300 kilometers south of Tokyo in the Pacific Ocean, with an area of 70 square kilometers and a population of 12,000. The island can be divided into two districts: area A, more urbanized, lies in the open area of the central part of the island; area B is a rural, highland community. In brief, A is the town, and B the village.

One hundred seventy-five psychiatric patients were found on the island. Curiously enough, the percentage of medically treated cases in district A was lower than in district B (32.5 percent vs. 44.9 percent). Analysis of various factors such as psychiatric diagnosis, age, occupation, economic status, and level of education could not explain this difference. The attitude toward religion appeared to be the significant factor to be taken into account.

We undertook to determine the percentage of families with religious adherents in districts A and B in terms of presence or absence of medical patients, somatic patients, psychiatric patients, and schizophrenic patients. Our random sample included approximately one-fifth of the families (households) on Hachijo. Respondents were asked if they, or any member of their family, had ever been treated by folk healers such as shamans or other religious practitioners or by participation in religious cult healings. We were concerned that the answers to such a query might not be too reliable, for Japanese, unlike Americans, are usually resistant to attitude sampling and evasive in their responses. So we also asked, "Apart from healing, have you or your family ever visited a sha-

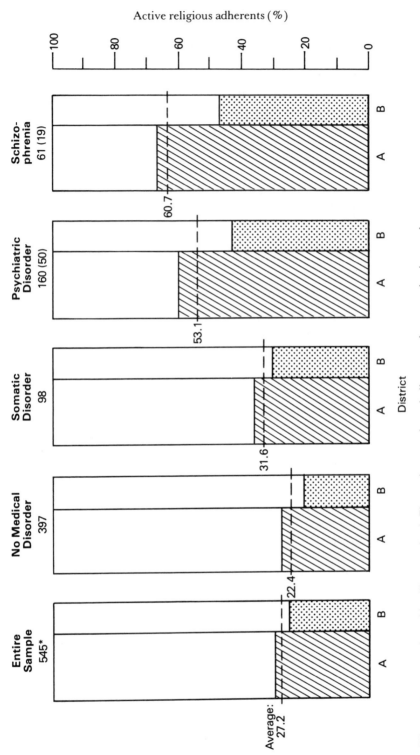

Active religious adherents (%)

District

Schizo-phrenia 61 (19)

Psychiatric Disorder 160 (50)

Somatic Disorder 98

No Medical Disorder 397

Entire Sample 545*

60.7

53.1

31.6

22.4

Average: 27.2

*Figures denote number of families examined. Figures in parentheses indicate number occurring in sample.

Districts A & B compared by active religious adherence and medical disorder in family

man?" and "Do you or your family have faith in some religion?" If they answered Yes they were counted as believers.

An average of 27.2 percent of the random sample of families indicated a religious commitment. When we compare the other four family groups—families without patients, with somatic patients, with psychiatric patients, and with schizophrenic patients—we can see that religious involvement rises with sickness, and especially so with psychiatric problems. Moreover, 66 percent of the believers in our random sample gave sickness as the motivation for becoming active religious adherents.

We also found a marked difference in religious commitment between districts A and B. Although that difference among the randomly sampled families was merely 4.4 percent and did not seem very significant, it increased to 20 percent among families with schizophrenic patients. This might indicate that patients in district B have access to more medical attention, but it is more likely, we feel, that the number of people who prefer to take recourse to, and/or who have access to, magico-religious practices is relatively greater in the urbanized segment than in the rural segment of the population.

I have good reason to believe that the foregoing findings for Hachijo Island can be taken as representative of contemporary Japan as a whole. In fact, this was corroborated at the Tokyo Metropolitan Mental Health Center, where I worked from 1966 to 1971. The facts that 44 percent of the cases at the center professed some faith in religion and that 83 percent of them belonged to one of the new religions indicate the importance of religion among urban mental patients. Therefore, religious healing has vital significance for mental-health professionals. For this reason we have given our attention to research on the new religions and their healing activities.

Healing in Two Contemporary Religious Sects

Although Japan has a variety of traditional folk therapies, those employed by the new religions can be regarded as the most important of the nonmedical therapies. Previously, my colleagues and I (Fujisawa et al. 1966) reported on several sects and their healing practices. Here I shall present two contrasting sects, S and K, as illustrative (see Table 1).

Sect S. Sect S is one of the largest new religions in contemporary Japan, claiming a membership of 1.5 million. It has a systematic doctrine, whereas Sect K is a small regional cult. At the 10-day summer training camp of Sect S, we administered 359 questionnaires. From among the 127 respondents who stated that they came to the camp to be cured of their illness, we interviewed and diagnosed 70 at the beginning of the camp and followed up on 59 of them at the end of the camp.

Table 1. Characteristics of Sects S and K

Characteristic	Sect S	Sect K
Doctrine	Systematic	Nonsystematic
Organization	National	Local
Number of adherents	1,500,000	About 500
Notion of cause of sickness	A shadow on the mind	Imbalance of mind and body
Notion of healing	Be thankful for everything	Accelerate metabolism, drive out toxin, absorb spirit of cosmos
Methods of healing	Lecture and discussion of personal experience; ritual activities	Kahli massage, spiritual-wave therapy

Among the latter group the case of a 48-year-old female, a beauty specialist, with an anxiety neurosis, may serve as illustrative.

On the second day of the training camp, she stated, "I have always been dissatisfied with my husband because of his stubborn personality. A few years ago my son joined the student movement *(zengakuren)*, since then I began to have palpitations and the fear of death every night. In spite of various medical and psychiatric treatments, my anxiety didn't get any better, and I was almost forced by a friend to join Sect S." At the second interview on the ninth day, her anxiety and sad expression were gone. She spoke with confidence and animation, "I have felt myself getting better these past several days. At last I could find the cause of my sickness. It is me! I am guilty! I have been lacking in gratitude to my husband. I will do my best for him after the camp. As for my heart, it can't be sick because it was created by God. I am no longer anxious, although I have some palpitations still." Six months after the camp, when we inquired how she was, she answered, "Quite well."

What actually happened at this training camp? It might be termed a severe brainwashing exercise in two parts. One part consists of lectures and confessions of personal experiences. Here the doctrine is strongly emphasized that the real man is harmonious and perfect, without sickness. The other part consists of religious rites that are, in effect, a combination of group therapy and work therapy.

Early every morning a loudspeaker awakens all the participants with religious songs. They salute one another, saying *Arigatō gozaimasu* ("Thank you very much"), with their hands pressed together in prayer. A variety of ritual activities, cleverly arranged, follow one after another. The rhythmic prayer *kanzen enman jissō* ("perfection, harmony, and real life") is repeated frequently. In the "laughter training" sessions the leader forces the participants to laugh. In other sessions they stand facing each other and pray that one another's unhappiness will diminish. As the sessions progress, the atmosphere of the camp becomes charged with excitement. In particular, the participants are enormously moved by their confessions of personal experiences, thus becoming highly suggestible and susceptible to cure.

Sect K. Sect K is a small local group with several hundred followers grouped around a healer in the suburbs of Tokyo. We have studied this sect from 1964 until the present, and we have followed up with periodic interviews 41 selected cases who visited the healer during the summer of 1965.

As shown in Table 1, the healing methods of Sect K are principally two, Kahli massage and spiritual-wave therapy. Kahli massage, which is derived from Yoga, consists of violent massage using a coinlike piece of metal after the entire body has first been covered with vegetable oil. This obtains from the sect doctrine that sickness is cured by driving the toxin out of the body by accelerating blood circulation and metabolism. In spiritual-wave therapy, the healer stands apart from the worshipers and holds up her hands, which are thought to transmit the spirit of the cosmos to the adherents through her fingertips. The whole or a part of the patient's body begins to vibrate spontaneously, which is called spiritual movement. During violent spiritual movement the patient is considered to be in a state of trance. Prior to treatment the suggestion is given to the patient that the sick part will move most violently. Here one case may suffice as illustrative.

A 52-year-old female, the wife of a farmer, had cancer phobia. Ten years before, her grandfather and her father had died of cancer in succession. Since then, suffering from nausea and hyperexia, she has visited many physicians one after another in her fear of gastric cancer. She received many diagnoses such as gastritis, gastric ulcer, gastroptosis, and even a clean bill of health. The differences in diagnosis made her more and more anxious, and she lost considerable weight. She was finally induced to enter the sect at her neighbor's suggestion.

The healer confidently diagnosed her condition. "Don't take any medicine, because it is toxic. You can eat everything. Your stomach is not sick." The confident diagnosis by the healer and the warm welcome by her "therapeutic brothers and sisters" quickly reduced her anxiety. She received both Kahli massage and spiritual-wave therapy, and as she entered into the spirit of the movement, her trust in the healer became very strong. She developed a good appetite and became quite happy.

Table 2 compares the characteristics of the cases we studied in Sects S and K. In terms of medical diagnosis, as shown in Table 3, more psychiatric disorders are found in Sect S, whereas in Sect K more somatic cases are found. This may be because a kind of physical therapy, Kahli massage, is employed by Sect K. As is shown in Table 4, which gives the effects of the sects' healing practices, remarkably favorable changes in neurotic clients are produced in both sects. Only epilepsy became worse as a result of the treatment. During the training period the two epileptics, who had discontinued taking their drugs, suffered grand mal attacks. Curiously enough, they felt happy despite their attacks and insisted that even epilepsy could be cured when their faith became more earnest. This poses a real problem for psychiatrists to think about. As to types of neuroses, hypochondria strikingly is dominant in Sect K, whereas no single type is so clearly predominant in Sect S, as is shown in Table 5.

For some adherents high expectations of being healed through cult participation are crucial factors, and they enter the faith willingly after many disappointments with long-term medical treatments. But these cases account for only a few, and the majority of our cases followed a course of taking both medical treatment and participating in cult healing. Such a practical course of action may be true of most of those who are ill among the followers of new religions in Japan. Unfortunately, there are some individuals who endanger their lives by consulting the healer without receiving any medical treatment, but their numbers are not great.

As to the question of how the patient's expectation is related to the effect of healing, we believed that there must be a close relationship but the results proved us wrong. The process of brainwashing was so skillfully designed that the results seemed almost inevitable, as if the adherents were traveling on a conveyer belt. In terms of the dynamics of psychotherapy the healing process has four stages. Stage one involves entrance into the faith and the process of acceptance. By having one's suffering accepted by others, one gains a new feeling of belonging. In stage two, intense relationships with the healer and the congregation develop. Some obtain a kind of oceanic feeling of unification with the cosmos, as in the second case described; some develop a great sense of gratitude toward others, as did the first case we described. Obligations and responsibilities toward the ancestors are utilized to the utmost. In stage three, conversion may take place, induced by suggestion and doctrine. The convert gains a new kind of insight and acquires a new sense of moral responsibility. Complete healing, the fourth stage, can only be achieved, it is believed, when one leads a religious life.

Table 2. Characteristics of Cases Interviewed

Characteristic	Sect S	Sect K
Number of cases	70 (23 male, 47 female)	41 (11 male, 30 female)
Distribution	national	local
Average age	34.0	46.5
Educational attainment (within compulsory education)	29.0%	53.8%
Occupation	various (6.6% farmer)	50.0% farmer

Table 3. Psychiatric Diagnosis of Cases Studied

Diagnosis	Sect S	Sect K
Schizophrenia	11	0
Schizophrenia?	0	1
Epilepsy	2	0
Neurosis	25	12
Alcoholism	2	0
Psychopathy	3	0
Organic psychosis	0	5
Somatic disease	19	23
Other*	8	0
Total	70	41

* These persons were in good health themselves but were participating on behalf of sick members of their families.

Table 4. Effect of Healing

Disorder	Change for the Worse	No Change	Some Change for the Better	Hard to Judge	Total
Sect S:					
Schizophrenia	0	6	4	0	10
Epilepsy	2	0	0	0	2
Neurosis	0	6	17	0	23
Alcoholics	0	0	0	2	2
Psychopathy	0	0	0	3	3
Somatic disease	0	15	3	1	19
Subtotal	2	27	24	6	59
Sect K:					
Schizophrenia?	0	0	1	0	1
Neurosis	0	1	11	0	12
Organic psychosis	0	3	2	0	5
Somatic disease	0	9	14	0	23
Subtotal	0	13	28	0	41
Total	2	40	52	6	100

Table 5. Disorders of Neurosis and Effect of Healing

Disorder	Number	No Change	Some Change for the Better
Sect S:			
Nervosity	6	1	5
Hypochondria	8	1	7
Anxiety Neurosis	5	4	1
Hysteria	4	0	4
Subtotal	23	6	17 (74%)
Sect K:			
Hypochondria	11	1	10
Anxiety Neurosis	1	0	1
Subtotal	12	1	11 (91%)
Total	35	7	28 (80%)

Summary

In Japan, despite modernization and Westernization, a large number of people are flocking to various nonmedical healers, especially among the new religions. Field studies and clinical experience have indicated that those who have a psychiatric problem seem especially inclined to take recourse to magico-religious cures. Moreover, it appears that the numbers of psychiatric cases pursuing such practices are relatively greater in the urban areas than in the rural. The question immediately occurs as to why such methods of healing would flourish with the availability of modern medicine. My field research and follow-up studies of selected cases reveal that remarkably favorable changes among neurotics can be achieved by magico-religious practices, and particularly by participation in some of the new religious cults that offer healing. Religious conversion apparently produces a beneficial change for neurotics by facilitating greater self-insight, social awareness, and moral responsibility. Comparing the insight induced through analytically oriented psychotherapy with that induced through religious conversion is a worthy subject for further research.

20

Self-Reconstruction in Japanese Religious Psychotherapy

TAKIE SUGIYAMA LEBRA

Introduction

PSYCHOTHERAPY as a form of persuasion must satisfy two general conditions to achieve its efficacy. First, its repertoire of messages, whether in diagnosis or treatment, must be embedded in the culture of its client so that it can tap his memory stored through enculturation. Second, the therapeutic messages, while they should thus sound familiar, also need to offer something novel or even stunning to arouse their receiver's curiosity and to capture his imagination. One way of combining these two prerequisites is to single out, simplify, elaborate, or exaggerate a segment of the total cultural fund. Most of the religious cults in Japan, which are known for their claimed records of healing and deliverance of sufferers, utilize this method. This paper focuses on one of these cults and analyzes the experiences of its members with reference to their "self-reconstruction."

The therapeutic or "divine" messages of the cult, which are meant to induce self-reconstruction, are deeply embedded in Japanese culture, particularly in its moral values. At the same time, they hyperbolize what the average Japanese would believe and practice. This is why outsiders—non-member Japanese—tend to be ambivalent toward the cult: on the one hand, they are impressed with the strong faith and moral commitment exhibited by the cult members; but on the other, they find the member's behavior odd, eccentric, or even "insane." This hyperbole turns out, as we shall see, to involve a bias for feminine values.

Although data are drawn from this particular cult, it is assumed that what is presented here can hold for most other healing cults in terms of the underlying belief systems, if not specific therapeutic techniques and, to an extent, for non-religious ethnopsychotherapies as well.

Reprinted from *Cultural Conceptions of Mental Health and Therapy*, ed. A. J. Marsella and G. M. White, 269–283. Copyright © 1982 by D. Reidel Publishing Company, Dordrecht, Holland.

The Cult and Data Gathering

The cult, which was introduced in my previous papers (Lebra 1974b, 1976a, 1976c) as the Salvation Cult, is actually called Gedatsukai, meaning "a society for deliverance." Founded in 1929 by a former businessman, Gedatsukai (or simply Gedatsu hereafter) not only survived the disastrous Second World War but has expanded as one of hundreds of "new religions" under the religious hospitality of postwar Japan. According to its own report in 1975, its membership rose to nearly 200,000, with more than 400 "teachers" engaging in missionary work at some 360 churches or branches (Japan, Bunkacho 1976). The founder, who died in 1948, is deified by his followers as "Sonja" (the most venerable one), or "Kongosama" derived from his posthumous name, "Gedatsu Kongo."

The Gedatsu is listed in the Shukyo Nenkan (yearbook of religions, published by Bunkacho, the Cultural Agency of the Japanese Government) as one of the Shingon Buddhist sects. The more amorphous sect called Shugendo, "the way of mastering magico-religous power" (Earhart 1970:ix), is also associated with Gedatsu's origins. According to Gedatsu superintendent Kishida (1964:56, and personal communication), the founder trained in the Shugendo and mastered magico-religious power, including that of healing. The Shugendo, supposedly started by a legendary figure called En no Ozunu in the late seventh century, represents a union of all religions—native and alien—with mystic emphasis. This eclectic legacy was fully inherited by the Gedatsu in that it accepts all conceivable supernatural entities as objects of worship. Gedatsu altars are occupied by imported Buddhas, native Shinto kami, dead humans, and the like. While national Shinto, as embodied by the Sun Goddess and her "descendants" (emperors), runs through its tenets, the Gedatsu is also faithful to local Shinto shrines which are generally identified as *ujigami,* and to the countless local kami (deities) associated with particular places or objects such as the water deity. Among animal deities, the fox and the snake are most often mentioned. Although the Gedatsu is preoccupied with the supernatural world and receptive to the mystic aspects of Taoism, the secular moral doctrine of Confucianism comprises an important part of Gedatsu teaching as well. Like all other Japanese cults, it manipulates the magical appeal of Chinese ideographs.

Most suggestive of its connection with the Shugendo and esoteric Shingon Buddhism is the possession ritual which is treasured as "unique" to the Gedatsu. In a dramatic setting in front of an altar, a leader, as a mediator between the spiritual and human worlds, invokes a spirit to enter a human host who is a member afflicted with illness or other disturbances and who seeks an explanation or treatment. Signaling its arrival by the sudden shaking of the hands of the host holding a charm, the spirit responds through the mouth of the host to the solicitous questions and requests of the mediator. The spirit thus discloses its identity—e.g., an ancestor, kami, or fox; male or female; its name, and so on. Oftentimes, as I observed, communication is facilitated by the mediator's offer of a binary choice of a yes or no answer as well as by sign communication allowed for a reticent spirit: the mediator may ask, "Are you an ancestor or kami? If you are a kami, raise your hands over your head; if an ancestor, stretch your hands straight forward." Once rapport is thus established, the spirit will reveal why its host is suffering from a particular problem, and give an instruction of what to do. When its message-providing mission is felt completed, the spirit is thanked and asked to return where it came from. If unwilling to leave, the spirit will receive *kundoki* (reproach) from the mediator. The whole ritual may be conducted by the mediator and host alone, but often is displayed like a theatrical performance in front of other members.

Intensive fieldwork was conducted during the summers of 1970 and 1971, centering around two ward branches of Eastern City, a provincial tourist town in central Japan. Membership of the two branches together was then estimated at about 200, each branch headed by an elderly woman. Young members were not totally absent—they were mostly children of the members—but a great majority was between the ages of 40 and 70.

The sex ratio of the participants varied depending upon the situations or activities. In registered membership, the number of women only doubled that of men (partly because some women still were in the habit of identifying themselves by the names of the househeads), but the attendance at branch meetings was in the ratio of about one to five in favor of female members; furthermore, in smaller, sub-branch gatherings and informal activities women were even more predominant. Conversely, "lecturers" sent from the cult's headquarters (honbu) in Tokyo or from prefectual divisions were almost all male; so were the counsellors or teaching staff who were giving advice to the pilgrims at Goreichi (the cult's central shrine complex in Saitama Prefecture). The meeting at the headquarters which I observed was attended by about 500 people with a ratio of one male to four females: the greater male representation here than at the local ward branches reflects the likelihood that more leaders attended the headquarters meetings. In short, it may be surmised that women are more predominant and active at a local level, in informal activities, or in the capacity of the rank and file; whereas their preponderance decreases at the center of the cult, in more formal, public activities, and is totally replaced by male predominance in central administration and teaching roles. It seems that males are motivated by chances for leadership to join or stay in the cult. Except for the central leadership, however, female predominance, in varying degrees, was observed in all situations and activities. This sex imbalance was a topic of discussion at a local meeting of ward "officers." The only male among 13 participants complained saying, "The most fundamental problem is that men do not attend. Whatever you say, after all it's men [who really count]. We must reflect upon our fault over this matter." The female officers agreed and admitted that male participation would be a measure of success of a ward branch.

Fieldwork included observations of meetings and rituals, participation in conversation with local members and leaders during intervals of formal activities, and interviews with 16 individuals (including two males). In addition, I observed activities at the headquarters and Goreichi, and interviewed several leaders and teachers stationed there. The cult's publications, especially members' autobiographical reports of their Gedatsu-inspired experiences which appear in every issue of the cult's monthly called *Gedatsu*,[1] were also consulted.

Aspects of Self-Reconstruction in Gedatsu Therapy
Self-Accusation

One of the primary messages which a Gedatsu inductee or member (female, unless otherwise specified) receives through her exposure to leaders, other members, meetings, rituals, or publications is that she blame herself for whatever plight she is experiencing. This pressure for self-accusation is deeply embedded in the Japanese moral system. De Vos found, in the TAT responses by a sample of rural Japanese, self-blame as a major reaction to stress. For example: "A husband comes home very late at night; the wife thinks it is for lack of her affection and tries hard; he finally reforms" (De Vos [1960] 1974:128); "An elder brother did something wrong and is examined by the policeman; he will be taken to the police station, but will return home and reform. The younger sister also thinks that she was wrong herself" (129). Sofue (1979:20) also delineates the Japanese "intropunitive" tendency on the basis of his sentence-completion-test results: in response to "I could not do it because . . ." the Japanese respondents tended to attribute the failure to the actor's fault such as "because I am not yet competent enough." The Japanese in general are socialized to reflect upon themselves *(hansei)* instead of accusing someone else suspected to be the source of frustration. A weekly hour of *hansei* used to be part of the school curriculum. *Hansei* is supposed to lead to guilt consciousness, remorsefulness, and apology. Lanham (1979:13) points out that a common ending of a story appearing in moral-education textbooks is a request for forgiveness or an apology, and that Little Red Riding Hood in a Japanese version has the fox tearfully ask for forgiveness.

As a step toward self-reconstruction, a Gedatsu member is persuaded not only to conform to this cultural norm of self-accusation but to go further in this direction. One's suffering is to be understood as a consequence of the sufferer's negligence of her duty as a daughter, wife, mother, descendant, or believer. A woman, suffering from whiplash of the neck vertebrae, learned from her acupuncturist, a member of the sect, that bone injury is caused by the victim's lack of gratitude to the gods. Furthermore, she was told that the location of the injured bone indicates what kind of virtue is deficient: injury above the neck means insufficiency of loyalty *(chu)*, injury above the chest signifies that of filial piety *(ko)*, injury above the abdomen is caused by the lack of benevolence *(jin)*, and so one down to the foot, involving two more virtues— justice *(gi)* and courtesy *(reisetsu)*.

Ego's fault causes others to suffer also. Put another way, one should blame onself if someone else is in misery. In despair over her daughter who had been bedridden with an intestinal disease for 10 years, another informant consulted a Gedatsu teacher and was told that the mother was responsible for the child's illness. Thereupon, "I realized how wrong I had been, felt remorseful, and cried, kneeling to my sleeping daughter so that my head would touch her spirit." The daughter soon recovered, which convinced the mother that a parent's moral defect *is* transferred to the child. The informant's guilt turned out to involve her own responsibility as a daughter and sister: her elder brother, childless, wanted to adopt her as a daughter[2] and lavished fatherly love on her (including giving a bath for her); her father, too, expected her, in order to perpetuate the *ie*, the stem-family household, to stay on with the family as successor to her brother and bring in an adopted husband to marry, instead of her marrying out. Ignoring their wishes, she moved out of her natal house to marry. Her lack of filial devotion *(oya-fuko)* was the cause of her child's affliction, she persuaded herself.

Interpersonal conflicts, as in marital relationships, tend to be attributed to an undesirable characteristic of a member, i.e., a strong ego, greed, aggressiveness, hostility, grudge and the like. She would be told that whatever she saw in her husband, such as his promiscuity, was only a reflection of her own disposition, that her suffering was an indication of the return of a noxious element originally emitted from herself. A victim of someone's aggression, then, should be awakened to her own aggression. This logic I called "the repercussion postulate" in a previous paper (Lebra 1974b). Even when wrongdoing is clearly attributed to another person, it is still ego who must apologize for "allowing the person to commit sin" *(tsumi o tsukuraseta)*.

Self-accusation is sometimes displayed in the possession ritual. The following exchange took place, as I observed, between a local leader as a mediator and a member (retired schoolteacher) as a spirit host. (Note that during the ritual the mediator plays two combined roles: a mediator and the unpossessed half of the host as a substitute since the host herself performs the role of the possessing spirit.)

> *Mediator:* Please show us how you are related to the *bontai* (secular body, namely, the host).
> *Spirit:* Listen, I am the guardian spirit [of the *bontai*]! (This was said in an authoritative, masculine tone.)
> *Mediator:* Thank you, sir, for using me daily. Thank you for your help. Would you like to give me any instruction or request?
> *Spirit:* This is my command to be taken seriously. Do whatever with a strong conviction. Get ready with your belly.[3] I am still displeased with you. You never finish what you start. I am displeased. You are the worst kind. I hate you.
> *Mediator:* I apologize. Please beat me with a whip and use me.

As soon as the ritual was over, the mediator resumed a leader's role which had been suppressed during the ritual, and reinforced the spirit message by telling the *bontai,* the message receiver, that her guardian spirit was really upset by her.

The hyperbolic self-blame is a common theme cutting across most healing cults. A ritual song of Tenrikyo to be chanted daily, for example, includes a passage like "Suffering is rooted in your own mind, blame not others, the fault is yours" (Thomsen 1963:47).

Allocentric Attribution

Paradoxical though it may sound, Japanese morality, along with self-directed aggression, stresses allocentric commitment involving the desirability of sensitivity to other people's feelings. One's experience is to be evaluated from another person's point of view *(aite no tachiba ni naru):* ego is supposed to be sensitive to the harm he may have done to alter. Such allocentricity further involves crediting alter, instead of ego, for a favorable consequence. This is where the ethic of *on* (beneficence) plays a crucial role to sensitize ego as a recipient of *on.* One's achievement should thus be attributed to a countless number of benefactors, known and unknown, alive and dead; every individual is born with an overwhelming debt to his forebears, to begin with (Benedict 1946; Lebra 1974b; Lebra 1976c:101–107). Japanese guilt is anchored in this sense of indebtedness (Lebra 1971).

The causal agent is thus reversed from ego to alter. Self is no longer a subject but an object of action. This ties in with the general passivity and obscurity characterizing the Japanese self. Linguistically, the Japanese speaker often uses the "passive" or the "passive causative" as in "[I] was caused to think . . ." instead of "I thought." Such expressions are not necessarily morally relevant; in fact they could serve as a means of attributing unpleasant outcomes to others as demonstrated by Niyekawa-Howard. In an attempt to establish a correlation between the grammatical options for the "adversative and passive causative" on the one hand and the sense of responsibility, Niyekawa-Howard discovered that "Japanese consistently showed a greater tendency to attribute responsibility to others than any other group tested [German, American, ethnic American]" (Niyekawa-Howard 1968:5).

Allocentric attribution and ego's passivity are elaborated in the Gedatsu, again, to an excessive degree. First, the Gedatsu follower is sensitized to her debts to all conceivable supernatural beings, forebears, people, and natural objects. Particularly important is the *on* owed to Sonja, leaders, fellow-members, especially those who brought one into the Gedatsu. Misfortune is often attributed to a lack of gratitude *(kansha)* as well as to a lack of remorsefulness *(zange)*. *Urami* (grudge) then must be converted into *kansha* and *zange*.

Gratitude is owed not only for a beneficial experience but for an adversity without which one would remain blind to the "truth." So thanks are expressed to a promiscuous husband, a rebellious son, a mean mother-in-law for awakening ego to her oversight, egocentrism, godlessness, and so on; marital disharmony is to be accepted with gratitude as providing an opportunity to discipline oneself, and a child's sickness as a message from the supernatural world which eventually will benefit ego.

Passivity is exaggerated in causative-passive-polite-grateful forms, as such expressions innundate the members' speech and writings. *"Ikiru"* (live) becomes *"ikasasete itadaku"* (am caused to live by [gods'] benevolence). One would be told: "Don't think you are living *(ikiru)* by yourself, but be grateful for *ikasasete itadaku."* One of the autobiographical reports, picked up by chance, happens to use this grammatical form 28 times within four pages *(Gedatsu,* March 1973:54–57).[4] "I learn" *(manabu)* or "I realize" *(kizuku)* is rephrased, without exception, as *manabasete itadaku* or *kizukasete itadaku.* Even a leg injury was experienced as *ashi o orasete itadaku* (was caused to break my leg by [divine] benevolence).

Passivity of self as an object, further, takes the form of possession or being controlled by a supernatural being. Illness and other misfortunes, while they are imputed to ego's fault as discussed above, also turn out to be signs of supernatural influence which have nothing to do with ego's volition. The sufferer is "caused to realize" that her suffering is due to a spirit that is, by means of the suffering, giving her some instruction or appealing for her help. Such a spirit, which is usually recruited from among ancestors, dead humans, dead infants and fetuses (miscarried), or animal spirits representing "guardian spirits," is wandering and suffering because it has not attained Buddhahood or has lost a divine status (*shinkaku*), and is thus seeking human help for its own salvation. An infant's spirit may cause breast pain or cancer in its mother as a way of notifying its helplessness. Mental disorder or "the head disease," as an informant puts it, is most likely to be caused by an angry spirit of a fox or snake.

Self-reconstruction here involves self as an *on*-debtor, a receiver of supernatural messages, and an object of solicitation and reliance. Passivity ultimately reaches the point where self is no longer self. Again, this is nothing unique to the Gedatsu. In Tenrikyo such passivity is articulated in the doctrine of *kashimono-karimono* (things lent and borrowed) according to which everything that a human being possesses, including his body, has been lent by God the Parent (Thomsen 1963:52).

Identity Interchange

There appears to be a logical contradiction between self-accusation and allocentric attribution in that one involves interiorization and the other exteriorization of the cause of illness. But for Gedatsu followers these two are consistent and complementary. What makes them compatible is the belief that there is no clear-cut demarcation line between self and other. The identity of self is actually interchangeable with that of another. Identity interchange is acceptable and morally plausible in Japanese culture insofar as identity is framed within the concept of social role. The ability or willingness to play another person's role, to act as if one were someone's parent (*oyagawari*), for example, is looked upon as a consequence of normal socialization. Furthermore, the cultural stress on solidarity and togetherness makes one susceptible to *ittaikan* (feeling of oneness) with another where one's self loses its boundary and melts into another's self. Identity interchange is also embedded in the Buddhist notion of *innen*, karmic bond of affinity, whereby one's identity is destined to replicate another's.[5] The *innen* usually, though not exclusively, connects two persons who are consanguineally related, such as parent and child, ancestor and descendant.

The Gedatsu psychotherapy manipulates this culturally acceptable identity interchange to, again, an extreme degree. First, one's behavior or suffering is often interpreted as a replica or "mirror reflection" of that of another. A "lecturer" tried to enlighten me by saying, "My wife's illness is mine; I am just borrowing her body. You really can't tell whose illness it is." More often, this kind of identity interchange involves a spirit: a daughter's disappearance from home is a replication of the behavior of her great-grandmother who led an unsettled life; one cries because an ancestor is crying; a daughter bleeds to near death because her great-grandfather (or great-grand uncle? the informant is not sure), drafted in the Sino-Japanese War (1894–95), is still bleeding.

Influence, furthermore, is mutually felt and exerted. If one's illness is a reflection of an ancestor's illness, the former, in turn, is reflected back onto the latter's mirror. A descendant's happiness then brings happiness for an ancestor, which then returns to the descendant, and so on, as if two mirrors were reflecting one another. Mutual reflection boils down to a complete overlap or fusion of two or more identities: "My ancestors, I, and my descendants—we are one and the same"; "Ancestor worship means self-worship." Underlying this reasoning is the assumption of the *innen* bond. Allocentric attribution, then, overlaps self-accusation in that as long as suffering lasts the sufferer should realize that an ancestor (or another spirit) is also suffering and she, the living sufferer, has been unable to alleviate the ancestor's suffering. That is not all. The sufferer must also blame herself for this negative *innen* to be inherited by her innocent children.

More elaborated in the Gedatsu beliefs and practices is identity interchange through role substitution. The spirit does not always cause suffering for the person for whom its message is meant, but may select another person as a substitute because the latter is more vulnerable, more responsive, more helpful, more attached to, or more strongly *innen*-bonded. A dead woman who has lost her way tries to draw attention from her son and daughter-in-law by causing mental disorder in her grandson simply because the latter is smarter than the parents. (This bright grandson, to the parents' astonishment, fell sudden victim to school phobia and joined a group of "hippies" on a mountain, but later returned home after the mother's "sincere" compliance with Gedatsu instructions.)

The substitutive role further involves the role of the vicarious sinner. The spirit which causes suffering for the living often turns out to have committed *tsumi* (sin) while it was in this world. A variety of *tsumi* is mentioned including homicide (usually by samurai ancestors), suicide (most often the unreciprocated love suicide by women), polluting a god-governed place with blood (for this reason any kind of bleeding is considered *tsumi*), power and greed with which the poor were exploited. What stands out among my informants is *shikijo no tsumi,* sin of sexual emotion, which takes various forms—adultery, rape, love suicide, divorce, remarriage, abortion, miscarriage, menstruation (killing eggs as well as polluting), and the like. The sinner is punished by an enraged god (or gods) and thus prevented from salvation. The sufferer in this world then turns out to be vicariously punished for the sin committed by a spirit: "Whenever I encounter trouble, I decide one of my ancestors committed a sin." The sexual sin by an ancestor is manifested in a variety of punishments for a descendant: gynecological disorders, uterine or breast cancer, sterility, miscarriage, unhappy marriage, concubinage, repeated divorce and remarriage, involuntary celibacy, and the like. Interestingly, interviews reveal that punishment may take the form of impotence or frigidity. Note that there is partial overlap between the sin and its punishment; miscarriage, for example, is both sin and punishment. This makes sense because the "real sinner" and the vicarious sinner are linked by *shikijo no innen* (*innen* of sexual emotion) which makes one replicate the other.

To redeem sin, the vicarious sinner and sufferer must repent and offer apologies to gods, usually stationed in one of the *ujigami* or other local shrines, again as a substitute for the sinner. *Owabi* (apology) offering in such a substitutive capacity is a major part of the discipline and rituals of Gedatsu. In front of the shrine, *owabi* is made with a vocal statement like "I apologize from the bottom of my heart as a substitute *(narikawatte)* for my ten-generation old ancestor, Matsuda Taro, for his *tsumi* in lacking respectfulness, faithfulness, and virtuousness. Please kindly forgive me." This vocal apology is reinforced by a written apology on a piece of paper *(wabijo)* submitted to the shrine. *Owabi* further involves *ohyakudo* (hundred times), meaning walking up and down to and from the shrine a hundred times to demonstrate the sincerity of the *owabi*-maker: "stepping *ohyakudo*" for Gedatsu means *owabi* offering. The shrine visit for *owabi* is repeated for as many days and as early in the morning (e.g., before dawn) as prescribed by the spirit through the possession ritual. Usually the spirit accompanies its substitute, but is so helpless that all initiative is taken by the substitute.

When the apology ritual is completed, the spirit may reappear in a possession ritual to inform its attainment of salvation and express its gratitude. The spirit is now ready to accept *kuyo* (nurturance through sutra, food, and special tea called *amacha*). The vicarious sinner is now able to take the role of a nurturant caretaker for the spirit.

Identity interchange thus involves a devotee to slip in and out of different identities, to assume multiple roles, and to split one identity into two. Indeed, some of the observed possession rituals revealed a vacillation between two levels of communication—spiritual and mundane—symbolized by formal and informal speech styles as well as high and low vocal pitches. In one such ritual, the host, after struggling hard to identify the possessing spirit, switched to her mundane role to confess, "I don't know." The mediator, irritated, became increasingly authoritative and insisted that the spirit be identified. On the basis of fragments of a sign message, the mediator finally worked out the information that the spirit was a seven-generation old male ancestor of the host. But of which household, the host's husband's or her natal one? The mediator began to ask, "Are you of the Yoshida House or," but could not recall the other name. Lowering her voice, and in a casual speech style, she asked the host, "What is your natal family's name?" This mundane question was answered immediately: "It's Watanabe." The pair then restored formality to resume spiritual conversation. The whole drama reminded me of ventriloquy.

The Gedatsu offers a special ritual which symbolizes identity-split in an unequivocal form. Every individual is believed, at least potentially, to carry his/her personal guardian spirit and assume its status. The status of the guardian spirit is promoted through its training at Goreichi. This is done by holding a sending-off ritual at a local shrine where some other members also participate. Upon completion of the training which lasts three weeks or so, the spirit returns to the same local shrine where the host and fellow-members gather to welcome the trainee back. During the spirit's absence, the host is supposed to go through the same kind of ascetic discipline at home as does the spirit at Goreichi. The returnee spirit, now accorded with a higher status, promotes the status of its host. The sending-off ritual and welcoming ritual seem to punctuate identity-split and identity-reunion.

Expurgation

Self-reconstruction through a hyperbolic version of self-accusation, allocentric attribution, and identity interchange, still remains incomplete without this final treatment—expurgation.[6] Purification constitutes the core of Shinto ritual, and the state of emptiness is a Buddhist ideal. The ultimate moral value in Japanese culture is represented by the pure heart, *magokoro* (true, sincere heart), *muga* (ego-lessness), or *mushin* (mind-lessness). What upsets the individual's health is the accumulation of impurities in him, which in turn are ingredients of ego itself. Removal of *ga* (ego) itself then is necessary for cure. Freedom from *ga* or attainment of *muga* or *mushin* entails a union of self with its environment or self's submission to nature.

The Gedatsu, like all other cults, stresses the need of abandoning *ga,* saying that obsessions with "I" are the cause of all troubles. Expurgatory rituals *(okiyome)* must be conducted to attain an empty self. Among such rituals is meditation, which is required of every new convert. In the "right" sitting style (with legs folded under the torso), one joins one's hands at eye level with a charm held between the palms, eyes closed. The meditation ritual, either in a group or individually, is repeated until purification is felt completed. Only after that is a convert entitled to host a spirit in the possession ritual. Otherwise the possession ritual could be as dangerous as "a madman carrying a knife."

Not only one's self but spirits must be cleansed for reasons made clear in the above analysis. In the logic of identity interchange, the expurgation of spirits means that of self, as well as vice versa. The spirits which are in need of purification are believed to hang on the *ihai* (mortuary tablets) which are placed in a pail at the altar of the household or the branch church. The expurgatory ritual for the spirits consists of repeatedly pouring *amacha* (the sacred tea) over the *ihai* while reciting a sutra. The Gedatsu goes to an extreme in expecting this ritual to take effect in a literal form: the spirits, under this *amacha* treatment, squeeze impurities out of themselves, which is verified by the defilement of the water: the muddier the water, the more purged and therefore "joyous" the spirits are. Gedatsu followers, thus, tell one another how thick their *amacha* has turned out. *Amacha* as a purgatory medium is also poured over whatever is believed to be a spirit's residence. Not only gravestones, but car tires also receive *amacha* treatment as they are regarded as causing traffic accidents because of polluted spirits hanging onto them.

Amacha turns out not just to wash away the pollutions on the surface of a spirit's body but to be consumed by the spirit, thereby purifying its internal system and expelling impurities out of the system. This belief is applied to human beings as well. *Amacha* is available for human consumption so that its drinker can clean up her physiological system—circulatory, digestive, eliminatory, etc. *Amacha* contains hydrangea which is evidently diuretic. Here is an equation between the spiritual and bodily expurgation, or between a metaphorical and literal meaning.

In addition to *amacha,* the cult prescribes "health foods," which are obtainable at the store run by the cult. A high rate of consumption of these foods can be inferred from the hyperactive trading observed at a local ward branch between the leader as a "middleman" and the followers buying them. When I visited the store, it had roughly 40 kinds of foods including a variety of tea, soybean products (bean paste, soy sauce), sesame seeds and oil, and seaweeds. All are supposed to be "natural foods" devoid of preservatives or other "artificial poisons." The most important among these seems to be *genmai,* unmilled brown rice. Again, its function is not so much nutritional as expurgatory. "Having a right diet," says a local member, "that is the shortest way to find yourself on the right track. *Genmai,* its germs in particular, has power to push everything filthy and harmful out of your body." The same belief apparently pertains to all other foods sold at the store. The business manager of the store stressed in the interview that all those foods are meant to cleanse the blood, to eliminate "poisons." In his view, clean blood and smooth elimination are essential to health maintenance.

The Gedatsu also runs its "health schools" and a "medical research institute." In an office of the latter, I was introduced to a machine whose vacuum glass balls, applied to the afflicted part of a patient's body, supposedly suck poison out of his blood, as proven, said a "doctor," through the glass blackened and air fouled.

The expurgatory therapy, which runs across all aspects of Gedatsu beliefs and practices, is further based upon the assumption that everybody is clean and healthy as long as he is left in nature, that illness is a result of the entry of unnatural elements, such as drugs, into the body. What is important is to go along with the law of nature, to be united with nature, or to dissolve self into nature. "To purify yourself means to harmonize yourself with nature." This "naturalism" joins hands with the abandonment of egoistic self or attainment of *muga*.

Conclusion

This paper analyzed a type of psychotherapy developed and practiced by a Japanese healing cult with a focus on self-reconstruction. Four aspects of self-reconstruction were delineated—self-accusation, allocentric attribution, identity interchange, and expurgation. It was noted that each of these is embedded in Japanese culture and is also exaggerated in the cult's teaching. All four aspects end up reinforcing in a hyperbolic manner the Japanese moral ideal of selflessness, self-denial, or self-abandonment.

Whether this kind of faith healing can be called "psychotherapy" or should be labeled "psychopathology," may be a matter of opinion. It should be reminded, however, that the above description of Gedatsu healing is not quite alien to some other non-religious ethnopsychotherapies which are perfectly respectable to professional psychiatrists. Naikan (Yoshimoto 1965; Okumura, Sato, and Yamamoto 1972; Murase 1974; Lebra 1976b:201–214), for example, concentrates on building up guilt in the client involving self-accusation and allocentric preoccupation. The acceptance of *arugamama* (things as they are) stressed in Morita therapy (Kora and Sato 1958; Morita 1960; Kora 1965; Kondo 1966; Lebra 1976b:215–231) overlaps Gedatsu therapy insofar as it recommends the acceptance of illness as fate, obedience to nature, and self-dissolution into nature. Yokoyama (1974), who was influenced by Morita and is practicing *seiza ryoho* (therapy by sitting), would sound familiar to Gedatsu followers when he recommends a renunciation of egocentric wishes, a replacement of one's mind with that of a baby, a development of infinite attachment to nature "as much as to be able to comprehend the language spoken by rice plants or wheat plants" (Yokoyama 1974:138). Further, both Naikan and Morita therapy in one phase intensify what might be regarded as pathological, as the Gedatsu does. If these therapies use the subsequent release of tension thus built up as a therapeutic leverage, so does the Gedatsu through confessions and expurgatory rituals and practice. The *innen* bond is recognized only to be nullified; the spirit is cared for only to become inactive. Naikan, Morita therapy, Gedatsu, and many other ethnopsychotherapies, religious and secular, all unite in stressing the renunciation of *ga* (ego— intellectual, emotional, or willful).

Despite these similarities, Gedatsu therapy is different from those mentioned above, most of all, in its manipulation of the supernatural hemisphere. Its therapeutic potentials may indeed derive from this difference since identity interchange with supernatural entities expands a spectrum of role options for self-reconstruction. If many psychiatric patients are driven by *amae* (dependency wish) as Doi (1974:146) claims about his patients, the option of taking the role of a helpless spirit may gratify the *amae* wish.

Another point of difference involves the feminine bias of the Gedatsu clientele. I speculate, as the final point of conclusion, on a link between the Gedatsu-inspired self-reconstruction and womanhood. It seems that female dispositions and/or expectations are played up in self-accusation, allocentric attribution, and identity interchange. Women are expected to be less self-assertive, less autonomous, more passive, and their identity more "relational" (Chodorow 1974). Motherhood in particular is exalted in the Gedatsu teaching and acted out in Gedatsu rituals. Maternal nurturance is symbolized by a member's caretaking ritual for an infant-like spirit; the woman's double identity of mother and child is acted out by her vicarious guilt and apology for the sake of a spirit.

A woman who is not feminine or maternal is, therefore, sanctioned against more severely than a male counterpart. A domineering wife is reminded of her place, and a voluntarily childless woman is accused of committing a grave sin. Traditional sex roles are thus imposed more upon females than males. The question remains whether this emphasis on femininity, motherhood, or female-role norms is peculiar to the Gedatsu and similar cults or whether the Japanese moral system tends to be skewed toward femininity which is only exaggerated by these cults. I prefer to leave the question open.

Notes

1. The two series of autobiographical testimonials are titled: *"Omoide"* (Recollections) and *"Yomigaetta jinsei"* (Revival).

2. Adoption of a younger sibling as a child and successor was not uncommon in prewar Japan.

3. The belly *(hara)* as the locus of the spiritual and bodily center is often referred to in Japanese speech particularly in the context of moral training.

4. See note 1.

5. The term *innen* is also used indiscriminately to refer to any kind of relationship, including a meeting of strangers.

6. The term "expurgation" is chosen, instead of the more common "purification," to convey the drastic nature of the cleansing process under discussion.

21

Japanese Attitudes toward Mental Illness and Mental Health Care

Tsunetsugu Munakata

Three Ways of Experiencing Illness

THERE are three basic ways in which illness is generally experienced: (1) as a loss of mental self-control, such as neuroses and psychoses; (2) as a loss of physical homeostasis, such as heart disease and diabetes; and (3) as a loss of behavioral self-control, such as sexual deviance and drug dependence. These experiences may appear mutually exclusive or the three aspects may overlap. In cases where they are mutually exclusive, those afflicted with somatized illness will avoid experiencing it as a loss of either mental or behavioral self-control; those afflicted with mental illness will avoid experiencing it as a loss of physical homeostasis or of behavioral self-control; and those afflicted with a loss of behavioral self-control avoid experiencing it as a loss of physical homeostasis or of mental self-control.

For example, widely observed in the field of occupational health in Japan are patients who experience pain in the neck and shoulders (neck and shoulder syndrome) as a symptom of the loss of physical homeostasis but who also suffer from a loss of mental self-control resulting from a depressive state evidenced by a loss of vitality and self-confidence coupled with a desire to die. In addition, they may suffer a loss of behavioral self-control as manifested by an inability to extricate themselves from their dependence on alcohol. However, to the extent that these patients mainly feel pain in their necks and shoulders as a loss of physical homeostasis, their mental symptoms and drinking and other deviant behaviors are regarded as minor symptoms. Moreover, when people

An earlier version of this paper was presented at the Modernization of East Asian Medicine Workshop, Institute of Culture and Communication, East-West Center, Honolulu, January 7–9, 1985. This paper has been substantially revised by the editors. Interested readers are urged to see the original (Munakata, in press).

realize that their health problems are not merely physical problems, they often may exhibit other serious symptoms such as a depressive state or alcohol dependence.

These three empirical aspects of illness—physical, mental, and behavioral—may differ according to sociocultural background. Dominant in East Asia, including Japan, is the notion that only the loss of physical homeostasis is socially permissible. Only this aspect of illness is acknowledged as what Parsons (1951) calls the "sick role" and only this role temporarily exempts the occupant from daily responsibilities and allows aid seeking from an authorized curer. In other words, illness associated with mental disorder or behavioral deviance lacks the "sense of being really sick." The loss of mental self-control is essentially viewed as a problem involving the afflicted person's willpower, something over which he or she is expected to exercise self-control. Japanese traditionally have been socialized to assume this health responsibility. Consequently, self-control is regarded as the responsibility of those suffering from neurosis, depressive state, and so on, as a matter of course. This leads others to urge the afflicted person to "Buck up!" although such expectations are most trying for those afflicted. While fatigue or malnutrition is an acceptable cause, psychological causes are generally not acceptable, and few would contemplate consulting a psychiatrist.

When a person neglects work, housekeeping, or child-rearing responsibilities as a result of the loss of self-control, or when he or she fails to observe social customs due to delusion or hallucination, the family is expected by society to control such mental illness and to help recovery. People will of course seek assistance from various advisers and curers, but these invariably only support the care provided by the family and do not in any way imply that the family has abandoned its role as the main provider of mental health care. Thus, in Japan such deviant behaviors as refusal to go to school or alcohol dependence are not considered illnesses that call for treatment by experts but are, above all, problems that families are expected to control and take care of. Difficulties within the family may occur as a result, but to abandon responsibility for such problems would call forth criticism and result in guilt feelings. Thus, the problem of deviant behavior tends to worsen because of the prevalence of excessive expectations on the part of society that families will control their members' deviance. It is often only when the family becomes completely exhausted and has lost its will to care that psychiatric treatment may be sought.

The social expectation, then, is that the responsibility for caring for illness associated with mental disorder and behavioral deviance is borne by the afflicted or by their families. Thus, mental illness is seldom experienced as something that requires professional treatment. Rather, it has tended to be regarded as a private *(uchiwa)*, family affair in which outsiders, even medical professionals, should not interfere.

Some Characteristic Features of Mental Health Care in Contemporary Japan

What is the actual state of Japan's mental health care system? Let us first ascertain some of the distinguishing features. According to my surveys and research (Munakata 1983a, 1983b, 1984a, 1984b), there are several characteristics which predominate.

First, the number of mental patients is relatively small, and the frequency of mental hospital admission and discharge is low. Second, and seemingly paradoxical, the average length of stay in a mental hospital is one of the longest in the world. Third, since there are relatively fewer nursing homes in Japan than in Europe and America, many older people end up staying in mental institutions, thus increasing the average length of stay. Fourth, mental hospitals in Japan are usually privately owned (about 86 percent), whereas in the United States almost exactly the reverse is true (about 8 percent). Fifth, Japanese mental hospitals tend to be relatively small, the average size being 250 beds. There have never been mental hospitals with thousands of beds as was once the case in Europe and the United States. Sixth, hospitalization for mental illness costs considerably less for the patient than in the United States, due to national health insurance and possibly lower maintenance expenditures. Seventh, Japan's medical insurance system is so set up that mental hospitals are, in effect, administratively encouraged to increase their patients' length of hospitalization. Eighth, although now being developed, community care for the mentally ill is still infrequent. Let us now examine the sociocultural background underlying these characteristics.

The Sociocultural Background of Japanese Mental Health Care

Like other East Asian societies such as Chinese and Korean, Japan has a concept and social norm different from the West's concerning the care of the mentally ill, the handicapped, and the elderly. This, as we have seen, is the notion that the primary care responsibility for children, adults, handicapped persons, and the elderly falls on their families and relatives. This has even been put into statutory form.[1]

In Western countries, families or relatives are, from my perspective, generally neither criticized nor made to feel guilty for not providing medical care or support to adult members who have become sick, handicapped, or old. Therefore, the responsibility for providing support is seldom written into law. There are of course families and relatives that accept the responsibility of providing medical care and support, but they do not do so out of a sense of social obligation or a feeling of guilt for neglecting their responsibility.

Under Japan's Mental Health Act, guardians (usually family members) are required to have their sick members receive treatment, to supervise them so that they will not injure themselves, and to manage their assets. Admission to a Japanese mental hospital requires the guardian's consent only. This allows, in the majority of cases, the patient to be admitted in a way which may be construed as compulsory hospitalization from the patient's perspective. Furthermore, the law is so broadly applied that the patient may be left in the hospital for good.

Facilities for the mentally ill are designed to complement the responsibility of the family to provide care for older patients as well as for handicapped persons. These facilities came into existence as substitutes, temporary or semipermanent, for families no longer able to provide assistance for sick or incapacitated members. During earlier days, when medical care and welfare facilities were unavailable, mental patients were often left alone in a cold, dark room of the house or in a barn (Kao 1979; Kure and Katada 1920). However, even when it took such an extreme form, this sort of action did not mean that families had abandoned their responsibility to provide care. Unlike the situation observed in other countries where large numbers of mental patients are thrown into the cold world outside, Japan has seldom witnessed such a public overflow of mental patients.

Thus, the mentally handicapped are left in the care of mental hospitals or various other types of facilities (Buddhist temples, faith-healing institutions) as substitutes only when families and relatives are unable to offer care. However, when families send their sick members to the hospital, telling them to remain and consider it their home, the patients for their part resign themselves to hospital life, feeling that they must not trouble their families and relatives by insisting on returning home even though they may wish to do so. (Recently, since hospitalization can be shortened thanks to the improved medical treatment and the availability of such social rehabilitation facilities as day-care centers, the situation is beginning to change slightly, especially among young patients.)

It usually requires an average of several years before a family gives up caring for a sick member and decides to leave him or her in the care of a mental hospital or some other care institution. In this process, features common to East Asians can be discerned. T. Lin (T. Lin et al. 1978) advances a five-phase sequence based on observations of his Taiwan Chinese patients. First, an attempt is made to reduce or eliminate the abnormal behavior of a sick member within the family using any and all methods available. Second, trusted outsiders, friends, and elders of the community, are asked for help. Third, outsiders such as religious healers, herbalists, or physicians are invited to treat the mentally ill person. Fourth, the patient is labeled mentally handicapped by outsiders whom the doctor and the family have consulted. Fifth, the family loses hope and accepts the misfortune of having a mentally ill member and often leaves the sick member in the care of a distant mental hospital. The coping behavior of the Chinese family is basically similar to that of the Japanese family.

According to public hospital statistics in Hawaii (Gudeman 1967; Kinzie 1974), Chinese and Japanese show a clear tendency to delay treatment at mental hospitals when compared with other ethnic groups. But once admitted, they tend to stay longer. Thus, statistics reflect the typical patterns of East Asian attitudes and behavior whereby families decide to leave their mentally ill members in the care of mental hospitals only after having actively cared for them for several years and finally realizing that they must give up.

Ideally, from the Japanese perspective, mental hospitals should be run like a family, and, in fact, families and relatives of the hospital owners and chief directors often live on the hospital premises and serve as primary staff members. For this reason the average number of mental hospital beds nationwide is about 250, which is deemed the maximum size for maintaining a familylike atmosphere. The fact that most mental hospitals are small and privately operated presumably helps to check the tendency toward bureaucratization so characteristic of publicly run mental hospitals.

Neurasthenia and Psychosomatic Disorder as Disguised Diagnoses

Mental illness as exemplified by schizophrenia does not "appear to be a real illness" as does physical illness resulting from a physical breakdown. Nevertheless, it is inevitably manifested through the loss of behavioral self-control. The general public finds it hard to believe that society has an obligation to care for its mentally ill members, as is the case in Western countries. As with Hansen's disease and tuberculosis, there is strong social prejudice among Japanese, especially the elderly, regarding mental illness. It is widely regarded as a problem of heritability, one that proscribes marriage with patient and family. Moreover, the mental hospital, at worst, conjures up an image of a place where the insane are dumped by their families. Since mental hospitals are closed institutions, what happens inside is as a rule rarely known to the outside world. When reported, as sometimes happens, the image created may be an unpleasant one involving hideous scandals, which further deepens the prejudice against mental hospitals. For these reasons, in mental illness, unlike ordinary illnesses, the diagnosis may cause patients to suffer from social disadvantages and psychological shock, engendering hopelessness and insecurity.

Generally speaking, because certain diagnoses, like schizophrenia or cancer, evoke social prejudice or anticipation of imminent death and raise expectations of serious psychological shock for the patient and family (due to an absence of effective treatment), the doctor will deliberately employ a disguised diagnosis. Depending on the people and circumstances surrounding the patient, such as company and school, not only the patient but his or her family may not be given the true diagnosis. Formerly schizophrenia was deliberately labeled as neurasthenia, presumably because the early stages of schizophrenia resemble neurasthenia and the term neurasthenia implies that the illness is partly physical.

It was against this background that the term neurasthenia spread even among laymen, being used to represent practically all forms of mental disorder. At one time doctors entered this term in their notes and submitted them officially to companies or families to be used as evidence for absence due to sickness. Doctors also often used the term neurasthenia in their explanations to their patients and families.

Disguising schizophrenia with a diagnosis of neurasthenia lost its effectiveness when the truth became too widely known. Instead, psychosomatic disorders and malfunctioning of the autonomic nervous system, which suggest a physical disorder, are frequently used today as diagnoses for what is actually schizophrenia. Such terms are seldom found in Western countries. Likewise, terms that do not call to mind a physical disorder, such as the term mental debility used in Great Britain or psychotic reaction used in America, are not generally employed in Japan because these terms do not connote a "real illness."

The phenomenon of coping with serious disadvantages and shocks to patients and their families by disguising the diagnoses is, as far as I know, not limited to Japan. It also occurs in other Asian countries, as well as Europe and America. But the extent to which this tactic is resorted to varies considerably from one country to the next. The general tendency seems to be that disguised diagnoses are not used for those engaged in occupations closely tied to public safety, such as soldiers and airplane pilots. In these cases true diagnoses will be more likely to be used.

However, the degree to which diagnoses are disguised in Japan seems

rather extreme. Given the previously noted prejudice against mental illness and the need for strong doctor-patient ties, characteristic of interpersonal relationships in Japanese society in general, Japanese doctors
seem compelled to provide a smoke screen for their diagnoses. The
same process occurs when doctors tell cancer patients that they have an
ulcer. The disguising of diagnoses is much more easily and frequently
resorted to in Japan than in Western countries. One example is a recent
incident in which a false diagnosis is suspected of having been used for
an airplane pilot with disastrous results. It involved a Japan Airlines
plane that crashed offshore of Haneda Airport in 1982, killing 24 and
injuring 147 passengers and crew. The pilot who caused the accident
had been diagnosed as suffering from a psychosomatic disorder, although he was actually a schizophrenic case. In order to understand the
way in which diagnoses are disguised in Japan, it is necessary to consider interpersonal relationships in Japanese society in general and doctor-patient relationships in particular.

Doctor-Patient Relationships

Generally speaking, Japanese interpersonal relationships are characterized by an effort to minimize psychological distance between the
interacting individuals. They do so by repressing their personal opinions and interacting frequently with each other for the purpose of establishing emotional ties before anything else. The quickness with which
the Japanese try to establish emotional ties may seem too abrupt for
Western people. Once the interacting individuals become friends, they
begin to feel that they can expect things of each other as if they were
members of the same family. They then become disinclined to say no to
each other's requests.

Weak followers will often obtain emotional and instrumental help
from their bosses by taking advantage of this type of interpersonal relationship. If the boss refuses to provide help, the follower will harbor a
strong grudge against him. But if the boss provides help, he will have
gained influence over the follower, who will then feel *on* (lasting obligation) toward the boss. To be recalled in this connection is Doi's *amae*
study (see chap. 8).

Moreover, in interpersonal relationships where the individuals
involved try their best to reduce the psychological distance, it is difficult
to say no directly to the other person's request because to do so would
make one feel guilty. The only thing that can be done in most cases is to
say yes or give some other vague response. Thus, it becomes necessary
not to regard another's response at face value but to exercise one's ability to guess *(sassuru)* whether the other person really means yes or is

merely giving a reluctant consent. To *sassuru* is to understand the other's feelings without relying on verbal communication or understanding. Parents train their children in the art of *sassuru*. They tell their children, "You should understand what other people are thinking before they say anything by merely looking at their faces. You have to be able to easily *sassuru* such a matter."

This pattern of interpersonal relationship, so typical of the Japanese, characterizes the relationship of doctor and patient as well (and that of doctor and the patient's family). The doctor takes over as the boss, and the patient and the patient's family become followers. Patient and family seek the doctor's indulgence and try to win his heart. Unless this sort of emotional exchange occurs, the patient and the patient's family feel anxious and dissatisfied.

To illustrate, I had a chance to observe an encounter between an American doctor and a Japanese-American (postwar immigrant) mental patient. The latter was extremely dissatisfied because he could not indulge himself in the way just described, and despite the fact that he was fluent in English, he refused to speak it. The doctor in charge summoned me to interpret for him, but instead of interpreting, I ended up serving as a substitute in the emotional discharge to satisfy the patient's need for interpersonal indulgence. The patient was able to satisfy this need by communicating with me, but I urged him to tell the doctor all this, since it was such an important issue. The patient took this advice and successfully explained his difficulties in English.

Another clinical scene I observed involved an American patient. The patient said, in effect, "I have such and such symptoms. I think I'm suffering from such and such illness. What sort of treatment can you give me?" The American doctor responded to the patient's questions at great length. If a patient talked like this in Japan, however, the doctor would probably be compelled to say, "Since you know your trouble in such great detail, I think you'd better cure it yourself." In other words, many Japanese doctors would be taken aback if their patients did not leave everything up to them. To behave in the manner of the American patient would be considered conceited by the doctor.

Thus, Japanese patients, unlike American patients, develop the kind of dependency on their doctors that children feel toward their mothers, and since Japanese doctors try to respond to their patients as if they belonged to the same family, they end up assuming the entire responsibility of treating and caring for their patients. Consequently, the doctor in charge often tries to have the last say in everything, even in matters that essentially concern nurses and caseworkers. He will, furthermore, feel a sense of guilt if he cannot fulfill this responsibility. Usually the doctor will avoid explaining anything unless he is absolutely certain. In this the Japanese doctor is quite different from the Western doctor. The Western doctor, to my knowledge, explains a great deal to his patient and the patient's family so as to enable them to make the necessary decisions. A Japanese patient and his family, on the other hand, must size up the situation from the doctor's nonverbal communication. In other words, the attending doctor must guess the wishes of the patient and family and assume the posture of taking full responsibility as if he were the head of the patient's family, whereas the patient and family are expected to guess the limits of what the doctor can do.

Some people will accurately guess the limits of what the doctor can do while others may not. Japanese doctors disguise their diagnoses so often and so frequently choose not to explain in detail the treatment they are giving that confusion may occur. Doctors are motivated by their desire to protect the patients and their families as much as possible from the loneliness, alienation, powerlessness, and hopelessness that might result from the knowledge of the terminal nature of their illness or the social prejudice associated with it. Indeed, doctors in the United States tend, in the Japanese view, to explain too much and leave too many medical decisions to their patients and families, who have little knowledge of the medical treatment being given. This, it is believed, generates a sense of powerlessness and hopelessness which the patients and their families may find hard to overcome.

Toward the Reconstruction of Mental Health Care Systems

I have focused thus far on the sociocultural factors particular to Japanese in order to understand their attitudes toward mental illness and mental health care. I have attempted to emphasize positive aspects of Japanese mental health care that might not be properly appreciated if European and American value standards were used. The family in the United States and other Western countries does not function adequately as a social network for the care of mental patients. When mental patients in these countries are discharged from mental hospitals, they are often abandoned in the local communities without proper care. They may become prey to criminal elements in society or end up staying in nursing homes or board and care homes. By contrast, mental patients in Japan can enjoy the protective care provided by their families and mental hospitals.

However, Japanese society tends to expect families to assume too much responsibility for their sick members. At the same time, and paradoxically, families have not made enough effort to comprehend the realistic limits of today's mental health care delivery system, relying excessively instead on mental hospitals or their family doctors to take care of their sick members. Moreover, the general public, those engaged in the care of the mentally ill, and the families of the mentally ill have tended to avoid looking squarely at the reality of mental illness. A smoke screen of ambiguity, symbolized by the widespread practice of disguising diagnoses, is allowed to conceal reality. Consequently, whether at home or in hospital, mental patients have been overprotected and deprived of their freedom as individuals. Further, it is not impossible that, given such total dependence of patients on doctors, profit-driven hospitals exploit patients in total disregard of their human rights. Thus, there are elements of the present system that must be improved before we can take full advantage of the potential beneficial aspects of Japanese culture while avoiding that which is detrimental to patients and their families.

First, to prevent families from abandoning their responsibility for the care of their sick members and overly relying on mental hospitals, it is important to improve the existing system of consultation in local communities. By doing so families will be able to make use of consultation soon after the outbreak of their members' illness. It is also important to establish a visiting care service whereby nurses and others could be sent to local communities to provide help for the mentally ill. In addition, there is a need to enrich social welfare resources in local communities. To back up these efforts, medical insurance and the existing system of health and welfare must be improved.

Second, to improve the self-reliance of mental patients, mental hospitals, instead of overprotecting patients, must focus treatment on providing social and psychological assistance. To accomplish this, the doctor in charge, however much the patient's family may have entrusted their sick member to him, must stop regarding paramedicals as mere assistants. The doctor must instead make positive efforts to establish a kind of relationship with these professionals that will fully utilize their talents as sociopsychological curers.

Note

1. Article 49, the Constitution of the People's Republic of China, p. 39, 1982. Although it is not stipulated in the Japanese Constitution, the relatives' "duty to furnish support" is stipulated in Article 877 of the Civil Code.

22

Fear of Eye-to-Eye Confrontation among Neurotic Patients in Japan

Yomishi Kasahara

I

Japanese psychiatrists have a terminology for phobia of interpersonal relations. This is not a peculiar kind of mental disorder specific in Japan (such as *amok* specific in Java, *koro* in Hong Kong, etc.) but is coincident with erythrophobia and allied conditions.[1] Since Casper in 1848, a dozen articles have been published concerning erythrophobia, or ereuthophobia, and some of them described it as dysmorphophobia, a variation of ereuthophobia. This is the fear of deformity of some specific parts of one's body. Such phobic symptoms are well known to psychiatrists and psychologists in every culture. A Japanese psychiatrist, S. Morita, however, placed ereuthophobia, along with its allied conditions including dysmorphophobia, etc., under the comprehensive category of "phobia of interpersonal relations" *(taijin kyōfu)*. Needless to say, a patient suffering from ereuthophobia actually fears that he may make a bad impression on others or make others become unpleasant by his blushing and, as a result, be humiliated by others. Consequently, patients may often withdraw from social relationships where there is a fear of this happening. In this sense, ereuthophobia and allied conditions are nothing but "fear of interpersonal relations."

It was in the early 1920s that Morita proposed this name and evolved for this group of neuroses a special method of treatment which was named after him. Since then, detailed studies of this variety of neurosis have been made by many authors.[2] This is simply because ereuthophobia and allied conditions have been the variety of neurosis most fre-

Reprinted from Working Papers, Culture and Mental Health Program, Social Science Research Institute, University of Hawaii, 1970. This paper was prepared while the author was in residence as a research fellow in a joint project of the East-West Center Senior Specialists Program and the SSRI's Culture & Mental Health Program (NIMH Grant MH-09243).

quently observed in Japan. This situation remains unchanged to this day. For instance, according to my statistics, of the 430 students who received psychiatric care at the Student Health Service of Kyoto University in 1968, one-half were neurotic. Out of these, 18.6 percent can be classified in the category with which we are concerned. This group ranks third after depressive reaction, accounting for 24 percent, and psychosomatic disorders, accounting for 20 percent.[3]

I wish to present here two subtypes of fear of interpersonal relations frequently found among Japanese youth with the hope that these data may be compared with neurotic patterns among youth in other cultures. The first is a fear of eye-to-eye confrontation, characterized by an anxiety of being looked at by others and an anxiety of unintentionally staring at others with strange looks. The second is a fear of emitting odor from one's body, classified as similar to fear of eye-to-eye confrontation. There are reasons to believe that in foreign countries these two types of neurosis do not occur as frequently as they do in Japan. Scattered references to the fear of emitting bodily odor are found in Western literature, but, to the best of my knowledge, the fear of eye-to-eye confrontation does not exist in the literature.[4]

II

A typical patient who has a fear of eye-to-eye confrontation complains as follows: "In the presence of others, I become tense and feel ill at ease. I am self-conscious of being looked at by others. At the same time, I am embarrassed as to where to direct my eyes. I cannot decide whether I should look away from other people's eyes or not. I cannot tell to what extent I should stare into the others' eyes. Meanwhile, my looks lose their naturalness and I end up by staring into others' eyes with piercing looks. Rather, it would be more accurate to say that my eyes become automatically glued to the other person's eyes. When this happens, rather than fear that I am being looked at, I feel that my eyes stare at others in an unnatural manner. This is because my unnatural piercing look hurts others by making them feel unpleasant. This is not merely imagination; it is indeed a fact for me. The reason I can insist on this is because I know intuitively by the way others behave towards me. Others look away from me, become restless, make grimaces, or leave their seat abruptly. It is psychologically so painful for me to embarrass people in this way that I end up avoiding people as much as possible."

The foregoing is a rough example of the complaints commonly made by severe cases of a fear of eye-to-eye confrontation. These symptoms usually develop between puberty and early adulthood. It is rather rare for these symptoms to persist with the same intensity after the age of 30, and after the age of 40 the onset of such a fear is extremely rare. In this sense, it can indeed be called a disorder peculiar to adolescence. There is no clear sex difference; however, it has been said that this pattern of neurosis is seen more among males. Blushing may be more acceptable socially for females than for males; therefore, the motivation to visit doctors may be weaker for females than for males. The more severe the symptoms of confrontation fear, the more restricted are the activities of daily life. Despite the persistence of their complaints and the intensity of their pathological convictions, patients appear to be normal. They tend to be more sociable than the average youth. A few cases border on overt schizophrenia.

Whereas in mild cases the fear of being looked at by others is predominant, in severe cases, as I indicated in the typical case cited, patients clearly suffer more from the fear of unintentionally staring at people with strange looks than from the fear of being looked at by others. It goes without saying that even in severe cases the fear of being looked at coexists. Thus, the combination of staring at and being stared at forms the pathological focus of this syndrome. Because the patient experiences the fear of eye-to-eye confrontation in the presence of others, I would like to further discuss complaints by patients in order to determine what kind of characteristics these other people have.

The patient does not experience any fear in the presence of doctors and counselors, or of his own relatives, with whom he has an intimate relationship. Conversely, he never experiences fear when he finds himself among total strangers in such places as a crowded street. The fear is induced in the presence of those who are neither particularly close nor totally strange, in other words, people of intermediate familiarity. This is especially so when he finds himself in a small group of several persons; he is most susceptible to fear in a small group where people are of about the same age and background as he. If they happen to be members of the opposite sex, the patient is particularly embarrassed. Male patients are usually too shy to make girl friends and tend to group among themselves, though they do not show overt signs of homosexuality. Needless to say, the patient does not welcome making a speech on a stage in the presence of a large audience nor does he welcome being in the presence of his superiors. However, compared with small-group situations such as those mentioned above, these large-group situations are much easier to bear. This is because large-group situations do not involve the complex interpersonal relationships of being stared at and of being unable to help staring at others.

I will try to describe in more detail what happens when a patient grows phobic in a small group situation. The patient feels relatively at home when talking tête-à-tête with any person who happens to be around. But if a third person enters this situation his presence upsets the patient, no matter who he happens to be. The patient automatically directs his sight to this third person, and the patient feels that this action is repulsive and hurts the other's feelings.

The foregoing can be interpreted in the following manner. The patient is able to take part in a dialogue situation in which he can play the role of either the speaker or the listener. However, he cannot take part in a triangular interpersonal constellation. In such a triangular situation, the patient automatically shifts his eyes away from the person at the side, who, rather than the person in front of him, engages his central concern. If he is on a train or in a classroom situation, those who concern him are the ones seated by his side. Some severe patients insist that they look from the sides of their eye-sockets and their look pierces the person sitting right next to them. Also, they frequently complain that their sight field is too expansive or that they can see sideways more than they want to, suffering from their side-glancing obsession. I wish to call this characteristic feature "phobia of side-glancing," borrowing these patients' nomenclature. To avoid glancing sideways, they tend to develop various kinds of counter-reactions. Some patients try to prevent people from entering their sight by seating themselves at the very end of the first row in the classroom and some others by wearing sunglasses. Still others stare straight ahead as much as possible in order not to glance sideways and end up by actually developing a piercing eye-look.

In supplement, I wish to present the case of a patient suffering from the fear of bodily odor. The patient is a 19-year-old male college student majoring in a natural science. Convinced that his body odor makes others unpleasant, he tries to avoid approaching people as much as possible. In a classroom he seats himself in the back row and leaves the classroom the moment the lecture is over. However, he cannot actually smell his body odor. At times he feels that the odor is peculiar, but most of the time he, himself, cannot understand the nature of his odor and consequently cannot describe it definitely when asked.

Therefore, the conviction that his body emits a peculiar odor is derived, not from his own perception but from observing the way others behave toward him. He intuitively feels that he is emitting a bad odor by observing people around him touching their noses with their hands, coughing, or laughing. Sometimes he can ascribe the sources of his odor to specific parts of his body such as the anus or genitals. Concluding from the foregoing, the form of this experience is not an olfactory hallucination but an idea of reference.

The preceding is an outline of the complaints commonly made by patients who fear their own body odor. This fear is similar to the fear of eye-to-eye confrontation on many important points. For instance, these patients do not give abnormal impressions, despite their delusional convictions. However, the fear of bodily odor is more serious than the fear of eye-to-eye confrontation because the former is more likely to show a short psychotic episode under stressful conditions than the latter.

It is obvious that patients with a phobia of interpersonal relations tend to suffer more from being repulsive than from being humiliated by others. Their complaints range from a fear of embarrassing others to a fear of giving an infectious look or radiating something from the body to paralyze others. What is of central concern in this context is the fear of hurting others. Therefore, we may be justified in labelling this kind of disorder as "altruistic phobia" as was suggested by Kaan (1892). This is to be set apart from "egoistic phobia" in which an external intrusion by phobogenic objects is feared.

However, as indicated previously, the patient suffering from altruistic phobia does fear humiliation by others. Actually, all phobias involve a fear of losing control of undesirable impulses and being humiliated as a result. For example, an elevator phobia is not the result of the possibility of physical danger involved in a falling elevator but is related to the necessity of being able to escape immediately from other people when one becomes anxious. The anticipation of panic, related to the need to move swiftly, causes anxiety to supervene and even a few seconds in going from one floor to the next floor become unendurable. If this interpretation is correct, the central problem of all phobias is the threat of public display of inadequacy and imperfection. Salzman (1968) states that "both phobia and obsession devices are attempts to control dangerous and undesirable impulses of a sexual or aggressive nature. It need not be necessarily a hostile or aggressive impulse. It may develop around the need to maintain pride and self-esteem. Loss of control and concern about humiliating consequences which might result are the factors that produce a phobia. The fear of losing control is in itself the threat of being humiliated." If this is true, there is no difference between altruistic and egoistic phobias, and consequently, concerning the threat of being humiliated, the phobia of interpersonal relations with which we are now concerned might be considered the most typical phobic reaction.

III

I would now like to consider these phenomena from a cross-cultural point of view. It should first be mentioned that it is extremely difficult to prove the hypothesis that a particular neurotic type is in the foregorund in a given culture in a given period. Data being limited, I do not want to assert that phobias of interpersonal relations are in the absolute majority in Japan. In order to clearly establish this hypothesis, a precise comparative study of neuroses is necessary. However, if a particular variation of phobias of interpersonal relations is more liable to occur in a given culture than in others, this phenomenon should then be considered in relation to its background.

Phobias of interpersonal relations are nothing but variations of hypochondria in the sense that patients are overly concerned about their bodily self. What differentiates these phobias from other manifestations of hypochondria is the fact that patients feel that they are simultaneously repulsive to themselves and to others. In connection with this, it should be noted that the only parts of the body which patients are hypochondriacally concerned about are external, such as the face, body shape, body odor, etc. If we compare such neurotic patients in different cultures, we may discover what parts of the bodily self are psychologically most vulnerable in a stressful, interpersonal situation.

Ereuthophobia and allied conditions as a whole seem not to have been in the limelight in Western psychiatry. According to Dietrich (1962), there has been only one paper dealing with dysmorphophobia as its main theme in European literature during the previous two decades. Dietrich went on to say that ereuthophobia is very rare in Germany. When dysmorphophobia is mentioned in Western literature, one's nose, skin, hair, chin, teeth, shape of the skull, breast, and body weight are enumerated as common objects of concern. Body odor is rarely mentioned and the eye not at all. The fear of eye-to-eye confrontation no doubt exists in other cultures, but it may fail to attract doctors' attention.

In contrast to this, Japanese psychiatrists encounter the fear of eye-to-eye confrontation and body odor almost every day, while little mention is made of one's skull, breast, nose, skin, etc., by patients. I have encountered 39 cases of the fear of interpersonal relations among students of a Japanese university: fear of body odor, 11 cases; fear of blushing, 6; fear of eye-to-eye confrontation, 5; fear of voicing and stuttering, 2; fear of negligible scars on their face, 2; fear of hand trembling, 2; miscellaneous fears, 11. From this it can be stated with considerable probablility that the fears of eye-to-eye confrontation and body odor are found frequently among young Japanese neurotics. This raises the questions of why Japanese people exhibit a marked propensity to the themes of eye and body odor in their phobias of interpersonal relations. However, to consider these phenomena in sociocultural terms is a task for the cultural anthropologist, not a psychiatrist. I shall attempt to answer this question in terms of my impressions received through therapeutic experiences with the patients.

Let us consider, first, the reason Japanese are concerned about the eye. In everyday interpersonal relationships, the act of staring at the person to whom one is talking is quite extraordinary and considered to be rude. To be continuously stared at creates displeasure for the Japanese, except among very intimate relations. To look intently at the person to whom one is talking does not, for the Japanese, signify respect. Rather, a tendency to look downward is appreciated even today, especially among females, and is thought to be suggestive of a certain elegance. Thus, there exists a cultural characteristic which causes Japanese to be hypersensitive about "looking at" and "being looked at." Even today, Japanese parents often discipline their children by saying, "Neighbors are watching whatever you do." It is conceivable that Japanese children grow into personalities which incessantly watch those outside of their family circle, either consciously or unconsciously. There is in Japan a traditional children's game, "Niramekko," played between two persons who keep staring at each other until one of them breaks into laughter. The one who laughs first is the loser. I feel that this game should be called the game of eye-to-eye confrontation. As Dr. Sakuda (1967), a sociologist, points out, this kind of game has a close relationship with the so-called "shame culture" of Japan. This may have its origin in counter-reaction to the fear of eye-to-eye confrontation.

In accordance with the avoidance of eye-to-eye confrontation in interpersonal relations, the mode of communication among Japanese is markedly nonverbal and indirect. Japanese culture esteems vague expressions and avoids frank talk. In this context, I feel that what those who fear eye-to-eye confrontation dread is another's rude, pointblank remarks in a given interpersonal situation. At the same time, they are also afraid that they may say something pointblank which is not in conformity with the established code of etiquette. The Japanese expect to understand and to be understood despite their use of vague expressions. Needless to say, these attitudes, in which we expect and depend upon another's benevolence, can be explained by the concept of *amae*, which has been illuminated by Doi (1962), one of the leading psychoanalysts in Japan, as the key concept for understanding Japanese personality structure.

It is also possible to detect some cultural influence in the "fear of side-glancing" observed among those who fear eye-to-eye confrontation. The sideward direction has a specific, intrinsic significance. The side, in contrast to above and below, represents a direction where equals are hand in hand, a space of friendship, or a space of conformity. It also implies something negative in that it could be a space where envy and competition lie. In making this point, recall the previous statement that a patient with a phobia of interpersonal relations finds it most difficult to deal with those who share similar backgrounds. Morita has also pointed out that, particularly in cases of shame, there lies a deep-rooted desire not to be defeated by equals and to surpass them. Psychoanalytic literature also points out that shame can be brought upon the individual in the process of comparing and competing with peers (siblings, school-mates, gang, professional group, social class, etc.), and social conformity achieved through shame will be essentially one of identification. It seems meaningful that the direction about which many patients are concerned is neither above nor below but to the side.

Next, I shall consider why bodily odor concerns Japanese with phobias of interpersonal relations. To consider this in sociocultural terms is far more difficult than analyzing fear of eye-to-eye confrontation, for case reports concerning the fear of body odor are found in every culture, i.e., U.S., Germany, and France. With regard to Japanese culture, it can be said that Japanese tend to appreciate odorlessness more highly than fragrance. To the Japanese, cleanliness is a state where there is no odor rather than a state where there is a pleasant odor, perhaps owing to their religions, Shintoism, and to a lesser degree, Buddhism.

IV

Finally, I would like to comment on the method of treatment for phobias of interpersonal relations in Japan. In Japan, the phobias are usually treated by Morita psychotherapy. In this therapy a patient is usually required to be hospitalized for two months during which he is forbidden to talk (even with his doctor) about his symptoms. However, he is allowed to write down whatever he wishes in his diary. Morita and his successors have stated that in order to come to terms with neurotic suffering, one must not search for the cause nor try to eliminate it; rather, one has to accept it without fighting the symptoms. The characteristics of Morita therapy are clearly stated by him, "You should become the world's most well-known shy person showing your face can blush more than anyone else's. Don't fight against having a blushing face." This therapy does not deal with a patient's life history and unconscious. Because of this, Morita therapy stands in a position contrary to psychoanalysis.

The aim of Morita therapy—"not fighting against symptoms, but rather getting used to them and even having a friendly feeling toward one's symptoms"—has had wide appeal in Japan. Most psychiatrists who are not practicing Morita therapy and are not advocates of this therapy are often aware that in their approach to patients they make use of many aspects of Morita's method. Though not widely practiced in Japan at present, Morita therapy remains a special type of therapy.

During the past ten years, psychiatrists have often claimed that patients suffering from phobias of interpersonal relations have not reacted positively to Morita psychotherapy. My experience has been the same. The symptom has not been decreasing, but at present young patients are unable to accept the aim of Morita therapy—"not fighting but just accepting symptoms as they are." Some patients are persuaded to be hospitalized for Morita therapy but often leave the hospital in a week or so. Few consider that a treatment originated forty years ago can be applied to the present generation. I believe that Japanese psychiatrists are facing a critical problem in the treatment of phobias of interpersonal relations. I am now tentatively trying two methods: psychoanalytically oriented group psychotherapy and behavioral therapy which Eysenck (Eysenck and Rochman 1965) advocates.

V

In the preceding, I have described some cases of ereuthophobia and allied conditions observed frequently among the Japanese youth of today, and discussed them briefly in relation to the Japanese cultural background. I hope that well-designed cross-cultural studies can be conducted on these patterns of neurosis. I feel it would be most effective to compare neurotic types prevailing among college students in various cultures. College students form a social stratum which is comparatively alike in many important respects in many cultures today, and it seems to be more useful for the present purpose to compare data furnished by campus psychiatry rather than to compare statistics gathered from in- and outpatients in general hospitals.

I wish to conclude this presentation by stating that further elucidation on the psychopathology of these fears is necessary in order to develop more effective treatment techniques for them.

Notes

1. In a strict sense, erythrophobia means "the fear of red." The fear of blushing taking place in the presence of others should be called ereuthophobia.

2. There are numerous English-language descriptions of Morita therapy. For a recent summary see Ikeda (1968).

3. The remainder comprised schizoid personality, obsessive neurosis, transient maladaptation, hypochondria, etc., each accounting for about 5 percent. The matrix group was ten thousand in number.

4. This is different from "stage fright" described by Fenichel (1945), because patients having a fear of eye-to-eye confrontation clearly suffer more from the fear of unintentionally staring at people with strange looks than from the fear of being looked at by others.

23

Naikan Therapy

TAKAO MURASE

NAIKAN therapy (*nai,* meaning "inside" or "within," and *kan,* "look-ing"[1]) is a form of guided introspection directed toward attitude and personality change. It has been practiced in Japan for the past thirty years. Developed by a lay practitioner, Mr. Inobu Yoshimoto, Naikan therapy was originally employed in correctional institutions but is now widely used in medical and educational settings as well.

Although the method was derived from the Jōdo-shin sect of Bud-dhism, the most popular Buddhist sect in Japan, it is unrelated to any professional psycho-therapeutic form, Eastern or Western. Naikan ther-apy is based upon the philosophy that the human being is fundamen-tally selfish and guilty, yet at the same time favored with unmeasured benevolence from others. In order to acknowledge these existential con-ditions deeply, one must become open-minded toward oneself, em-pathic and sympathetic toward others, and must courageously confront his own authentic guilt. Only then will he achieve new identity.

This Naikan philosophy is intimately related to Japanese culture and, at the same time, is firmly based upon the universal nature of the human mind. Both the culture-bound and the more universal aspects are found in the specific Naikan procedures and clients' behavior in Naikan setting. Let me start by describing the specific Naikan proce-dures.

The Method

In short, Naikan therapy is a process of continuous meditation based upon highly structured instruction in self-observation and self-reflec-tion. Accordingly, the content of instructions and themes for meditation

Reprinted from *Culture-Bound Syndromes, Ethnopsychiatry, and Alternate Therapies,* vol. 4 of *Mental Health Research in Asia and the Pacific,* ed. W. P. Lebra. An East-West Center Book. © 1976 The University Press of Hawaii.

or reflection, as well as the way of giving instructions are of central significance.

The volunteer Naikan patient is asked to examine himself in relationship to others from the following three perspectives: (1) "Recollect and examine your memories of the care and benevolence that you have received from a particular person during a particular time in your life." (Beginning as a rule with an examination of his relationship to his mother, the client proceeds to examine, reexperience, and reflect relationships with other family members and with other persons whom he has been close to, from childhood to the present.) (2) "Recollect and examine your memories of what you have returned to that person." (3) "Recollect and examine the troubles and worries you have given that person." These three perspectives can be named, for the sake of convenience, "benevolence given," "benevolence returned," and "trouble given to others."

The examination is conducted in a boldly moralistic manner, placing the burden on the patient rather than on the "other." No excuses, rationalizations, or aggressions toward others are permitted except in the earliest meetings, when the counselor is more passive and tends merely to listen to what the patient describes to him. Following the introductory session, however, the counselor places more demands on the patient and is prepared to lead him if the patient faithfully follows the instructions. Mr. Yoshimoto used to give his clients such instructions as, "Examine yourself severely, like a prosecutor indicting the accused."

The patient begins his Naikan recollections and reflections at 5:30 in the morning and continues them until 9:00 in the evening. He sits in a quiet place surrounded on two sides by a Japanese screen and walls on the other two so that he is cut off from distractions and is free to concentrate exclusively on his inner world. Since he is not allowed to leave this very narrow space except to visit the bathroom or go to bed, the place inside the screen constitutes his whole environment. Such small confines facilitate concentrated self-reflection. For seven successive days he follows the same schedule so that at the end he has sat more than 100 hours almost continuously except while sleeping. This continuation of the same mental activity is essential for Naikan insight.

The counselor interviews the patient briefly (five minutes average) approximately every 90 minutes to ask what he has been examining. Total interview time amounts to 40–50 minutes a day. The role of the Naikan counselor is very different from the ordinary role of the professional counselor or therapist. The primary function of the Naikan counselor is to directly supervise the patient in a highly specific routine of private meditation. He is mainly concerned with making sure that his patient is following instructions and reflecting successfully on the topics assigned for his self-examination. In this respect, the Naikan therapist is more concerned with procedure than with content or with the counselor-patient relationship. In other words, it is not necessary for the counselor to achieve a full, empathic understanding of the patient's intricate inner world. The counselor accepts and respects the patient as a person, as one who has the potential to realize himself; at the same time, the counselor is negative and critical about any non-Naikan or anti-Naikan attitude that the patient might have toward himself. In this sense, the basic counselor-patient relationship in Naikan is authoritarian. Although direct contact with the patient is sporadic, it is nevertheless intensive and highly directive. Accordingly, transference is kept as uncomplicated as possible.

Patients following the instructions often find them rather difficult. At first they may be unable to concentrate on specific themes in the way they are instructed. For some the psychological and physical isolation or confinement is too much to stand. The counselor uses several techniques to help them overcome the first barriers. Usually it takes two to three days for the patients to adjust to the new situation.

Occasionally and unexpectedly, forgotten memories come up and sporadic or diffuse guilt feelings and gratitude are experienced. At the same time, various kinds of resistance against the practice may come out, usually not the deeply rooted idiosyncratic resistance observed in psychoanalysis, but rather a more conscious reaction to such an unusual, harsh situation as Naikan. Patients are free to discontinue the method if it proves to be too difficult for them. Simple emotional catharsis is observed in some cases.

As the process goes on, the patient becomes more and more meaningfully involved with his past. For some the process is gradual, whereas for others abrupt insights into the guilty aspects of their present and past emerge. Insights into other people's love for them and their dependence upon them for this love also occur. Toward the end of therapy they accept the newly recognized guilt along with feelings of self-criticism and repentance. They also feel truly grateful for love from others and become empathic with the pain and suffering that they experienced.

The Outcome

The most common result of successful Naikan therapy is an improvement in the patient's interpersonal relationships. The improvement is brought about by the increase in, or the fresh appearance of, real feelings of gratitude for others; an inclination toward self-examination rather than an extra-punitive or impulsive attitude; empathic and sympathetic ability; regard for others; and the realization of one's responsibility for his social role(s). From another angle, the establishment of identity; strengthening of ego-ideal; and achievement of security, confidence, and self-disclosure may be the most obvious factors in the improvement.

This method has proven effective with various types of patients, except psychotics, without any modifications of technique. Notable success has been achieved with delinquents, criminals, and drug addicts. Even though few scientifically rigorous follow-up studies have been done, in many correctional institutions the Naikan method has proven more effective than other methods of treatment.

Contraindications and Ill Effects

As a rule Naikan is ineffective for patients who are diagnosed as having an endogenous psychosis. Severely self-punitive types of compulsive neurotics difficult to treat by any method may gain nothing from Naikan. It must be emphasized, however, that the depressive state that is accompanied by strong feelings of guilt is not necessarily a contraindication for Naikan, because the guilt and the self-criticism stemming from the systematic examination of objective experiences in Naikan differ essentially from feelings observed among depressed patients. This will be illustrated in the first case study, below.

Case Studies

Case 1: a woman suffering from depressive reaction. Mrs. N. was a middle-class housewife, 32 years old, when she began Naikan treatment. Previously she had worked as a primary schoolteacher. When she came in for treatment, she had been in a depressive state for 10 months, manifested by an increasing loss of interest in activities and a certain amount of obsession about her inability to accomplish things as she had before. She suffered from serious insomnia and had at times contemplated suicide. Her depressive reaction seemed to be precipitated by two incidents: maladjustment to her work following a change of teaching assignment two years previously, and an unexpected pregnancy several months before admission. The pregnancy increased her despair because losing her job as a result would have had harsh economic consequences for her family. Prior to these difficulties, she had reported no previous serious depressions. There were no reported familial or hereditary factors that might have effected her psychological disturbance. Medication given prior to Naikan treatment had been totally ineffective.

When she arrived for treatment, her motivation for Naikan was quite low. She cooperated with the treatment but in a very passive and almost reluctant manner. For three days she was not deeply involved in meditation but devoted most of her time to making accusations about her own incapacity and worthlessness. She seemed unable to adapt to the situation and was on the point of asking her father to take her back home. Her father, however, strongly encouraged her to continue trying. Mrs. Yoshimoto also strenuously encouraged the client to continue. Following this, after the third day, the patient suddenly began to be able to carry out the practice of Naikan. She accepted the method with seriousness. She was then able to examine what her mother-in-law had done for her and through this was able to feel how deeply her mother-in-law cared for her. Following this emotional insight her whole attitude toward life underwent a drastic change. She found everything shiny and bright. Let me cite an interview from that time. Mr. Yoshimoto asked, "What have you been examining?" Mrs. N. replied, holding back the tears:

> Last year we bought a piano for our daughter. I realize now that this was only made possible by using the money that my mother-in-law had saved. I had forgotten this and thought that I had bought it with my own money, completely forgetting her contribution. I was so egocentric.
>
> When she was hospitalized, I only visited her once, bringing her a small gift, although my father-in-law visited her more frequently. (This was accompanied by a lot of self-deprecatory crying.) When I was hospitalized after the delivery of my last child, she visited me almost daily, bringing expensive fruits and walking up to the fifth floor to see me in spite of her heart condition. At this time she very, very kindly took care of me and really acted like a loving mother. I think about that now and I am aware at last how egocentric and unaware I had been as a *yome* ("daughter-in-law"). I really don't know how I can express my gratitude to her now. I am full of the feeling that I wish to beg her pardon on my knees right now.

She spent the hours following this revelation reflecting on her relationship with her father-in-law, thinking about how he had expressed love and shown care for his daughter-in-law. She again realized how relatively ungrateful she had been, not only to her father-in-law but also to her real father.

Thinking about the troubles that she had given her father-in-law in the past, she realized that she had not been *sunao,*[2] "obedient." She described herself as feeling like a "poisonous snake." She also said that she had become increasingly aware of a tremendous amount of guilt toward people in her home and worried that she could not beg her father-in-law to forgive her for her faults and imperfections.

On the fifth day of Naikan exercise, Mr. Yoshimoto felt that she had become in some ways too dramatic and excited to continue the practice of Naikan properly. He therefore asked her father to come and discuss taking her back.

The father, on seeing her daughter's drastic change, was quite over-whelmed. They reunited, embracing each other in joyous tears. The day following her return home her excitement subsided but her im-proved state of mind continued.

When about two weeks had passed, she became unstable and a little depressed. But this time the amount of depression was significantly less than she had experienced prior to Naikan. She overcame the crisis by employing Naikan exercises at home by herself. Through this she regained courage and hope. Her former rigid attitudes toward life changed, and she became more flexible and accepting. She could relate herself to everything with gratitude, warmth, and naturalness.

Although at the time of my second follow-up study (one year and four months following her Naikan treatment) there was still a possibility of her becoming depressed in the future, her attitude toward life had fun-damentally changed as a result of Naikan treatment. The likelihood of subsequent psychological disturbance seemed lessened following her treatment.

To summarize, this woman recovered from a severe depressive reac-tion by undergoing Naikan therapy for only a few days. Naikan brought her the insight that she had been very selfish and without any real regard for beneficence and love from others, especially her family members. This insight was accompanied by the deep feeling of authen-tic guilt and gratitude. Her strong defensiveness, which may have been mainly due to her distrust of others, was remarkably decreased, and her aggression toward herself seemed to disappear. She came to have a much better understanding of the feelings of others and gained vital hope for the future.

Case 2: a male student with ego-identity problems. Mr. M. was a male undergraduate student studying to be a primary schoolteacher. Al-though superficially his social and academic adjustments were normal, he seemed to be worried by emotional problems and wanted to "change himself." In the initial interview he told me that he had a feeling his per-sonality was composed of a lot of small sins, which he was extremely afraid of facing. He had asked himself whether he could be a "real" adult since he realized he was dirty and "diffused."

After two days of the introductory stage he gradually became in-volved in examining himself. He kept thinking of his "dark" self and asking, "Who am I," and wondering how he could go on living. He recollected the warm treatment he received from his primary school-teachers and realized that he had done nothing for them. He felt espe-cially lonesome, miserable, and remorseful when he recollected an epi-sode in which he accidentally broke a window in the school and his teacher did not reprimand him at all. With tears in his eyes, he kept on thinking about this incident. Then suddenly he felt alive, full of determination and insight. Sobbing, he told Mr. Yoshimoto, "Right now, at this very moment, I clearly realize what I should do right after graduation from the university; I must bring up children the way my primary school teachers did me. I believe this is my mission. That's all." Following this incident, when he was recollecting and examining his memory of the relationship with his mother, he had another experience of extremely strong emotion and feeling. When he was eight years old he still wet his bed, and whenever it happened his mother would change the wet sheet and let him come into her own bed. The recollection of the warmth of his mother's bed was combined with the recollection of another kind of warmth he experienced more directly in his babyhood, when he was carried by his mother in her arms or on her back. When he realized that he had completely forgotten this warmth up to the present, he felt so sad and sorry that he could not help but burst into tears. Sobbing, he went to Mr. Yoshimoto and asked for permission to go back to his parents immediately in order to do anything he could for them and also to tell them how his feelings and thoughts had changed. Mr. Yoshimoto advised him not to be so overwhelmed by sheer emotion but to try harder to examine himself. He simmered down and reached a tranquil state of mind.

Both of these experiences are primarily based on the acknowledgment of warmth from others. He said, "My mother and my first-grade teacher, these two persons are now closer to me, I feel."

In recollecting and reflecting upon his relationship with his father, he remembered one incident about which he felt deeply ashamed. Once when his father suddenly lost consciousness, his first worry was taking over his father's debts. Mainly for this reason he wished for his father's recovery. He also had to admit to himself that he had been jealous of his brother and had hated and distrusted him in spite of his brother's kindness to him. He found himself always being exploitative, not only of his brother but of others as well.

On the final day of his Naikan treatment he said, "Before Naikan, I wished I could completely forget such bad memories as having been slapped by my teacher or being a truant in junior high school days; but right now, I keenly feel that I exist here, now, only after I have done those things. That's why I really think I must not forget my sinful past." He felt strong enough to face the guilt squarely and found it most meaningful.

According to the follow-up interview and psychological testing carried out three months after he finished concentrated Naikan therapy, his interpersonal relationships in general showed marked improvement. His previous exploitative and antagonistic attitude toward others changed to a cooperative, accepting, and open-minded one. He began to listen to others and to see himself from another person's point of view. He also began to be more responsible, stable, and confident of himself, with greater hope for the future. The fundamental change in his attitude toward life made it possible for him to speak very easily in front of nearly 200 people in church. That he could do such a thing was beyond his imagination before Naikan therapy.

We must note, however, that in spite of the marked improvement in his attitude toward life, according to the TAT, his essentially negative relationship with his father seemingly remained almost unimproved.

Tentative Analysis of the Therapeutic Function of Naikan

The major task that the Naikan patient is asked to accomplish is to see himself in another's position and reflect on both the beneficence given to him and the harm he has done to others.

In vividly recollecting memories of "having been loved and cared for,"[3] especially by maternal figures, the Naikan patient reexperiences the deep security and satisfaction that he once had in his relationship with the person being recalled.[4] The Naikan setting reinforces the positive aspect of the client's image of others, especially his mother. His deep gratitude for his parents is transferred to others in general and he becomes more accepting of himself and others. He discloses himself, moves toward others, and becomes more empathic with them.

It may be also reasonable to assume that to recollect the experience of "having been loved and cared for" in earlier days gives the patient a feeling of inherent continuity and consistency between his present self and his basic trust of the world. This experience brings about a more solid and more integrated ego identity.

From the cultural standpoint, the character of the Japanese mother,[5] who is essentially very nurturant and interdependent with her child, may contribute in creating the above-mentioned therapeutic condition.

One additional significant therapeutic aspect of the acknowledgment of "having been loved and cared for" is that it prepares the ground for confronting and accepting one's guilt. One can never have authentic guilt feelings toward a person whom he feels he does not love or who he feels does not love him. This is probably the most decisive aspect of recollecting benevolence, because acknowledging guilt is, after all, the central experience of Naikan therapy.

Now let me discuss the therapeutic meaning of the acknowledgment of guilt. In contrast to the prevalent idea of guilt as being more or less negative and very often pathological, Naikan emphasizes the existentially positive meaning of guilt-consciousness if one is able to confront it. Experiences related to guilt-consciousness tend to be forgotten and alienated from the ego unless one dares to face them. Once the person examines his past guilty conduct, relates himself directly with it, and accepts it as belonging to himself, he naturally changes his self-image and re-orients it toward responsibility, courage to be, and a humble attitude toward life. (He then achieves a broader and more integrated identity.) His selfish attitude and lack of empathy or sympathy lessens, often radically, when he realizes he is not qualified to demand and criticize others without respecting and understanding their feelings.

It is necessary to note that for a Japanese to do harm to those close to him, such as parents, is a severe violation of social morals. Thus, the acknowledgment of such misconduct produces especially strong guilt feelings in the Japanese. As R. Bellah (1957) and G. De Vos (1960) proposed, *on* obligation is very closely related with guilt among the Japanese. Naikan seems to facilitate guilt-consciousness skillfully by reinforcing the sense of *on* obligation, particularly the *on* obligation regarding one's mother. It is interesting to note that among Westerners, superego anxiety is said to have its origin in the father-son relationship, which is basically determined by fear of authority perceived in conjunction with sexual rivalry as well as by the more or less "universalistic" nature rather than by the "particularistic" one. Japanese guilt, on the other hand, seems to be very closely related with the mother-son relationship, in which the fundamentally empathic and sympathetic attitude of the son toward his mother brings about guilt in him when he realizes he has done harm to his beloved mother, who may have raised her child in a rather "moral masochistic" (devotive), self-punitive way. He also tends to feel guilty when he realizes that he has had an unconscious intent to hurt his mother, due to the natural ambivalence that arises from living under very close parental control. The whole traditional social system of *on* obligation may reinforce this profound personal attitude toward guilt.

Thus, Naikan therapy utilizes very effectively such basic characteristics of the Japanese personality as strong potential guilt feelings, *on*-consciousness, the predominant significance of mother, and specific moral values in the context of highly "particularistic" interpersonal relationships. The more universal basis of Naikan may be found in its emphasis on insight into, and a positive relating with, one's guilt, in contrast to the mere feeling of guilt.[6]

Notes

1. *Kan* literally means "observation" but carries a specific meaning in the context of Japanese Buddhism. It implies observing or visually imagining an object during meditation with intensively integrated states of mind.

2. The Japanese word *sunao* is almost impossible to translate into English. It contains such implications as naturalness, naiveté, straightforwardness, simplicity, frankness, open-mindedness, mildness or gentleness, and compliance. Japanese culture attaches high moral value to this trait, and the word is often used in negative form by Naikan patients when they criticize themselves.

3. Discussing the dynamics underlying Naikan method may pose some difficulty for Westerners, since the recollection of affection for a parent (along with guilt about one's transgressions against the parent) is usually said to be discovered only after the analysis of unconscious anger toward the parent. Furthermore, for Westerners, hostility toward the parent often is deliberately intensified through the process of recollection and free association. This is much less prominent in Japanese patients than in Western patients. The cultural differences responsible for this may have to do with the different ways of gratifying dependency in Japanese culture when contrasted with a culture originating in Continental Europe (see Doi 1961, 1962). The relative absence of aggression in Japanese family life cannot be accounted for simply on the basis of repression but is due to significantly different cultural practices in child-rearing and family life. I think that recognition of guilt and the realization of love in a way exacerbates and intensifies the conflict within the patient over his responsibilities for other people in his life.

4. In connection with the recollection of early experiences of being loved, it may be necessary to discuss the possibility of regression in Naikan therapy. We notice that many Naikan patients experience something similar to regression, though very mildly and temporarily. Since Naikan is an exclusively conscious and judgmental procedure, even though regression tends to occur, it is in conflict with the conscious, self-observational, and reality-directed way of thinking in Naikan and thus is readily and quickly suppressed. Although the therapeutic meaning of this oscillating process of repeatedly arising mild conflict and its resolution is not clear to the author yet, he assumes that the regression-like experience in Naikan must be therapeutic to a certain degree in making the patient relatively free from his perceived-reality-bound and rigidly patterned way of experiencing.

5. Those interested in the character of the Japanese mother can refer to Tomomatsu (1939), Yamamura (1971), and Caudill (1961). Yamamura, a Japanese sociologist, analyzed the image of mother among Japanese delinquents treated by Naikan therapy. In his findings almost all of the delinquent boys who underwent Naikan therapy realized either that they had returned evil for their mother's kindness or that they had been given love and care by their mothers in spite of the harsh treatment they gave their mothers.

6. Yasunaga (1967), a Japanese psychiatrist, contends that the significant therapeutic meaning of pure guilt-consciousness, which is defined as the feeling accompanied by the realization that one sees himself responsible for his conduct, is that he also has done harm to a particular person. In this sense this "pure feeling of guilt" differs from the ordinary feeling of guilt. Yasunaga noticed that this kind of guilt feeling is brought about by a truly empathic understanding of another's pain and suffering. This experience of pure guilt has the positive effect of (1) melting away even the very strongest defense, (2) resolving one's *amae,* or dependent attachment on others, (3) successfully overcoming one's bitter consciousness of being hurt by others, and (4) increasing the possibility of confronting oneself honestly.

References

ABEGGLEN, J. C.
1958 *The Japanese Factory: Aspects of Its Social Organization.* Glencoe, Ill.

ADAMS, J. S.
1965 Inequality in Social Exchange. In *Advances in Experimental Social Psychology,* vol. 2, ed. L. Berkowitz. New York.

AKIMOTO, H., ET AL.
1964 An Epidemiological, Genetic, and Social-Psychiatric Study of Mental Disorders on the Isolated Island of Hachijo. *Psychiatria et Neurologia Japonica* 66:951–986.

ALYSWORTH, K.
1946 Rocks, Water and Wood—Japan's Reverence of Nature. *Story Paper for Boys and Girls in Elementary V-VI* 2, no. 6. Methodist Church.

AMES, W. L.
1981 *Police and Community in Japan.* Berkeley and Los Angeles.

ARAI, S., J. ISHIKAWA, AND K. TOSHIMA
1958 Développement psychomoteur des enfants japonais. *La revue de neuropsychiatrie infantile et d'hygiene mentale de l'enfance* 6:262–269.

ARIÈS, P.
1962 *Centuries of Childhood.* New York.

ARIGA, K.
1948 Nihon kodai kazoku [The Japanese family in ancient times]. In *Shakaigaku taikei* [Outline of sociology], vol. 1, *Kazoku,* ed. J. Tanabe. Tokyo.

ASQUITH, P. J.
1981 Some Aspects of Anthropomorphism in the Terminology and Philosophy underlying Western and Japanese Studies of the Social Behavior of Non-Human Primates. Ph.D. diss., Oxford University.

ASTON, W. G.
1896 *Nihongi: Chronicles of Japan from the Earliest Times to A.D. 697.* Supplement to *Transactions and Proceedings of the Japan Society.* London.

AUSTIN, L.
1976 *Japan: The Paradox of Progress.* New Haven.

AXLING, W.
1932   *Kagawa*. London.

AZUMA, H.
1984   Receptive Diligence and Teachability: A Cross-Cultural Discussion of Motivation in Education. Paper presented at International Congress of Psychology, Acapulco.

BALINT, M.
1952a The Final Goal of Psychoanalytic Treatment. In *Primary Love and Psychoanalytic Technique*. London.
1952b Critical Notes on the Theory of the Pregenital Organizations of the Libido. In *Primary Love and Psychoanalytic Technique*. London.

BAYLEY, D. H.
1978   *Forces of Order: Police Behavior in Japan and the United States*. Berkeley and Los Angeles.

BEARDSLEY, R. K., J. W. HALL, AND R. E. WARD
1959   *Village Japan*. Chicago.

BEFU, H.
1966   Gift-giving and Social Reciprocity in Japan: An Exploratory Statement.
-67   *France/Asie* 21:161–178.
1971   *Japan: An Anthropological Introduction*. San Francisco.
1980   *The Group Model of Japanese Society and an Alternative*. Rice University Studies 66. Houston.

BELLAH, R.
1957   *Tokugawa Religion*. Glencoe, Ill.

BENDASAN, I.
1970   *Nipponjin to Yudayajin* [Japanese and Jews]. Tokyo.

BENEDICT, R.
1946   *The Chrysanthemum and the Sword: Patterns of Japanese Culture*. Boston. Reprinted, 1961.

BLACKER, C.
1964   *The Japanese Enlightenment: A Study of the Writings of Fukuzawa Yukichi*. Cambridge.

BLALOCK, H. M., JR.
1960   *Social Statistics*. New York.

BLAU, P. M.
1964   Justice in Social Exchange. *Sociological Inquiry* 34:193–206.

BLOCH, M.
1975   *Political Language and Oratory in Traditional Society*. London.

BLOOD, R. O., JR.
1967   *Love-Match and Arranged Marriage: A Tokyo-Detroit Comparison*. New York.

BOTT, E.
1957   *Family and Social Network*. London.

BRADSHAW, E. O.
1952   *Unconquerable Kagawa.* St. Paul.

BRANDT, V. S. R.
1971   *A Korean Village: Between Farm and Sea.* Cambridge, Mass.

BURTON, R. V., AND J. W. M. WHITING
1961   The Absent Father and Cross-Sex Identity. *Merrill-Palmer Quarterly* 7:85–95.

CAUDILL, W.
1958   *Effects of Social and Cultural Systems in Reactions to Stress.* Social Science Research Council, Pamphlet 14. New York.
1961   Around the Clock Patient Care in Japanese Psychiatric Hospitals: The Role of the *Tsukisoi. American Sociological Review* 26:204–214.
1962   Patterns of Emotion in Modern Japan. In *Japanese Culture: Its Development and Characteristics,* ed. R. J. Smith and R. K. Beardsley. Chicago.
1970   The Study of Japanese Personality and Behavior. In *The Study of Japan in the Behavioral Sciences,* ed. E. Norbeck and S. Parman. Rice University Studies 46. Houston.

CAUDILL, W., AND G. DE VOS
1958   Achievement, Culture, and Personality: The Case of the Japanese Americans. *American Anthropologist* 58:1102–1126.

CAUDILL, W., AND L. T. DOI
1962   Patterns of Emotion in Modern Japan. In *Japanese Culture: Its Development and Characteristics,* ed. R. J. Smith and R. K. Beardsley. Chicago.
1963   Interrelations of Psychiatry, Culture and Emotion in Japan. In *Man's Image in Medicine and Anthropology,* ed. I. Galdston. New York.

CAUDILL, W., AND T. Y. LIN, EDS.
1969   *Mental Health Research in Asia and the Pacific.* Honolulu.

CAUDILL, W., AND D. W. PLATH
1966   Who Sleeps by Whom? Parent-Child Involvement in Urban Japanese Families. *Psychiatry* 29:344–366. *(See also chapter 15 of this volume.)*

CAUDILL, W., AND H. A. SCARR
1962   Japanese Value Orientations and Culture Change. *Ethnology* 1:53–91. Reprinted, 1974, in *Japanese Culture and Behavior: Selected Readings,* 1st ed., ed. T. S. Lebra and W. P. Lebra. Honolulu.

CAUDILL, W., AND C. SCHOOLER
1969   Symptom Patterns and Background Characteristics of Japanese Psychiatric Patients. In *Mental Health Research in Asia and the Pacific,* ed. W. Caudill and T. Lin. Honolulu.

CAUDILL, W., AND H. WEINSTEIN
1970   Maternal Care and Infant Behavior in Japanese and American Urban Middle-Class Families. In *Families in East and West,* ed. R. Hill and R. König. Paris.

CHAMBERLAIN, B. H.
1882   *Kojiki, Records of Ancient Matters.* Supplement to vol. 10, *Transactions of the Asiatic Society of Japan.*

CHIN, S.
1971   *Nipponjin to Chūgokujin* [Japanese and Chinese]. Tokyo.

CHODOROW, N.
1974   Family Structure and Feminine Personality. In *Woman, Culture, and Society,* ed. M. Rosaldo and L. Lamphere. Stanford.

COHEN, J.
1965   Some Statistical Issues in Psychological Research. In *Handbook of Clinical Psychology,* ed. B. Wolman. New York.

COLBY, B. N.
1966   Behavioral Redundancy. In *Communication and Culture: Readings in the Codes of Human Interaction,* ed. A. G. Smith. New York.

COLE, R.
1970   *Japanese Blue Collar.* Berkeley and Los Angeles.

COLE, R., AND B. KARSH
1968   Industrialization and the Convergence Hypothesis. *Journal of Social Issues* 24:45–64.

COLEMAN, S.
1983   *Family Planning in Japanese Society: Traditional Birth Control in a Modern Urban Culture.* Princeton, N.J.

CONROY, M., ET AL.
1980   Maternal Strategies for Regulating Children's Behavior: Japanese and American Families. *Journal of Cross-Cultural Psychology* 2:153–172.

COOLEY, W. W., AND P. R. LOHNES
1962   *Multivariate Procedures for the Behavioral Sciences.* New York.

CRANE, P. S.
1967   *Korean Patterns.* Seoul.

DENZIN, N. K.
n.d.   Producing and Accounting for the Insanity and Alienation of Place. MS.

DE VOS, G.
1960   The Relation of Guilt toward Parents to Achievement and Arranged Marriage among the Japanese. *Psychiatry* 23:287–301. Reprinted, 1974, in *Japanese Culture and Behavior: Selected Readings,* 1st ed., ed. T. S. Lebra and W. P. Lebra. Honolulu. *(See also chapter 6 of this volume.)*
1962   Deviancy and Social Change: A Psychocultural Evaluation of Trends in Japanese Delinquency and Suicide. In *Japanese Culture: Its Development and Characteristics,* ed. R. J. Smith and R. K. Beardsley. Chicago.
1966   Role Narcissism and the Etiology of Japanese Suicide. *Transcultural Psychiatric Research* 3:13–17.
1973   *Socialization for Achievement: Essays on the Cultural Psychology of the Japanese.* Berkeley and Los Angeles.

1978   The Japanese Adapt to Change. In *The Making of Psychological Anthropology,* ed. G. D. Spindler. Berkeley.

DE VOS, G., AND A. WAGATSUMA
1959   Psycho-cultural Significance of Concern over Death and Illness among Rural Japanese. *International Journal of Social Psychiatry* 5:6–19.

DE VOS, G., AND H. WAGATSUMA
1961   Value Attitudes toward Role Behavior of Japanese Women in Two Japanese Villages. *American Anthropologist* 63:1204–1230.

DE VOS, G., AND H. WAGATSUMA, EDS.
1966   *Japan's Invisible Race.* Berkeley and Los Angeles.

DIETRICH, H.
1962   Uber Dysmorphophobie (Missgestaltfurcht) [On dysmorphophobia]. *Archiv fur Psychiatrie und Nervenkrankheiten,* no. 203.

DOI, L. T.
1956   Japanese Language as an Expression of Japanese Psychology. *Western Speech* 20:90–96.
1958   Shinkeishitsu no seishin-byōri [Psychopathology of *shinkeishitsu*]. *Psychiatria et Neurologia Japonica* 60:733–744.
1960   Jibun to amae no seishin-byōri [Psychopathology of *jibun* and *amae*]. *Psychiatria et Neurologia Japonica* 61:149–162.
1961   Sumanai to Ikenai [*Sumanai* and *ikenai*]: Some Thoughts on Super Ego. *Japanese Journal of Psychoanalysis* 8:4–7.
1962   *Amae:* A Key Concept for Understanding Japanese Personality Structure. In *Japanese Culture: Its Development and Characteristics,* ed. R. J. Smith and R. K. Beardsley. Chicago. Reprinted, 1974, in *Japanese Culture and Behavior: Selected Readings,* 1st ed., ed. T. S. Lebra and W. P. Lebra, Honolulu. *(See also chapter 8 of this volume.)*
1971   *Amae no Kōzō* [The structure of *amae*]. Tokyo.
1973   *The Anatomy of Dependence.* Tokyo, San Francisco, New York.
1981   ———. 2d ed. Tokyo.
1985   *Omote to ura* [Front and back]. Tokyo.

DORE, R. P.
1958   *City Life in Japan.* Berkeley and Los Angeles.
1973   *British Factory–Japanese Factory: The Origins of National Diversity in Industrial Relations.* Berkeley and Los Angeles.
1978   *Shinohata: A Portrait of a Japanese Village.* New York.

EARHART, H. B.
1970   *A Religious Study of the Mount Haguro Sect of Shugendo.* Tokyo.

ELIOT, C.
1935   *Japanese Buddhism.* London.

EMBREE, J.
1939   *Suye Mura: A Japanese Village.* Chicago.

ERIKSON, E. H.
1956   The Problem of Ego Identity. *Journal of the American Psychoanalytic Association* 4:56–121.

EYSENCK, H. J., AND S. ROCHMAN
1965   *The Causes and Cures of Neurosis.* San Diego.

FENICHEL, O.
1945   *The Theory of Neurosis.* New York.

FIRTH, R.
1954   Social Organization and Social Change. *Journal of the Royal Anthropological Institute* 84:1–20.

FISHER, J. L., AND T. YOSHIDA
1968   The Nature of Speech According to Japanese Proverbs. *Journal of American Folklore* 8:34–43.

FRAGER, R., AND T. ROHLEN
1976   The Future of a Tradition: Japanese Spirit in the 1980's. In *Japan: The Paradox of Progress,* ed. L. Austin. New Haven.

FRENCH, T. M.
n.d.   Guilt, Shame, and Other Reactive Motives. Unpublished paper.

FRISCH, J. E.
1963   Japan's Contribution to Modern Anthropology. In *Studies in Japanese Culture,* ed. J. Roggendorf. Tokyo.

FUJISAWA, T., ET AL.
1966   A Social-Psychiatric Study of Religious Movements in Japan (in Japanese). *Seishin igaku* 8:928–932.

FURUKAWA, T.
1952   Giri [Social obligation]. *Nihon shakai minzoku jiten* [Dictionary of Japanese ethnography and folklore], vol. 1. Tokyo.

GANS, H. J.
1962   *The Urban Villagers.* New York.

GLEASON, A. H.
1964   Postwar Housing in Japan and the United States: A Case in International Comparison. In *Studies on Economic Life in Japan.* University of Michigan Center for Japanese Studies, Occasional Papers, no. 8. Ann Arbor.

GOFFMAN, E.
1952   Cooling the Mark Out: Some Aspects of Adaptation to Failure. *Psychiatry* 15:451–463.
1971   *Relations in Public.* New York.

GONDO, Y.
1970   A Study on the View of Life Held by Korean Students (in Japanese). *Research Bulletin, The Research Institute of Comparative Education and Culture, Kyushu University* 1:81–102.

GORER, G.
1943 Themes in Japanese Culture. *Transactions of the New York Academy of Sciences* 2:106–124.

GOULDNER, A. W.
1960 The Norm of Reciprocity: A Preliminary Statement. *American Sociological Review* 25:161–178.

GUDEMAN, H. G.
1967 Evaluation of the Unit System, Hawaii State Hospital. Mimeo.

HALL, R. K.
1949 *Shūshin: The Ethics of a Defeated Nation.* New York.

HAYASHI, K.
1983 Adolescent Sexual Activities and Fertility in Japan. *Bulletin of the Institute of Public Health* 32, no. 2: 88–94.

HEARN, L.
1905 *Japan: An Attempt at Interpretation.* New York.

HENRY, J.
1955 Docility or Giving Teacher What She Wants. *Journal of Social Issues* 11:33–41.

HOLLINGSHEAD, A. B., AND F. C. REDLICH
1958 *Social Class and Mental Illness.* New York.

HOMANS, G. C.
1958 Social Behavior as Exchange. *American Journal of Sociology* 63:597–606.

IKEDA, K.
1968 Morita's Theory of Neurosis and Its Application to Japanese Psychotherapy. In *Modern Perspectives in World Psychiatry,* vol. 2, ed. J. G. Howells. London.

INKELES, A., AND P. H. ROSSI
1956 National Comparisons of Occupational Prestige. *American Journal of Sociology* 61:329–339.

ISHIDA, E.
1963 Unfinished but Enduring: Yanagita Kunio's Folklore Studies. *Japan Quarterly* 10:35–42.
1974 *Japanese Culture: A Study of Origins and Characteristics.* Honolulu.

ISONO, F.
1960 Ie to jiga-ishiki [Family and self-consciousness]. In *Kindai Nippon shisōshi kōza* [History of thought in modern Japan], vol. 6. Tokyo.

JAPAN. BUNKACHŌ [NATIONAL CULTURAL AGENCY]
1976 *Shūkyō nenkan* [Yearbook of religion]. Tokyo.

JAPAN. MINISTRY OF HEALTH AND WELFARE
1961 *The National Survey on the Aged.* Tokyo.

JAPAN. MOMBUSHŌ [MINISTRY OF EDUCATION]
1935
-1939   *Jinjō shōgaku shūshin-sho* [Elementary school moral training]. Tokyo.

JAPAN. NATIONAL COMMISSION FOR UNESCO
1958   *Japan: Its Land, People and Culture.* Tokyo.

JAPAN. OFFICE OF THE PRIME MINISTER
1962a   *1960 Population Census of Japan.* Vol. 2, *One Percent Tabulation.* Part 1, "Age, Marital Status, Legal Nationality, Education and Fertility." Tokyo.
1962b   *1960 Population Census of Japan.* Vol. 2, *One Percent Tabulation.* Part 5, "Household." Tokyo.
1964   *General Report on the Family Income and Expenditure Survey.* Tokyo.

JAPAN INFORMATION SERVICE
1966   Survey Taken on Finances of Young Japanese Workers. *Japan Report* 12, no. 8 (April 30): 5-7.

KAAN, H.
1892   *Der neurasthenische Angstaffekt bei Zwangsvorstellungen und der primordiale Grubelzwang.* Wien and Leipzig.

KAIGO, T.
1963   A Short History of Postwar Japanese Education. *Journal of Social and Political Ideas in Japan* 1:15-23.

KAPLEAU, P.
1965   *The Three Pillars of Zen.* Tokyo.

KARASAWA, T.
1965   Morality from Now On: Concerning the Moral Guidance Data. *Contemporary Religions in Japan* 6:42-57.

KARDINER, A.
1939   *The Individual and His Society.* New York.

KASAHARA, Y.
1984   *The Apathy Syndrome among Educated Young Adults in Japan* (in Japanese). Tokyo.

KAWAI, H.
1976   *Bosei shakai: Nihon no byōri* [The pathology of Japan as a maternal society]. Tokyo.

KEYSERLING, H.
1925   *The Travel Diary of a Philosopher.* 2 vols. New York.

KINZIE, J. D.
1974   A Summary of Literature on Epidemiology of Mental Illness in Hawaii. In *People and Cultures in Hawaii,* ed. W. Tseng et al. Honolulu.

KISHIDA, E.
1964   *Gedatsu Kongō to sono kyōgi* [The Gedatsu founder and his teachings]. Tokyo.

KITSUSE, I. J., A. E. MURASE, AND Y. YAMAMURA
In   Kikokushijo: The Emergence and Institutionalization of an Educational
press Problem in Japan. In *Studies in the Sociology of Social Problems*, ed. J. W.
       Schneider and J. I. Kitsuse. Norwood, N.J.

KONDO, A.
1966   Morita ryōhō [Morita therapy]. *Seishin igaku* 8:707–715.

KORA, T.
1965   Morita Therapy. *International Journal of Psychiatry* 1:611–645.

KORA, T., AND K. SATO
1958   Morita Therapy: A Psychotherapy in the Way of Zen. *Psychologia* 1:219–
       225.

KOYAMA, T.
1962   Changing Family Structure in Japan. In *Japanese Culture: Its Development
       and Characteristics*, ed. R. J. Smith and R. K. Beardsley. Chicago.

KROEBER, A. L.
1951   The Novel in Asia and Europe. *University of California Publications in Semitic
       Philology* 11:233–241.

KUMURA, T., T. AMANO, AND I. UCHIMI, EDS.
1965   *Shōgaku dōtoku* [Primary school moral education text], vols. 1–6. Osaka.

KURANO, K., ED.
1957   *Kojiki taisei* [Kojiki: Comprehensive edition]. Vol. 6, Hombun-hen [Text].
       Tokyo.

KURATA, I.
1943   Toshidama kō [The new year's gift]. *Minkan denshō* 8:497–502.
1944   Kōden no konjaku [The funerary gift: Past and present]. *Minkan denshō*
       10:457–463.

KURE, S., AND G. KATADA
1920   *Seishin-byōsha shitaku kanchi no jikkyō oyobi sono tōkei-teki kansatsu* [Statistics
       and case analysis of custodial home care for the mentally ill]. Tokyo. Rev.
       ed., 1973.

LAEVELL, U. W.
1961   *Teacher's Guide Book*. American Book Co.

LAEVELL, U. W., AND M. L. FRIEBELE
1961   *Golden Rule Series*. Vols. 1–3. American Book Co.

LAEVELL, U. W., M. L. FRIEBELE, AND T. CUSHMAN.
1964   *Golden Rule Series*. Vols. 4–6. American Book Co.

LANHAM, B. B.
1956   Aspects of Child Care in Japan: Preliminary Report. In *Personal Character
       and Cultural Milieu*, 3d rev. ed., ed. D. G. Haring. Syracuse.
1966   The Psychological Orientation of the Mother-Child Relationship in
       Japan. *Monumenta Nipponica* 21:322–333.
1974   Relation of History and Prospectives of the Future: Japan's Youth of the
       Past and Present. *Asian Profile* 2:519–535.

1979   Ethics and Moral Precepts Taught in Schools of Japan and the United States. *Ethos* 7:1–18. *(See also chapter 16 of this volume.)*

LANHAM, B. B., AND M. SHIMURA
1967   Folktales Commonly Told American and Japanese Children: Ethical Themes of Omission and Commission. *Journal of American Folklore* 80:33–48.

LEBRA, T. S.
1971   The Social Mechanism of Guilt and Shame: The Japanese Case. *Anthropological Quarterly* 44:241–255.
1974a Intergenerational Continuity and Discontinuity in Moral Values among Japanese. In *Youth, Socialization, and Mental Health.* Vol. 3 of *Mental Health Research in Asia and the Pacific,* ed. W. P. Lebra. Honolulu.
1974b The Interactional Perspective of Suffering and Curing in a Japanese Cult. *International Journal of Social Psychiatry* 20:281–286.
1976a Ancestral Influence on the Suffering of Descendents in a Japanese Cult. In *Ancestors,* ed. W. H. Newell. The Hague.
1976b *Japanese Patterns of Behavior.* Honolulu.
1976c Taking the Role of the Supernatural "Other": Spirit Possession in a Japanese Healing Cult. In *Culture-Bound Syndromes, Ethnopsychiatry and Alternate Therapies,* ed. W. P. Lebra. Honolulu.
1983   Shame and Guilt: A Psychocultural View of the Japanese Self. *Ethos* 11:192–209.
1984   *Japanese Women: Constraint and Fulfillment.* Honolulu.

LEBRA, W. P.
1966   *Okinawan Religion: Belief, Ritual, and Social Structure.* Reprinted, 1985. Honolulu.

LEE, C., AND G. DE VOS, EDS.
1981   *Koreans in Japan: Ethnic Conflict and Accommodation.* Berkeley and Los Angeles.

LEE, O-Y.
1982   *Chijimi shikō no nihonjin* [Japanese miniaturism]. Tokyo.

LÉVI-STRAUSS, C.
1966   *The Savage Mind.* London.

LIFTON, R. J.
1963   Youth and History: Individual Change in Postwar Japan. In *The Challenge of Youth,* ed. E. Erickson. New York.

LIN, T. Y., ET AL.
1978   Ethnicity and Patterns of Help-Seeking. *Journal of Culture, Medicine and Psychiatry* 2:3–13.

McGUFFEY, W. H.
1879   *McGuffey's Eclectic Readers.* American Book Company.

MARUYAMA, M.
1956   *Gendai seiji no shisō to kōdō* [Ideology and action in contemporary politics]. Tokyo.

1960 Chūsei to hangyaku [Loyalty and rebellion]. In *Kindai Nippon shisōshi kōza* [History of thought in modern Japan], vol. 6. Tokyo.

1972 Rekishi ishiki no kosō [The ancient layer of historical consciousness]. In *Nippon no shisō* [Japanese ideology], vol. 6, ed. M. Maruyama. Tokyo.

MAUSS, M.
1954 *The Gift: Forms and Functions of Exchange in Archaic Societies.* Glencoe, Ill.

MERTON, R. K.
1949 *Social Theory and Social Structure.* Glencoe, Ill.

MILLER, D. R., AND G. F. SWANSON
1958 *The Changing American Parent.* New York.

MILLET, K.
1973 A Personal Discovery. *Ms* 1:56–59, 113–115.

MINAMI, H.
1953 *Nihonjin no shinri* [The psychology of the Japanese]. Tokyo.

MINZOKUGAKU KENKYŪJO [ETHNOLOGICAL RESEARCH INSTITUTE], ED.
1951 *Minzokugaku jiten* [Dictionary of ethnology]. Tokyo.

MOERAN, B.
1982 A Survey of Modern Japanese Pottery. Parts 1–4. *Ceramics Monthly* 30,
–83 nos. 8–10; 31, no. 1.
1983 The Language of Japanese Tourism. *Annuals of Tourism Research* 10.
1984 *Lost Innocence: Folk Craft Potters of Onta, Japan.* Berkeley and Los Angeles.

MOGAMI, T.
1935 Kōeki no hanashi [Trade]. In *Nihon minzokugaku kenkyū* [Studies in Japanese folklore], ed. K. Yanagita. Tokyo.

MORI, A.
1985 Morita shinkeishitsu jūni nenkan no tōkei-teki kōsatsu [A statistical study of Morita *shinkeishitsu* for twelve years]. *Tokyo Jikei-kai Ika Daigaku zasshi* 100:293–307.

MORI, Y.
1937 Mura no kōsai to giri [Social interaction and obligations among villagers]. In *Sanson-seikatsu no kenkyū* [Life in mountain villages], ed. K. Yanagita. Tokyo.

MORITA, S.
1960 *Shinkeishitsu no hontai to ryōhō* [The essential characteristics and therapy of *shinkeishitsu*]. Tokyo.

MORRIS, V. D.
1972 Idioms of Contemporary Japan. Part 3: Maihōmushugi. *The Japan Interpreter* 7:383–395.

MOSS, H. A.
1967 Sex, Age, and State as Determinants of Mother-Infant Interaction. *Merrill-Palmer Quarterly* 13:19–36.

MUNAKATA, T.
  1983a Tōkei ni miru bunretsū-byōsha to seishin iryō taikei [Mental health care
         delivery system for the schizophrenia patient: A sociological perspective].
         Psychiatria et Neurologia Japonica 85, no. 10:660–671.
  1983b Nihon no seishin iryō taikei ni okeru shakai-bunka-teki haikei [Socio-cul-
         tural background of mental health care delivery system in Japan]. *Japanese
         Journal of Mental Health* 30:135–148.
  1984a Socio-Cultural Background of Mental Health Care Delivery System in
         Japan as Compared with Western Countries. Paper presented at the
         meeting of the World Psychiatric Association Regional Symposium,
         Helsinki.
  1984b *Seishin iryō no shakaigaku* [Sociology of mental health care]. Tokyo.
  In   Socio-cultural Features of Japanese Attitudes toward Mental Illness and
  press Mental Health Delivery Systems. In *Proceedings of the Modernization of East-
         Asian Medicine Workshop*, ed. David Wu. Honolulu.

MURASE, T.
  1974   Naikan Therapy. In *Japanese Culture and Behavior: Selected Readings*, 1st ed.,
         ed. T. S. Lebra and W. P. Lebra. Honolulu. *(See also chapter 23 of this vol-
         ume.)*
  1982   Sunao: A Central Value in Japanese Psychotherapy. In *Cultural Conceptions
         of Mental Health and Therapy*, ed. A. J. Marsella and G. M. White.
         Dordrecht.

NAKAMURA, H.
  1960   *Ways of Thinking of Eastern Peoples: India, China, Tibet, Japan.* Tokyo.
         Reprinted, 1964, Honolulu.

NAKAMURA, S., ED.
  1966   *Nōryoku kaihatsu keikaku* [A plan for the development of ability]. Tokyo.

NAKANE, C.
  1965   Toward a Theory of Japanese Social Structure. *Economic Weekly* [Bombay],
         annual no. 17 (February): 197–216.
  1967   *Tate shakai no ningen kankei* [Human relations in a vertical society]. Tokyo.
  1970   *Japanese Society.* Berkeley and London. *(Excerpt, chapter 12 of this volume.)*
  1978   *Tate-shakai no rikigaku* [The dynamics of a vertical society]. Tokyo.

NAKAYAMA, I.
  1965   *Nihon no kindaika* [Japan's modernization]. Tokyo.

NAMIHIRA, E.
  1984   *Byōki to chiryō no bunka-jinruigaku* [Anthropology of illness and treatment].
         Tokyo.

NIHON SHAKAI GAKKAI CHŌSA IINKAI [RESEARCH COMMITTEE OF THE JAPAN
SOCIOLOGICAL SOCIETY], ED.
  1958   *Nihon shakai no kaisō-teki kōzō* [The class structure of Japanese society].
         Tokyo.

NISHIHIRA, S., ET AL.
1970 *A Study of Japanese National Character,* vol. 2. Tokyo.

NITOBE, I.
1905 *Bushido: The Soul of Japan.* Rutland, Vt. Reprinted, 1969.

NIYEKAWA-HOWARD, A.
1968 A Psycholinguistic Study of the Whorfian Hypothesis Based on the Japanese Passive. Paper presented at the 13th Annual National Conference on Linguistics, New York.

NORBECK, E.
1955 Yakudoshi: A Japanese Complex of Supernatural Beliefs. *Southwestern Journal of Anthropology* 11:447–448.
1978 *Country to City: The Urbanization of a Japanese Hamlet.* Salt Lake City.

NORBECK, E., AND G. DE VOS
1972 Culture and Personality: The Japanese. In *Psychological Anthropology,* ed., F. L. K. Hsu. Cambridge, Mass.

NORBECK, E., AND M. NORBECK
1956 Child Training in a Japanese Fishing Community. In *Personal Character and Cultural Milieu,* ed. D. G. Haring. Syracuse.

ODAKA, K.
1964 The Middle Classes in Japan. *Contemporary Japan* 28 (1964): 10–32; 28
–65 (1965): 268–296.

ODAKA, K., AND S. NISHIHIRA
1965 Social Mobility in Japan: A Report on the 1955 Survey of Social Stratification and Social Mobility in Japan. *East Asian Cultural Studies* 4, nos. 1–4: 83–126.

OKUMURA, N., K. SATO, AND H. YAMAMOTO, EDS.
1972 *Naikan ryōhō* [Naikan therapy]. Tokyo.

ŌMACHI, T.
1935 Kankon-sōsai no hanashi [Ceremonies for initiation, marriage, funeral, and ancestors]. In *Nihon minzokugaku kenkyū* [Studies in Japanese folklore], ed. K. Yanagita. Tokyo.

OSARAGI, J.
1952 *Munakata kyōdai* [Munakata brothers]. Tokyo.

OSHIBA, M.
1961 Moral Education in Japan. *School Review* 69:227–244.

PARKIN, D.
1976 Exchanging Words. In *Transaction and Meaning,* ed. B. Kapferer. Philadelphia.
1978 *The Cultural Definition of Political Response.* London.

PARSONS, T.
1951 *The Social System.* Glencoe, Ill.

PASSIN, H.
1970   *Japanese Education: A Bibliography of Materials in the English Language.* New
        York.

PEARLIN, L. I., AND M. L. KOHN
1966   Social Class, Occupation, and Parental Values: A Cross-National Study.
        American Sociological Review 31:466–479.

PEASE, D.
1961   Some Child Rearing Practices in Japanese Families. *Marriage and Family
        Life* 23:179–181.

PEIPER, A.
1963   *Cerebral Function in Infancy and Childhood.* New York.

PELZEL, J. C.
1970   Human Nature in the Japanese Myths. In *Personality in Japanese History,*
        ed. A. M. Craig and D. H. Shively. Berkeley and Los Angeles. *(See also
        chapter 1 of this volume.)*
1977   Japanese Personality in Culture. *Culture, Medicine, and Psychiatry* 1:299–
        315.

PIERS, G., AND M. B. SINGER
1953   *Shame and Guilt.* Springfield, Ill.

PLATH, D. W.
1964   *The After Hours: Modern Japan and the Search for Enjoyment.* Berkeley and Los
        Angeles.
1967   Utopian Rhetoric: Conversion and Conversation in a Japanese Cult. In
        *Essays on the Verbal and Visual Arts: Proceedings of the 1966 Annual Spring Meet-
        ing of the American Ethnological Society,* ed. J. Helm. Seattle.
1980   *Long Engagements: Maturity in Modern Japan.* Stanford.

RAMSEY, C. E., AND R. J. SMITH
1960   Japanese and American Perceptions of Occupations. *American Journal of
        Sociology* 65:475–482.

REDEKOP, W. B.
1964   Education for Loyalty in Prewar and Postwar Japan. Ph.D. diss., Uni-
        versity of British Columbia.

REISCHAUER, E. O.
1957   *The United States and Japan.* Rev. ed. Cambridge, Mass.

RETTIG, S., AND B. PASAMANICK
1959   Moral Codes of American and Korean College Students. *Journal of Social
        Psychology* 50:65–73.

REYNOLDS, D. K.
1969   Directed Behavior Change: Japanese Psychotherapy in a Private Mental
        Hospital. Ph.D. diss., University of California, Los Angeles.
1983   *Naikan Psychotherapy: Meditation for Self-Development.* Chicago.

REYNOLDS, V.
1976   The Origins of a Behavioural Vocabulary: The Case of the Rhesus Monkey. *Journal for the Theory of Social Behavior* 6:105–142.

RHEINGOLD, H. L.
1960   The Measurement of Maternal Care. *Child Development* 31:565–575.

RIESMAN, D.
1950   *The Lonely Crowd.* New Haven.

RILKE, R. M.
1939   *Dunio Elegies,* trans. and ed. J. B. Leishman and S. Spender. New York.

RIN, H.
1972   Roundtable Discussion: Past, Present, and Future of Psychiatric Discipline and Treatment in Asia and the Pacific (in Japanese). *Seishin igaku* 14:980–1001.

ROHLEN, T.
1969   Shinnyū-shain kyōiku no Nihon-teki tokuchō: Amerika no shanai kyōiku to hikaku kōsatsu [The special Japanese qualities of new employee training: Considerations based on a comparison with company training in America]. *Kyōiku to igaku* 17, no. 11: 33–40.

1970a Nōryoku-shugi jidai no seishin kyōiku [Spiritual education in an era emphasizing objective ability]. *Sangyō kunren* 16:41–48.

1970b Sponsorship of Cultural Continuity in Japan: A Company Training Program. *Journal of Asian and African Studies* 5:184–192. Reprinted, 1974, in *Japanese Culture and Behavior,* 1st ed., ed. T. S. Lebra and W. P. Lebra. Honolulu.

1971   The Organization and Ideology of a Japanese Bank: An Ethnographic Study of a Modern Organization. Ph.D. diss., University of Pennsylvania.

1974   *For Harmony and Strength: Japanese White-Collar Organization in Anthropological Perspective.* Berkeley and Los Angeles.

1983   *Japan's High Schools.* Berkeley and Los Angeles.

RUBENSTEIN, J.
1967   Maternal Attentiveness and Subsequent Exploratory Behavior in the Infant. *Child Development* 38:1089–1100.

SAKUDA, K.
1967   *Haji no bunka saikō* [The shame culture reexamined]. Tokyo.

SAKURADA, K.
1954a Zōtō [Gift exchange]. In *Nihon shakai minzoku jiten* [Dictionary of Japanese ethnography and folklore], vol. 10, ed. N. M. Kyōkai. Tokyo.

1954b Noshi [The symbolic attachment to a formal gift]. In *Nihon shakai minzoku jiten* [Dictionary of Japanese ethnography and folklore], vol. 3, ed. N. M. Kyōkai. Tokyo.

SALAMON, S.
1977   Family Bounds and Friendship Bonds: Japan and West Germany. *Journal of Marriage and the Family* 39:807–820.

SALZMAN, L.
1968   *The Obsessive Personality.* New York.

SANGYŌ KUNREN [INDUSTRIAL TRAINING]
1968   Seishin kyōiku tokushū [Special issue on spiritual education]. *Sangyō Kunren* 14, no. 9.

SASAKI, Y.
1969   Psychiatric Study of the Shaman in Japan. In *Mental Health Research in Asia and the Pacific,* ed. W. Caudill and T. Y. Lin. Honolulu.
1984   *Okinawa no bunka to seishin eisei* [Okinawan culture and mental health]. Tokyo.

SCHOOLER, C., AND W. CAUDILL
1964   Symptomatology in Japanese and American Schizophrenics. *Ethnology* 3:172–178.

SEGAWA, K.
1964   *Nihonjin no ishokujū* [The food, clothing, and shelter of the Japanese]. Tokyo.

SEWARD, G., ED.
1958   *Clinical Studies in Culture Conflict.* New York.

SHIIBASHI, Y.
1942   Amazake to kisetsu [Sweet rice-wine and seasons]. *Minkan denshō* 8:21–23.

SHŌGAKUKAN, ED.
1965   Akazukin [Little Red Riding-Hood]. In *Shōgakukan no yoiko ehon series* [Shōgakukan series of illustrated books for children]. Tokyo.

SMITH, R. J.
1978   *Kurusu: The Price of Progress in a Japanese Village 1951–75.* London.
1983   *Japanese Society: Tradition, Self, and the Social Order.* Cambridge.

SMITH, R. J., AND E. L. WISWELL
1982   *The Women of Suye Mura.* Chicago.

SNEDECOR, G. W.
1946   *Statistical Methods.* 4th ed. Ames, Iowa.

SOFUE, T.
1979   Aspects of the Personality of Japanese, Americans, Italians, and Eskimos: Comparisons Using the Sentence Completion Test. *Journal of Psychological Anthropology* 2:11–52.

STEPHENS, W. N.
1963   *The Family in Cross-Cultural Perspective.* New York.

STRONG, N. O.
1978   Patterns of Social Interaction and Psychological Accommodation among Japan's *Konketsuji* Population. Ph.D. diss., University of California.

SUGIHARA, Y.
1962   *Shinkyō buraku* [The Shinkyo community]. Tokyo.

SUGIURA, K.
1935 Minkan-shinkō no hanashi [Folk religion]. In *Nihon minzokugaku kenkyū* [Studies in Japanese folklore], ed. K. Yanagita. Tokyo.

SUZUKI, D. T.
1959 *Zen and Japanese Culture.* New York.
1965 *The Training of the Zen Buddhist Monk.* New York.

SUZUKI, T.
1984 *Words in Context.* Tokyo.

TAEUBER, I. B.
1958 *The Population of Japan.* Princeton, N.J.

TAKAGI, M.
1954 *Nihonjin no seikatsu-shinri* [Japanese psychology of daily life]. Tokyo and Osaka.

TAUT, B.
1958 *Houses and People of Japan.* Tokyo.

THOMSEN, H.
1963 *The New Religions of Japan.* Tokyo.

TOLAND, J.
1970 *The Rising Sun: The Decline and Fall of the Japanese Empire 1936–1945.* New York.

TOMOMATSU, E.
1939 *Boshin* [The mind of mother]. Tokyo.

TOPPING, H. F.
1935 *Introducing Kagawa.* Chicago.

TOSHIMA, K.
1958 Tōhoku chihō ni okeru nyūyōji seishin hattatsu ni kansuru kenkyū [A study of the mental development of infants in the Tohoku area]. *Nihon Shōnika-Gakkai zasshi* 62:1444–1450; 1550–1556; 1557–1563.

TOTOKI, A.
n.d. Zero Defect Movement in Japan: Its Development and Future Aspect. In *Experiences with Zero Defect Program and Movement in Japanese Industries: A Participative Problem Solving Approach for Productivity and Quality Improvement.* Japan Management Association. Tokyo.

TSENG, W.-S., AND J. HSU
1969 Chinese Culture, Personality Information and Mental Illness. *International*
-70 *Journal of Social Psychiatry* 16:5–14.

UCHIMI, I., AND T. AMANO, EDS.
n.d. *Shōgaku dōtoku shidōsho* [Primary school moral education text: Teacher's guide], vols. 1–6. Osaka.

UMESAO, T.
1960 *Nihon tanken* [Exploring Japan]. Tokyo.

VOGEL, E. F.
1963   *Japan's New Middle Class: The Salary Man and His Family in a Tokyo Suburb.*
       Berkeley and Los Angeles. 2d ed., 1971.
1979   *Japan as Number One: Lessons for America.* Cambridge, Mass.

VON MEHREN, A., ED.
1963   *Law in Japan.* Cambridge, Mass.

WAGATSUMA, H.
1957   Japanese Values of Achievement—The Study of Japanese Immigrants
       and Inhabitants of Three Japanese Villages by Means of T.A.T. Master's
       thesis, University of Michigan.

WAKAMORI, T.
1944   Shakō to kyōyō [Social interaction and cultural sophistication]. *Minkan
       denshō* 10:447–448.
1947   *Nihon minzoku-ron* [Japanese folklore]. Tokyo.
1951   *Rekishi to minzoku* [History and folklore]. Tokyo.
1953   *Nihonjin no kōsai* [Social interaction among Japanese]. Tokyo.

WALLER, W.
1938   *The Family.* New York.

WATANABE, M.
1974   The Conception of Nature in Japanese Culture. *Science* 183 (Jan. 25):
       279–282.

WATANABE, S.
1963   *Old People in Transitional Japan.* Tokyo.

WEISBERG, P.
1967   Social and Non-Social Conditioning of Infant Vocalizations. In *Behavior in
       Infancy and Early Childhood,* ed. Y. Brackbill and G. G. Thompson. Glen-
       coe, Ill.

WHITE, L. A.
1959   *The Evolution of Culture.* New York.

WHITING, R.
1977   *The Chrysanthemum and the Bat: Baseball Samurai Style.* New York.

WHITING, J. W. M., R. KLUCKHOHN, AND A. ANTHONY
1958   The Function of Male Initiation Ceremonies at Puberty. In *Readings in
       Social Psychology,* ed. E. E. Maccoby, T. M. Newcomb, and E. L.
       Hartley. New York.

WILLIAMSON, J.
1978   *Decoding Advertisements.* London.

WIMBERLEY, H.
1969   Self-Realization and the Ancestors: An Analysis of Two Japanese Ritual
       Procedures for Achieving Domestic Harmony. *Anthropological Quarterly*
       42:37–51.

WINDLE, J. F.
  1968 Feeding Infants in Japanese and American Urban Middle Class Families. Master's thesis, American University of Washington, D.C.
WOLF, M.
  1972 *Women and the Family in Rural Taiwan.* Stanford.
WOLFF, P. H., AND I. HURWITZ
  1966 The Choreiform Syndrome. *Developmental Medicine and Child Neurology* 8:160–165.
YAMAMURA, Y.
  1971 *Nihonjin to haha* [Mother for Japanese]. Tokyo.
YANAGITA, K.
  1940 *Shokumotsu to shinzō* [Food and heart]. Tokyo and Osaka.
YASUNAGA, H.
  1967 Chiyu-kiten to zaiakukan [Healing and guilt feelings]. *Seishin Igaku* 9:281–285.
YOKOYAMA, K.
  1974 *Seiza ryōhō* [Therapy by sitting]. Osaka.
YOSHIMOTO, I.
  1965 *Naikan yonjūnen* [Forty years of Naikan]. Tokyo.
YOUNG, M., AND P. WILLMOTT
  1957 *Family and Kinship in East London.* Baltimore.
YUCHTMAN, E.
  1972 Reward Distribution and Workrole Attractiveness in the Kibbutz: Reflections on Equity Theory. *American Sociological Review* 37:581–595.

Contributors

Pamela J. Asquith, presently Killam Scholar in Anthropological Research, University of Alberta, is the author of "Some Aspects of Anthropomorphism in the Terminology and Philosophy Underlying Western and Japanese Studies of the Social Behavior of Non-Human Primates" (1981).

Harumi Befu is professor of anthropology at Stanford University, and author of *Japan: An Anthropological Introduction* (1971).

Vincent S. R. Brandt has taught at Dartmouth University and is the author of *A Korean Village: Between Farm and Sea* (1971).

William Caudill was chief of the Section of Personality and Environment, Laboratory of Socio-Environmental Studies, National Institute of Mental Health, Bethesda, Maryland. He coedited (with T. Y. Lin) *Mental Health Research in Asia and the Pacific* (1969).

George De Vos is professor of anthropology at the University of California, Berkeley. Among his publications is *Socialization for Achievement: Essays on the Cultural Psychology of the Japanese* (1973).

L. Takeo Doi, who is currently affiliated with St. Luke's Hospital, Tokyo, was formerly professor of health sciences at Tokyo University and director of the National Institute of Mental Health in Japan. His publications include *Omote to ura* [Front and back] (1985).

Eiichirō Ishida was professor of anthropology at Tokyo University and author of *Japanese Culture: A Study of Origins and Characteristics* (1974).

Yomishi Kasahara, director of Nagoya University Hospital and professor/chairman of psychiatry, Nagoya University, authored *Apathy Syndrome among Educated Young Adults in Japan* (1984).

Hayao Kawai is professor of psychology at Kyoto University. He is a Jungian analyst and author of *Bosei shakai Nippon no byōri* [The pathology of Japan as a maternal society] (1976).

Betty B. Lanham, professor of anthropology, Indiana University of Pennsylvania, Indiana, Penn., authored "Relation of History to Prospectives of the Future: Japan's Youth of the Past and Present" (1974).

Takie Sugiyama Lebra is professor of anthropology at the University of Hawaii. Among her publications is *Japanese Women: Constraint and Fulfillment* (1984).

William P. Lebra was professor of anthropology at the University of Hawaii. His publications include *Okinawan Religion: Belief, Ritual, and Social Structure* (1966).

Brian Moeran is lecturer in Asian Anthropology at the School of Oriental and African Studies, University of London. Among his publications is *Lost Innocence: Folk Craft Potters of Onta, Japan* (1984).

Tsunetsugu Munakata is chief of medical sociology research at the National Institute of Mental Health, Japan, and author of *Seishin iryō no shakaigaku* [The sociology of mental health treatment] (1984).

Takao Murase, professor of psychology at Rikkyo University, authored "Sunao: A Central Value in Japanese Psychotherapy" (1982).

Chie Nakane is professor of anthropology at the Institute of Oriental Studies, Tokyo University. She is author of *Japanese Society* (1970).

John C. Pelzel, emeritus professor of anthropology, Harvard University, authored "Japanese Personality in Culture" (1977).

David W. Plath is professor of anthropology at the University of Illinois, Urbana. His publications include *Long Engagement: Maturity in Modern Japan* (1980).

Thomas P. Rohlen has taught at the University of California, Santa Cruz, and Harvard University, and authored *Japan's High Schools* (1983).

Sonya Salamon is associate professor of human resources and family studies at the University of Illinois, Urbana. She is author of "Family Bounds and Friendship Bonds: Japan and West Germany" (1977).

Yuji Sasaki, professor of health sciences, Tokyo University, edited *Okinawa no bunka to seishin eisei* [Okinawan culture and mental health] (1984).

Takao Suzuki is professor of linguistics at Keio University. He is the author of *Words in Context* (1984).

Helen Weinstein was research assistant, Section on Personality and Environment, Laboratory for Socio-Environmental Studies, National Institute of Mental Health, Bethesda, Maryland.

Index

Acceptance: in Morita therapy, 343; sensitivity to social, 295; of unpleasant tasks, 330–331
Achievement, 80, 331, 339; attributed to benefactors, 359; behavior, 83; demand for, 340; drive, 81, 88; educational, xiv; motive for, 85
Addressor-addressee, linguistic analysis of, 142–156
Adolescence: disorder peculiar to, 381; and suicide, 271
Adoption: of husband, 358; of son-in-law, 174
Aggression, 358; out of frustrated *amae*, 123; of nature, 12; Western and Japanese, 99. *See also* Violence
Agrarian culture, 37–39
Akirame, 21
Alcohol dependence, 370
Altruism, 65; altruistic donation, 166
Amae, xv, 105, 121–129, 341, 375, 385; behavior, 139; definition of, 121; as expressed through tyranny, 138, 141; Korean version of, xv; and *ninjō*, 64; and *on*, 340; of psychiatric patients, 367; related terms, 122–124; wife's, on her mother, 140
Ancestors, 356, 361; homecoming of, 66; at the household altar, 159–160; obligation toward, 350; worship of, 284, 362
Anxiety, 82, 383; of child, 305; neurosis, 348; reduction, 312, 313, 349; of rejection and isolation, 320
Apology, 289, 358, 363; to gods, 363
Arranged marriage, xvii, 24, 80, 131; rejection of, 84. *See also* Love marriage
Authority, 333; househead's, 181; parental, 291

Benevolence, 65, 284, 358; given and returned, 389; from others, 343, 388. See also *On*

Blushing, 381. *See also* Ereuthophobia; Erythrophobia; Phobia: of interpersonal relations
Brainwashing, 348, 350
Bride's status in Japan and India, 178
Buddhism, 4, 343, 386; Buddhahood, 21, 361; Buddhas, 355; Buddhist culture, 39; Buddhist influence, 58; Buddhist rite for animals, 4, 32; Buddhist thought, 98; and discipline, 295; Jōdo-Shin sect, 388; Shingon, 355. *See also* Zen
Bushidō, 66

Cancer phobia, 349
Caretaking, 205; American and Japanese, 220; passive presence, 224. *See also* Infant care; Mother; Mother-infant communication
Catharsis, 334; through Naikan, 390
Ceremony, 313. *See also* Ritual
Change, xv–xx, 295; in gift-giving patterns, 163–167; and high economic growth, 302, 304; postwar decline of *chū*, *kō*, and *on*; postwar increase in maternal control, 300–301; in sleeping arrangement, 198; social, 275, 295; in social organization, 177. *See also* Individuation; Modernization; Westernization
Character: development, 48–49, 284, 307; improvement, 314; perfection of, 314; strength, 316
Child rearing, 291. *See also* Infant care; Mother-child communication; Socialization
Chū (chu), 70, 358. *See also* Loyalty
Cleanliness, 386
Cohesion, 59; familial, 271; group, 114, 333. *See also* Solidarity
Commensality, 160, 161
Communes, co-sleeping in, 272–273